In Garageland
Rock, Youth and Modernity
Johan Fornäs, Ulf Lindberg and Ove Sernhede

The Crisis of Public Communication
Jay G. Blumler and Michael Gurevitch

Glasgow Media Group Reader, Volume 1
News Content, Language and Visuals
Edited by John Eldridge

Glasgow Media Group Reader, Volume 2
Industry, Economy, War and Politics
Edited by Greg Philo

The Global Jukebox
The International Music Industry
Robert Burnett

Inside Prime Time
Todd Gitlin

Talk on Television
Audience Participation and Public Debate
Sonia Livingstone and Peter Lunt

Media Effects and Beyond
Culture, Socialization and Lifestyles
Edited by Karl Erik Rosengren

We Keep America on Top of the World
Television Journalism and the Public Sphere
Daniel C. Hallin

A Journalism Reader
Edited by Michael Bromley and Tom O'Malley

Tabloid Television
Popular Journalism and the 'Other News'
John Langer

International Radio Journalism
History, Theory and Practice
Tim Crook

Media, Ritual and Identity
Edited by Tamar Liebes and James Curran

De-Westernizing Media Studies
Edited by James Curran and Myung-Jin Park

British Cinema in the Fifties
Christine Geraghty

Ill Effects
The Media Violence Debate, Second Edition
Edited by Martin Barker and Julian Petley

Media and Power
James Curran

Remaking Media
The Struggle to Democratize Public Communication
Robert A. Hackett and William K. Carroll

Media on the Move
Global Flow and Contra-Flow
Daya Kishan Thussu

An Introduction to Political Communication
Fourth Edition
Brian McNair

The Mediation of Power
A Critical Introduction
Aeron Davis

Television Entertainment
Jonathan Gray

Western Media Systems
Jonathan Hardy

Narrating Media History
Edited by Michael Bailey

News and Journalism in the UK
Fifth Edition
Brian McNair

Political Communication and Social Theory
Aeron Davis

Media Perspectives for the 21st Century
Edited by Stylianos Papathanassopoulos

Journalism After September 11
Second Edition
Edited by Barbie Zelizer and Stuart Allan

Media and Democracy
James Curran

Changing Journalism
Angela Phillips, Peter Lee-Wright and Tamara Witschge

Misunderstanding the Internet
James Curran, Natalie Fenton and Des Freedman

Critical Political Economy of the Media
An Introduction
Jonathan Hardy

Journalism in Context
Practice and Theory for the Digital Age
Angela Phillips

News and Politics
The Rise of Live and Interpretive Journalism
Stephen Cushion

Gender and Media
Representing, Producing, Consuming
Tonny Krijnen and Sofie Van Bauwel

Misunderstanding the Internet
Second Edition
James Curran, Natalie Fenton and Des Freedman

Misunderstanding the Internet

"Fully updated, the second edition of *Misunderstanding the Internet* speaks more clearly and critically than ever to today's hyperbolic claims, utopian and dystopian, about the internet. By presenting a wealth of data that problematises easy claims of democratisation, the authors issue an urgent call to action to embed public values in the internet of the future."

Sonia Livingstone, *Professor of Media and Communications, London School of Economics and Political Science*

"By updating their authoritative work on the Internet, James Curran, Natalie Fenton and Des Freedman have done scholars, students and concerned citizens an enormous favor. *Misunderstanding the Internet* remains the single most important book for someone to read to grasp the history and political economy of the digital revolution."

Robert W. McChesney, *Professor of Communication, University of Illinois at Urbana-Champaign*

"This is a very important book, it offers critical insights to contemporary political and economic power, the role of social media and how mass publics are informed, correcting many false assumptions - an absolute must read for students and academics in social and political sciences, as well as media and communications."

Gregory Philo, *Professor of Communications and Social Change, University of Glasgow*

The growth of the internet has been spectacular. There are now more than 3 billion internet users across the globe, some 40% of the world's population. The internet's meteoric rise is a phenomenon of enormous significance for the economic, political and social life of contemporary societies.

However, much popular and academic writing about the internet continues to take a celebratory view, assuming that the internet's potential will be realised in essentially positive and transformative ways. This was especially true in the euphoric moment of the mid-1990s, when many commentators wrote about the internet with awe and wonderment. While this moment may be over, its underlying technocentrism – the belief that technology determines outcomes – lingers on and, with it, a failure to understand the internet in its social, economic and political contexts.

Misunderstanding the Internet is a short introduction, encompassing the history, sociology, politics and economics of the internet and its impact on society. This expanded and updated second edition is a polemical, sociologically and historically informed guide to the key claims that have been made about the online world. It aims to challenge both popular myths and existing academic orthodoxies that surround the internet.

James Curran, Natalie Fenton and Des Freedman are professors in the Department of Media and Communications at Goldsmiths, University of London, UK.

Communication and Society
Series Editor: James Curran

This series encompasses the broad field of media and cultural studies. Its main concerns are the media and the public sphere: on whether the media empower or fail to empower popular forces in society; media organisations and public policy; the political and social consequences of media campaigns; and the role of media entertainment, ranging from potboilers and the human-interest story to rock music and TV sport.

Glasnost, Perestroika and the Soviet Media
Brian McNair

Pluralism, Politics and the Marketplace
The Regulation of German Broadcasting
Vincent Porter and Suzanne Hasselbach

Potboilers
Methods, Concepts and Case Studies in Popular Fiction
Jerry Palmer

Communication and Citizenship
Journalism and the Public Sphere
Edited by Peter Dahlgren and Colin Sparks

Seeing and Believing
The Influence of Television
Greg Philo

Critical Communication Studies
Communication, History and Theory in America
Hanno Hardt

Media Moguls
Jeremy Tunstall and Michael Palmer

Fields in Vision
Television Sport and Cultural Transformation
Garry Whannel

Getting the Message
News, Truth and Power
The Glasgow Media Group

Advertising, the Uneasy Persuasion
Its Dubious Impact on American Society
Michael Schudson

Nation, Culture, Text
Australian Cultural and Media Studies
Edited by Graeme Turner

Television Producers
Jeremy Tunstall

What News?
The Market, Politics and the Local Press
Bob Franklin and David Murphy

Misunderstanding the Internet

Second edition

James Curran, Natalie Fenton
and Des Freedman

Routledge
Taylor & Francis Group

LONDON AND NEW YORK

Second edition published 2016
by Routledge
2 Park Square, Milton Park, Abingdon, Oxon OX14 4RN

and by Routledge
711 Third Avenue, New York, NY 10017

Routledge is an imprint of the Taylor & Francis Group, an informa business

First edition published by Routledge 2012

British Library Cataloguing-in-Publication Data
A catalogue record for this book is available from the British Library

Library of Congress Cataloging-in-Publication Data
Curran, James.
Misunderstanding the Internet / James Curran, Natalie Fenton and
Des Freedman. — Second edition.
pages cm—(Communication and society)
Includes bibliographical references and index.
1. Internet—Social aspects. 2. Internet—Economic aspects.
3. Internet—Political aspects. 4. Social networks. I. Fenton, Natalie.
II. Freedman, Des, 1962- III. Title.
HM851.C87 2016
302.23'1—dc23
2015033280

ISBN: 978-1-138-90620-4 (hbk)
ISBN: 978-1-138-90622-8 (pbk)
ISBN: 978-1-315-69562-4 (ebk)

Typeset in Times New Roman
by Swales & Willis Ltd, Exeter, Devon, UK
Printed and bound in Great Britain by
Ashford Colour Press Ltd, Gosport, Hampshire

Contents

Preface   viii

1 The internet of dreams: reinterpreting the internet   1

2 The internet of history: rethinking the internet's past   48

3 The internet of capital: concentration and commodification
   in a world of abundance   85

4 The internet of rules: critical approaches to online
   regulation and governance   117

5 The internet of me (and my 'friends')   145

6 The internet of radical politics and social change   173

7 The internet we want   203

Index   210

Preface

This book is a spin-off from a research programme at Goldsmiths, University of London generously funded by the Leverhulme Trust. The programme has resulted in numerous specialist books, journal articles and computer applications. This book is different: an overview rather than a monograph. While it was prompted and informed by our empirical research, it grew out of our background reading of the relevant literature on the internet, and of our increasingly sceptical response to it.

So what began as a briefing for ourselves grew into a book-length overview, indeed almost a maverick textbook. But technology (and its uses) evolves quickly. The first edition of *Misunderstanding the Internet* was well received, and has been translated into Chinese and Korean. This encouraged us to return to the book some three years later, and to revise it in a way that takes account of both developments in the internet and research about it. The internet continues to transform our communicative experiences from shopping, to chatting to friends, to searching out information, to political activism. Social media has expanded exponentially in reach, transforming personal relationships and business. From social movements such as Occupy Wall Street and the Indignados in Spain to protests against the closure of a public park in Istanbul, the internet facilitates the sharing of our experiences and the building of solidarities across the world. Advances in mobile technology ensure we are ever more tuned in and connected at all times. At the same time, all of our digital comings and goings are tracked and our data collected to sell on to those who have become more sophisticated at profiting from it. We now know that digital surveillance is far more commonplace than we ever thought, and privacy is an ever more important concern. And all the while, multi-media conglomerates continue to replicate patterns of dominance of legacy media. The internet is so much a part of our daily lives that we rarely stop to think what it might mean for our own identities, our relationships, our working lives, our institutions, our citizenship, our democracies. This second edition of *Misunderstanding the Internet* hopes to persuade readers, once more, to do just that.

This second edition has not only been updated in detail with significant rewrites of chapters, but has also increased substantially in size to address new developments and debates.

Although each chapter has been written by one by-lined author, it has been commented upon and even edited by the two others. The book is a collective effort, and a shared pleasure.

Chapter 1

The internet of dreams

Reinterpreting the internet

James Curran

In the 1990s, leading experts, politicians, public officials, business leaders and journalists predicted that the internet would transform the world.[1] The internet would revolutionise, we were told, the organisation of business, and lead to a surge of prosperity (Gates 1995).[2] It would inaugurate a new era of cultural democracy in which sovereign users would call the shots, and old media leviathans would decay and die (Negroponte 1996). It would rejuvenate democracy – in some versions by enabling direct e-government through popular referenda (Grossman 1995). All over the world, the weak and marginal would be empowered, leading to the fall of autocrats and the reordering of power relations (Gilder 1994). More generally, the global medium of the internet would shrink the universe, promote dialogue between nations and foster global understanding (Jipguep 1995; Bulashova and Cole 1995). In brief, the internet would change society permanently and irrevocably, like the invention of print and gunpowder.

These arguments were mostly inferences derived from the internet's technology. It was assumed that the distinctive technological attributes of the internet – its interactivity, global reach, cheapness, speed, networking facility, storage capacity and alleged uncontrollability – would change the world beyond all recognition. Underlying these predictions was a widely shared internet-centrism, a belief that the internet was a determining technology that would reconfigure all environments.

These predictions gained ever greater authority when, seemingly, they were fulfilled. The internet entered every domain of social life, changing the way people searched for information, communicated, met, shopped and spent their time. The notion that anyone could live their life entirely offline seemed so absurd that it became the subject of satire (Portlandia, n.d.). Indeed, 15-year-olds in economically advanced countries spent around three hours online on a typical weekday in 2013 (OECD 2014: 13).

Numerous experts continued to affirm in the 2000s that the internet was transforming society. The internet was supposedly engendering a shift from passive consumption to active participation (Shirky 2010); causing markets to fragment (Anderson 2006); and rendering society more open and egalitarian (Leadbetter 2009). The 2011 popular uprisings in the Middle East – immediately hailed as the 'Twitter Revolutions' – seemed to offer final confirmation that the internet was a transformative force. As the world-famous sociologist, Manuel Castells, exulted in a book hymning the power of the internet: 'dictatorships could be overthrown with the bare hands of the people' (Castells 2012: 1).

Thus, it seemed as if only technophobes, stuck in a time warp of the past, remained blind to what was apparent to everyone else: namely that the internet was remaking the world. But as pronouncements about the internet's impact shifted from the future to the present tense, and became ever more assured, some analysts had second thoughts. In 1995, Sherry Turkle had celebrated anonymous online encounters between people on the grounds that they could extend imaginative insight into the 'other', and forge more emancipated sensibilities (Turkle 1995). Sixteen years later, she changed tack. Online communication, she lamented, could be shallow and addictive, and get in the way of developing richer, more fulfilling interpersonal relationships (Turkle 2011).[3] Another apostate was the Belarus activist Evgeny Morozov. His former hope that the internet would undermine dictators was, he declared, a 'delusion' (Morozov 2011). There were also others whose initial, more guarded belief in the emancipatory power of the internet turned into outright scepticism. Typical of this latter group was John Foster and Robert McChesney who wrote in 2011 that 'the enormous potential of the Internet . . . has vaporized in a couple of decades' (2011: 17).

We are thus faced with a disconcerting difference of expert opinion. Most informed commentators view the internet as a transforming technology. Seemingly, their predictions are being confirmed by events. Yet a confident minority decries the majority view as perverse. Who – and what – is right?

We will attempt to sketch an answer in this introductory chapter by identifying four key sets of predictions about the impact of the internet, and then check to see whether they have come true.[4] This will lead to a brief consideration of the conditions that result in the internet having a greater or lesser effect.

Economic transformation

In the 1990s, it was widely claimed that the internet would generate wealth and prosperity for all. This was the central conclusion of a long article in *Wired*, the bible of the American internet community, written by the magazine's editor, Kevin Kelly (1999). Its title and standfirst set the article's tone: 'The Roaring Zeros: The good news is, you'll be a millionaire soon. The bad news is, so will everybody else'.

This was merely one exuberant example of the speculative fever that took hold of mainstream media. 'The Internet gold rush is under way', declared the *Seattle Post-Intelligencer* (6 December 1995). 'Thousands of people and companies are staking claims. Without a doubt there is lots of gold because the Internet is the beginning of something immensely important.' Across the Atlantic Ocean, the same message was being proclaimed with undisguised relish. The 'fortunes' of 'Web whiz-kids', according to the *Independent on Sunday* (25 July 1999), 'reduce National Lottery jackpots to peanuts and make City bonuses seem like restaurant tips'. Punters could become rich too, it was promised, if they invested in whiz-kids' IPOs (initial public offerings). This invitation to personal enrichment was backed up by authoritative reports in the business press that the internet would generate increased prosperity. 'We have entered the Age of the Internet', declared *BusinessWeek* (October 1999). 'The result: an *explosion* of economic and productivity growth first in the U.S., with the rest of the world soon to follow' (emphasis added).

Bullish comments about the dynamic economic impact of the internet subsided when the dotcom bubble burst in 2001, but were reprised from the mid-2000s onwards. While this second wave of prophecy was not as flamboyant as the first, its general tenor was still strongly upbeat. One standard argument was that past predictions had been wrong only because they had been premature. But the internet is now moving allegedly into its full deployment phase, and coming into its own (Atkinson et al. 2010). Indeed, as time passed and memory of the internet crash faded, forecasts tended to become ever more optimistic (e.g. OECD 2014).

Central to this resilient prophetic tradition is the idea that the internet and digital communication has given birth to the 'New Economy'. While this concept is mutable and sometimes opaque, it is associated with certain recurrent themes. The internet provides, we are told, a more efficient means of connecting suppliers, producers and consumers. It is a disruptive technology that is generating a Schumpeterian wave of innovation, and attendant surge of productivity. And it is contributing to the growth of an information and communication economy that will compensate for the decline of manufacturing in de-industrialising, Western societies.

At the heart of this theorising is a mystical core (which was especially prominent in the 1990s). The internet is supposedly changing the terms of competition by establishing *a level playing field* between corporate giants and small companies. As Steve Jobs asserted in 1996, the internet is an 'incredible democratiser', since 'a small company can look as large as a big company and be accessible' (cited in Ryan 2010: 179). This has supposedly renewed the dynamism of the market, and unleashed a whirlwind force of creativity and growth. The internet has also created new market opportunities by enabling small start-ups to bypass dominant retailers and service agencies. It has lowered costs and extended exports, enabling new producers to prosper by catering for niche markets. More generally, the internet favours, we are told, horizontal, flexible network enterprise, able to respond rapidly to changes in consumer demand, unlike heavy-footed, top-down, Fordist, giant corporations. 'Small' is not only nimble but empowered and gifted with opportunity in the internet-based New Economy.

The presentation of these themes is often cloaked in specialist language. To understand its insights, it is seemingly necessary to learn a new vocabulary: to distinguish between portal and vortal, to differentiate between internet, intranet and extranet, to grasp the meaning of phrases like 'click-and-mortar' and 'data-warehousing', and to be familiar with endless acronyms like CRM (customer relationship management), VAN (value-added network), ERP (enterprise resource planning), OLTP (online transaction processing) and ETL (extract, transform and load). To be part of the novitiate who understands the future, it is first necessary to master a new catechism.

It is not easy to assess whether this vision of the future has come true because the economic impact of the internet is ongoing and incomplete. An added complication arises from the fact that the internet was preceded by earlier electronic data interchange systems like the telex and fax, and widespread business use of computers for data analysis (Bar and Simard 2002). Change has been cumulative.

Even so, it is possible to make a preliminary assessment. The first conclusion is that the internet has indeed modified the nerve system of the economy by changing the interactions between suppliers, producers and consumers, the configuration of markets, the volume and velocity of global financial transactions, and the nature of data processing and communication within business organisations. The internet has also given rise to the creation of major corporations like Google, and assisted the growth of lucrative enterprises like online gaming.

Perhaps the aspect of this economic restructuring that has most affected everyday material life is the rise of online retailing. In 2013 almost 50% of the adult OECD population bought something online. However, this average conceals very large variations between countries. Within the OECD bloc of affluent nations, the British and Danes are the most disposed to shop online: over three quarters did so in 2013. Yet, in the same year, only 10% of people in Turkey and 2% of people in Mexico ordered goods and services online (OECD 2014: 42).

While many now shop online, the *volume* of online shopping is still small in relative terms. This is for two main reasons: online sales take place mainly within nations rather than between nations, and are uneven across different retail and service sectors. To put the rise of online selling in perspective, e-commerce sales made up just 6.5% of total retail sales in the United States in 2014 (Bucchioni et al. 2015). By comparison, e-commerce accounted for 4% of total sales in Europe in 2007 (European Commission 2009), though the proportion will have risen since then.

Online sale of goods and services will continue to expand in the future. The relatively recent inroads made by Uber, which connects drivers with passengers, and Airbnb, which connects hosts with paying guests, are examples of an ongoing transformation. Factors holding back the rise of online retailing will diminish in importance over time. Even so, the obstacles in the way of an international online revolution – low internet access in some countries, language difficulties, security fears, differences in broadband speed and in the reliability of postal services, national variations in custom procedures and taxes, local corruption, differences of legislation respecting the cross-border transfer of personal details, the high cost of insurance and much else besides – remain formidable (Swedish National Board of Trade 2012; cf Groot 2011). There will also continue to be people who enjoy offline shopping, want to try out a product before purchase, or wish to buy without delay.

The second conclusion is that the internet has not been a geyser of wealth cascading down to all. There was an enormous increase in the stock market value of internet companies between 1995 and 2000. But this was fuelled by ignorance and the credit boom produced by financial de-regulation in the mid-1990s (Blodget 2008; Cassidy 2002). The bubble was exacerbated by financial incentives that encouraged investment analysts to recommend unsound investments in the internet sector (Wheale and Amin 2003), and by a group-think belief that conventional investment criteria did not apply to the New Economy (Valliere and Peterson 2004). In the event, most dotcom start-ups that attracted heavy investment folded without ever making a profit (Cellan-Jones 2001). These losses were so severe that they helped to cause a downturn of the US economy in 2001.

During the late 1990s and early 2000s, there was a rapid diffusion of internet use in the West. But this did not give rise to a sustained economic boom. Quite the contrary: the credit crunch of 2007 and the financial crash of 2008 marked the beginning of the longest recession of the Western economy since the 1930s (Blinder 2015; Bordo et al. 2013; Cattaneo et al. 2010). More generally, the internet era was a time of deepening economic inequality when the rich became much richer, and the incomes of many others flat-lined or even declined (Piketty 2014; Cingano 2014; OECD 2011; Stone et al. 2015). Manifestly, the internet was not a fountain of prosperity that reached all.

The third, related conclusion is that the internet's anticipated contribution to the economy was greatly overstated. Detailed, authoritative estimates of the internet's contribution range from 0.8% to 7% of GDP (OECD 2013: 19). Thus, a Harvard Business School study, using an employment income approach, concluded that the advertising-supported internet contributed approximately 2% to the US's GDP, or perhaps 3% if the internet's indirect contribution to domestic economic activity is taken into account (Deighton and Quelch 2009). An alternative calculation estimated that business-to-consumer e-commerce in Europe accounted for 1.35% of GDP (Eskelsen et al. 2009). A McKinsey Report (du Rausas et al. 2011) concluded that the internet's direct economic input averaged 3.4% of the GDP of the G8 countries and five other major economies. Different methods of measurement (that can assign speculative values to societal welfare and consumer gains) produce different results.[5] But whatever method of measurement is adopted, the internet's total economic contribution is small by comparison with what was hoped for in the 1990s.

The fourth conclusion is that the internet did not create a level playing field between small and large enterprise. The belief that it would was the principal evangelical component of the 'New Economy' thesis, and lay at the heart of its conviction that the internet would generate a surge of innovation and growth.[6] This article of faith proved to be wrong on several counts.

It underestimated the advantages of size.[7] Large corporations have bigger budgets, and greater access to capital, than small companies. This gives the former a competitive advantage, which they can exploit by lowering prices and increasing promotion. In general, large companies also have other built-in advantages: large economies of scale, enabling lower unit costs of production; economies of scope, based on the sharing of services and cross-promotion; and concentrations of expertise and resources that facilitate the launch of new products and services. While there can also be diseconomies of scale, large companies can renew themselves through acquiring dynamic young companies.

These advantages help to explain why large corporations continued to dominate leading market sectors, from car manufacture to grocery supermarkets. Indeed, in the leading economy (US), the number of *manufacturing* industries, in which the largest four companies accounted for at least 50% of shipment value, steadily increased between 1997 and 2007 (Foster et al. 2011: chart 1). There was also a truly remarkable increase between 1997 and 2007 in the market share of the four largest firms in leading sectors of the US *retail* industry. To take just two examples, the big four computer and software stores' share soared from 35% to 73%, while the share of the big four merchandising stores rose from 56% to 73%, during this period (Foster et al. 2011: table 1).

The trend towards corporate dominance was not confined to the offline world. In January 2011, 73.5% of the world's internet users visited either Google or its subsidiary, YouTube (Naughton 2012: 269). In the same month, the iTunes Store accounted for an estimated 71% of worldwide online digital music sales (Naughton 2012: 277–8). Amazon became the dominant online retailer (aided by economies of scale and scope), while Facebook became the leading social media site due partly to network effects (the bigger the service, the more useful it becomes). These corporations' rise to a position of ascendancy in a new industry, in so short a time, illustrates the underlying logic of the capitalist system: the natural processes of competition tend to diminish competition.

There is also compelling evidence that large companies proved to be better adapted to exploiting the opportunities offered by the internet than small companies. In 2012, 40% of large enterprises (with more than 250 employees) in OECD countries were engaged in e-commerce, compared with 20% of small businesses (with under 50 employees) (OECD 2014a: 42). E-commerce sales represent about 20% of all sales for large enterprises, but only 7% for small firms (OECD 2014a: 139). E-commerce proved particularly challenging for small and medium-sized enterprises in developing countries, for numerous reasons including inadequate infrastructure and high bandwidth costs (World Trade Organization 2013).

In brief, the economic impact of the internet was filtered through the unequal relations of competition in the marketplace. The prediction that small business would triumph in the internet era was never fulfilled. Corporate Goliaths continued to squash undersized Davids armed only with a virtual sling and pebble.

Global understanding

During the 1990s, there was a broad consensus that the internet would promote greater global understanding. 'The internet', declared the Republican politician Vern Ehlers (1995), 'will create a community of informed, interacting, and tolerant world citizens'. The internet, concurred Bulashova and Cole (1995), offers 'a tremendous "peace dividend" resulting from improved communications with and improved knowledge of other people, countries and cultures'. One key reason for this, argues the writer Harley Hahn (1993), is not just that the internet is a global medium but also that it offers greater opportunity for people to communicate with each other than do traditional media. 'I see the Net', he concludes, 'as being our best hope . . . for the world finally starting to become a global community and everybody just getting along with everyone else'. Another reason for optimism, advanced by numerous commentators, is that the internet is less subject to state censorship than traditional media, and is thus better able to host a free, unconstrained global discourse between ordinary citizens. It is partly because 'people will communicate more freely and learn more about the aspirations of human beings in other parts of the globe', opines Frances Cairncross (1997: xvi), that 'the effect will be to increase understanding, foster tolerance, and ultimately promote worldwide peace'. These themes – the internet's international reach, user participation, and freedom – continued to be invoked in the 2000s as grounds for thinking that the internet would bond the world in growing amity.

These arguments have been given a distinctive academic imprint by critical cultural theorists. Jon Stratton (1997: 257) argues that the internet encourages the 'globalization of culture' and 'hyper-deterritorialization' – by which he means the loosening of ties to nation and place. This argument is part of a well-established cultural studies tradition which sees media globalisation as fostering cosmopolitanism, and an opening up to other people and places (e.g. Tomlinson 1999).

Critical political theorists advance a parallel argument (Fraser 2007; Bohman 2004; Ugarteche 2007, among others). Their contention is that what Nancy Fraser (2007: 18–19) calls the 'denationalization of communication infrastructure' and the rise of 'decentered internet networks' are creating webs of communication that interconnect with one another to create an international public sphere of dialogue and debate. From this is beginning to emerge allegedly a 'transnational ethic', 'global public norms' and 'international public opinion'. This offers, it is suggested, a new basis of popular power capable of holding to account transnational economic and political power. While these theorists vary in terms of how far they push this argument (Fraser 2007, for example, is notably circumspect), they are advancing a thesis that goes beyond the standard humanist understanding of the internet as the midwife of global understanding. The internet is presented as a stepping-stone in the building of a new, progressive social order.

The central weakness of these optimistic perspectives is that they are based on inference from internet technology rather than evidence. Yet the readily available information tells a different story. The impact of the internet does not follow a trajectory dictated solely by its technology, but is filtered through the structures and processes of society. This constrains in at least seven different ways the role of the internet in promoting global understanding and a new social order.

Seven constraints

First, the world is unequal, and this limits participation in an internet-based global dialogue. In 2014, the richest 1% owned 48% of global wealth. The remaining 52% of the world's wealth was owned unequally, much of it by the richest 20% (Oxfam 2015). The distribution of income is also sharply unequal, and this disparity has increased (Piketty 2014). Indeed, the gap between rich and poor is currently the highest it has been in most OECD countries in 30 years (OECD 2014a).

Economic inequality is reproduced as a structure of access to the internet. Thus, 87% of North Americans, 72% of people in Oceania/Australia and 70% of those in Europe – the three richest regions in the world – are internet users, compared with 27.5% of the population in the poorest region, Africa (Internet Worlds Stats (IWS) 2015a). This disparity is even more marked when comparing rich and poor nations. In wealthy Norway and Sweden, 95% use the internet, compared with 15% of the population in low-income Pakistan, and 6% in impoverished Afghanistan (IWS 2015b).

Inequalities of internet use are determined not only by geography but also by inequalities within nations. In 2013, 92% of homes with an income of $100,000 or more used the internet in the United States, compared with 48% of households with an income of less than $25,000 (File and Ryan 2014). Similarly, Dutton et al. (2013) found that, in Britain, close to 100% of the highest income group use the internet, compared with only 58% of those in the lowest income group (less than £12,500). In emerging and developing countries, the poor, less educated and old are much less likely than the average to use the internet (Pew 2015). Gender is also an important determinant of use in developing countries, with especially low levels of use among women in Sub-Saharan Africa and some parts of the Middle East (Antonio and Tuffley 2014; Intel 2013).

Differences will be modified over time, as emergent economies grow. But because the world is so unequal, it will be a very long time before developing countries even approach current levels of net penetration in economically developed societies. Meanwhile, the internet is not bringing the world together: it is bringing primarily the advantaged into communion with each other. The total proportion of the population in December 2014 who are internet users is estimated to be 42% (IWS 2015c). The majority of the world is thus *not* part of the internet circle of 'mutual understanding'.

Second, the world is divided by language.[8] Most people speak only one language, and cannot understand foreigners when they speak in their own tongue. The nearest thing to a globally shared language is English which, according to the International Communications Union (2010), only 15% of the world's population understands. The next most widely shared language is Chinese, but this is little understood outside China and its diaspora. The role of the internet in bringing people together is thus severely hampered by mutual incomprehension.

Third, language is a medium of power. Those communicating online in English can reach, in relative terms, a substantial public due to Britain's imperial legacy and the US's international soft power. Mid-scale, those conversing in Arabic – the legacy of a once great power – communicate with 5% of internet users (IWS 2015d). Further down the scale, the Marathi-speaking population has only a very limited chance of being understood online outside Western India. Who gets attention on the internet, the 'medium of global understanding', depends on what language they speak.

Fourth, people have different degrees of cultural capital to draw upon. Some are eloquent, speak multiple languages, can deploy relevant expertise, and have flexible work hours, while others lack these assets. This can influence who gets to be heard. Take, for example, *openDemocracy*, an e-zine that publishes intelligent, informed comment about public affairs for an international public. It is dedicated to 'facilitating argument and understanding across geographical boundaries', and to ensuring that 'marginalized views and voices are heard' (OpenDemocracy n.d.). Despite these noble aspirations, 81% of its authors have elite occupations, and 71% live in North America or Europe (Curran and Witschge 2010, tables 6.2 and 6.3: 110–11). More generally, leading bloggers often come from elite backgrounds in Britain, America and elsewhere (Cammaerts 2008).

Fifth, the world is divided by conflicts of value, belief and interest. For example, ISIS has generated a storm of hatred. It is reviled in the West (e.g. *Daily Telegraph*, 4 April 2015) and in much of the Middle East (e.g. *Al Jazeera Online*, 1 September 2014) because its ambition to create a caliphate under religious law is a threat to neighbouring regimes, and is a direct challenge to the strategic objectives of the United States and its allies. ISIS is also abhorred because it is a bigoted, violent, repressive organisation with a punitive policy towards those it regards as Muslim heretics and apostates.

For its part, ISIS claims to be returning to an early, pure form of Islam. It is viewed by some as an inspiring beacon of uncorrupted Islamic renewal which strikes terror among its enemies, among them 'crusaders' from the West. ISIS's online beheadings secured global visibility. It has also skilfully used Twitter, Facebook and Instagram to proselytise, recruit, radicalise and raise funds (Farwell 2014). This has included developing a Twitter app to enable users to gain the latest information about ISIS, and the skilful manipulation of hashtag posts to dominate trending posts. At least 46,000 Twitter accounts were used by ISIS supporters between September and December 2014 (Berger and Morgan 2015). Yet ISIS is only the most recent, prominent example of a terrorist organisation using the internet to win converts and extend international links, in addition to transferring and laundering money (Conway 2006; Hunt 2011; Freiburger and Crane 2008).

But while indignant attention centres on Islamic militancy, it is worth noting that the Christian West has a rich tradition of online hatred. Indeed, race hate groups in the US were internet pioneers, with former Klansman Tom Metzger, then leader of White Aryan Resistance, setting up a community bulletin board as early as 1985 (Gerstenfeld et al. 2003). From these cyber-frontier origins, racist websites proliferated. The Raymond Franklin list of hate sites runs to over 170 pages (Perry and Olsson 2009), while the Simon Wiesenthal Centre (2011) documents 14,000 social network websites, forums, blogs, Twitter sites and other online sources in its *Digital Terror and Hate* report. Some of these websites built a large base: Stormfront, one of the earliest 'white-only' websites, had 52,566 users in 2005 (Daniels 2008: 134).

Detailed studies of race hate sites conclude that they maintain and promote racism in a variety of ways (Back 2001; Perry and Olsson 2009; Gerstenfeld et al. 2003). They can foster a sense of collective identity, reassuring militant racists that they are not alone. This can be accomplished not only through features like an 'Aryan Dating Page' but also through more conventional content such as forums discussing health, fitness and home making. The more sophisticated hate websites are adept at targeting children and young people by offering, for example, online games and practical help. Some have developed international networks of support in which ideas and information are shared. At the core of these websites is a message of racial hatred, typified by warnings of the 'demographic time bomb' of alien procreation in 'our' midst. These 'white fortresses' of cyberspace not only promote disharmony. There is a relationship between racist discourse and racist violence (Akdeniz 2009).

This illustrates one central point: the internet can spew out hatred, foster misunderstanding and perpetuate animosity. Because the internet is both international and interactive, it does not mean that it automatically encourages 'sweetness and light'.

Sixth, nationalist cultures are strongly embedded in most societies, and this constrains the internationalism of the web despite its global reach. Nation-centred cultures, sometimes nourished over centuries, are supported by television that is organized primarily on a national basis (with international channels like CNN usually drawing small audiences in most countries). Thus, in 2007 American network TV news devoted only 20% of its time to foreign news, while even its counterparts in two internationalist Nordic countries allocated just 30% (Curran et al. 2009: 13). Likewise, Aalberg et al. (2013: 8) found that, in eight out of 11 countries, the newscasts of leading television channels allocated less than a quarter of their time to foreign news in 2010; and Stepinska et al. (2013: 31) concluded that popular television channels in 17 countries devoted an average of only 22% of news items to purely foreign news in 2008. This national introversion, supported by national television, influences the content of the web. Thus, leading news websites in nine countries devoted, in 2010, only 23% of their content to exclusively international news, a proportion that was not much higher than their press and television rivals (Curran et al. 2013, table 5: 889).

National cultures can also influence web interactions. For example, China is a strongly nationalistic society. This is a consequence of national humiliations visited upon it by Western and Eastern imperial powers in the past; pride in the country's remarkable economic success; and the product of the Communist regime's deliberate cultivation of nationalism as a way of maintaining public support and social cohesion. Intense nationalism finds expression in Chinese websites and in online chat rooms. This can spill over into visceral hostility towards the Japanese in which not much understanding is displayed (Morozov 2011).

Seventh, authoritarian governments have developed ways of managing the net and of intimidating would-be critics. These will be discussed more fully later.[9] It is sufficient to note here that in many parts of the world people cannot, without fear, interact and say what they want online. Global internet discourse is distorted by state intimidation and censorship.

In short, the idea that cyberspace is a free, open space where people from different backgrounds and nations can commune with each other and build a more deliberative, tolerant world overlooks a number of things. The world is unequal and mutually uncomprehending (in a literal sense); it is torn asunder by conflicting values and interests; it is subdivided by deeply embedded national and local cultures (and other nodes of identity such as religion and ethnicity); and some countries are ruled by authoritarian regimes. These different aspects of the real world penetrate cyberspace, producing a ruined Tower of Babel with multiple languages, hate websites, nationalist discourses, censored speech and over-representation of the advantaged.

Yet there are forces of a different kind advancing greater cosmopolitanism. Cheap travel, mass tourism, increased migration, global market integration and the globalisation of entertainment have encouraged an increased sense of trans-national connection. Some of these developments find support in the internet. YouTube showcases shared experience, taste, music and humour from around the world that promote a 'we-feeling' (revealing, for example, that stand-up comedy in Chinese can be very funny, overriding the deadening effect of subtitles).[10] The internet also facilitates the rapid global distribution of arresting images that strengthen a sense of solidarity with beleaguered groups, whether earthquake victims or protesters facing repression in distant lands. The internet has the potential to assist the building of a more cohesive, understanding and fairer world. But the mainspring of change will come from society, not the smartphone.

One key way of effecting change is through democratic politics. Has the prediction that the internet would empower people, and revitalise democracy, been borne out by what has happened?

Empowerment

At the turn of the century, numerous scholars proclaimed that the internet would undermine dictators by ending their monopoly of information (e.g. Fukuyama 2002). The internet would also install, it was suggested, a new form of participatory democracy. 'It will not be long', proclaimed cultural studies guru Lawrence Grossman (1995), 'before many Americans sitting at home or at work will be able to use telecomputer terminals, microprocessors, and computer-driven keypads to push the buttons that will tell their government what should be done about any important matter of state'. More generally, it was thought that the internet would rejuvenate democracy because the public would gain unprecedented access to information, and be better able to control government (Toffler and Toffler 1995). The internet would also undermine elite control of politics because, according to Mark Poster (2001: 175), it would lead to 'empowering previously excluded groups'. Top-down communication between elites and the general public would be displaced by horizontal communication between social groups. In this brave new world the grassroots would reclaim power and inaugurate a 'renaissance of democracy' (Agre 1994). Thus, the funding of electoral candidates by ordinary citizens through the internet would overtake, we were told, corporate funding, bringing to an end the domination of money over politics.

Limits on empowerment

The often repeated claim that the internet would sound the death knell of dictatorship will be examined more closely in the next chapter. But it is worth noting here that this forecast failed to predict that authoritarian regimes would find a way of censoring the internet. Take, for example, Saudi Arabia, where an internet connection was first established in 1994. Public access to the internet was deferred until 1999, to give the government adequate time to organise an effective system of censorship. This included funnelling all international connections through the state-controlled Internet Services Unit, the pre-set blocking of proscribed websites, and the creation of a volunteer vigilante force to police the net (Boas 2006). In China, a still more sophisticated system was established to cope with a much larger volume of internet traffic. In essence, this came to rely on three tiers of control (King et al. 2013; Qiang 2012). The first, often referred to as the 'the Great Firewall of China', is the blocking of specified websites from operating in the country. The second is the blocking of 'keywords', which prevents users from posting things that contain banned words or phrases. The third is a system of licensed compliance which requires each site to be responsible for monitoring and censoring content, or be shut down. This has generated a legion of site censors, backed up by a large state internet police force. In addition, the state deploys an enormous number of both paid employees and volunteers to promote official thinking online (Hvistendahl 2014). This censorship system has evolved into a flexible regime that permits individual criticism of the government but aims to prevent organised protest and collective action. It can lead, when deemed necessary, to draconian measures including the localised disconnection of the internet (Mackinnon 2012).

Authoritarian states' internet censorship, though not comprehensive, has been effective enough in normal circumstances to contain online subversion. Indeed, the internet has often been enrolled as a state PR agency. A comparative study of eight nations concludes that 'many authoritarian regimes are proactively promoting the development of an Internet that serves state-defined interests rather than challenging them' (Kalathil and Boas 2003: 3). As we shall see in the next chapter, censorship can be undermined when dictators face organised resistance. But even in these circumstances, the internet strengthens rather than causes opposition to autocracy.

The hope that the internet would inaugurate a new era of direct democracy was also dashed. There were strong objections to online plebiscites on the grounds that they were contrary to the principle of *representative* democracy. The 'e-government' that did emerge usually took the form of inviting the public to comment, petition or otherwise respond online to an official website. This could be useful: for example, in Britain, 30% of online responses to a proposed new law in 1997 came from private individuals – a much higher proportion than in the era before online consultation (Coleman 1999). However, cumulative evidence suggests that online dialogue with government has, in general, three limitations (Slevin 2000; Chadwick 2006; Livingstone 2010). Citizens' inputs are often disconnected from real structures of decision making. Citizens are disinclined to take part in these consultations partly for this reason: thus, 10% or less report taking part in online consultations or voting in European Union countries (Seybert and Reinecke 2013). Sometimes 'e-democracy' means no more than one-sided communication in which the government provides information about services and promotes their use. In short, online consultation adds something to the functioning of democracy without making a great deal of difference.[11]

Nor did online funding end the political domination of money in the country where this hope was most frequently voiced. Politics in the US is especially driven by corporate and financial interests because of the country's failure to regulate effectively election campaign funding, and limit television political advertising which accounts for a high proportion of campaign expenditure (Curran 2011). The belief that all this would change as a consequence of the internet came to be embodied by an outsider candidate, Barack Obama, in the run-up to the 2008 Presidential election. In fact, the internet did help Obama to raise substantial financial contributions from ordinary citizens, and to win votes in the primaries and subsequent presidential election. But Barack Obama still had to secure large corporate donations as well as citizen funding to finance a $235.9 million television political advertising campaign, in addition to a large outlay on online campaigning and expensive professionals (Curran 2011). The dominance of money over politics remained fundamentally unchanged, even if the style of campaigning was modified to incorporate new as well as old methods.

Indeed, the 2012 US presidential election was the most expensive ever. As before, television advertising accounted for the largest chunk of campaign outlay: Obama spent $580 million on advertising in 2012, while Romney spent $470 million (Washington Post 2012). While the Obama team raised money through small individual donations, they raised substantially more from major corporations and wealthy individuals (OpenSecrets 2012). Even their use of the internet in 2012 was directed more towards managing voters than engaging with them in a meaningful way. For example, they invested heavily in data analytics and behaviour modelling to help them send different, crafted communications to different audiences (Bimber 2014).

The hope that the internet would empower the excluded and marginalised has also not been fully fulfilled. To understand why, it is necessary to situate the internet in its wider context.

A recurrent finding of political studies is that those on high incomes participate more in public affairs than those on low incomes. This has long been true of the United States (Schlozman et al 2012; Weeks 2013). It also holds for Britain where, in 2010, 'individuals in the highest income group were 43% more likely to vote than those in the lowest income group' (Birch et al. 2013: 8). It is true more generally of European countries not merely in relation to voting but to political participation in other ways (Lancee and Van de Werfhorst 2012). And the evidence from comparative research suggests that this is a more general, worldwide phenomenon (Solt 2008; Walker et al. 2013).

The principal explanation for differential participation is that those on low incomes tend to have lower self-esteem and a weaker sense of political efficacy than those who are better off. This has to do partly with how the poor are treated by others; this can be reinforced by the discourse of public anti-poverty policy; and it can arise also from a personal sense of inadequacy in which those on low incomes attribute their poverty to personal deficiency irrespective of structural factors (Sutton et al. 2014; Walker et al. 2013; Barry and Flint 2010). Social stigma can encourage a sense of powerlessness, while 'long-term poverty can make people feel that it is impossible to change things' (The UK Commission on Poverty, Participation and Power 2000: 4). Internalising individual deficiency explanations of poverty can also encourage the poor to turn away from collective political solutions (Lister 2004). Studies also show repeatedly that children of poor families can acquire low expectations and a diminished sense of confidence and entitlement through early socialisation (Hirsch 2007; Sutton et al. 2007; Horgan 2007). In some countries, most notably the United States, those on the lower end of the socioeconomic spectrum consume less news and talk less frequently about public affairs than those higher up the social scale. Politics is less frequently a feature of their everyday life (Smith 2013). In a comparative study of 22 nations, Frederick Solt (2008) also found that economic inequality depresses political interest, political discussion and voting, save among the affluent. One reason for this, Solt suggests, is that in unequal societies the privileged have a powerful incentive to participate in politics because they know from experience that they tend to do well out of it, while the disadvantaged have less reason to think this.

There are thus deep-seated social factors that encourage different levels of political participation in society. This is carried over into the online world. Di Genarro and Dutton (2006) found that in Britain the politically active tend to be drawn from the higher socioeconomic groups, the more highly educated and older people. Those engaged in political online participation are even more skewed towards the affluent and highly educated, though they are more often younger.[12] Di Genarro and Dutton's conclusion is that the internet seems to be promoting political exclusion rather than inclusion. Similarly, Oser et al. (2013: 99) found that 'the advantaged are more active in both online and offline participation' in the 2008 US election. In the subsequent 2012 US election, Smith (2013) found that online participation like offline participation was dominated by the well educated and well off. The same conclusion has been reached in some studies of political protest. For example, an ethnographic study of the Occupy Movement in Boston in 2011 noted that, while the protesters included the homeless and destitute, their overall social composition was 'skewed to the upper end of the spectrum of socioeconomic power and privilege' (Juris 2012: 265).

History shows that sustained collective action can mitigate the social disempowerment of poverty.[13] But this requires an enormous effort of collective organisation, institution building, cultural reformation, political leadership, electoral achievement and a progressive legislative programme, usually over a long period of time. It is not something that just happens effortlessly as a consequence of a new communications technology.

The internet has also failed to reinvigorate democracy in ways that were hoped for, due to the brake imposed by widespread political disengagement. A comparative study of 11 nations in four continents found that, in line with other surveys, 35% of respondents overall agreed or agreed strongly with the statement: 'no matter who people vote for, it won't make any difference to what happens'. Around half emerged as relatively disconnected from politics. Fifty-four per cent agreed that 'politics is so complicated a person doesn't understand what is happening', with the same percentage also saying that they feel themselves to be less informed than other people. The survey also revealed a low level of political knowledge (Curran et al. 2014).

The extent of political disconnection varies between countries, making it difficult to generalise about its causes. In part, political detachment would seem to be a disgruntled response to the perceived shortcomings of particular polities. Political disengagement is also the outcome of wider societal influences: in particular, it is claimed, the less representative nature of political systems in general (Gray and Caul 2000), increased individualism (Bauman 2001), greater social fragmentation (Couldry, Livingstone and Markham 2007), the legacy of patriarchy (Curran and Hayashi 2013) and a perceived lack of individual influence (Schudson 1997).

Indeed, the fact that large numbers of people are turned off politics helps to explain the prevailing pattern of internet use. Thus, a Pew survey of American internet users found that on a typical day 38% go online 'just for fun' or 'to pass the time', compared with 25% who say that they go online for news or information about politics (Pew 2009a). A more recent time-budget survey in the US found that the principal uses made of the internet were, in order of precedence: social networking, e-mails, doing searches and playing online games (GFK and IAB 2014: 18). In the case of the UK, the three principal uses were reported to be, in order of frequency: emailing, finding information about goods and services and, third, reading or downloading news, newspapers and magazines (Office for National Statistics 2014). Thus, accessing diverse information to hold government to account is not a priority concern of most internet users.

Far from fostering a democratic renaissance, it is not even clear that internet use has even increased overall political participation. The academic evidence on this is contradictory, suggesting at best a weak relationship between internet/social media use and increased political participation, but uncertainty about the direction of causation in this possible relationship (for a useful summary, see Boulianne 2015). The cautious tone of this literature is typified by this summary of a recent two-wave study:

Facebook use is positively related to civic and entertainment-oriented, but not to online or offline political, participation. Further analysis using structural equation modelling shows that prior levels of civic participation have a stronger effect on Facebook use than Facebook use has on civic participation. Facebook use only leads clearly to entertainment-centred participation.

(Theocharis and Quinteler 2014: 1)

The only evidence that supports the internet democratic regeneration thesis is case studies that suggest the internet has increased the effectiveness of activists. It is worth summarising some of these since this is an important outcome.

Empowered activists

In October 2010, a group of around 10 activists met in a north London pub. Some of them had read a recent article in the satirical magazine *Private Eye* about how the giant corporation Vodafone had avoided paying full tax by negotiating a 'sweetheart' deal with the tax authorities. This was also a time when a recently elected Conservative-Liberal Democrat Coalition government had announced major spending cuts. This prompted the group to initiate a campaign that linked the two issues together. They set up a website called UK Uncut, calling for direct action against tax avoidance at a time of public austerity. Their first demonstration temporarily closed down the Oxford Street branch of Vodafone. It was followed by other mass sit-ins and teach-ins in the premises of corporations 'dodging' tax, and was extended to banks under the slogan 'bail-in' to cuts, to coincide with the announcement of large bank executive bonuses.

Without the internet, this small group would not have been able to mobilise flash crowds and win media attention. Within six months, UK Uncut protests had been reported in numerous TV and radio reports, and had featured in around 40 articles (some hostile) in leading newspapers,[14] partly because these protests were thought to connect to an undercurrent of public indignation. This media coverage persisted for the next two years, helping to put corporate tax avoidance on the public agenda.

UK Uncut was helped by the climate of opinion at the time in Britain. However, the next example illustrates the way in which the internet can assist activists to huddle together when they are out of step with the national mood. MoveOn was set up in America to oppose militarism in the wake of the 9/11 terrorist attacks. Interviews and ethnographic observations suggest that MoveOn's online activity provided a safe haven for dissent at a time of intimidating patriotism. It also put sympathisers in touch with other like-minded people in their district, and spurred some armchair dissenters into becoming politically active. In a rapid expansion facilitated by the internet, MoveOn grew from 500,000 members in 2001 to 3 million in the US by December 2005 (Rohlinger and Brown 2008). A relative failure in terms of its campaign objectives, MoveOn nevertheless rallied and sustained dissent.

The internet has also been effective in facilitating the organisation of activist networks on an international scale. However, international coordination has happened on an extensive basis before with more limited communication technology – a point illustrated by a successful campaign at the dawn of the mass internet. Jody Williams had been alerted to the terrible injuries that left-behind landmines could inflict when she visited Nicaragua. She started an educational campaign in the United States, but made little progress. Realising that there were numerous anti-landmine organisations in other countries, she concluded that the way forward was to link them together. In 1992 she and her colleagues set up the International Campaign to Ban Land Mines, and relied initially on post, phone and fax (and only latterly the net). Yet they were able to bring together more than 700 groups in a concerted campaign for an international treaty. Their efforts were rewarded with the signing of the 1997 [anti-personnel] Mine Ban Treaty by 120 states (not including China and the US), leading to the award of a Nobel Peace prize (Klotz 2004; Price 1998).

The internet made it easier for activists to connect, interact, proselytise and mobilise. This is borne out by the campaign launched in 1997 against the Multilateral Agreement on Investments (MAI). Although the MAI's rationale was to promote international investment, its effect would have been to make it more difficult for elected governments to regulate international investors. This became clear when a draft of the proposed agreement was leaked, prompting a general mobilisation of international civil society. Progressive activists around the world were deluged with e-mails warning that MAI would lead to an international race to the bottom in terms of labour, human rights, the environment and consumer regulation. Within a remarkably short period of time, different progressive groups in international civil society (and some governments of developing countries) came together to exert concerted pressure. They found a champion in the French socialist government, which opposed the MAI (and also publicly applauded the internet campaign). This effectively prevented the MAI's adoption in 1998, owing to the OECD's consensus procedures (Smith and Smythe 2004).

This was followed by mass protests organised by the movements for global justice at the World Trade Organization meeting in Seattle (1999), the G8 summit at Genoa (2001) and subsequent meetings of world leaders, greatly assisted by the internet (Juris 2005). This led to a mass mobilisation at the G8 meeting at Gleneagles, in 2005, when debt relief measures for poorer countries were publicly proclaimed (though in fact only partly honoured).

The MAI campaign had an aftermath in the campaign against the Transatlantic Trade and Investment Partnership (TTIP) draft free trade agreement proposed between the European Union and the United States. Details of the draft agreement were only leaked relatively late in the negotiations to a German newspaper in 2014. This occasioned an online red alert, because the draft agreement would again make it more difficult to regulate investors. Among other things, it would enable large corporations to protect their interests by suing national governments in international arbitration tribunals. Environmental, consumer and labour movement groups came out in opposition, and organised petitions and demonstrations. At the time of writing, this campaign has not yet built up a head of steam of the kind that killed off the MAI.[15]

The internet has also enabled activists to make a general appeal to consumer power. Thus, an internet-aided campaign was initiated against Nike in the 1990s on the grounds that its expensive trainers were being made by workers who were employed for long hours in unsafe conditions, earning subsistence wages. The company responded by saying that it was not responsible for conditions in factories that it did not own. Increasing public pressure alerted the company to the danger that its brand could be seen as uncool and heartless. Nike then shifted its position and gave a public undertaking in 2001 that it would exert 'leverage' on contractors if they were bad employers. The campaign responded by holding Nike to account, and by publicly evaluating its claims to greater corporate responsibility (Bennett 2003).

Similarly, a part-time British DJ, Jon Morter, and his friends decided to launch a protest against the commercial manipulation of pop music. They chose as their target the way in which the winner of the television talent show *X Factor* in the UK regularly headed the Christmas music chart. Through Facebook and Twitter, they launched a counter-campaign for Rage Against the Machine, selecting as their Christmas choice a track that included the line: 'Fuck you, I won't do what you tell me'. The campaign took off, securing celebrity endorsements and extensive media publicity. The protest track secured the No. 1 Christmas spot in 2009, in a collective expression of resentment against commercial control.

The internet can also enable citizens to hold the media to account. Thus, in 2002, Senator Trent Lott – one of America's top politicians as Senate majority leader – made a speech at a birthday party attended by the Washington press corps, in which he referred approvingly to the race segregation politics of the 1940s. It received minimal attention, with a small item on the ABC news website. The blogosphere hummed with indignation, belatedly prompting Paul Krugman to endorse the protests in his *New York Times* column. This triggered further investigations by the TV networks and the *Washington Post*, which revealed that Senator Lott had made similar remarks in the past. In the ensuing political row President Bush, speaking to a mostly black audience, publicly rebuked the Senator. Trent Lott was forced subsequently to stand down as Senate majority leader. Thus, protests expressed through the internet persuaded mainstream media to conclude that an event that they had judged to be a non-story was in fact important (Scott 2004). This led to the fall of a leading politician, and the tacit redrawing of the boundaries of legitimate consent. Nostalgia for the racist politics of the past was defined as unacceptable in a political leader.

The internet can also enable the police to be held to account. In the hierarchy of news credibility, police statements ordinarily rank high. So when the Metropolitan Police (Met) said that Ian Tomlinson, a street newspaper seller who had got caught up in the London G20 protests in 2009, had died of natural causes, it was automatically believed. Equal credence was given to the Met's claim that the first contact police officers had with Tomlinson was when they attempted to give him first aid, despite being exposed to missiles from protesters. Thus, the London *Evening Standard* (2 April 2009) reported unquestioningly: 'Police Pelted with Bricks as They Help Dying Man'. The police account was supported by the Independent Police Complaints Commission (IPCC) which relied initially on the local police to investigate what had happened. It was then corroborated by Home Office Pathologist, Dr Freddy Patel, whose autopsy concluded that Ian Tomlinson had died of natural causes. This, seemingly, was the end of the matter.

But, in fact, something other than the official version of events had taken place. An apparent attempt to manage presentation of Tomlinson's death[16] was blown apart when a New York investment fund manager, who had filmed what had happened, belatedly sent the footage to the *Guardian*. It showed Tomlinson being struck, and then pushed to the ground, by a police officer. The video was published on the *Guardian* website, and then went viral on the web. The police sought, without success, to have the footage removed from the website. This merely increased the public pressure to find out what had really happened.

The media adopted a more questioning approach when visual evidence became available online on 7 April 2009. Thus, the previously credulous *Evening Standard* disputed the IPCC's claim that there were no CCTV cameras in the area where Tomlinson had died, pointing out that there were six. The regulator backed down, prompting the paper to report 'We Were Wrong over CCTV, Says Police Watchdog' (*Evening Standard*, 14 April 2009). A more critical tone also informed the reporting of mainstream broadcast channels (e.g. BBC Radio 4, 9 April 2009), and indeed of leading Conservative newspapers (e.g. *Times*, 9 April 2009 and *Sunday Telegraph*, 5 July 2009). Attention temporarily shifted from protestor violence, the focus of initial reporting, to police violence.

In response to this pressure, the truth gradually trickled out. A second and third post-mortem revealed that Ian Tomlinson had died partly as a consequence of the fall he had sustained. The official inquest concluded that Ian Tomlinson, who was already in poor health, had been unlawfully killed (Inquest 2009). The IPCC, belatedly galvanised into undertaking a proper investigation, found that the police officer, Simon Harwood, had been a marauding presence at the G20 protest, and was the person who struck and pushed Ian Tomlinson to the ground. Onlookers, who had attempted to come to the aid of Tomlinson as he lay on the ground, had been forced away by the police. It was not the case, as reported earlier, that the police had been obstructed by a barrage of missiles, when they eventually helped Tomlinson. Harwood was subsequently tried, admitted that he had made mistakes, but denied that he intended serious harm. He was found not guilty of manslaughter by the jury which took four days to reach its verdict. Harwood was later found guilty of gross misconduct by a police disciplinary panel, and sacked. The police made a strongly self-critical apology (reflecting a continuing commitment to consent-based policing), and paid compensation to Ian Tomlinson's family. After a careful scrutiny of his record, Dr Patel was struck off the medical register.

What happened in London is part of a wider pattern. The so-called 'Miami Model' of mass protest policing, based on a more militarised mode of operation, an emphasis on containment ('kettling') and targeted response, was increasingly adopted in Western countries after its successful piloting in 2003 (Monaghan and Walby 2012; Milberry and Clement 2014). Protesters adapted to more coercive policing by using mobile phones to monitor police conduct in so-called counter-surveillance.

Thus, the follow-up G20 mass protest in Toronto in 2010 led to angry confrontations with the police, and the arrest of over 1000 people (most of whom were released without charge). Those charged included Adam Nobody (his real name), after an encounter that was filmed and put on YouTube. The footage shows him with his face down, his arms behind his back and a police officer's fist smashing into his face. A leading local paper (*Globe and Mail*, 30 November 2011) reported that when Adam Nobody was asked who he was, and gave his name, a police officer thought it was provocative and gave him a further beating. Nobody sustained a fractured cheekbone and broken nose, requiring several hours of surgery.

The YouTube video became a focus of public debate, with the local police chief, Bill Blair, claiming that it had been tampered with. This escalated the political row, and led to the appointment of an official enquiry by the independent police regulator. His report was sharply critical of the police's poor training, inadequate planning, excessive force and violation of human rights during and after the protest (McNeilly 2012: vi–vii ff.). The charges against Nobody were withdrawn: a police officer, Babak Andalib-Goortani, was subsequently found guilty of assaulting him (CBC News, 29 January 2015).

The mobile phone also became a way of calling police to account in the US. In 2014–15, online videos of the police killing Michael Brown, Eric Garner and Walter Scott and of the lead-up to the fatal police injuring of Freddie Gray – all African Americans – generated a storm of online indignation, followed by protests across America. Again, actual visual online evidence caused some mainstream news media, including network TV news reporting to be more critical.

Cumulative public pressure had a variable effect. It led to a federal investigation into Michael Brown's slaying which concluded that there was overwhelming racial bias in the town's policing, and recommended a root and branch reform of the local police. No action was taken in relation to the death of Eric Garner, even though the city medical examiner concluded that Garner had been killed as a consequence of police action. By contrast, Michael Slager, the police officer who shot Walter Scott, was charged in 2015. Six police officers, suspected in relation to Freddie Gray's death, were suspended, and a separate investigation by the US Department of Justice authorised.

Case studies of online protest seem to be skewed towards progressive causes. This may be because there has been an increase of predominantly left-wing political protest in the West due to the international economic crisis, deepening inequality and the crisis of political legitimacy in a growing number of countries (Castells 2015). It may also reflect the selective interests of academic researchers, resulting in an unrepresentative sample of case studies. But there is no reason to suppose that the internet is inherently left-wing. Indeed, from the start, conservatives became better organised online than liberals in the United States (Hill and Hughes 1998). The internet has continued to be important for the American right, as evidenced by the role of the internet in the rise of the Tea Party Movement (Thompson 2010). All that can be claimed perhaps is that because the press tends to favour the right in many countries, the creation of a new space of communication potentially accessible to different viewpoints is of disproportionate significance for the left.

But in general the use of the internet by activists of different persuasions has strengthened the infrastructure of democracy. By making activists (of all persuasions) more effective, better able to forge links with other networks and in a stronger position to communicate their concerns to a wider public and mobilise support, the internet has helped to energise civil society.

Wider disempowerment

However, this enhancement has been offset by other trends that have resulted in a greater concentration of power. Big business accounts for a greatly increased share of global trade, and is more mobile than before. This places large corporations in a stronger position to play governments off against each other, pay less tax and secure market-friendly policies. The deregulation of global capitalism, and the growth of financial markets, has further diminished the ability of national governments – and of national electorates – to hold economic power to account, and manage their economies (Panitch and Gindin 2012; Crouch 2004; Curran 2002). The faltering development of a global system of governance has failed to offset this decrease of national state power. As Peter Dahlgren (2005) notes, 'there are simply few established mechanisms for democratically based and binding *transnational* decision making' (emphasis added). Meanwhile, political power in many national democracies has become more centralised; politicians have become sometimes less representative; and their interactions with the electorate more manipulative, more guided by public relations and more media-distorted (Esser and Stromback 2014; Davis 2010; Hay 2007; Marquand 2008, among others). If the internet has increased the impact of political activists – and there is good reason to think that it has – this is in the context of polities that have become more strongly influenced by economic and political elites. Paradoxically, the internet-based empowerment of activists is taking place in a wider political context of greater disempowerment.

To sum up, the forecast that the internet would rejuvenate democracy and empower the people was based on an extrapolation from its technology. It has been fulfilled to the extent that the internet has enabled activists to have greater impact. But the internet has not given rise to direct democracy, reduced the power of money in American politics, turned the public into news junkies holding government to account, enfranchised the excluded or even substantially increased overall political participation. What predictions failed to take into account was that the empowering effects of the internet would be constrained by the demoralising effects of poverty, growing public disconnection from politics, and the increasing preponderance of political and economic elites.

But surely all this is changing because the wider communications environment is being transformed. Is not top-down control of the media being undermined? Cannot ordinary people speak to millions in a way that was impossible before? After all, this is what people, who were in a position to know, told us would happen.

Renaissance of journalism

The internet, according to Rupert Murdoch, is democratising journalism. 'Power is moving away', he declares, 'from the old elite in our industry – the editors, the chief executives and, let's face it, the proprietors', and is being transferred to bloggers, social networks and consumers downloading from the web (Murdoch 2006). This view is echoed by the leading British conservative blogger Guido Fawkes, who proclaimed that 'the days of media conglomerates determining the news in a top-down Fordist fashion are over . . . Big media are going to be disintermediated because the technology has drastically reduced the cost of dissemination' (cited in Beckett 2008: 108). The radical academic lawyer Yochai Benkler (2006) concurs, arguing that a monopolistic industrial model of journalism is giving way to a pluralistic networked model based on profit and non-profit, individual and organised journalistic practices. The radical press historian John Nerone goes further, believing that the media's *ancien régime* has been superseded already. 'The biggest thing to lament about the death of the old order [of journalism]', he chortles, 'is that it is not there for us to piss on any more' (Nerone 2009: 355). Numerous commentators, drawn from the left as well as the right, and including news industry leaders, citizen journalists and academic experts, have reached the same conclusion: the internet is bringing to an end the era of media moguls and conglomerate control of journalism.

The second related theme of this euphoric commentary is that the internet will lead to the reinvention of journalism in a better form. The internet will be 'journalism's ultimate liberation', according to Philip Elmer-Dewitt (1994), because 'anyone with a computer and a modem can be his own reporter, editor and publisher – spreading news and views to millions of readers around the world'. One version of this vision sees traditional media being largely displaced by citizen journalists who will generate 'a back-to-basics, Jeffersonian conversation among the citizenry' (Mallery, cited in Schwartz 1994). An alternative version sees professional journalists working in tandem with enthusiastic volunteers to produce a reinvigorated form of journalism (e.g. Beckett 2008; Deuze 2009). This is a view now coming out of the heart of the news industry. 'Journalism will thrive', proclaims Chris Ahearn, Media President at Thomson Reuter, 'as creators and publishers embrace the collaborative power of new technologies, retool production and distribution strategies and we stop trying to do everything ourselves' (Ahearn 2009).

The dethroning of traditional news controllers and the renewal of journalism are thus the two central themes of this forecast. Indeed, it is now argued that these changes are upon us. The technological development of the internet, notably the shift to Web 2.0, has given ordinary people a 'voice' and ended traditional gate-keepers' monopoly of mediation. New words – such as 'prosumer', 'prosumption' and 'produsage' – have been coined to capture the boundlessly creative role of the public in a new, more open system of journalistic production and consumption. Once again a new vocabulary has to be learnt, it seems, to comprehend the magnitude of the changes that are taking place.

Indeed, the possibilities opened by up by new technology are said by some to go even further than the transformation of journalism. We are entering, according to Manuel Castells (2012: 8), a new era of 'mass self-communication' which will transform power relations in the network society. The democratisation of communication opens the way, in his view, to the building up of counter-power and a new insurgent politics (Castells 2015).[17]

These accounts all fail to grasp the extent to which traditional media gatekeepers are still in control. For a start, television remains the principal source of news. This is the case in 10 out of 11 countries surveyed by Papathanassopoulos et al. (2013), in nine out of 10 countries surveyed by Newman and Levy (2014), and in all eight countries examined by Nielsen and Schrøder (2014). The continuing primacy of television as a source of news is confirmed also by recent, authoritative national studies (for example, Ofcom 2014a; Mitchell and Page 2015).

The media pecking order is in a process of transition. In general, the old are more oriented towards to TV news and less towards online news than the young.[18] In South Korea and Finland, the net has overtaken TV as the main source of news (Papathanassopoulos et al. 2013; Newman and Levy 2014). Both countries have very high internet penetration rates, and their experience is probably a portent of things to come. But while it is likely that the news hierarchy will change, this has not yet happened in most countries.

More importantly, television and newspaper organisations – so-called 'legacy' media – colonised the news segment of cyberspace. They were quick to set up their own news websites to gain first mover advantage. Most legacy media also subsidised these new ventures by making available their news-gathering resources, and giving away online content for free.

This strategy succeeded in securing for legacy media a lead position in online news. The top news websites in a nine-nation survey were found to be owned overwhelmingly by legacy media organisations (Curran et al. 2013). National sources suggest that this success has not been confined to the first league but often extends in depth. Thus, the 10 most viewed news websites in the United States in 2015 are Yahoo-ABC News, CNN Network, NBC News Digital, Huffington Post, CBS News, USA Today, BuzzFeed, New York Times, Fox News Digital Network and Mail Online/Daily Mail (Mitchell and Page 2015: 11). Eight out of these 10 are controlled by legacy news organisations. Similarly, in the UK, the 10 most viewed news sites in April 2014 were the BBC, Mail Online, Guardian,

Telegraph, Trinity Mirror Nationals, Huffington Post, Independent, CNN Digital Network, Newsquest Media Group and Yahoo News Websites (Johnson 2014). Again, eight out of the 10 are owned by legacy organisations.

So, when people consume news online, it is generally supplied by legacy organisations. Not very surprisingly, this online news is very similar to their other news output. Indeed, a nine-nation survey found that public affairs news on leading TV, print and online outlets even cite very similar sources – most notably, the state and powerful institutions (Curran et al. 2013: 886, table 3).

Legacy media also succeeded in weakening the challenge of new online start-ups. Legacy media's superior resources, established brand names and early online success deterred competition. Crucially, the decision of most media managements to establish free news websites made it difficult for new independents to charge for content. This was a way of preventing a business model from taking root that would sustain competition.[19]

Consequently, few online independents made an impact, and most struggled to survive. While there have been some successes in the West (Huffington Post (acquired by AOL in 2011), BuzzFeed and more recently Vice News among them), they are the exceptions. A survey of online independents in the US concluded that 'despite enthusiasm and good work, few if any of these are profitable or even self-financing' (Pew 2009b). Similarly, a Columbia Journalism Review study concluded that 'it is unlikely that any but the smallest of these [independent web-based] news organisations can be supported primarily by existing online revenue' (Downie and Schudson 2010). A follow-up Pew survey concluded bleakly that digital-only news organisations have 'had bumpy rides' (Mitchell and Page 2015). To judge from a transnational survey, many online media start-ups 'are not challenging the legacy media' but merely supplementing them 'by serving smaller niche audiences' as a strategy for staying afloat (Cook and Sirkkunen 2012: 117).

The weak challenge posed by online news independents has had a knock-on effect on what has been accessed through content aggregators. These are algorithm-driven organisations oriented towards frequency of use in much the same way that advertising-based commercial TV companies are driven by audience ratings. Redden and Witschge (2010) explore the implications of this by analysing how the two most important aggregators, Google and Yahoo, covered five major news stories in 2007–8. They found that the majority of first-page items for all five stories in both aggregators derived from leading news websites. The remainder came from establishment sources: not one came from an 'alternative source' (Redden and Witschge: 2010: 180–1). This selection matters, Redden and Witschge point out, because research shows that most users do not venture beyond the first page of search results. In other words, the selection criteria adopted by Google and Yahoo for giving prominence to news stories has had the effect of reproducing the ascendancy of the main news media, and of the principal institutional sources they draw upon.

Potentially, the rise of social networking sites (SNS) could have undermined the ascendancy of legacy media, and their online subsidiaries.[20] SNS could have become a parallel space in which people independently seek out, share, create and consume an alternative corpus of news. But, in ordinary circumstances, this is not what is happening. Nielsen and Schrøder (2014) compare the use made of SNS in eight economically advanced nations. Less than a third of online users say that they use social media as a source of news – fewer, even, than those who cite print media (Nielsen and Schrøder 2014: 479, table 2). In six out of eight countries, less than a quarter say that SNS is their main way of finding news online (Nielsen and Schrøder 2014: 483, table 4). In the same six countries, less than a fifth share or comment on a story on SNS, share a story via email or comment on one via a website. Established media are still the prime movers in the supply, selection and dissemination of news, in a top-down way.

The larger claim made that the internet has inaugurated the era of mass self-communication, and created conditions conducive to political transformation, also seems overblown. A recent comparative survey found that only between 1 and 5% of online users produce a blog, depending on the country (Nielsen and Schrøder 2014: 484). Even in the United States, the country with the highest proportion of bloggers in this survey, only a minority are interested in political blogs. Twelve per cent of Americans regularly read blogs about politics and current affairs, with a further 21% saying that they read them sometimes (Kohut et al. 2012). Most bloggers are amateurs, who need their regular day job to pay their way (Couldry 2010). This makes it more difficult for them to research stories or secure a large audience, unlike the very small number of professional bloggers.

Of course, the internet places a cheap tool of communication in the hands of citizens. But an enhanced ability to communicate at low cost should not be equated with being heard. Although Twitter encompasses public affairs, it is not the citizen's megaphone that it is sometimes represented to be. Celebrities – like the British actor, Stephen Fry, who had 11.6 million 'followers' in 2015 (https:// twitter.com/stephenfry/followers) – reach a much larger audience than ordinary individuals.

Activist groups have found it difficult to get the attention of mainstream media (Fenton 2010b). This is confirmed by a study that found that, in 2010, civil society organisations accounted for less than 15% of the sources cited in political and policy issue stories in leading media in nine countries (and 5% or less, in the case of Colombia, South Korea and Japan) (Tiffen et al. 2014: 385, table 9b).

What activist groups say can also be lost on the web. This is partly because their statements tend to get a low search engine listing. As Hindman (2009: 14) succinctly puts it, the internet is not 'eliminating exclusivity in political life: instead, it is shifting the bar of exclusivity from the production to the filtering of political information'. And while SNS offer a new space of communication, they are used more for social than for political purposes. Thus, in the UK, more Twitter users (72%) say that they follow their friends than follow the news (45%) (Ofcom 2014b). In the US, only 34% of SNS users say that they post thoughts or comments on political issues (Smith 2013). In the EU, less than 20% of people report posting opinions on civic or political issues via websites (Seybert and Reinecke 2013).

But at least it seems reasonable to suppose that the internet has greatly enhanced the quality of journalism. After all, as a consequence of the internet, journalists have faster access to more information and to a wider range of news sources. This should make it easier to verify stories and give expression to different viewpoints. Journalists can also draw more easily upon feedback and input from their audiences.

Declining quality

However, this optimistic assessment leaves out the devastating consequences of lost advertising. The internet is cheap, and good at targeting specific groups of consumers. After a slow start, these attributes generated a meteoric rise in internet advertising at the expense of both the press and television. Internet advertising now accounts for the largest share of media advertising in Canada and the UK, and is thought likely to gain the largest share in the US by 2016 (IAB Canada 2014; Advertising Association/Warc 2015; Forrester Research 2014), with similar trends elsewhere.

Loss of advertising would not have mattered if advertising was merely being diverted from legacy to online news, with dying newspapers being replaced by thriving news websites. But in fact, some of this diverted advertising went to advertising-only websites, content aggregators and other websites unrelated to news production. This erosion of commercial subsidy for journalism (exacerbated by the recession) has led to a reduction in the number of journalists. Nel (2010) estimates that the number employed in the UK's 'mainstream journalism corps' shrank by between 27% and 33% between 2001 and 2010. US newsroom employment declined from 55,000 to 36,700 between 2006 and 2013 (Barthel 2015). In Canada, about 10,000 media jobs were lost between 2008 and 2013 in print and broadcast sectors (Wong 2013). In Australia, it has been estimated there was a 20% cut in the mainstream journalism workforce between 2012 and 2014 (O'Donnell et al. 2015).

Editorial budget cuts have caused the quality of journalism to deteriorate. Thus, in the case of the American media, the FCC (2011) mourns the decline of 'accountability reporting' in local TV news, while a damning Pew report concludes that there has been a narrowing of the news agenda on local television and more low-cost opinion at the expense of reporting on cable news (Jurkowitz et al. 2013). Major savings have been made in international reporting. This has contributed to the halving of the amount of airtime on US network evening newscasts devoted to overseas reporting in 2013 compared with the late 1980s. It is also why the number of international reporters working for US newspapers declined by 24% between 2003 and 2010 (Mitchell and Page 2014: 5).

A major study of British journalism also concludes that a pervasive process of deterioration is taking place (Fenton 2010a; Lee-Wright et al. 2011), in marked contrast to hyped predictions of regeneration. It found that fewer journalists are being called upon to produce more content, as a consequence of newsroom redundancies, the integration of online and offline news production, and the need to update stories in a 24-hour news cycle. This is encouraging journalists to rely more on tried-and-tested, mainstream news sources as a way of boosting output. It is also fostering the lifting of stories from rivals' websites as a way of increasing productivity, even to the extent of using the same news frames, quotes and pictures. Depleted resources are contributing in general to increased reliance on scissors-and-paste, deskbound journalism. This is exacerbating an endemic weakness of British journalism (Davies 2008; Jackson and Moloney 2015). A similar trend towards imitative journalism and the 'spiral of sameness', partly driven by increased financial pressures, has also been found in Argentina and elsewhere (Boczkowski 2010: 4).

The emergence of not-for-profit, investigative news organisations has offset, to a small degree, editorial cost saving. Thus ProPublica, an investigative newsroom in Washington, has researched a number of important stories (including one winning a Pulitzer Prize) and secured an audience for these stories by working in collaboration with established media outlets (Curran 2012). But a recent survey of this not-for-profit sector shows that it has failed to build an autonomous revenue base, and relies perilously for 58% of its revenue from charitable sources (Knight Foundation 2015).

To sum up, legacy news organisations have entrenched their ascendancy because they now have a commanding position in *both* the offline and online production of news. They have not been deposed by independent news websites because these usually have limited funds and small audiences. They have not been displaced by SNS because these are generally used for social rather than political purposes. And the rise of content aggregators has extended rather than subverted their domination.

The prediction that the internet would regenerate journalism now also looks fallible. It is true that the internet makes it easier for journalists to do a good job by quickly accessing diverse information, including inputs from the public. However, citizen journalism in a fully developed partnership form, with professionals working closely together with amateurs, has been rare. And what was not anticipated was that the rise of the internet would cause advertising support for journalism to shrink (at least for now). This has resulted in fewer journalists writing more stories, often less well. This is making for imitative, conventionally sourced, deskbound journalism.

Even the belief that the internet has inaugurated individual mass communication that will give rise to political transformation looks highly questionable. The rise of blogging was overhyped. SNS is not ordinarily a politicised alternative communication system. Those seeking to change society can network between themselves more effectively – something that is really important. But they still have the problem of gaining a hearing from increasingly entertainment-centred news media.

Yet this overall picture conceals significant variations. An unduly sceptical assessment can blank out important exceptions. There have been places where citizen journalism has triumphed, and where social media have been politicised and played a pivotal role in mobilising dissent. What gives rise to this variance is something that needs to be investigated, and understood better.

Different contexts/different outcomes

In Britain, citizen journalism has been a relative flop, whereas in South Korea it was for a time a powerful force. The explanation for this divergence lies in the different political and social circumstances of the two countries.

At the turn of the century there was limited pressure for radical political and cultural change in Britain. A youth-based cultural revolt had taken place more than a quarter of a century earlier. There was growing disengagement from politics, reflected in the lowest ever turnout in the 2001 general election (Couldry et al. 2007).

So when the public affairs website *openDemocracy* (OD) started in 2001, it was in a relatively becalmed period when the winds of change, both political and cultural, had died down in Britain. OD was also an international project, only partly connected to a British base. With substantial foundation support, an able team at the centre and drawing upon a talented network of unpaid or poorly paid contributors, the website became the leading British venture of its kind. Its total, gross number of visitors per month peaked at 441,000 in 2005 before falling rapidly thereafter. The venture then went into financial crisis in 2007 (Curran and Witschge 2010), from which it has never fully recovered

By contrast, there was a pressure-cooker build-up in favour of political and cultural change in South Korea at the turn of the century. The short-lived attempt to create a parliamentary democracy in 1960 had been overtaken by a military coup. However, the democracy movement gained increased momentum in the subsequent period, securing major constitutional reforms in 1987. A civilian president was elected in 1992, and this opened the way to further liberalisation. The number of civil society organisations doubled in the 1990s, having doubled in the previous decade (Kim and Hamilton 2006: 553, table 5). There was also a long-running campaign for greater media independence from government that gained support from increasingly disaffected journalists (Park et al. 2000). Public attacks were made on collusion between big business and government, the neoliberal policies pursued in the wake of the Asian 1997–8 economic crisis and the continued presence of a large, unaccountable American army in the country. The politician Roh Moo-hyun came to represent the gathering tide of radical reformism, and was elected President in 2002. This upsurge of political radicalism was accompanied by a growing cultural revolt against authoritarian conformity.

OhmyNews (OMN) was launched in 2000 by a young, radical journalist, Yeon Ho Oh, with a modest launch fund of $85,000. It initially had a skeletal staff of four, supported by 727 volunteer 'citizen journalists' (Kim and Hamilton 2006). But it was different from the three dominant national dailies, all of which were closely identified with the establishment. It quickly became a leading platform of political and cultural dissent, and grew rapidly at a time of popular radicalisation.

The website's registered citizen journalists rose to 14,000 in 2001 and more than doubled to 34,000 by 2004. Its core staff in 2004 had expanded to 60 people (of whom 35 were full-time journalists). This was accompanied by a meteoric growth in OMN's readership. A survey undertaken for an independent investor company estimated that in 2004, OMN had 2.2 million visitors a month. Winning this volume of young, mostly affluent users solved the perennial problem of independent web publishing – lack of income. OMN became profitable by 2003 because it attracted substantial online advertising. By contrast, the donations and voluntary subscriptions from users remained relatively low, very much less than the modest proceeds of its print edition (Kim and Hamilton 2006: 548, table 1).

OMN 'reinvented' journalism by skilfully harnessing professionals and amateurs in a joint venture. By the mid-2000s, its core group of professional journalists wrote only about 20% of the website content. However, they selected and edited the articles sent in by 'citizen journalists' that were published in the main sections of the website. Space was created beside articles for readers' responses, and the website hosted chat rooms on different topics. Citizen journalists received a token payment if their articles were accepted in the main section. Articles, unpaid and unedited, were also published in the 'kindling' sections of the website. The whole operation was overseen by a committee made up of both professionals and representatives of citizen journalists. By 2004, OMN published between 150 and 200 articles each day, becoming in effect a website 'daily'.

This remarkable achievement – attracting a legion of volunteers, building a mass audience, achieving solvency and influencing public life – made OMN one of the world's most successful experiments in 'pro-am' journalism. However, this success was created in the crucible of radical expectation, when it seemed as if South Korea was going to make a decisive break with the past. As it turned out, anticipated reforms were not enacted, or were discontinued in the face of determined political and business opposition, during the Roh ministry. The Korean economy also underperformed under Roh's watch. In the next presidential election (2007), the Conservative (GNP) candidate won in a low poll. In 2009, former President Roh – facing the prospect of criminal charges for bribery and corruption – committed suicide. There followed a period of conservative domination culminating in the election of Park Geun-hye as President in 2013. She is the daughter of the right-wing general who overthrew the democratic government in a military coup in 1961.

OMN suffered as a consequence of its close association with a 'failed' President, and from the decline of the left. The proliferation of new websites also meant that OMN ceased to be the natural home of cultural dissent. It also became apparent, in retrospect, that its volunteer base was unrepresentative: in 2004, 77% were men, and were drawn disproportionately from 'Greater' Seoul (Joyce 2007: 'exhibit' 2). The website ceased to be profitable in 2006, and ran into increasing financial difficulty thereafter. OMN is now a shadow of its former self.

New technology was central to OMN's initial success because it lowered costs, facilitated contributions from volunteers and enabled lively interactions on its website. But OMN only became a world leader in citizen journalism because bottled-up expectations in the early 2000s caused the project to lift off. When the political wind subsided, OMN fell to the ground.

The importance of the external context in enabling or disabling the realisation of the technological potential of the internet can also be illustrated by what happened to OMN's sister website launched in Japan in 2006. The project had substantial resources because OMN went into partnership with a telecommunications corporation. However, Japan, a strongly consensual, democratic corporatist society, offered less fertile soil for the new venture than polarised South Korea. OMN Japan found it difficult to recruit good left-wing journalists. Those they did recruit tended to be professionally oriented, and clashed with volunteers who objected to heavy editing. Web traffic stayed low, and amateur contributors to OMN Japan remained less than a tenth of their counterparts in Korea (Joyce 2007). An attempt was made to save the website by giving it a softer, lifestyle focus, but to no avail. The venture closed in 2008, a failure from the very outset.

In 2004 OMN also set up an English-language, international website. OMN International attracted a relatively small number of contributors and users. This detracted from its quality (reflected in its very erratic and uneven coverage of news and issues around the world), and saddled it with financial problems (Dencik 2011). It is still in existence but struggling. Unlike its parent website, it never connected to a strong headwind of popular radicalism.

Control/empowerment

The importance of political context can be illustrated in another way by comparing two neighbouring countries, Singapore and Malaysia. In one country, the internet has been largely tamed, whereas in the other it has become an important channel of dissent.

This difference has not arisen because internet penetration is higher in Malaysia. Quite the contrary; the percentage of the population who use the internet in Singapore (79%) is appreciably larger than it is in Malaysia (66%) (Internet World Stats 2015e). Nor is the difference attributable to divergent censorship arrangements. While Singapore's internet policy is notionally more restrictive, since it entails formal website licensing, in actual practice it is little different from that in Malaysia (George 2007; Weiss 2014). Both countries have an authoritarian framework of law but have adopted a relatively liberal policy towards the internet to further their economic modernisation programmes.

The role of the internet has diverged in Singapore and Malaysia principally because the two countries have different structures of power. Singapore is ruled by a single, united party (PAP) which has been in office since 1965 when the country became independent. PAP dominates directly or indirectly all aspects of life in the small city state. It uses coercive methods to perpetuate its rule, from the annual licensing of civil society organisations to the ruthless pursuit of political opponents through the law courts in defamation suits. But the regime also enjoys consensual support based on its remarkable economic success, the appeal of its national ideology stressing Asian values, public morality and social harmony, and the tacit backing of the media controlled by corporations with close links to government (George 2007; Worthington 2003; Rodan 2004). This dominance has resulted in a largely quiescent civil society which works with rather than against the government. And it has produced a succession of general election results in which the ruling party has powered to overwhelming victories. Only in 2011 did a significant opposition – the centre-left Workers Party – make a breakthrough by winning six seats. Even then, the remaining 81 constituency-based seats were monopolised by the ruling party.

So great has been the ruling elite's domination of Singaporean society that the internet has been largely neutralised as a space of dissent. Even a critical website, which operated outside Singapore's jurisdiction in the early 2000s, stayed largely within the framework of official ideology due to its hegemonic reach (Ibrahim 2006). Indeed, when Andrew Kenyon (2010) undertook a comparative analysis of critical reporting in three countries – Australia, Malaysia and Singapore – he had to omit Singaporean online content because there were too few critical articles to constitute an adequate sample.

This online domination was modified when the ban on online campaigning in elections was lifted in 2011, and the Workers Party gained significant minority support. But while the Workers Party is outspokenly critical on issues like affordable housing, it does not challenge the legitimacy of the regime. Meanwhile, powerful pressures to conform in Singapore's authoritarian society persist. As Meredith Weiss (2014: 98) notes, limited internet activism 'has yet to undo decades of socialization towards self-censorship'.

Superficially, the politics of Malaysia appear similar to those of Singapore. One ruling group, the Barisan Nasional (BN), has been in power since national independence. The regime combines coercive measures – most notably the Sedition Act inherited from British colonial rule – with a national ideology stressing nation building, racial harmony and social responsibility. But there the resemblance stops. The ruling group is a political coalition, not a single party as in Singapore. It has been at times rancorous and divided, unlike the remarkably cohesive PAP. The first major split within BN occurred in 1997 when the Deputy Prime Minister, Ibrahim Anwar, was sacked, and subsequently jailed for what were widely thought to be trumped-up charges of sodomy and corruption. The second fracture happened when Prime Minister Abdullah Badawi was in effect ousted in 2009, following sustained criticism from his long-serving predecessor, Mohamad Mahathir, and other prominent critics within his party. And in 2015, new tensions surfaced when the government became engulfed in a corruption scandal, eliciting yet more criticism from the outspoken former premier, Mohamad Mahathir. The ruling group is thus partly dysfunctional. Although it has presided over economic growth, BN has not attained the same degree of spectacular economic success as its counterpart in Singapore.

Malaysia has long been a more divided society than Singapore in terms of its ethnic composition and religious affiliation. This helped to generate a stronger

political opposition. The general tenor of this opposition also became more viru-
lent than in Singapore, culminating in the last decade in accusations of systemic
racism, irreligion, violent intimidation and organised electoral fraud that implic-
itly attack the legitimacy of the regime (Postill 2014). In addition, Malaysia has a
more active civil society than in Singapore with civil rights, constitutional reform,
Hindu rights, Islamic groups and other prominent organisations (George 2007).

Against this background, the internet became an increasingly important space
of dissent and criticism in Malaysia. Civil society groups set up independent websites. A dissenting minority press that had survived in Malaysia also developed
an online presence. By the mid-2000s, internet activists became organised, and
developed strong links with each other, in a way that did not happen in Singapore.
Cherian George (2005) found that Malaysian websites in the early 2000s more
frequently updated their content, were better resourced, were more critical and
reached a very much larger audience than their counterparts in Singapore.

Indeed, there were three key moments when the internet played a significant
role in fanning dissent in Malaysia (Postill 2014). In 1998–9 Reformasi, a Muslim
reformist organisation, was launched in response to the jailing of the heir apparent, Ibrahim Anwar, with the support of over 50 pro-Anwar websites. At its 1999
peak, the Laman Reformasi site received more than 5 million visits. Opposition
news sites, listservs and forums served as virtual meeting places in a country
where the right of assembly was severely curtailed. They were supplemented in
rural areas with more traditional modes of communication.

Reformasi made inroads into BN's heartland, and this happend again when
the three main opposition groups formed a temporary alliance to contest the 2008
general election. Their campaign was boosted by blogs (with a number of prominent bloggers winning seats), alternative websites and YouTube clips to offset the
limited coverage of the opposition in mainstream media. For the first time, BN
lost its two-thirds majority in parliament.

The third key moment was the mobilisation of civil society and opposition
groups in the Bersih 2.0 Protests in 2011. This was the second series of demonstrations that had begun in 2007 calling for free and fair elections, but this time
enrolling large numbers with the help of Facebook and Twitter. These protests
were eventually contained through repressive policing and a new restrictive law.
But mass protests helped to initiate young people into politics, and to build a
cross-sectional sense of oppositional identity that paved the way for a further election upset (Weiss 2014). In 2013, BN had the worst result in its history, winning
a bare majority of the vote.

As mentioned earlier, a new political crisis centred on corruption developed in
2015. Investigative reports in the *Wall Street Journal*, and other Western media,
accused Prime Minister Najib Razak of diverting cash from a troubled public project (1MDB) into his private bank account. This became a topic of ridicule on social
media, generating jokes like '42 Billion Shades of Debt' and 'The Debt Knight
Rises' (Pak 2015). The government could still rely on mainstream media support
through its links to the principal media owners, but it did not control the internet.

The government publicly considered introducing a new online censorship system. But it abandoned the idea partly in response to voluble opposition. It would also have meant going back on a much-trumpeted commitment, and was at odds with its policy of economic modernisation. For the moment BN has responded by mobilising its supporters and media allies in an online counter-offensive. But it is faced with a problem that the government in Singapore does not have: an internet that is undermining support for the regime.

In brief, the wider political context encouraged the development of the internet as an agent of dissent in Malaysia, but of co-option and control in Singapore. This illustrates our concluding point: different contexts produce different outcomes, something that is repeatedly obscured by overarching theories of the internet centred on its technology.

Conclusion

Initial assessments of the impact of the internet were based on inferences derived from its technology. The internet would foster global understanding, it was reasoned, because the internet is a global medium. The internet would empower the people because it makes an effective means of communication available to all. The internet would transform journalism because it is cheap and interactive. The internet would render the small company equal to the large one because its transformative technology would be accessible to both. These were all plausible prophecies because they drew attention to what the internet could do if its technological potential was fully realised.

But they all had one enormous error at their centre. They failed to recognise that the impact of technology is filtered through the structures and processes of society. Thus when internet experts predicted that the internet would foster global understanding, they were thinking only about the new technology's global reach and interactivity. Conse failed to register that the world speaks in different tongues, is enormously unequal and its constituent parts have different values, interests and affiliations; and that all this would shape how the internet would develop. Consequently they failed to anticipate that the internet's global dialogue would be conducted in mutually incomprehensible languages; that it would be a communion between the affluent rather than between all; and that it would give expression to hate and intolerance as well as to friendship and empathy, reflecting the divisions of the offline world.

This same mistake – the same failure to recognise that the internet would be shaped by society, not just its technology – was played out again and again. Thus, the prediction that the internet would empower the public and rejuvenate democracy overlooked the political, economic and cultural factors that could inhibit this outcome. Poverty disempowers people, and lowers their participation in public life: and this is carried over into the online world in which the poor generally play a less active political role. Increasing numbers of people feel disconnected from politics, and this encourages them to use the internet more for social than for public purposes.

Similarly, the expectation that the internet would dethrone news conglomerates was confounded by the way these companies used their enormous resources to colonise online journalism, often giving away content free in a way that made it difficult for newcomers to compete against them. Likewise, the prediction that the internet would create a level playing field between small and big companies failed to register the enormous advantages that large corporations would still have in terms of economies of scale (and often of scope).

In all these instances, the nature of society and economy had the effect of limiting the anticipated impacts of the internet. But at this point, the argument becomes more complicated because the technology of the internet is not irrelevant. On the contrary, it has brought into being large corporations like Google and Amazon that have radically disrupted the markets in which they operate; it has led to a cumulative retail revolution; and it has changed the operation of business enterprise. It has also created social media that facilitate social connection and are a profound source of pleasure. And it has greatly increased the networking effectiveness of political activists, and in this way strengthened civil society. This list could easily be extended.

So, neither society nor technology solely determines the nature of the internet's impact. The issue is rather which of these influences is more important, and how do they interact with one another? The rest of the book seeks to answer these questions. From this initial overview, organised around prophecy, we now examine and re-evaluate the history of the internet, and then move on to consider the ways in which the internet has contributed to changes in the spheres of economics, regulation, identity and radical politics.

Notes

1 My thanks for the exceptional research assistance of Joanna Redden. My thanks also go to Nick Couldry for commenting on a first edition of this chapter, and Colin Lusk for doing the same for the second edition.

2 The Harvard reference system turns multiple citations into rebarbative obstructions between sentences that interrupt the flow of meaning. In this opening paragraph, only one publication per theme has been cited, for the sake of accessibility. Numerous other examples of these arguments will be encountered later in this chapter.

3 Sherry Turkle did not change tack by 180 degrees, since what she wrote in both her optimistic and pessimistic phases was hedged with qualifications.

4 This audit approach differs from that of Mosco (2005) who usefully views internet prophecy as a discourse that illuminates the assumptions and contexts in which they are formulated; and from that of Anderson (2005), who examines internet predictions in a descriptive way.

5 For a helpful assessment of different ways of measuring the internet's contribution to the economy, see OECD (2013).

6 A subsidiary theme of the New Economy thesis is that companies, with structures and operations well adapted to the internet, do well. For example, Castells (2001: 68) presents Cisco Systems as 'the pioneer of the [network] business model' that is forging

ahead in the internet era. In 2000–1, Cisco's shares declined by 78%, and the company laid off 8,500 workers. In 2011, Cisco announced further mass lay-offs. The company's rollercoaster history illustrates one simple point: a network business network, adapted to the internet, is no guarantee of sustained success.

7   For useful introductions to a very extensive relevant literature, see Porter (2008a and b); Dranove and Schaefer (2010); and Ghoshal (1992).

8   The language barrier is lowered a little by the unrepresentative nature of internet users. It is estimated that 28% of world internet users communicate in English, while another 23% communicate in Chinese (IWS 2015d).

9   See pages 65–66 in Chapter 2.

10 For an example of good Chinese stand-up comedy, see http://www.youtube.com/ watch?v=iailMSUVenA (accessed 12 October 2015).

11 Coleman and Blumler (2008: 169 ff) argue eloquently that online consultation could make more of a difference if a *publicly supported* 'civic commons in cyberspace' is created that is linked to political decision making.

12 See also Chapter 6.

13 In many Northern European countries, trade unions expanded from the labour aristocracy of skilled workers to include the semi-skilled and unskilled. These mass trade union movements grew out of the working class, with its own institutions and cultures. They helped to fund and sustain social democratic parties which constructed social alliances, won elections and built welfare states.

14 See http://www.ukuncut.org.uk/press/coverage?articles_page=5 (accessed 4 April 2011).

15 See Chapter 6.

16 It subsequently emerged that three police officers told their supervisor that they had seen another police officer, whom they did not know, strike a man from behind and push him to the ground. This information was not forwarded to the IPCC or to the pathologist.

17 See Chapter 5.

18 Even so, in many countries, young people are more frequently exposed to the news on TV than online (see Curran et al. 2013: 885, table 2).

19 This was not the only reason why content was given away for free. The managements of many media enterprises also convinced themselves – misguidedly – that building a mass audience through online giveaways would lead to the generation of mass digital advertising revenue.

20 See Chapter 5.

References

Aalberg, T. et al. (2013) 'International TV News, Foreign Affairs Interest and Public Knowledge', *Journalism Studies*, 14 (3): 387–406.

Aalberg, T. and Curran, J. (2012) (eds) *How Media Inform Democracy*, New York: Routledge.

Advertising Association/Warc (2015) 'Drive to Digital sends UK Advertising to its Highest Growth for Four Years', Advertising Association, 21 April. Online. Available HTTP: <http://expenditurereport.warc.com/FreeContent/Q4_2014.pdf> (accessed 13 June 2015).

Agre, P. (1994) 'Networking and Democracy', *The Network Observer*, 1 (4). Online. Available HTTP: <http://polaris.gseis.ucla.edu/pagre/tno/april-1994.html> (accessed 4 May 2011).

Ahearn, C. (2009) 'How Will Journalism Survive the Internet Age?', *Reuters*, 11 December. Online. Available HTTP: <http://blogs.reuters.com/from-reuterscom/2009/12/11/how-will-journalism-survive-the-internet-age/> (accessed 10 June 2011).

Akdeniz, Y. (2009) *Racism on the Internet*, Strasbourg: Council of Europe Publishing.

Anderson, C. (2006) *The Long Tail*, London: Random House Business Books.

Anderson, J. (2005) *Imagining the Internet*, Lanham, MD: Rowman and Littlefield.

Antonio, A. and Tuffley, D. (2014) 'The Gender Digital Divide in Developing Countries', *Future Internet*, 6: 673–687.

Atkinson, R., Ezell, S. J., Andes, S. M., Castro, D. D. and Bennett, R. (2010) 'The Internet Economy 25 Years After .Com: Transforming Commerce and Life', The Information Technology & Innovation Foundation. Online. Available HTTP: <http://www.itif.org/files/2010–25-years.pdf> (accessed 2 February 2011).

Back, L. (2001) 'White Fortresses in Cyberspace', UNESCO Points of View. Online. Available HTTP: <http://www.unesco.org/webworld/points_of_views/back.shtml> (accessed 4 June 2011).

Bar, F. with Simard, C. (2002) 'New Media Implementation and Industrial Organization', in L. Lievrouw and S. Livingstone (eds) *The Handbook of New Media*, London: Sage.

Barry, E. and Flint, J. (2010) *Self-Esteem, Comparative Poverty and Neighbourhoods*, York: Joseph Rowntree Foundation.

Bartels, L. M. (2008) *Unequal Democracy: The Political Economy of the New Gilded Age*, Princeton: Princeton University Press.

Barthel, M. (2015) 'Newspapers: Fact Sheet', State of the News Media 2015, Pew Research Center, April. Online. Available HTTP: <http://www.journalism.org/2015/04/29/newspapers-fact-sheet/> (accessed 16 June 2015).

Bauman, Z. (2001) *The Individualised Society*, Cambridge: Polity Press.

Beckett, C. (2008) *Supermedia*, Oxford: Blackwell.

Benkler, Y. (2006) *The Wealth of Networks*, New Haven, CT: Yale University Press.

Bennett, L. W. (2003) 'Communicating Global Activism', *Information, Communication & Society*, 6 (2): 143–168.

Berger, J. and Morgan, J. (2015) 'The ISIS Twitter Census: Defining and Describing The Population Of ISIS Supporters On Twitter', Brookings Center for Middle East Policy. Online. Available HTTP: <<<http://www.brookings.edu/~/media/research/files/papers/2015/03/isis-twitter-census-berger-morgan/isis_twitter_census_berger_morgan.pdf> (accessed 22 May 2015).

Bimber, B. (2014) 'Digital Media in the Obama Campaigns of 2008 and 2012: Adaptation to the Personalized Political Communication Environment', *Journal of Information Technology & Politics*, 11 (2): 130–150.

Birch, S., Gottfried, G. and Lodge, G. (2013) 'Divided Democracy: Political Inequality in the UK and Why it Matters', IPPR. Online. Available HTTP: <http://www.ippr.org/assets/media/images/media/files/publication/2013/11/divided-democracy_Nov2013_11420.pdf?noredirect=1> (accessed 23 May 2015).

Blinder, A. (2015) 'What Did We Learn from the Financial Crisis, the Great Recession, and the Pathetic Recovery?' *The Journal of Economic Education*, 46 (2): 135–149.

Blodget, H. (2008) 'Why Wall Street Always Blows It . . .', *The Atlantic Online*. Online. Available HTTP: <http://www.theatlantic.com/magazine/archive/2008/12/whywall-street-always-blows-it/7147/> (accessed 12 February 2011).

Boas, T. C. (2006) 'Weaving the Authoritarian Web: The Control of Internet Use in Nondemocratic Regimes', in J. Zysman and A. Newman (eds) *How Revolutionary*

Was the Digital Revolution? National Responses, Market Transitions, and Global Technology, Stanford, CA: Stanford Business Books.

Boczkowski, P. (2010) *News at Work*, Chicago: University of Chicago Press.

Bohman, J. (2004) 'Expanding Dialogue: The Internet, the Public Sphere and Prospects for Transnational Democracy', *Sociological Review*, 131–155.

Bordo, M., Jonung, L. and Markiewicz, A. (2013) 'A Fiscal Union for the Euro: Some Lessons from History', *CESifo Economic Studies*, 59 (3): 449–488.

Boulianne, S. (2015) 'Social Media Use and Participation: A Meta-analysis of Current Research', *Information, Communication & Society*, 18 (5): 524–538.

Bucchioni, P., Liu, X. and Weidenhamer, D. (2015) 'Quarterly Retail E-Commerce Sales, 4th Quarter 2014', U.S. Census Bureau News, U.S. Department of Commerce, Washington, D.C., 17 February. Online. Available HTTP: <https://www.census.gov/retail/mrts/www/ data/pdf/ec_current.pdf> (accessed 12 May 2015).

Bulashova, N. and Cole, G. (1995) 'Friends and Partners: Building Global Community on the Internet', paper presented at the Internet Society International Networking Conference, Honolulu, Hawaii, June.

Cairncross, F. (1997) *The Death of Distance*, Boston: Harvard Business School Press.

Cammaerts, B. (2008) 'Critiques on the Participatory Potentials of Web 2.0', *Communication, Culture and Critique*, 1 (4): 358–377.

Cassidy, J. (2002) *Dot.con: How America Lost its Mind and Money in the Internet Era*, New York: Harper Collins.

Castells, M. (2001) *The Internet Galaxy*, Oxford: Oxford University Press.

Castells, M. (2012) *Networks of Outrage and Hope*, Cambridge: Polity Press.

Castells, M. (2015) *Networks of Outrage and Hope*, 2nd edition, Cambridge: Polity Press.

Cattaneo, O., Gereffi, G. and Staritz, C. (2010) 'Global Value Chains in a Postcrisis World: A Development Perspective', Washington, D.C.: The World Bank. Online. Available HTTP: <http://www.cggc.duke.edu/pdfs/Gereffi_GVCs_in_the_Postcrisis_World_Book.pdf> (accessed 15 June 2015).

Cellan-Jones, R. (2001) *Dot.bomb: The Rise and Fall of Dot.com Britain*, London: Aurum.

Chadwick, A. (2006) *Internet Politics: States, Citizens and New Communication Technologies*, Oxford: Oxford University Press.

Chrysostome, E. and Rosson, P. (2004) 'The Internet and SMES Internationalization: Promises and Illusions', paper delivered at Conference of ASAC, Quebec, Canada, 5 June. Online. Available HTTP: <http://libra.acadiau.ca/library/ASAC/v25/articles/Chrysostome-Rosson.pdf> (accessed 23 October 2011).

Cingano, F. (2014) 'Trends in Income Inequality and its Impact on Economic Growth', *OECD Social, Employment and Migration Working Papers*, No. 163, OECD Publishing. Online. Available HTTP: <http://dx.doi.org/10.1787/5jxrjncwxv6j-en> (accessed 15 June 2015).

Coleman, S. (1999) 'New Media and Democratic Politics', *New Media and Society*, 1 (1): 62–74.

Coleman, S. and Blumler, J. (2008) *The Internet and Democratic Citizenship*, Cambridge: Cambridge University Press.

Commission on Poverty, Participation and Power (2000) 'Listen Hear: The Right to be Heard', Report of the Commission on Poverty, Participation and Power, Bristol: Policy Press. Online. Available HTTP: <http://www.jrf.org.uk/publications/listen-hear-right-be-heard> (accessed 10 January 2011).

Conway, M. (2006) 'Terrorism and the Internet: New Media – New Threat?', *Parliamentary Affairs*, 59 (2): 283–298.

Cook, E. (1999) 'Web Whiz-kids Count Their Cool Millions', *Independent*, 25 July, p. 10.

Cook, C., Sirkkunen, E. and Pekkala, P. (2012) 'Conclusions', Chasing Sustainability on the Net: International Research on 69 Journalistic Pure Players and Business Models, Sirkkunen, Esa and Cook, Clare (eds), Tampere Research Centre for Journalism, Media and Communication. Online. Available HTTP: <http://tampub.uta.fi/bitstream/handle/10024/66378/chasing_sustainability_on_the_net_2012.pdf?sequence=1> (accessed 13 June 2015).

Couldry, N. (2010) 'New Online Sources and Writer-Gatherers', in N. Fenton (ed.) *New Media, Old News*, London: Sage.

Couldry, N., Livingstone, S. and Markham, T. (2007) *Media Consumption and Public Engagement*, Basingstoke: Palgrave Macmillan.

Crouch, C. (2004) *Post-Democracy*, Cambridge: Polity Press.

Curran, J. (2002) *Media and Power*, London: Routledge.

Curran, J. (2011) *Media and Democracy*, London: Routledge.

Curran, J. (2012) 'The Internet and the Transformation of Journalism' in J. Lloyd and J. Winter (eds) *Media, Politics and the Public*, Stockholm: Ax:son Johnson Foundation.

Curran, J. and Witschge, T. (2010) 'Liberal Dreams and the Internet' in N. Fenton (ed.) *New Media, Old News: Journalism and Democracy in the Digital Age*, London: Sage.

Curran, J., Lund, A., Iyengar, S. and Salovaara-Moring, I. (2009) 'Media System, Public Knowledge and Democracy: A Comparative Study', *European Journal of Communication*, 24 (1): 5–26.

Curran, J. and Hayashi, K. (2013) 'Politically Disinterested', *Society Now*, 17, 22–23.

Curran, J. et al. (2013) 'Internet Revolution Revisited: A Comparative Study'. *Media, Culture and Society*, 35 (7): 880–897.

Curran, J. et al. (2014) 'Reconsidering "Virtuous Circle" and "Media Malaise" Theories of the Media: An 11-Nation Study', *Journalism*, 15 (7): 815–833.

Dahlgren, P. (2005) 'The Internet, Public Spheres, and Political Communication: Dispersion and Deliberation', *Political Communication*, 22: 147–162.

Daniels, J. (2008) 'Race, Civil Rights, and Hate Speech in the Digital Era' in A. Everett (ed.) *Learning Race and Ethnicity: Youth and Digital Media*, The John D. and Catherine T. MacArthur Foundation Series on Digital Media and Learning, Cambridge, MA: MIT Press, 129–154.

Davies, N. (2008) *Flat Earth News*, London: Chatto and Windus.

Davis, A. (2010) *Political Communication and Social Theory*, London: Routledge.

Deighton, J. and Quelch, J. (2009) *Economic Value of the Advertising-Supported Internet Ecosystem*, Cambridge, MA: Hamilton Consultants Inc.

Dencik, L. (2011) *Media and Global Civil Society*, Basingstoke: Palgrave Macmillan.

Deuze, M. (2009) 'The People Formerly Known as the Employers', *Journalism*, 10 (3): 315–318.

Di Genarro, C. and Dutton, W. (2006) 'The Internet and the Public: Online and Offline Political Participation in the United Kingdom', *Parliamentary Affairs*, 59 (2): 299–313.

Downie, L. and Schudson, M. (2010) 'The Reconstruction of American Journalism', *Columbia Journalism Review*. Online. Available HTTP: <http://www.cjr.org/reconstruction/the_reconstruction_of_american.php> (accessed 10 January 2010).

Dranove, B. and Schaefer, S. (2010) *Economics of Strategy*, 5th edn, Hoboken, NJ: John Wiley.

du Rausas, P., Manyika, J., Hazan, E., Bughin, J., Chui, M. and Said, R. (2011) 'Internet Matters: The Net's Sweeping Impact on Growth, Jobs and Prosperity'. McKinsey

Global Institute. Online. Available HTTP: <www.mckinsey.com/Insights/MGI/Rese arch/Technology_and_Innovation/Internet_matters> (accessed 5 May 2014).

Dutton, W., Blank, G. with Groselj, D. (2013) 'Cultures of the Internet: The Internet in Britain', Oxford Internet Survey 2013. Oxford Internet Institute, University of Oxford. Online. Available HTTP: <http://oxis.oii.ox.ac.uk/wp-content/uploads/2014/11/OxIS-2013.pdf> (accessed 18 May 2015).

Edmunds, R., Guskin, E. and Rosenstiel, T. (2011) 'Newspapers: Missed the 2010 Media Rally', *The State of the News Media 2011*, Pew Research Center's Project for Excellence in Journalism. Online. Available HTTP: <http://stateofthemedia.org/2011/newspaper-sessay/> (accessed 20 August 2011).

Ehlers, V. (1995) 'Beyond the Cyberhype: What the Internet Means to the Congressman of the Future', *Roll Call*, 1 October.

Elmer-Dewitt, P. (1994) 'Battle for the Soul of the Internet', *Time*, 144 (4): 50–57.

Eskelsen, G., Marcus, A. and Ferree, W. K. (2009) *The Digital Economy Fact Book*, 10th edn, The Progress and Freedom Foundation. Online. Available HTTP: <http://www.pff. org/issues-pubs/books/factbook_10th_Ed.pdf> (accessed 2 April 2011).

Esser, F. and Stromback, J. (eds) (2014) *Mediatization of Politics*, Basingstoke: Palgrave Macmillan.

European Commission (2009) *Eurostat*. Online. Available HTTP: <http://epp.eurostat.ec. europa.eu/portal/page/portal/eurostat/home/> (accessed 14 August 2011).

Farwell, J. (2014) 'The Media Strategy of ISIS', *Survival: Global Politics and Strategy*, 56: 6, 49–55.

FCC (2011) 'The Information Needs of Communities: The Changing Media Landscape in a Broadband Age', Federal Communications Commission. Online. Available HTTP:<https://apps.fcc.gov/edocs_public/attachmatch/DOC-307406A1.pdf>(accessed 17 June 2015).

Fenton, N. (2008) 'Mediating Hope: New Media, Politics and Resistance', *International Journal of Cultural Studies*, 11: 230–248.

Fenton, N. (ed.) (2010a) *New Media, Old News: Journalism and Democracy in the Digital Age*, London: Sage.

Fenton, N. (2010b) 'NGOs, New Media and the Mainstream News: News from Everywhere' in N. Fenton (ed.) *New Media, Old News*, London: Sage.

File, T. and Ryan, C. (2014) 'Computer and Internet Use in the United States: 2013', U.S. Department of Commerce, U.S. Census Bureau. Online. Available HTTP: <<http:// www.census.gov/content/dam/Census/library/publications/2014/acs/acs-28.pdf> (accessed 22 May 2015).

Forrester Research (2014) 'Digital Ad Spend to Reach $103B by 2019', Media Resources, 4 November. Online. Available HTTP: <https://www.forrester.com/digital+ad+spend+ to+reach+103b+by+2019/-/e-pre7448> (accessed 13 June 2015).

Foster, J. and McChesney, R. (2011) 'The Internet's Unholy Marriage to Capitalism', *Monthly Review* (March). Online. Available HTTP: <http://monthlyreview.org/ 110301foster-mchesney.php> (accessed 4 June 2011).

Foster, J., McChesney, R. and Jonna, R. (2011) 'Monopoly and Competition in Twenty-First Century Capitalism', *Monthly Review*, 62: 11.

Fraser, N. (2007) 'Transnationalizing the Public Sphere: On the Legitimacy and Efficacy of Public Opinion in a Post-Westphalian World', *Theory, Culture and Society*, 24 (4): 7–30.

Freiburger, T. and Crane, J. S. (2008) 'A Systematic Examination of Terrorist Use of the Internet', *International Journal of Cyber Criminology*, 2 (1): 309–319.

Fukuyama, F. (2002) *Our Posthuman Future*, New York: Farrar, Straus and Giroux.

Gates, B. (1995) 'To Make a Fortune on the Internet, Find a Niche and Fill it', *Seattle Post-Intelligencer*, 6 December.

George, C. (2005) 'The Internet's Political Impact and the Penetration/Particpation Paradox in Malaysia and Singapore', *Media, Culture and Society*, 27 (6): 903–920.

George, C. (2007) *Contentious Journalism and the Internet*, Seattle: University of Washington Press.

Gerstenfeld, P. B., Grant, D. R. and Chiang, C. (2003) 'Hate Online: A Content Analysis of Extremist Internet Sites', *Analyses of Social Issues and Public Policy*, 3 (1): 29–44.

GFK and IAB (2014) 'Original Digital Video Consumer Study', GFK Media & Entertainment, April. Online. Available HTTP: <http://www.iab.net/media/file/GfKIAB2014OriginalDigitalVideoReport.pdf> (accessed 24 May 2015).

Ghoshal, S. (1992) 'Global Strategy: An Organizing Framework', in F. Root and K. Visudtibhan (eds) *International Strategic Management: Challenges and Opportunities*, New York: Taylor and Francis.

Gilder, G. (1994) *Life After Television*, New York: Norton.

Gray, G. and Caul, M. (2000) 'Declining Voter Turnout in Advanced Industrial Democracies, 1950 to1997: The Effects of Declining Group Mobilization', *Comparative Political Studies*, 33 (9): 1091–1112.

Groot, Sietske de (2011) *Small Businesses and Online Trading*. Federation of Small Businesses. Online. Available HTTP: <http://www.fsb.org.uk/policy/assets/fsb1144%20online%20trading%20report_web.pdf> (accessed 14 May 2015).

Grossman, L. K. (1995) *The Electronic Republic: Reshaping Democracy in the Information Age*, New York: Viking.

Hahn, H. (1993) *Voices from the Net*, 1.3, 27 October. Online. Available HTTP: <http://www.spunk.org/library/comms/sp000317.txt> (accessed 7 November 2010).

Hay, C. (2007) *Why We Hate Politics*, Cambridge: Polity Press.

Hill, K. and Hughes, J. (1998) *Cyberpolitics*, Lanham, MD: Rowman and Littlefield.

Hindman, M. (2009) *The Myth of Digital Democracy*, Princeton: Princeton University Press.

Hirsch, D. (2007) 'Experiences of Poverty and Educational Disadvantage', Joseph Rowntree Foundation. Online. Available HTTP: <http://www.jrf.org.uk/publications/experiences-poverty-and-educational-disadvantage> (accessed 5 January 2011).

Horgan, G. (2007) The Impact of Poverty on Young Children's Experience of School', Joseph Rowntree Foundation. Online. Available HTTP: <http://www.jrf.org.uk/publications/impact-poverty-young-childrens-experience-school> (accessed 20 January 2011).

Hunt, J. (2011) 'The New Frontier of Money Laundering: How Terrorist Organizations use Cyberlaundering to Fund Their Activities, and How Governments are Trying to Stop Them', *Information & Communications Technology Law*, 20 (2): 133–152.

Hvistendahl, M. (2014) 'Study Exposes Chinese Censors' Deepest Fears', *Science*, 345 (6199): 859–860.

IAB Canada (2014) '2013 Actual + 2014 Estimated Canadian Internet Advertising Revenue Survey', Interactive Advertising Bureau of Canada, 17 September. Online. Available HTTP: <http://iabcanada.com/files/Canadian-Internet-AdRev-Survey_2013-14.pdf> (accessed 13 June 2015).

Ibrahim, Y. (2006) 'The Role of Regulations and Social Norms in Mediating Online Political Discourse', PhD dissertation, LSE, University of London.

Inquest (2009) 'Briefing on the Death of Ian Tomlinson', Inquest, June 2009. Online. Available HTTP: <inquest.org.uk/pdf/INQUEST_ian_tomlinson_briefing_jun_2009.pdf> (accessed 14 October 2015).

Intel (2013) 'Women and the Web: Bridging the Internet Gap and Creating New Global Opportunities in Low and Middle-Income Countries'. Online. Available HTTP: <http://www.intel.com/content/www/us/en/technology-in-education/women-in-the-web.html> (accessed 18 May 2014).

International Telecommunications Union (2010) 'ITU Calls for Broadband Internet Access for Half of the World's Population by 2015', *ITU News*, 5 June. Online. Available HTTP: <http://www.itu.int/net/itunews/issues/2010/05/pdf/201005_12.pdf> (accessed 10 January 2011).

Internet World Stats (2015a) 'Internet Users in the World: Distribution by World Regions'. Online. Available HTTP: <http://www.internetworldstats.com/stats.htm> (accessed 18 May 2015).

Internet World Stats (2015b) 'Internet World Statistics: Usage and Population Statistics'. Online. Available HTTP: <http://www.internetworldstats.com/stats4.htm> (accessed 17 May 2015).

Internet World Stats (2015c) 'Internet World Statistics: the Pig Picture'. Online. Available HTTP: <http://www.internetworldstats.com/stats.htm> (accessed 16 May 2015).

Internet World Stats (2015d) 'Internet World Users by Language'. Online. Available HTTP: <http://www.internetworldstats.com/stats7.htm> (accessed 22 May 2015).

Internet World Stats (2015e) 'Asia Internet Users'. Online. Available HTTP: <http://www.internetworldstats.com/asia.htm> (accessed 16 July 2015).

Jackson, D. and Moloney, K. (2015) 'Inside Churnalism: PR, Journalism and Power Relationships in Flux', *Journalism Studies* (ahead-of-print), 1–18.

Jackson, J. (2013) 'Datawatch: Global Newspaper Circulation in Decline as Disruption Reaches Emerging Economies', The Media Briefing, 11 February 2013. Online. Available HTTP: <http://www.themediabriefing.com/article/datawatch-circulation-decline-developing-economies> (accessed 11 July 2013).

Jipguep, J. (1995) 'The Global Telecommunication Infrastructure and the Information Society', Proceedings ISOC INET '95. Online. Available HTTP: <http://www.isoc.org/inet95/proceedings/PLENARY/L1–6/html/paper.html> (accessed 10 January 2010).

Johnson, N. (2014) 'Nielsen Data Report: April 2014', Mediatel Newsline, 10 June. Online. Available HTTP: <http://mediatel.co.uk/newsline/2014/06/10/nielsen-data-report-april-2014/> (accessed 11 June 2015).

Joyce, M. (2007) 'The Citizen Journalism Web Site "OhmyNews" and the 2002 South Korean Presidential Election', Berkman Center for Internet and Society of Harvard University. Online. Available HTTP: <http://cyber.law.harvard.edu/sites/cyber.law.harvard.edu/files/Joyce_South_Korea_2007.pdf > (accessed 24 July 2011).

Juris, J. (2005) 'The New Digital Media and Activist Networking within Anti-Corporate Globalization Movements', *The Annals of the American Academy*, 597: 189–208.

Juris, J. (2012) 'Reflections on #Occupy Everywhere: Social Media, Public Space, and Emerging Logics of Aggregation', *American Ethnologist*, 39 (2): 259–279.

Jurkowitz, M. et al. (2013) 'The Changing TV News Landscape', The State of the News Media 2013, The Pew Research Center's Project for the Excellence in Journalism. Online. Available HTTP: <http://www.stateofthemedia.org/2013/special-reports-landing-page/the-changing-tv-news-landscape/> (accessed 17 June 2015).

Kalapese, C., Willersdorf, S. and Zwillenburg, P. (2010) *The Connected Kingdom*, Boston Consulting Group. Online. Available HTTP: <http://www.connected-kingdom.co.uk/downloads/bcg-the-connected-kingdom-oct-10.pdf> (accessed 14 August 2011).

Kalathil, S. and Boas, T. C. (2003) *Open Networks, Closed Regimes: The Impact of the Internet on Authoritarian Rule*, Washington, D.C.: Carnegie Endowment for International Peace.

Kelly, K. (1999) 'The Roaring Zeros', *Wired*, September. Online. Available HTTP: <http://www.wired.com/wired/archive/7.09/zeros.html> (accessed 10 December 2010).

Kenyon, A. (2010) 'Investigating Chilling Effects: News Media and Public Speech in Malaysia, Singapore and Australia', *International Journal of Communication*, 4: 440–467.

Kim, E.-G. and Hamilton, J. (2006) 'Capitulation to Capital? OhmyNews as Alternative Media', *Media, Culture and Society*, 28 (4): 541–560.

King, G., Pan, J. and Roberts, M. (2013) 'How Censorship in China Allows Government Criticism but Silences Collective Expression', *American Political Science Review*, 107 (2): 1–18.

Klotz, R. J. (2004) *The Politics of Internet Communication*, Lanham, MD: Rowman and Littlefield.

Knight Foundation (2015) 'Gaining Ground: How Nonprofit News Ventures Seek Sustainability'. Online. Available HTTP: <http://knightfoundation.org/features/non-profitnews-2015-summary/> (accessed 16 June 2015).

Kohut, A., Doherty, C., Dimock, M. and Keeter, S. (2012). 'In Changing News Landscape, even Television is Vulnerable', Pew Internet & American Life Project. Online. Available HTTP: <http://www.people-press.org/2012/09/27/in-changing-news-land-scape-even-television-is-vulnerable/> (accessed 30 May 2015).

Lancee, B. and Van de Werfhorst, H. (2012) 'Income Inequality and Participation: A Comparison of 24 European Countries', *Social Science Research*, 41: 1166–1178.

Lane, D. (2004) *Berlusconi's Shadow*, London: Allen Lane.

Lauria, J. (1999) 'American Online Frenzy Creates Overnight Billionaires', *Sunday Times*, 26 December.

Leadbetter, C. (2009) *We-Think*, 2nd edn, London: Profile Books.

Lee-Wright, P., Phillips, A. and Witschge, T. (2011) *Changing Journalism*, London: Routledge.

Lister, R. (2004) *Poverty*, Cambridge: Polity Press.

Livingstone, S. (2010) 'Interactive, Engaging but Unequal: Critical Conclusions from Internet Studies' in J. Curran (ed.) *Media and Society*, 5th edn, London: Bloomsbury Academic.

Mackinnon, R. (2012) 'China's "Networked Authoritarianism"' in L. Diamond and M. Plattner (eds) *Liberation Technology*, Baltimore: Johns Hopkins University Press.

Mandel, M. J. and Kunii, I. M. (1999) 'The Internet Economy: The World's Next Growth Engine', *Business Week Online*, 4 October. Online. Available HTTP: <http://www.businessweek.com/1999/99_40/b3649004.htm?scriptFramed> (accessed 2 February 2011).

Marquand, D. (2008) *Britain Since 1918*, London: Phoenix.

McNeilly, Gerry (2012) 'Policing the Right to Protest: G20 Systemic Review Report', Office of the Independent Police Review Director, Independent Police Review Director. Online. Available HTTP: <www.oiprd.on.ca/EN/PDFs/G20-Systemic-Review-2012_E.pdf> (accessed 27 May 2015).

Milberry, K. and Clement, A. (2014) 'Policing as Spectacle and the Politics of Surveillance at the Toronto G20' in K. Milberry and A. Clement (eds) *The State on Trial: Policing Protest*, Vancouver, BC: UBC Press, 127–147.

Mitchell, A. and Page, D. (2014) *State of the News Media 2014*, Pew Research Center, 26 March. Online. Available HTTP: <http://www.journalism.org/files/2014/03/Overview.pdf> (accessed 17 June 2015).

Mitchell, A. and Page, D. (2015) 'State of the News Media 2015', Pew Research Center, April. Online. Available HTTP: <http://www.journalism.org/files/2015/04/FINAL-STATE-OF-THE-NEWS-MEDIA1.pdf> (accessed 6 June 2015).

Monaghan, J. and Walby, K. (2012) '"They Attacked The City": Security intelligence, the sociology of protest policing and the anarchist threat at the 2010 Toronto G20 summit', *Current Sociology*, 60 (5): 653–671.

Morozov, E. (2011) *The Net Delusion*, London: Allen Lane.

Mosco, V. (2005) *The Digital Sublime*, Cambridge, MA: MIT Press.

Murdoch, R. (2006) 'Speech by Rupert Murdoch at the Annual Livery Lecture at the Worshipful Company of Stationers and Newspaper Makers', *News Corporation*, 3 March. Online. Available HTTP: <http://www.newscorp.com/news/news_285.html> (accessed 1 September 2010).

Naughton, J. (2012) *From Gutenberg to Zuckerberg*, London: Quercus.

Negroponte, N. (1995; 1996) *Being Digital*, rev. edn, London: Hodder and Stoughton.

Nel, F. (2010) *Laid Off: What Do UK Journalists Do Next?* Preston: University of Central Lancashire. Online. Available HTTP: <http://www.journalism.co.uk/uploads/laidoffreport.pdf> (accessed 20 August 2011).

Nerone, J. (2009) 'The Death and Rebirth of Working-class Journalism', *Journalism*, 10 (3): 353–355.

Newman, N. and Levy, D. (2014) 'Reuters Institute Digital News Report 2014: Tracking the Future of News', Reuters Institute for the Study of Journalism, University of Oxford. Online. Available HTTP: <https://reutersinstitute.politics.ox.ac.uk/sites/default/files/Reuters%20Institute%20Digital%20News%20Report%202014.pdf> (accessed 10 June 2015).

Nielsen, R. and Schrøder, K. (2014) 'The Relative Importance of Social Media for Accessing, Finding, and Engaging with News', *Digital Journalism*, 2 (4): 472–489.

O'Donnell, P., Zion, L. and Sherwood, M. (2015) 'Where do Journalists Go After Newsroom Job Cuts?' *Journalism Practice* (ahead-of-print), 1–17.

OECD (2011) 'Divided We Stand—Why Inequality Keeps Rising' in *An Overview of Growing Income Inequalities in OECD Countries: Main Findings*, OECD. Online. Available HTTP: <www.oecd.org/els/social/inequality> (accessed 14 June 2015).

OECD (2013) 'Measuring the Internet Economy: A Contribution to the Research Agenda', *OECD Digital Economy Papers*, No. 226, OECD Publishing. Online. Available HTTP: <http://dx.doi.org/10.1787/5k43gjg6r8jf-en> (accessed 12 May 2015).

OECD (2014a) *Measuring the Digital Economy: A New Perspective*, OECD Publishing. Online. Available HTTP: <http://dx.doi.org/10.1787/9789264221796-en> (accessed 12 May 2015).

OECD (2014b) 'Focus on Inequality and Growth – December 2014'. Online. Available HTTP: <www.oecd.org/social/inequality-and-poverty.htm> (accessed 18 May 2015).

Ofcom (2010a) 'Perceptions of, and Attitudes towards, Television: 2010', PSB Report 2010 – Information Pack H, 8 July. Online. Available HTTP: <http://stakeholders.of.com.org.uk/binaries/broadcast/reviews-investigations/psb-review/psb2010/Perceptions.pdf> (accessed 8 November 2010).

Ofcom (2010b) *International Communications Market Report*, London: Ofcom. Online. Available HTTP: <http://stakeholders.ofcom.org.uk/binaries/research/cmr/753567/icmr/ICMR_2010.pdf> (accessed 23 August 2011).

Ofcom (2014a) 'News Consumption in the UK: 2014 Report'. Online. Available HTTP: <http://stakeholders.ofcom.org.uk/binaries/research/tv-research/news/2014/News_Report_2014.pdf> (accessed 6 June 2015).

Ofcom (2014b) 'Adults' Media Use and Attitudes Report 2014', Ofcom, April. Online. Available HTTP: <http://stakeholders.ofcom.org.uk/binaries/research/media-literacy/adults-2014/2014_Adults_report.pdf> (accessed 31 May 2015).

Office for National Statistics (2014) 'Internet Access – Households and Individuals 2014', 7 August. Online. Available HTTP: <http://www.ons.gov.uk/ons/dcp171778_373584.pdf> (accessed 24 May 2015).

Olmstead, K., Mitchell, A. and Rosenstiel, T. (2011) 'Navigating News Online', Pew Research Center, Project for Excellence in Journalism. Online. Available HTTP: <http://pewresearch.org/pubs/1986/navigating-digital-news-environment-audience> (accessed 20 August 2011).

ONS (2008) *Internet Access 2008: Households and Individuals*, London: Office of National Statistics.

OpenDemocracy (n.d.) 'About OpenDemocracy'. Online. Available HTTP: <http.//www.opendemocracy.net/node/440> (accessed 9 October 2008).

OpenSecrets (2012) '2012 Presidential Race', OpenSecrets.org. Online. Available HTTP: <https://www.opensecrets.org/pres12/> (accessed 30 June 2015).

Oser, J., Hooghe, M. and Marien, S. (2013) 'Is Online Participation Distinct from Offline Participation? A Latent Class Analysis of Participation Types and Their Stratification', *Political Research Quarterly*, 66 (1): 91–101.

Oxfam (2015) 'Wealth: Having it all and Wanting More', Oxfam Issue Briefing. January. Online. Available HTTP: <https://www.oxfam.org/sites/www.oxfam.org/files/file_attachments/ib-wealth-having-all-wanting-more-190115-en.pdf> (accessed 18 May 2015).

Pak, J. (2015) '1MDB: The Case That's Riveting Malaysia', BBC News online, 8 July 2015. Online. Available HTTP: <http://www.bbc.co.uk/news/world-asia-33447456> (accessed 16 July 2015).

Panitch, L. and S. Gindin (2012) *The Making of Global Capitalism*, London: Verso.

Papathanassopoulos, S. et al. (2013) 'Online Threat, But Television is Still Dominant: A Comparative Study of 11 Nations', *Journalism Practice*, 7 (6): 690–704.

Park, M.-Y., Kim, C.-N. and Sohn, R.-W. (2000) 'Modernization, Globalization and the Powerful State: The Korean Media' in J. Curran and M.-Y. Park (eds) *De-Westernising Media Studies*, London: Routledge.

Perry, B. and Olsson, P. (2009) 'Cyberhate: The Globalization of Hate', *Information & Communications Technology Law*, 18 (2): 185–199.

Pew (2009a) Pew Project for Excellence in Journalism, *State of the News Media 2009*, Pew Research Center Publications, 16 March. Online. Available HTTP: <http://www.stateofthemedia.org/2009/narrative_overview_intro.php?cat=0&media=1> (accessed 10 December 2009).

Pew (2009b) 'Trend Data', Pew Internet & American Life Project. Online. Available HTTP: <http://www.pewinternet.org/Static-Pages/Trend-Data/Online-Activities-Daily.aspx> (accessed 2 April 2010).

Pew Research Center (2011) 'Internet Gains on Television as Public's Main News Source', 4 January. Online. Available HTTP: <http://pew research.org/pubs/1844/poll-main-source-national-international-news-internet-television-newspapers> (accessed 7 January 2011).

Pew Research Center (2013) 'Civic Engagement in the Digital Age'. Online. Available HTTP: <http://pewinter-net.org/Reports/2013/Civic-Engagement.aspx> (accessed 1 June 2015).

Pew Research Center (2015) 'Internet Seen as Positive Influence on Education but Negative Influence on Morality in Emerging and Developing Nations'. Online. Available HTTP:

<http://www.pewglobal.org/files/2015/03/Pew-Research-Center-Technology-Report-FINAL-March-19–20151.pdf> (accessed 22 May 2015).

Piketty, T. (2014) *Capital in the Twenty-First Century*, Cambridge, MA: Belknap Press.

Porter, M. (2008a) *On Competition*, Boston: Harvard Business School Press.

Porter, M. (2008b) 'The Five Competitive Forces that Shape Strategy', *Harvard Business Review*, January: 79–93.

Portlandia (n.d.) 'Social Bankruptcy' (season 4, episode 3 excerpt) reproduced on YouTube. Online. Available HTTP: <https://www.youtube.com/watch?v=zz-7d3HZE7o> (accessed 15 May 2015).

Poster, M. (2001) *What's the Matter with the Internet*, Minneapolis: University of Minnesota Press.

Postill, J. (2014) 'A Critical History of Internet Activism and Social Protest in Malaysia, 1998–2011', *Asiascape: Digital Asia Journal*, 1–2: 78–103.

Price, R. (1998) 'Reversing the Gun Sites: Transnational Civil Society Targets Land Mines', *International Organization*, 52 (3): 613–644.

Qiang, X. (2012) 'The Battle for the Chinese Internet' in L. Diamond and M. Plattner (eds) *Liberation Technology*, Baltimore: Johns Hopkins University Press.

Redden, J. and Witschge, T. (2010) 'A New News Order? Online News Content Examined', in N. Fenton (ed.) *New Media, Old News*, London: Sage.

Rodan, G. (2004) *Transparency and Authoritarian Rule in Southeast Asia*, London: RoutledgeCurzon.

Rohlinger, D. and Brown, J. (2008) 'Democracy, Action and the Internet after 9/11', *American Behavioral Scientist*, 53 (1): 133–150.

Ryan, J. (2010) *A History of the Internet and the Digital Future*, London: Reaktion Books.

Schlozman, K. L., Verba, S. and Brady, H. (2012) *The Unheavenly Chorus: Unequal Political Voice and the Broken Promise of American Democracy*, Princeton: Princeton University Press.

Schudson, M. (1997) *The Good Citizen: A History of American Civic Life*, New York: Simon and Schuster.

Schwartz, E. I. (1994) 'Power to the People: The Clinton Administration is Using the Net in a Pitched Effort to Perform an End Run Around the Media', *Wired*, 1 January. Online. Available HTTP: <http://www.wired.com/wired/archive/2.12/whitehouse_pr.html> (accessed 10 January 2010).

Scott, E. (2004) '"Big Media" Meets the "Bloggers": Coverage of Trent Lott's Remarks at Strom Thurmond's Birthday Party', Kennedy School of Government Case Study C14-04–1731.0, Cambridge, MA: John Kennedy School of Government, Harvard University.

Scott, T. D. (2008) 'Blogosphere: Presidential Campaign Stories that Failed to Ignite Mainstream Media' in M. Boler (ed.) *Digital Media and Democracy: Tactics in Hard Times*, Cambridge, MA: MIT Press.

Seybert, H. and Reinecke, P. (2013) 'Internet Use Statistics – Individuals', Statistics in Focus, Eurostat, European Commission. Online. Available HTTP: <http://ec.europa.eu/eurostat/statistics-explained/index.php/Internet_use_statistics_-_individuals> (accessed 31 May 2015).

Shirky, C. (2010) *Cognitive Surplus*, London: Allen Lane.

Simon Wiesenthal Centre (2011) '2011 Digital Terrorism and Hate Report Launched at Museum of Tolerance New York'. Online. Available HTTP: <http://www.wiesenthal.com/site/apps/nlnet/content2.aspx?c=lsKWLbPJLnF&b=4441467&ct=9141065> (accessed 8 July 2011).

Sklair, L. (2002) *Globalization*, 3rd edn, Oxford: Oxford University Press.

Slevin, J. (2000) *The Internet and Society*, Cambridge: Polity Press.

Smith, A. (2013) 'Civic Engagement in the Digital Age', Pew Research Center. Online. Available HTTP: <http://pewinter-net.org/Reports/2013/Civic-Engagement.aspx> (accessed 1 June 2015).

Smith, A., Schlozman, L., Verba, S. and Brady, H. (2009) 'The Internet and Civic Engagment', Pew Internet & American Life Project, 1 September. Online. Available HTTP: <http://www.pewinternet.org/Reports/2009/15–The-Internet-and-Civic-Engagement.aspx> (accessed 10 May 2010).

Smith, P. and Smythe, E. (2004) 'Globalization, Citizenship and New Information Technologies: from the MAI to Seattle' in M. Anttiroiko and R. Savolainen (eds) *eTransformation in Governance*, Hershey, PA: IGI Publishing.

Solt, F. (2008) 'Economic Inequality and Democratic Political Engagement', *American Journal of Political Science*, 52 (1): 48–60.

Stepinska, A., Porath, W., Mujica, C., Xu, X. and Cohen, A. (2013) 'The Prevalence of News: Domestic, Foreign and Hybrid' in A. Cohen (ed). *Foreign News on Television*, New York: Peter Lang.

Stone, C., Trisi, D., Sherman, A. and DeBot, B. (2015) 'A Guide to Statistics on

Historical Trends in Income Inequality', Center on Budget and Policy Priorities. Online. Available HTTP: <http://www.cbpp.org/sites/default/files/atoms/files/11–28-11pov. pdf> (accessed 15 June 2015).

Stratton, J. (1997) 'Cyberspace and the Globalization of Culture' in D. Porter (ed.) *Internet Culture*, London: Routledge, 253–276.

Sutton, E., Pemberton, S., Fahmy, E. and Tamiya, Y. (2014) 'Stigma, Shame and the Experience of Poverty in Japan and the United Kingdom', *Social Policy and Society*, 13 (1): 143–154.

Sutton, L., Smith, N., Deardon, C. and Middleton, S. (2007) 'A Child's-eye View of Social Difference', Joseph Rowntree Foundation: The Centre for Research in Social Policy (CRSP), Loughborough University. Online. Available: <http://www.jrf.org.uk/ publications/childs-eye-view-social-difference> (accessed 10 January 2011).

Swedish National Board of Trade (2012) *E-commerce – New Opportunities, New Barriers: A Survey of e-Commerce Barriers in Countries Outside the EU*. World Trade Organization. Kommerskollegium, 4. Online. Available HTTP: <https://www.wto.org/ english/tratop_e/serv_e/wkshop_june13_e/ecom_national_board_e.pdf> (accessed 14 May 2015).

Taubman, G. (1998) 'A Not-so World Wide Web: The Internet, China, and the Challenges to Nondemocratic Rule', *Political Communication*, 15: 255–272.

Theocharis, Y. and Quintelier, E. (2014) 'Stimulating Citizenship or Expanding Entertainment? The Effect of Facebook on Adolescent Participation', *New Media & Society*, online first edition, 27 August, 1–12.

Thompson, D. (2010) 'The Tea Party Used the Internet to Defeat the Internet President', *The Atlantic*, 20 November. Online. Available HTTP: <http://www.theatlantic.com/ business/archive/2010/11/the-tea-party-used-the-internet-to-defeat-the-first-internet-president/65589/> (accessed 22 August 2011).

Tiffen, R. et al. (2014) 'Sources in the News: A Comparative Study', *Journalism Studies*, 15 (4): 374–391.

Toffler, A. and Toffler, H. (1995) *Creating a New Civilization*, Atlanta, GA: Turner.

Tomlinson, J. (1999) *Globalization and Culture*, Cambridge: Polity Press.

Turkle, S. (1995) *Life on the Screen*, New York: Simon and Schuster.

Turkle, S. (2011) *Alone Together*, New York: Basic Books.

Ugarteche, O. (2007) 'Transnationalizing the Public Sphere: A Critique of Fraser', *Theory, Culture and Society*, 24 (4): 65–69.

Valliere, D. and Peterson, R. (2004) 'Inflating the Bubble: Examining Investor Behaviour', *Venture Capital*, 4 (1): 1–22.

Volkmer, I. (2003) 'The Global Network Society and the Global Public Sphere', *Development*, 46 (1): 9–16.

Walker, R. et al. (2013) 'Poverty in Global Perspective: Is Shame a Common Denominator?', *Journal of Social Policy*, 42 (2): 215–233.

Washington Post (2012) '2012 Presidential Campaign Finance Explorer', Campaign 2012. Online. Available HTTP: <http://www.washingtonpost.com/wp-srv/special/politics/campaign-finance/> (accessed 23 May 2015).

Weeks, D. (2013) 'Democracy in Poverty: A View from Below', Harvard University, Edmond J. Safra Center for Ethics, 16 May. Edmond J. Safra Working Papers, No. 10.

Weiss, M. (2014) 'New Media, New Activism: Trends and Trajectories in Malaysia, Singapore and Indonesia', *International Development Planning Review*, 36 (1): 91–109.

Wheale, P. R. and Amin, L. H. (2003) 'Bursting the Dot.com "Bubble": A Case Study in Investor Behaviour', *Technological Analysis*, 15 (1): 117–136.

Witschge, T., Fenton, N. and Freedman, D. (2010) *Protecting the News: Civil Society and the Media,* London: Carnegie UK. Online. Available HTTP: <http://www.carnegieuktrust.org.uk/getattachment/1598111d-7cbc-471e-98b4-dc4225f38e99/Protecting-the-News–Civil-Society-and-the-Media.aspx> (accessed 9 June 2011).

Wong, J. (2013) 'Thousands of Cuts in the Media Industry', Canadian Media Guild, 19 November. Online. Available HTTP: <http://www.cmg.ca/en/2013/11/19/thousands-of-cuts-in-the-media-industry/> (accessed 17 June 2015).

World Trade Organization (2013) 'E-commerce in Developing Countries: Opportunities and Challenges for Small and Medium-Sized Enterprises'. Online. Available HTTP: <https://www.wto.org/english/res_e/booksp_e/ecom_brochure_e.pdf> (accessed 13 May 2015).

Worthington, R. (2003) *Governance in Singapore*, London: RoutledgeCurzon.

Chapter 2

The internet of history

Rethinking the internet's past

James Curran

Introduction

When the internet expanded in the 1980s and early 1990s, it was cloaked in romance.[1] The internet's pioneer users developed a distinctive argot, introducing acronyms like MOO and MUD (which refer to adventure and role-playing games). To use the internet in this period was like belonging to a cult, with its own inner secrets, sub-cultural style and tough entry requirement of technical competence. Users were overwhelmingly young, and in the know.

Even when the internet entered the mainstream in the mid-1990s, it still retained something of its early exotic allure. Long articles appeared in the prestige press, explaining how the internet worked and the amazing things that it could do. Words like 'cyberspace', derived from internet pioneers' romance with science fiction, entered the general vocabulary.

It was around this time that the first serious attempts were made to research the origins and development of the internet. However, these early histories were conditioned by the awestruck period in which they were written, something that was reflected in the way they all spelt the internet with a capital 'I' (Abbate 2000; Gillies and Cailliau 2000; Berners-Lee 2000; Rheingold 2000; Banks 2008; Ryan 2010).[2] Their view of the internet was largely uncritical.

There is a clear parallel between these histories of the internet and pioneer histories of the British press, published in 1850–87. British press historians were so awed by the advent of mass journalism, and the power for good that it represented, that they reverently used capital letters to spell Newspaper Press (e.g. Hunt 1850: 178; Grant 1871–2: 453). They, too, were uncritical.

Indeed, an uncritical orientation is almost built into the way in which most internet history is written. Conventional internet history concentrates on the early development of the internet, its Edenic phase, and tells the history of the internet as a Western story. The trouble with this approach is that the internet is much more subject to commercial and state control than it was 30 years ago. And although the internet was a Western invention, it is now a global phenomenon. Updating and de-westernising the history of the internet changes its trajectory. It ceases to be a simple story of progress.

Technical development of the internet

The technical history of the internet can be briefly summarised. The internet began as a small, publicly owned computer network established in 1969 in the United States. This network expanded with the development of a shared computer language and set of protocols. E-mail (or network mail, as it was first called) was introduced in 1972. The term 'internet' emerged in 1974 as a simple abbreviation for *internetworking* between multiple computers. The modern internet dates from 1983, with the establishment of a network of networks wholly independent of the US armed forces.

A US-centred network expanded into a fully international network during the 1980s. A key moment of transition was when CERN, the European Organization for Nuclear Research, adopted internet protocol (IP) for its internal network of computers in 1985, and opened its first external IP connections in 1989. The internet also reached Asia by the late 1980s, though it was not until 1995 that Africa established its first home-grown internet services. By 1998 the internet reached every populated country in the world. However, the diffusion of internet use remained geographically uneven.

The internationalisation of the internet was accompanied by its popularisation. The first key applications of the internet were e-mails, bulletin boards and listservs deployed during the pioneer phase of 1970–90. This was followed by the killer application of the 1990s: the world wide web publicly launched in 1991, the introduction of a graphical browser in 1993 which made the web easier to use, and the development of search engines in the late 1990s that in effect simplified the web, and made it easier to navigate. The 2000s saw the rise of social media and user-generated content, exemplified by the launch of Facebook in 2004. This was followed in the 2010s by the take-off of smartphones which became an integral part of many people's lives. These different uses and applications resulted in the internet being taken up by a widening gyre of users, estimated to be 3.1 billion people in 2014 (Internet World Stats 2015).

Underpinning this remarkable phenomenon were four distinct strands of technical innovation. One was the transformation of the computer from a vast machine occupying an entire room, and requiring the attendance of a white-coated priesthood, into a powerful, easy-to-use artefact that can sit on a lap or be held in a hand. Another was the development of computer networking from the development of shared codes for transporting and addressing communications through to the development of cloud computing supported by massive server farms. A third was the transformation of connective software that facilitated the accessing, linking, storage and generation of information from the read-only technology of the world wide web to the read-write technology that made possible the rise of social media. A fourth strand was the development of communications infrastructure. The internet was able to 'piggy back' on phone lines and cable that had already been established to enable interoperability between countries. Its subsequent massive expansion was facilitated by the development of high-bandwidth cable and also the growth of cellular wireless networks.

However, the evolution of the internet was not simply a technological process determined by scientific innovation. It was also shaped by the objectives of the people who funded, created and fashioned it. Their objectives were to clash, culminating in a battle for the 'soul' of the internet.

Military–scientific complex

It is a much-remarked-upon paradox that although the internet can be viewed as an agency of peace, it was a product of the Cold War. When, in 1957, the Soviet Union launched a satellite orbiting the Earth, it won the first lap of the 'space race'. This galvanised the Pentagon into setting up the Advanced Research Projects Agency (ARPA), whose many projects included a scheme to promote interactive computing through the creation of the world's first advanced computer network (ARPANET). Although the network was conceived originally as a way of sharing expensive computer time, and enabling communication between computers with different operating systems and interfaces, it acquired another rationale. Computer networking could facilitate, it was argued, the development of a sophisticated military command and control system capable of withstanding a nuclear attack from the Soviet Union. The recasting of this project led to major public investment (Edwards 1996; Norberg and O'Neil 1996).

It also resulted in the design of the early internet being influenced by military objectives, in a form that is increasingly downplayed in internet history (e.g. Hafner and Lyon 2003). One overwhelming military concern was the creation of a computer network that would withstand Soviet attack. This led the military to sponsor a devolved system without a command centre that could be destroyed by the enemy. It resulted in a network that was difficult not only to 'take out' but also to control. This also accorded with the concerns of computer scientists who designed the new system, and who did not want to be subject to a centralised, hierarchal chain of command.

Military considerations also led to the development of network technology that would enable the system to function even if parts of it were destroyed. A key military attraction of packet-switching (central to the development of the internet) was that it dispensed with vulnerable, open lines between sender and receiver. Instead, messages were disaggregated into units ('packets') before dispatch, sent through different routes depending on traffic and network conditions, and reassembled on arrival. Each packet was wrapped in a kind of digital envelope with transport and content specifications. The open, peer-to-peer neutrality of the system not only suited military objectives but also accorded with the ethos of academic science.

A further military concern was to have a networking system that could serve different, specialised military tasks. This encouraged the creation of a diverse system that allowed different networks to be incorporated, once minimum requirements had been met. It also led to the addition of satellite and wireless for internetworking, since these were well adapted to communication with jeeps, ships and aeroplanes. But if the internet's modular structure served the military need for flexibility, it also suited academics who wanted to enhance the internet's value as a research tool by incorporating more networks. The add-on nature of the internet thus met the objectives of both partners.

Mutual tact seems also to have prevented the raucous campus protests against the Vietnam War in the later 1960s and early 1970s from souring the harmonious relationship between scientists and the military (Rosenzweig 1998). When a serious clash of priorities developed over the issue of security, this was resolved amicably through the division of the internet into military and civilian networks in 1983.

The mutual trust that developed between the military and scientists resulted in the latter having considerable autonomy. As a consequence, the culture of academic science became part of the founding tradition that shaped the early development of the internet. This culture stressed the importance of public disclosure, collective dialogue and intellectual cooperation to further scientific advance. It gave rise to the cooperative development of networking protocols, and their open release – something that had to be defended subsequently.

The US state thus bankrolled the network design and development of the internet. It also assisted indirectly the building of the internet in other ways. The US defence budget funded the first American electronic digital computer in 1946, and subsidised the subsequent technical advance of the US computer industry (Edwards 1996). The American state also supported the American space programme, whose by-product – orbiting satellites – also contributed to the later development of the internet.

In effect, the American state underwrote a major part of the internet's initial research and development costs. This was not something that the private sector was willing to do. Indeed, in 1972 the telecommunication giant AT&T declined the government's offer to take over ARPANET, the forerunner of the modern internet, on the grounds that it was not likely to make a profit. A computer network linked to the defence programme had, in the corporation's view, no commercial future. Yet, after supporting the research and development costs of the internet, and also shouldering the financial burden of building a significant user base, the American state 'shepherded' the internet to market. In 1991, the ban on commercial use of the public internet was lifted; and in 1995 the public internet was privatised.

The internet thus had a curious beginning. It was a *Dr Strangelove* project, whose subtext resembled the subtitle of the satirical 1964 film: 'How I learned to stop worrying and love the Bomb'. It was also the progeny of an activist state, functioning in a classic social-democratic way to promote growth and jobs, in a country whose political culture celebrates small government. And as a consequence of the relative autonomy accorded to scientists by the military, the design of the internet was imbued from the outset with the values of academic science.

Countercultural values

If the military–scientific complex shaped the early internet, its subsequent development was strongly influenced in the 1980s by the American counterculture (and later by its European counterpart). This counterculture had different strands, although these were often intertwined. A communitarian strand aimed to promote togetherness through the fostering of mutual empathy and understanding. A hippy sub-culture sought individual self-realisation by breaking free from repressive convention, while a radical sub-culture hoped to transform society through the transfer of power to the people. These different currents within the counterculture influenced how the emerging internet was used.

In a strikingly original study, Fred Turner (2006) documents the way in which hip journalists and cultural entrepreneurs acted as mediators, bringing together two divergent groups and sustaining a creative partnership between them. Their brokerage skill lay in flattering the two groups, and awakening hope. They told computer scientists, accustomed to being viewed as nerds, that they were cool messiahs destined to transform the world; and they briefed activists in the counterculture – already in steep decline by the 1980s – that a technology existed that could make their fading dreams come true. Together, computer scientists and activists, they proclaimed, could free the computer from its utilitarian purpose, and make it work for humanity.

A promethean partnership between scientists and activists was forged that played an important role in re-imagining the computer. Thus local area networks in California, usually funded as low-subscription-based services supported by volunteer labour, were created as virtual communes in the 1980s. This was typified by the WELL (Whole Earth 'Lectronic Link), established in the San Francisco area in 1985, originally as a dial-up bulletin board system. It was the brainchild of Stewart Brand, then a radical rock concert impresario, and Larry Brilliant, a left-wing doctor and Third World campaigner. Brilliant enrolled numerous fellow former members of The Farm, a large, self-sufficient agricultural commune in Tennessee. They created an electronic commune that grew into 300 computer-mediated 'conferences' which brought together social and political activists, as well as enthusiasts of all kinds. One of the WELL's largest sub-groups was fans of the radical rock group the Grateful Dead. Deadheads (as they were disrespectfully called) spent hours online discussing the Grateful Dead's enigmatic lyrics and exchanging music recorded at live gigs – something that the rock group supported as part of its public stand *in favour* of the 'pirating' of its music. However, participation in the WELL diminished after a few years. The electronic commune was bought in 1994 by a shoe manufacturer, Bruce Katz. The internecine conflict that followed the takeover led to its steep decline (Rheingold 2000: 331–4).

Similar communal experiments occurred in Europe, typically with the local state acting as a midwife. The best known of these was Amsterdam's Digital City (called DDS in the Netherlands). This began as a pilot project sponsored by the local council in 1994, and was reconstituted in 1995 as a 'virtual city' with a Foundation grant. Different squares in the 'city' were given over to specific topics (such as politics, film and music), and in each of these squares, cybercafés were created as meeting places. The experiment captured the imagination of radical activists, university students, workers in the creative industries and others living in Amsterdam. At its height, the project involved thousands of people, facilitated popular access to online services and mobilised online voting on a range of issues. However, public involvement fell away in the later 1990s after the initial excitement wore off. The project was then weakened by internal conflicts, and failed to secure long-term funding.

More enduring were experiments that linked geographically dispersed grassroots networks, some influenced by radical American students (Hauben and Hauben 1997). These included Usenet (1979), BITNET (1981), FidoNet (1983) and PeaceNet (1985). Usenet newsgroups, built around the UNIX system, proved to be the most important of these networks. Set up initially to discuss issues to do with UNIX software and troubleshooting, they diversified to cover a wide spectrum of topics from abortion to Islam. Usenet newsgroup sites rose from just three in 1979 to 11,000 by 1988, and over 20,000 by 2000 (Naughton 2000: 181–2). This poor relation started as a dial-up service was subsequently allowed to ride on the ARPA network. It was then carried by the internet.

Meanwhile, the hippy strand of the counterculture helped to turn the computer into a playground. During the early 1990s, a cult was created around text-based adventure games in which participants could take on assumed identities and interact with others, freed from the visual markers of age, gender, ethnicity, class and disability. Celebrants hailed this as a space in which people could explore their real selves, break free from the constraints and prejudices of everyday life, attain greater empathy with others and build a better world based on liberated subjectivities (Turkle 1995). Others saw it as a liberating context in which people could have promiscuous, virtual sex freed from the conventions of the offline world (and sometimes pass themselves off as being younger and more attractive than they were in real life) (Ito 1997).

The counterculture also contributed to the emergence of hip computer capitalism. Thus, Steve Jobs and Steve Wozniak, who launched Apple in 1980, came out of the alternative movement. Jobs had travelled to India in a quest for personal enlightenment, while Wozniak was heavily involved in the radical rock scene. In 1982, Wozniak personally funded the organisation of a rock festival dedicated to the Information Age. At the festival, which attracted more people than Woodstock, there was a giant video screen on which was projected a simple message:

> There is an explosion of information dispersal in the technology and we think this information has to be shared. All great thinkers about democracy said that the key to democracy is access to information. And now we have a chance to get information into people's hands like never before.
>
> (Cited in Flichy 1999: 37)

The counterculture thus reconceived how the computer could be used to advance its vision of the future. Its activists transformed the internet from being the tool of a techno-elite into becoming the creator of virtual communities, a sub-cultural playground and an agency of democracy.

European public service

The third formative influence shaping cyberspace was a European welfarist tradition that had created great public health and broadcasting systems. While the internet was born in the United States, the world wide web was created by Tim Berners-Lee in the publicly funded European Particle Physics Laboratory at CERN.

Tim Berners-Lee was inspired by two key ideas: that of opening up access to a public good (the storehouse of knowledge contained in the world's computer system) and that of bringing people into communion with each other. The son of two mathematicians, Berners-Lee found fulfilment in serving the community. While not automatically anti-market, he resented the exaltation of market values above all else. He is often asked in the United States (though less frequently in Europe), he says, whether he regrets not making money out of the invention of the world wide web. His response is a typical reaction of a public servant:

> What is maddening is the terrible notion [implied in this question] that a person's value depends on how important and financially successful they are, and that this is measured in terms of money. . . Core in my upbringing was a value system that put monetary gain well in its place.
>
> (Berners-Lee 2000: 116)

Berners-Lee's desire not to promote the web through a private company was prompted by his conviction that it would trigger competition and lead to the subdivision of the web into private domains. This would subvert his conception of 'a universal medium for sharing information' and undermine the purpose of his project. He persuaded the management of his publicly funded agency to release the world wide web code in 1993 as a gift to the community. He subsequently became the head of the agency regulating the web (World Wide Web Consortium (W3C)) to 'think about what was best for the world, as opposed to what would be best for one commercial interest' (Berners-Lee 2000: 91).

Thus, the bequest of the web made freely available a vast cornucopia of knowledge and information. It was inspired by the ideal of serving society rather than self.

Commercial honeymoon

However, the 'openness' advocated by technologists took the form of championing scientific access and disclosure rather than opening up the internet to mass consumption. The communards who adapted the internet for new purposes were members of minority sub-cultures who were driven to acquire the necessary expertise. Even the first manifestation of the world wide web, hatched in a scientific laboratory, required significant computer skills to access. The internet still belonged to an exclusive world.

The fourth influence shaping the development of cyberspace was the marketplace. The lifting of the commercial ban on use of the public internet in 1991 had seemingly a wholly benign effect. The arrival of web browsers that displayed images with texts was, as Berners-Lee (2000: 90) acknowledges, 'a very important step for the Web'. It was followed by commercial search engines that made the web easy to explore. The market, it seemed, was all about popularising the internet, and democratising its use.

In the mid-1990s, all aspects of the internet seemed enormously positive. Even if the internet was a product of a superpower war machine, its military origins had been terminated (in effect, when ARPANET handed over control of the public internet backbone to the National Science Foundation in 1990). A combination of academic, countercultural and public service values had given rise to an internet that was independent, decentralised, diverse and open to innovation. The ways in which the internet could be used had been greatly extended. The growing influence of commerce seemed merely to extend the benefits of this new medium to more people, without detracting from its fundamental nature.

The largely uncritical reception given to the commercialisation of the net during the mid-1990s accorded with the ethos of the time. This was a period of triumphalism when democracy and capitalism had defeated communism, with the collapse of the Soviet Union in December 1991 (Fukuyama 1993). The mood music of that era was accompanied by the lyrics of internet experts. The MIT guru Nicholas Negroponte wrote a celebrated book in 1995, which portrayed the internet as an integral part of a democratising digital revolution. The public, he predicted, will *pull* what it wants from the internet and digital media, rather than accept what is *pushed* at them by media giants. Media consumption, he continued, is becoming 'customised' according to individual taste, and 'the monolithic empires of mass media are dissolving into an army of cottage industries', making obsolete 'industrial-age cross-ownership laws' (Negroponte 1996: 57–8 and 85). Similarly Mark Poster (1995), another revered net expert, concluded that the world was entering the 'second media age', in which monopoly would be replaced by diversity, the distinction between senders and receivers would be dissolved, and the ruled would become rulers. In these, and most other contemporary commentaries, the market was viewed not as a limitation but as an asset.

The coalition that had created the pre-market internet began to fracture during the 1990s. Some academic computer scientists set up internet companies and became millionaires. Others quietly acquiesced to software licensing restrictions, while university administrators looked for ways to make money out of their computer science departments. A new generation of computer industry leaders emerged, whose casual clothes and populism seemed to set them apart from the stuffy corporate culture of their predecessors. Their companies appeared caring and different. Google, for instance, had as its company slogan 'Don't Be Evil', and set up a non-profit, philanthropic wing in 2004. Even the imagery used to describe digital capitalism changed. The early metaphor of the 'information superhighway', with its 1950s association of statist modernism, gave way to the sci-fi electronic sublime of 'cyberspace' (Streeter 2003).

In this environment, digital capitalism seemed cool: the way to make money, express individuality and avoid state control. Indeed, everything to do with the internet in the 1990s – including its commercialisation – seemed wondrous, transformative and positive.

Commercial transformation

Commercialisation extended the legacy of innovation initiated by public investment. In particular a great university, Stanford, produced skilled, enterprising students who flourished in a dense network of expertise supported by investors. Its adjacent area of Palo Alto and Mountain View, extending to the wider Bay Area tech scene, became an incubator of new enterprises from the launch of Google in 1998 through to the creation of Instagram in 2010.

But commercialisation also changed the character of the internet. The adoption in 1997 of a standard protocol for credit card transactions gave an important boost to online sales. The internet became in part a shopping mall: a place where virtual shops did business, and where products and services were sold. This clearly met a public need. It gave rise to a retail revolution which, so far, has been primarily national rather than international.[3]

Online content (as distinct from offline products and services) proved more difficult to sell. The content that sold best was pornography and games. By 2006, the adult entertainment industry in the US – in which online porn came to play a significant part – made $2.8 billion in 2006 (Edelman 2009). Online gaming proved to be a still greater success, reaping in 2011 an estimated $19 billion in worldwide revenue (with China having the highest proportion of gamers among internet users) (Statistics Portal 2015; cf. DFC Intelligence 2010). Its online triumph enabled the video-gaming industry to overtake the Hollywood movie industry in terms of revenue (Movie Picture Association in America 2013; Newzoo 2013).[4] By contrast, journalism was a much less commercially successful online product.

Commercialisation also led to the growth of online advertising. While some advertising sites like craigslist and Gumtree proved to be immensely popular, online advertising could also be intrusive. The advertising industry introduced first of all the banner advertisement (a horizontal strip, reminiscent of early press display advertisements). This was followed by advertisements of different shapes such as 'button', 'skyscraper' and pop-up 'interstitials' and, later, audio-visual advertisements (more like television commercials).

The growth of advertising was accompanied by the proliferation of spam. The first recorded example of spam occurred in 1978. It proliferated to the point when, according to John Naughton (2012: 82), it accounted for well over half of global e-mail traffic in 2009. The technically proficient were able to filter out this tidal wave of mostly unwanted information.

Advancing market influence also introduced unobtrusive controls. Internet corporations lobbied government for changes in the law that served their interests. In particular, they pressed for the legal protection of intellectual property rights in a way that threatened to undermine the open, collaborative tradition on which the internet had been built (Lessig 1999; Weber 2004). In 1976, the United

States passed a Copyright Act which extended copyright to software. This was buttressed in 1998 by the Digital Millennium Act, which greatly strengthened legal provision against piracy that threatened digital media companies. Its effect, however, was to overprotect intellectual property rights at the expense of legitimate 'fair use' of web content (Lessig 2001) in so restrictive a form that it was difficult to enforce. More recently, some leading internet and telecommunications companies have been pressing for the abandonment of net neutrality – the cornerstone of the open, peer-to-peer design of the internet – to optimise revenue. So far, their lobbying has been unsuccessful.[5]

Commercialisation also established more subtle forms of control based on market power. The beguiling vision of boutiques, cottage industries and sovereign consumers, conjured up by Nicholas Negroponte (1996), proved to be a fantasy. At an international level, a small number of corporations established a leading position in different sectors of the internet. Indeed, four of these had in 2015 a level of capitalisation that made them among the biggest companies in the world: Apple ($700bn), Google ($430bn), Microsoft ($380bn) and Oracle ($175bn). A detailed national market breakdown complicates this picture a little. For example, although Google is the foremost search engine in the world, Baidu dominates in China, as do Yandex in Russia and Yahoo in Japan (Haucap and Heimeshoff 2013: 55, table 2). But in their respective national markets, one search engine dominates. A similar picture applies in relation to news. A small number of large news organisations (overwhelmingly legacy media) dominate online news consumption in their respective countries, with a small elite group of news organisations like the *New York Times* and Globo building an international audience in their respective language markets (Curran et al. 2013).

Some leading internet companies used their market power in ways that were exclusionary. For example, Apple iPhones and iPads do not allow the addition of applications that have not been approved beforehand by Apple. Disobey the Apple Way, and your handheld computer is liable not to work. The fact that smartphones are tethered to controlled mobile networks in contrast to the way that freely programmable computers are connected via landline networks has enabled the imposition of this new layer of control (Naughton 2011; cf. Lametti 2012).

Indeed, a number of internet leaders sailed so close to the wind, or were judged to be so anti-competitive, that they ran into trouble with the authorities. The European Commission recently imposed a fine on Microsoft, and is currently investigating Google and Amazon (EC 2015; EC 2013). Apple is under investigation by the US Federal Trade Commission (Golson 2015), while Facebook faces investigations in five European countries (Schechner 2015).

Digital capitalism turned out to be not very different from other forms of large-scale corporate capitalism. Indeed, the leading digital corporations could be a good deal more ruthless while seeming to be more caring and informal. Their sharp edge was epitomised by Steve Jobs, the driving force behind Apple. He undertook a product test on his pregnant, long-term girlfriend, asking in a survey of almost 100 friends whether he should opt for her or another woman he fancied. Which, he asked, was the prettier? Who did they like better? Who should he marry? (Isaacson 2011: 272). Although capable of inspiring intense loyalty, Jobs was also insensitive. When one candidate droned on in a job interview, Jobs broke in saying: 'Gobble, gobble, gobble, gobble'. The interview panel cracked up with laughter, prompting the poor man to get up and leave, saying: 'I guess I'm not the right guy' (Isaacson 2011: 142).

Jobs studied under a Zen Master but this did not prevent his company from being exploitative. Apple's elegant products were manufactured partly through Foxconn, a company whose factories in China are notorious for their long hours, low wages and soulless, crowded dormitories. When a number of Foxconn workers committed suicide in 2010, the company response was not to improve working conditions but to build a safety net around its facilities (Mosco 2014: 161). While this put Apple in an unwelcome spotlight, Amazon, Google, Microsoft, Cisco and HP also outsourced work to low-wage contractors with poor records. Likewise, an undercover investigation into Amazon UK found that workers walk miles every day to fulfil exacting packaging and shipping targets for just above the minimum wage. The company relies heavily on agency and seasonal staff, without the security and higher pay of permanent employees (Cadwalladr 2013).

Apple, Facebook, Amazon, Microsoft and Google all made strenuous efforts to dodge taxes (Sikka 2015). Thus, Amazon channelled 15 billion euros to a subsidiary in Luxembourg in 2013 to evade taxes in countries where it made large amounts of money (Bergin 2014). Similarly, Google has taken advantage of tax treaties 'to channel more than $8 billion in untaxed profits out of Europe and Asia each year' into a Bermuda tax haven (Bergin 2014).

More recently, internet companies have come under attack from environmentalists. Their profligate use of energy in industrial-scale server warehouses is giving rise, it is argued, to needlessly large carbon emissions (Glanz 2012). There has also been an explosive growth of non-recyclable e-waste caused by dumped computers, monitors, mobile phones, DVD players, iPods, iPads and microchips, positively encouraged by the way new products are deliberately launched with a short life span (Gabrys 2013). The 'immaterial', it turns out, has a large environmental footprint.

Commercialisation of the internet also gave rise to the development of a new regime of commercial surveillance from the 1990s onwards (Schiller 2007; Deibert et al. 2008; Zittrain 2008). One method entailed monitoring data and traffic over a network (for example, Google searches) in a form that tracks users, gathers information about which websites are visited and what users do on these sites. Another method was to install software that monitored the activities of a specific computer and its user. This software had the potential to enter the 'backdoor' of other computers, enabling the monitoring of their activity. The third approach was to collate data from different sources to compile a social network analysis about the personal interests, friendships, affiliations and consumption habits of users.

Surveillance technology came to be deployed very extensively. In the United States, an estimated 92% of commercial websites aggregated, sorted and used for economic purposes data about people's use of the net (Lessig 1999: 153). Most people made themselves vulnerable to this monitoring by waiving their rights of privacy to gain free access. 'Human rights' protection of privacy was relatively weak in the United States, although stronger in Europe.

This technology came to be used in ways that had not been intended. According to a study released in 2000, 73% of US firms routinely checked on their work-force's use of the net (Castells 2001: 74). More importantly, autocratic governments adopted – as we shall see – commercial surveillance software to monitor and censor the internet. Methods developed to assist marketers and advertisers were deployed to support autocracy.

It used to be widely thought that this was a problem confined to authoritarian states. Monitoring communications in the West was directed, it was assumed, at specific people and undertaken solely for legitimate purposes such as preventing serious crime and terrorism. It is now becoming clear that national security agencies are seeking to collect big data streams, and then process them afterwards (Andrejevic and Gates 2014). There are various ways of collecting this information. The Snowden leaks reveal that the NSA can compel private companies like Google, Microsoft, Facebook and Skype to hand over consumer data without users themselves knowing (Bauman et al. 2014; Greenwald 2014; Lyon 2014). Another way of collecting information entails placing data interceptors on the global submarine cables that are the primary arteries of the internet (Brown 2014). This is something that the UK's Government Communications Headquarters is seemingly doing: other national security agencies in Europe are also routinely tapping internet cables (Bauman et al. 2014). There is now a growing demand for the public to be told more clearly how extensive is this shift towards mass monitoring of communications; what safeguards are in place to prevent abuse; and what protection is available for public interest whistle-blowers.

In short, the commercialisation of the internet played an important part in popularising the internet, and making it accessible to a wider public. It also extended investment and innovation, after an initial public outlay. But commercialisation also had strongly negative features. It gave rise to economic concentration and the abuse of market dominance. It led to the creation of global digital giants, some of which dodged tax, exploited workers and lobbied for changes in the law that served their interests rather than the public interest.[6] And it led to a system of commercial surveillance that was adapted by dictatorships to repress dissent, and is now being used in liberal democracies in ways that potentially threaten civil liberties.

Revolt of the nerds

However, the steady advance of commercialism was resisted. The first people to take a stand were computer scientists who opposed the imposition of 'proprietary software' by large corporations.

The nerds' revolt began in 1984, when Richard Stallman, a radical programmer at MIT, set up the Free Software Foundation. He had been outraged when a colleague had refused to pass on a printer code on the grounds that it was now restricted by licence. This seemed to Stallman an enforced form of private selfishness that violated the norm of cooperation on which his professional life had been based. His outrage turned to anger when AT&T announced its intention to license the widely used and previously unrestricted UNIX operating system. In his view, this amounted to the corporate capture, with the full authority of the law, of a program that had been produced communally.

Richard Stallman, a bearded figure with the appearance of an Apostle, gave up his secure job and set about almost single-handedly building a free alternative to the UNIX operating system. It was called GNU (standing for 'GNU is Not UNIX'). Between 1984 and 1988, Stallman designed an editor and compiler, which were hailed as masterpieces of skill and ingenuity. Then, Stallman's hands sustained repetitive strain injury, and he slowed down. The GNU project was still some way from completion. A then unknown Finnish student, Linus Torvalds, who had heard Stallman give a charismatic talk in Helsinki, filled the breach. With the help of his friends, Torvalds developed the missing kernel of the GNU system in 1990. The computer community collectively improved the resulting GNU/ Linux operating system, making it one of the most reliable in the world. Such was its sustained success that IBM decided in 1998 to hitch its wagon to the protest movement. It officially backed the Linux system, agreeing to invest money in its further development without seeking to exercise any form of proprietary control.

IBM also embraced, on the same terms, the Apache server. This derived from a program released freely by a publicly funded agency, the National Center for Supercomputing Applications (NCSA) at the University of Illinois. Initially full of bugs, it was transformed by the hacker community through cumulative improvements ('patches') and renamed Apache. It became a widely used free server – its success again accounting for its open-source adoption by IBM.

This was followed by the launch of the freely available client software Mozilla Firefox, in 2003–4. By 2011, it had become the second most widely used web browser in the world, having grown against the odds at the expense of Microsoft's Internet Explorer. One of Mozilla Firefox's attractions was that it provided a way of blocking online advertising.

What partly underpinned the effectiveness of this concerted protest was that it enlisted the protection of the state (something that radical libertarians tend to ignore). The Free Software Foundation set up by Stallman released its projects under a General Public Licence (GPL). This contained a 'copyleft' clause (the wordplay is typical computer nerd humour) requiring any subsequent improvement in free software to be made available to the community, under the GPL. Contract and copyright law was thus deployed to prevent companies from modifying free software and then claiming the resulting version as their property. It was also used to ensure that future refinements in free software were 'gifted' back to the community.

The successful open-source (OS) movement kept alive the tradition of the open disclosure of information. It perpetuated the cooperative norms of the scientific community in which people make improvements, or develop new applications (like the world wide web), on the basis of open access to information and then return the favour by making the basis of their discoveries freely available. It also kept faith with the values of academic science, with its belief in cooperation, freedom and open debate in pursuit of scientific advance. The result was the creation of a practical alternative to proprietary software.

The OS movement drew upon highly trained computer scientists at universities, research laboratories and in the computer industry, as well as skilled hackers. OS activists tended to have a shared belief that the power of the computer should be harnessed for the public good, and were inclined to view any form of authority with suspicion. While their motives were altruistic, they also gained satisfaction from the thrill of creativity and recognition from their peers (Levy 1994). The OS community was also guided by standards, rules, decision-making procedures and sanctioning mechanisms. It was partly this that made it so effective (Weber 2004).

User-generated content

The OS campaign was linked to the drive to participate in the creation of online content. The OS champion, Richard Stallman, had been one of the people who had argued in the 1990s that there should be a web-based online encyclopaedia which would be generated and revised collectively in much the way that OS code is produced. This dream was fulfilled when Jimmy Wales and Larry Sanger launched Wikipedia in 2001.

It became one of the largest collaborative ventures in the world. By 2015, Wikipedia was the seventh most popular website globally (Alexa 2015a). It had almost 35 million articles in 288 languages, attracted nearly 500 million unique visitors every month, and had reached 18 billion page views by 2014 (Wikipedia 2015). It has established itself as an invaluable (though not always reliable) source of information on a wide spectrum of topics. This achievement was underpinned by the self-correcting mechanism of collective revision, a team of some 70,000 active editors (in 2015), a shared norm of adhering to factual accuracy, unobtrusive safeguards, editorial transparency and an academic tail of footnotes and hypertextual links (Dariusz 2014; Zittrain 2008).

The rise of Wikipedia was followed by the even more spectacular take-off of Facebook. It was set up by Harvard students in 2004, prospered as a young elite social networking site, and then grew exponentially when it became open to all in 2006. It enables users to publish in effect to their friends, while excluding unwanted attention. In 2015, Facebook was the second most popular website in the world (Alexa 2015b), with 1.4 billion monthly active users. Half its users in 2011 logged in once a day (Naughton 2012: 97) – an indication of its importance in people's lives.

Facebook's flotation was accompanied by the launch of numerous other successful social networking sites (SNS), such as LinkedIn (2003), Flickr (2004), Twitter (2007), Gays.com (2008), Jiepang (2010) and Instagram (2010). Most of these had different functions (Flickr, for example, enables the sharing of photographs and videos), reached different communities or communicated in different languages (Chinese in the case of Jiepang). In normal circumstances, they were primarily social sites, as their name suggests.

Most of these sites were commercial in origin, and were increasingly controlled by major digital groups. But they were free at the point of use, and were sustained by the collective talents, interests and resources of the community they served. For example, YouTube, the video-hosting website (acquired by Google in 2006), offers a space in which users can circulate what they enjoy, and also distribute content they have created, edited or manipulated, often using software tools made available free from OS programmes. The success of this and other similar websites, and the mushrooming of SNS in general, marks the renewal of the do-it-yourself, communal tradition initiated by experiments like the WELL and Amsterdam's Digital City.

The radical strand of the early internet also found expression in the founding of WikiLeaks in 2006. A small, non-profit organisation, it receives, processes and makes publicly available information supplied by whistle-blowers and others. It caused a sensation in 2010 when it released footage of an American helicopter gunning down Iraqi civilians and two journalists in Baghdad in 2007, with the chilling combatant comment 'Light 'em all up. Come on, fire!'. This was followed by the mass leaking of US diplomatic cables, which, among other things, provided a revealing insight into America's informal empire. WikiLeaks overcame the potential problem of being overlooked in the web's vast emporium by forming strategic alliances with leading media organisations. In effect, WikiLeaks sought to turn the tables: governments rather than users were to be scrutinised through data stored on computers.

But the impact of the diplomatic cable leaks was weakened by the way in which numerous media in the UK, the US and elsewhere failed to follow up allegations raised by the leaks, downplayed their novelty, questioned the legitimacy of the leaks on security grounds and subsequently focused on accusations levelled against Julian Assange, and the retribution levied on the whistle-blower, Chelsea Manning, who was sentenced to 35 years' imprisonment (Schlosberg 2013; Benkler 2011). This showed that traditional media gatekeepers, and their close allies, were still able to see off a networked Fourth Estate, at least on this occasion.

Recalcitrant users

The nerd revolt and the revival of communally generated content were effective partly because they were backed up by recalcitrant users. The pre-market internet had accustomed people to expect web content and software to be free. For this reason, it proved difficult to re-educate them into becoming paying consumers.

This is illustrated by early attempts to monetise the web. In 1993, the publicly funded agency NCSA (National Center for Supercomputing Applications) released its pioneer browser, Mosaic, on the net for free. Within six months, a million or more copies were downloaded. Members of the Mosaic team then set up a private company and offered an improved, commercial version, Netscape, on a three-month, free-trial basis. However, demands for payment, after the free trial, were widely ignored. Netscape's management then had to decide whether to insist on payment or change tack. It opted to make its service free because it feared – probably rightly – that continued attempts to charge would cause people to migrate to a free alternative. Netscape turned instead to advertising and consultancy as its main source of revenue (Berners-Lee 2000: 107–8).

Initially, there was considerable hostility to the idea of net advertising. Indeed, two thirds of Americans said they did not want any online advertising in a 1995 survey (cited by McChesney 1999: 132). In the previous year, the US law firm Canter and Siegel had been punished for overstepping the mark. It had posted an advertisement for its immigration law advice service to thousands of newsgroups, only to be inundated the next day with so many abusive replies ('flames') that its internet service provider repeatedly crashed (Goggin 2000). Over time, resistance to advertising was successfully overcome, especially after software became available for filtering out e-mailed spam.

Attempts to persuade consumers to pay for online content met with less success. Companies that charged website fees in the 1990s tended to fail (Schiller 2000; Sparks 2000). The music industry, after a long and disastrous delay, found a compromise solution to the online pirating of music: in effect, it opted for charging very much less for online tracks. A growing number of newspaper publishers attempted in 2010–12 to charge for content that they had previously made freely available. Sometimes they attempted to smooth the transition by offering a limited number of articles free. The audit results are now coming through, and suggest that the experiment has been a failure (save in the case of specialised financial journalism). Thus, an extensive cross-national study found that newspaper paywalls were softening (with more content being offered free), while user charges were declining, and now accounted for only about 10% of newspaper audience revenue (Myllylahti 2014). Likewise, another major comparative study concluded that the income gained from paywalls was limited, and growth in paywall and apps revenue typically stalled once 'the supply of loyal users ran out' (Newman and Levy 2014: 12).

A tacit détente has been reached. Consumers seem willing to waive their rights to privacy, and put up with a limited quota of advertising, while continuing to resist paying for online content. Meanwhile a growing number of people have imposed their own imprint by generating, sharing and commenting on online content.

The rapid diffusion of smartphones in the 2010s deepened people's involvement with the internet. In the US, 64% of adults had smartphones in 2014 (Pew 2014), similar to the 61% of adults who had smartphones in the UK (Ofcom 2014a). Smartphones are becoming Americans' ever-present companion: 65% of US smartphone users check their phones within 15 minutes of waking up and within 15 minutes of going to bed (Twohig 2015). In the case of the UK, the diffusion of smartphones and tablets appears to have extended people's love affair with the media. Ofcom reports that the average adult in the UK now spends more time using media and communications than sleeping (2014b). These two countries are part of a wider trend towards mass adoption of new mobile technology. In 2014 there were estimated to be 2.6 billion smartphones in use, with an especially high distribution in the West (GSMA 2015).

Looking back

The history of the Western internet is thus a chronicle of contradiction. In its predominantly pre-market phase, the internet was powerfully influenced by the values of academic science, American counterculture and European public service. Originating as a research tool linked to a military project, the internet acquired multiple new functions – as the creator of virtual communities, a playground for role-playing and as a platform for interactive political debate. The crowning culmination of this first phase was the gift of the web to the world, creating a storehouse of information freely available to all.

However, this early formation was overlaid by a new commercial regime. A determined attempt was made to charge for software that had previously been free. Major media organisations established well-resourced websites. Search engines, seeking to harvest advertising, signposted visitors to popular destinations. The growth of online entertainment tended to side-line political discourse. New commercial surveillance technology was developed to monitor user behaviour, accompanied by legislation strengthening intellectual property rights. Dominant internet corporations became established, sought to limit competition and belied their 'Don't be evil' image by exploiting outsourced workers and evading taxes in countries where they made large profits.

Yet the old order refused to surrender without a fight. Dissenting computer workers collectively developed and made available OS software. Users, conditioned by the norms of the early internet, often refused to pay for online content and shifted to sites that were free. The spirit that had re-imagined the computer and discovered new uses for it in the 1980s was powerfully renewed in the 21st century. It led to the creation of the user-generated Wikipedia, SNS and the whistle-blower website WikiLeaks.

If the main progressive effort in the West was to combat market censorship and control of the web, and is only now becoming concerned about the excesses of national security surveillance of the internet, its counterpart in the East had a different emphasis. Its efforts were overwhelmingly directed towards opposing and thwarting state censorship. It is to this that we now turn, in a necessarily preliminary attempt to widen the scope of internet history.

March to democracy

It was widely predicted in the 1990s that the global diffusion of the internet would assist the march to democracy. The keyboard, we were told, would prove mightier than the bullet: dictatorships would fall like dominoes because the internet would inspire a clamour for freedom.[7]

This view is refuted by a comparative analysis of internet diffusion rates and measurements of democratic change in 72 countries between 1994 and 2003 (Groshek 2010). It found that 'Internet diffusion was not a specific causal mechanism of national democratic growth' (Groshek 2010: 142). Even in three instances (Croatia, Indonesia and Mexico) where the internet appears to have had a significant democratising influence, the processes of causation were complex. The internet should be seen as a 'coincidental developmental condition', an aspect of larger social and political change that contributed to a nation's democratic development (Groshek 2010: 159).

One reason why the 'internet as the grave-digger of dictatorship' thesis proved to be overstated was that it failed to appreciate that democracy is only one source of governmental legitimacy. Economic success (Singapore), fear of a strong neighbour (pre-1996 Taiwan), nationalism (China), ethnic affiliation (Malaysia), God's will (Iran) and identification with national liberation (Zimbabwe) are just some of the alternative sources of legitimation sustaining resilient authoritarian regimes. In addition to brute force, authoritarian governments have also deployed non-coercive strategies for sustaining their rule, such as co-opting powerful interests, developing clientelist systems of patronage that reward their supporters and adopting a policy of divide and rule (Gandhi and Przeworski 2007; Magaloni 2008). Above all, authoritarian governments can often count on pragmatic acceptance based on the absence of a realistic alternative, the personal struggle to make ends meet or get on and the narcotic of an entertainment-centred popular culture.

The second thing that the 'technology of freedom' thesis got wrong was that it mistakenly assumed that the internet was uncontrollable. It was widely argued in the 1990s that because the internet is a decentralised system in which information is transmitted via independent, variable pathways through dispersed computer power, it could not be controlled by location-bound government. Dissident communications, we were told, could be produced outside the jurisdictional control of national government and downloaded in the privacy of people's homes. Freedom would take wing because it could no longer be suppressed in the internet era.

This failed to take account of the multiple methods developed by authoritarian regimes around the world to censor the internet, and intimidate critics. Authoritarian governments can inculcate a general climate of fear by killing, torturing or imprisoning dissidents. They can require all domestic websites and internet service providers to be licensed, and withdraw these licences if they breach restrictive laws. Authoritarian regimes can outsource censorship by requiring all internet service providers to filter out access to any website on an official blacklist, irrespective of where in the world it originates from. They can monitor the internet behaviour of potential dissidents through surveillance software by, for example, planting a malignant link to a critical petition. They can deploy automated software to identify 'harmful' internet communications, such as critical, anonymous posts, and promptly have them wiped. They can unleash programming to defeat evasion, including the identification of proxy sites, and disable critical sites through DDOS (Distributed-Denial-of-Service) attacks. The ultimate weapon is to pull the plug – closing down internet communication in a region (China), suspending the texting of messages for a period (Cambodia) or stopping mobile phone coverage in a city (Iran) (Morozov 2011; cf. Deibert et al. 2008; Freedom House 2009; OpenNet Initiative 2015). But internet censorship has always been a work in progress in which fresh measures have been taken to respond to new developments. Thus, to take an example almost at random, the Saudi Arabian government introduced new restrictions on user-generated content, including on Facebook, in 2013 (Noman 2013).

Governments have also sought to make the internet a propaganda tool – what Morozov (2011: 113) calls 'spinternet' – not merely through the creation of official websites but also through more indirect methods. For example, the Chinese government has long seeded support groups to proselytise online, while in Russia the principal internet entrepreneur, Konstantin, is a close government ally. In Iran, the arrest of dissidents facilitated – through gaining access to their e-mail and mobile phone contacts – the rapid round-up of oppositional networks in 2009–10. New technology proved, in this case, to be a more efficient method of identifying and apprehending enemies of the state than the old-fashioned Soviet methods of bugging and trailing suspects.

The extent to which the internet was controlled in practice by authoritarian governments varied greatly. This depended partly on their capacity, and partly also on their wider policy objectives. Some authoritarian regimes, like those in Iran, China and Uzbekistan, became undisputed leaders in censoring the internet; others, like those in Ethiopia and Yemen, were ineffectual because they were dysfunctional as governments; while others still, like the authorities in Malaysia and Morocco, chose to adopt relatively liberal internet regimes to advance economic modernisation (OpenNet Initiative 2011, 2015).

How much control was exercised also depended on the wider context. Some authoritarian governments could rely on poverty as the ultimate censor (as in Myanmar). Other regimes, such as that in Singapore, controlled the internet as a consequence of the hegemonic support that they enjoyed.[8] By contrast, large-scale alienation (as in Iran) could produce activists adept at evading censorship.

In brief, those who predicted that the rise of the internet would lead to the fall of authoritarian regimes were confounded by the way most of these regimes survived in the internet era. Many authoritarian governments across the world had greater resources at their disposal, and were better able to censor the internet, than was appreciated in the cyber-utopian moment of the mid-1990s.

But there is a recent exception where, it is claimed, new communications technology inspired people to rise up against dictators. This claim has been repeated so often that it warrants closer scrutiny.

Arab uprisings

On 18 December 2010, mass street protests took place in Tunisia. They were followed by tumultuous demonstrations, rallies and occupations that caused

President Ben Ali to flee the country on 14 January 2010. The contagion of discontent spread to Egypt, where popular protests forced, on 11 February, the resignation of President Hosni Mubarak after almost 30 years of rule. During January and February, popular protests occurred across much of the region. Some of these were placated by promises of liberalising reform, as in Jordan and Morocco. But there were sustained protests in six 'insurgent' countries: Bahrain, Yemen, Libya and Syria, in addition to Tunisia and Egypt.

Since protests happened over so short a period, and were supported by digital technology, some have called them the 'Twitter' or 'Facebook' revolutions (e.g. Taylor 2011). Social media, it is claimed, enabled flash demonstrations to take place, and encouraged protests to spread across national frontiers. What made this situation unprecedented, it is argued, is that people could communicate with each other on a mass scale and gain strength from each other in ways that could not be controlled by the authorities. Typically, this analysis foregrounds the drama of the uprisings and the enabling role of communications technology, while paying limited attention to the past or to the wider political and social context (e.g. El-Nawawy 2011; Mullany 2011).

A closer examination suggests that these first drafts of history are seriously flawed. The Middle East and North Africa (MENA) region was not especially primed by new information communication technology to erupt. An analysis of 52 million Twitter users found that only 0.027% identified their locations as Egypt, Yemen and Tunisia (Evans 2011). The Facebook penetration rate in the region's trouble spots was not high: a mere 1% in Syria and 5% in Libya, though it was 17% in Tunisia (Dubai School of Government (DSG) 2011: 5, figure 6). In 2010, less than a quarter of the population in Egypt and Syria were internet users, a proportion that fell to 6% in Libya (DSG 2011: 10, figure 12). This was much lower than in many other authoritarian nations in Asia (Internet World Stats 2011a). This suggests that it was not information communications technology (ICT) that made the MENA region especially combustible.

Indeed, out of the six 'insurgent' countries, Bahrain alone featured in the top five rankings of MENA countries for Facebook user penetration or for internet use in 2010 (DSG 2011: 5, figure 6; and 12, figure 15). In other words, what the great bulk of insurgent countries had in common was that they were *not* part of the ICT vanguard in the Arab region. So, to take a specific example, 24% of Egyptians were internet users, compared with 41% of Moroccans, 44% of Saudi Arabians and 69% of those living in the UAE in 2010 (Internet World Stats 2011b). Yet these latter countries with higher internet penetration rates did not turn on their dictators. This suggests that there were underlying causes – rather than the mere presence of the internet and social media – that were mainly responsible for the Arab uprisings.

This is corroborated by the history of insurgent countries. The Arab uprisings were the culmination of dissent fermented over decades (Wright 2008; Hamzawy 2009; Alexander 2010; Joshi 2011; Ottaway and Hamzawy 2011; Dawisha 2013, among others). In Syria, the 2011 uprising had been preceded by the 1982 rebellion, which had been put down with enormous brutality. Yemen had a civil war in 1994, and was approaching the condition of a failed state by the time of the 2011 uprising. Bahrain, Egypt, Libya and Tunisia had recurrent protests in the 1980s, 1990s and 2000s. Bahrain had become a beleaguered police state after its parliament had been suspended in 1975. In Egypt, the Kefaya Movement had united disparate anti-government groups in 2004–5. In the first three months of 2008 alone, there had been some 600 protests in the country. A powder keg was waiting to blow.

Underlying this incendiary situation was a mixture of factors – some that were common to all insurgent Arab countries, and others that were country specific. One common factor was growing opposition to regimes that were viewed as corrupt and repressive. Resentment was particularly strong in those countries, like Tunisia and Libya, where it was felt that the benefits of economic development were funnelled towards those closest to the regime (Durac and Cavatorta 2009).

Another factor common to most of the affected countries was high youth unemployment, compounded by rising expectations. Countries across the region expanded their higher education and post-15 education rates (Cassidy 2011; Barro and Lee 2010). But the more highly educated young found that the labour market did not offer the opportunities they had been educated for. The anger and disappointment this generated was a key driving force of the political turmoil that shook the Arab world (Campante and Chor 2011), in much the way that it had been a destabilising element in the former British Empire.

The highly educated, urban young were also especially influenced by Western liberal ideas and values, stressing the importance of freedom and democracy. This increased their antagonism towards the authoritarian governments that had 'failed' them. There was also a feminist, anti-patriarchal undercurrent in some of the protests, most notably in Egypt.

In addition, there were very specific economic causes. There was high, general unemployment and underemployment in all the affected countries. In some states, neoliberal policies had led to the loss of public subsidies and jobs. In general, rising food prices added to discontent. Economic factors were especially important in generating opposition in Tunisia, where resistance began in the poorer areas, and in Egypt, where trade unions played a significant role.

Intra-elite tensions, tribal conflicts and religious enmities were also important contributory factors in the uprisings. Thus, there was strong Shia opposition to the Sunni ruling minority in Bahrain; fundamentalist Islamist opposition to the government in Yemen; and Muslim opposition to the 'secular' regimes in Syria, Egypt and Tunisia. Tribal rivalry was an especially important factor in Libya and Yemen where the government was closely associated with regionally based tribal groupings. There were tensions within the hierarchy of power in a number of countries, not least in Egypt where there was growing antagonism between the military and the Gamal Mubarak faction of the government.

In brief, there was a common thread of active opposition to the regimes in all the insurgent countries, which extended back over decades. This dissent had deep-seated political, economic, cultural and religious causes. This was the principal reason why the six insurgent countries erupted in 2010–11. The radicalisation of their digital media was the expression of this discontent rather than its cause.

The authorities in these insurgent countries attempted to control the media. In Tunisia, the two main TV channels initially played down both the unrest and civilian casualties, and then attempted to demonise the protesters as thugs and outlaws (Miladi 2011). The Tunisian government also jammed critical content on Facebook and blogs, and stepped up 'phishing' for personal information to disable dissident networks. In Egypt, the authorities attempted to pull the plug after mass demonstrations on 25 January 2011 by blocking Twitter, Facebook and mobile phone messages in quick succession, before shutting down the entire internet on 27 January. Similarly, a complete blackout of the internet was ordered in Libya. But in all three countries the authorities moved too late, and the clampdown was not fully effective. Indeed, the Egyptian government lifted its internet blackout partly because it was ineffectual.

The ability of a small number of techie dissidents to outwit the authorities, with external support, was strategically important. Activists reached phone numbers abroad that automatically forwarded messages to foreign computer networks that sent these back to the country through a variety of means (Castells 2015). Arab activists from across the regions exchanged codes and software that allowed dissidents to access the internet, despite government blockades (Harb 2011). Google stepped in, supplying new software in 2011 that enabled protesters to 'tweet' over the phone (Oreskovic 2011). Arab activists across the region also acted, over a long period, as informal publicists, translating content and relaying visual footage – functioning, in the words of the Tunisian blogger Sami bin Gharbia, as 'the echo chamber of the struggle on the street' (cited in Ghannam 2011). This echo chamber was further amplified by Twitter sympathisers in the West.

Mobile phones, personal computers and social media all played a part in fanning the embers of dissent, supported by the more traditional methods of leafleting and gatherings in mosques. Facebook posts and blogs explained the reasons for protests; Twitter, e-mails and SNS coordinated demonstrations and occupations; mobile phones recorded police and military brutality; and the satellite TV channel, Al Jazeera, based in Qatar, used citizen video recordings to report what was happening across the region. This alternative media power not only facilitated the organisation of opposition but also encouraged protesters to persist in the face of brutal repression.

In short, the uprisings had deep underlying causes and were prefigured by protests over many years, largely ignored in the West. But the emergence of new media – in particular the mobile phone, internet and pan-Arab satellite TV – contributed to the build-up of dissent, facilitated the actual organisation of protests and disseminated news of the protests across the region and to the wider world. If the rise of digital communications technology did not cause the uprisings, it strengthened them.

But it did not strengthen them enough. Two of the insurgent countries had authoritarian upgrades. The Bahrain regime brought in Saudi Arabian troops to put down protests in 2011. In Egypt, a military coup led by General al-Sisi in 2013 led to the jailing of the first democratically elected President in some 50 years – Mohammed Morsi – who was subsequently sentenced to death. This was accompanied by the killing of dissidents and draconian censorship of the media.

Three insurgent countries were militarised, and plunged into civil wars exacerbated by foreign power interventions (Hinnebusch 2015; Stacher 2015). At the time of writing, Libya is run by rival militia, and has two governments. The authoritarian government in Syria has lost control of substantial tracts of territory now occupied by rival oppositions, who are also fighting each other. Yemen has in effect divided into two countries in a civil war that is not yet resolved. Only Tunisia has made a transition to a peaceful and sustained democracy. Thus, in five out of six countries, the gun proved mightier than the microchip.

In hindsight, the Arab Spring was the subject of enormous simplification, even by some leading experts. For example, Jeffrey Alexander, Co-Director of the Centre of Cultural Sociology at Yale University, wrote an instant book about the 2011 Egyptian Revolution in which he claimed it was a triumph of liberal values, digital media and the power of international civil society (Alexander 2011). The Egyptian military stayed neutral, in his account, for two reasons: the cultural power of liberal ideas, enacted in a 'performative revolution' by the Egyptian people, and the power of Western public opinion that led the American government to exert a restraining influence on the Egyptian military leadership. The only trouble with this analysis is that the military did not stay neutral but overthrew Egypt's short-lived democracy, and the American government accepted the new dictatorship for geopolitical reasons and gave generous military aid to it. This underlines the limits of cultural power and of the digital media that allegedly sustain it.

Advance of women

If one momentous historical change has been the faltering march to democracy, another has been the advance of women. Sharp inequalities persist between men and women in terms of income, life chances and public influence, but they have lessened over time – albeit in an uneven way – across the world (Hufton 1995; Rowbotham 1997; Kent 1999; Sakr 2004, among others). Underpinning this historic shift has been the rise of service industries, increasing female participation in the paid workforce, the decline of social ascription, improved education, better contraception, the emergence of feminism and the erosion of gender theories legitimating inequality.

One way the development of the internet connected to this historic trend was to provide a tool for the *organised* women's movement. In Islamic countries, the rise of leading Muslim reformers at the end of the nineteenth century encouraged the spread of more liberated perspectives (Hadj-Moussa 2009). By the 1980s, the women's movement had become a political force in the MENA region. Feminists generated intense controversy by talking about taboo subjects such as domestic violence, sexual harassment, female genital mutilation and rape (Skalli 2006), and gained a growing influence, especially among young women from elite or educated backgrounds. But this was in a region where internet use among women was especially limited (Wheeler 2004: 139, table 9.1). It was also a context where female literacy was sometimes low.

Despite these obstacles, important gains were made. Thus, in Morocco, a new generation of women's organisations emerged in the 1980s that operated outside formal political circles. By the early 2000s they had incorporated the internet as part of their campaigning activity, helped by the fact that Morocco had a higher internet penetration rate than its neighbours. The main target of the women's movement was the Moudawana, the family code governing marriage, divorce and child custody, which had previously provided women with few rights. In 2003 campaigners secured reform of the Moroccan family code in a way that raised the minimum age of marriage from 15 to 18, removing the need for women to have a guardian's approval before marriage and giving women the right to divorce their husbands (Tavaana 2011).

This and other successes arose from a concerted campaign conducted through the full spectrum of the media across the region. This produced a sustained backlash that led to the murder of the female Kuwaiti editor Hedaya Al-Saleem by a policeman (subsequently convicted) and the killing of female journalists in Algeria (Skalli 2006: 41). This persecution encouraged a growing sense of cohesion among campaigners, extending across frontiers and supported by frequent online communication between Arab-speaking members of the women's movement.

However, the strongest outpost of the women's movement in MENA was the Persian-speaking theocracy of Iran. Between 1978 and 2005, the number of women's rights NGOs increased from 13 to 430. The growth of the women's movement found expression online partly because women accounted in 2003 for 49% of internet users in Iran, a much higher proportion than in most of the region. The issues discussed on Iran's most popular feminist blogs included divorce, stoning, banning female participation in sporting events and discriminatory laws in general (Shirazi 2011). These were supplemented by other progressive blogs that engaged with personal politics, such as that written by the popular blogger Lady Sun (Sreberny and Khiabany 2010).

This portrayal of the net as an arm of the organised women's movement in the Middle East needs to be qualified in two ways. First, much web content was conditioned by patriarchal values, and was hostile to women's liberation. Second, probably only a small minority of women read online content originating directly from the women's movement. Feminist blogs and publications do not feature, for example, in Wheeler's (2007) small-scale study of young female Egyptian internet users in 2004. Her subjects, who often spent hours each week in internet cafés, emerge as quite instrumental – for example, getting information for essays or seeking to improve their English to get a better job. It was primarily through their online interactions with other women – rather than through any link to an organised movement – that they derived support for negotiating the constraints of their socially conservative environment.

Online campaigning championed women's rights elsewhere in the world. Thus, the #BringBackOurGirls hashtag agitation publicised Boko Haram's abduction of school girls in Chibok, Nigeria in 2014. It is reported to have reached over a million tweets, and helped to transform a story that initially received limited national and international media coverage into a global cause célèbre (Tomchak 2014). Similarly, the #DelhiGangRape hashtag campaign drew attention to the 2012 gang rape of a young woman in Delhi. She was travelling on a bus and was raped by six men including the bus driver, and subsequently died from her injuries. The campaign mobilised street demonstrations, gained international media publicity and contributed to the government's decision to incorporate specific anti-rape provisions in the criminal code (Sharma 2014).

These campaigns against violence directed towards women had international traction because they affronted global social norms. But progress on other women's issues often proved more difficult. Many women had limited access to new communications technologies. In some countries, online female activists were subject to government censorship, exposed to online abuse, and, in a general way, experienced negative media stereotyping. Their access to power and decision making could also be limited. Gender imbalance at the top was reflected in the fact that women in parliaments, around the world, accounted for a mere 11% in 1995 and only 22% in 2014 (Loiseau and Nowacka 2015).

If one response to gender inequality was to try to change it through organised political action, another was to seek to advance in the world as a purposive individual and triumph against the odds. Youna Kim (2010) presents a vivid portrait of young Asian women with high expectations, encouraged by educational success and sometimes privileged backgrounds, encountering – or facing the prospect of entering – the male-dominated world of work in Korea, Japan or China. In this case study, their 'rebellion' took the form of flight to the West, postgraduate education and the search for new opportunities to realise their talents and ambitions. One inspiration for their flight was Hollywood images of independent women who took control of their lives. While respondents recognised that these were fictional idealisations, they also hoped that they were in part true. These dramas contributed to a utopian self-imagining in which respondents aspired to remake themselves, in a Western context, as autonomous women who placed themselves at 'the centre of [their] biography' (Kim 2010: 40).

An unrelated study provides a glimpse into how the internet features in this cultural dynamic. Yachien Huang (2008) found that university-educated women in Taiwan tended to watch the American TV series *Sex and the City* on their computer screens instead of on family television sets, which were often dominated by male surveillance and choice control. Internet bulletin boards also provided these women with an opportunity to discuss and debate aspects of this series. Its appeal for these young women arose partly from changing gender relations in Taiwan. Rising female consumer power and economic expectations had not been mirrored by a corresponding change in the traditionalist culture of Taiwanese society, with its expectation of demure female behaviour, duty and self-sacrifice. The series, projecting a hedonistic world of independent, affluent women in Manhattan, provided a 'cultural resource' for Taiwanese women seeking to negotiate their obligation to be a 'good girl' with their desire to have more 'individualistic lifestyles and open sexuality' (Huang 2008: 199). It was an inspiration for 'their struggle for agency' in a male-dominated world, but one that tended to take a personal, individualised route. As one interviewee put it, the lesson of the series is 'choose what you want, and don't make yourself miserable' (Huang 2008: 196).

The history of the internet is thus bound up with the struggle for greater gender equality. The internet provided a tool for an organised campaign for women's liberation in the Middle East and elsewhere. It also distributed depictions of autonomous women that inspired the seeking of personal solutions to gender inequality.

Internet and individualism

This last response is one aspect of another important historical change. There has been a cumulative shift from values and beliefs that prioritise the collective good of the community, and of groups within it, to ones that give priority to the satisfaction of the needs, desires and aspirations of the individual. This has been encouraged by, among other things, the rise of the market system, increasing mobility, the weakening of custom and tradition, and the declining influence of the family and collective organisations (Beck and Beck-Gernsheim 2001).

Some see the internet as encouraging this more individual-centred orientation because this is supposedly wired into the internet's DNA. According to Barry Wellman and associates (2003):

> The development of personalization, wireless portability, and ubiquitous connectivity of the Internet all facilitate networked individualism as the basis of community. Because connections are to people and not to places, the technology affords shifting of work and community ties from linking people-in-places to linking people at any place. Computer-supported communication is *everywhere*, but it is situated *nowhere*. It is I-alone that is reachable wherever I am: at a home, hotel, office, highway, or shopping center. The person has become the portal.
>
> (Wellman et al. 2003)

Rainie and Wellman (2012) have returned more recently to this theme, arguing that the incorporation of the smartphone into everyday life has strengthened their argument. 'People are not hooked', they write, 'on gadgets – they are hooked on each other. . . . In the world of networked individuals, it is the person who is the focus: not the family, not the work unit, not the neighborhood, and not the social group' (Rainie and Wellman 2012: 4).

There is clearly some truth in this. However, networked individualism also led to the forging of new communal identities. Thus, Kavada (2015) argues that use of social media contributed to the formation of Occupy's collective voice and sense of community, while Juris (2012) emphasises that online mobilisation to a shared physical space was also central to the bonding that took place in the Boston occupy movement.

More importantly, communalism can shape online experience, and reaffirm a prior sense of collective identity. Thus, Miller and Slater (2000) found that strong nationalist sentiment in Trinidad gave rise to nationalist web content. Even chat rooms conveyed a sense of being 'Trini' through the display of 'ole talk' and 'liming' – the ability to communicate, be expressive and warm, and to be witty about everyday things – because this was viewed as being part of the island's distinctive national culture. Online encounters with foreigners also led some Trinidadians to feel that they should act as informal national ambassadors. Strong national consciousness thus infused Trinidadians' online experience in ways that supported their national identity. Underlying this intense sense of national belonging, argue Miller and Slater, was the historical experience of slavery, migration and social dislocation.

Similarly, Madhavi Mallapragada's study of expatriate and diasporic Indians (2000) concluded that the internet was widely used to stay connected to a distant homeland. Her subjects sought out web content that displayed India's rich cultural heritage. Some discussed how to deal with their assimilating children, who were turning their backs on their Indian identity. A small number even used the net to facilitate arranged marriages between members of their family and people living in India. Likewise, Larry Gross (2003) argues that the internet provides emotional support, practical advice and a sense of belonging among gay men encountering persecution or prejudice in different parts of the world. In both these instances, the internet supported pre-existing collective identities based respectively on nation and sexuality.

Likewise, the collectivist culture of Japan generated the distinctive Nico Nico Dougwa (NND) video-sharing website in which comments are overlaid on the screen rather than written beneath it. The comments are pithy, often witty and limited to ten. Any user can delete a comment and replace it with another. This creates an atmosphere of live, collective viewing not unlike watching a football match, with spontaneous comments from the crowd.

The website developed a mass following, with some 5 million regular users in 2008. Its acolytes developed a culture of 'kuuki' – 'the shared atmosphere of appreciation that one needs to catch, if one wants to comment appropriately and to understand the joy of being a Nico Chuu [fan]' (Bachmann 2008a: 2). This group togetherness is reinforced by the anonymity of those making comments, in which even a pseudonymous tag is omitted. However, if a distinctive style is recognised, the group may bestow the honour of conferring a nickname.

Nico Nico Dougwa is very obviously the product of a collectivist culture. Yet 'tag wars', reflecting divergent responses to a video, can sometimes occur, causing group cohesion to break down. Online anonymity can also provide a cover for expressing controversial views that would not be acceptable in the offline world. This is a more pronounced feature, notes Bachmann (2008b), of the Japanese internet forum 2channel. His overall conclusion is that the online experiences in

Japan which he studied both reflect and reaffirm group togetherness, while also
sometimes giving expression to a desire to escape from it.

The unifying thread of these case studies, mostly located outside the West, is
that strongly communal life in the real world can penetrate the online experience,
and result in the internet offering support – though sometimes in a complex or
contradictory way – for the maintenance of communal identities. The implication
of this is that the social impact of the internet is likely to have been different in the
collectivist East than in the more individual-centred West.

However, the dynamic of change is towards greater individualism. The internet
can provide a space for the expression of individual identity even in collectivist
societies. Thus, a study of Japanese students' use of advanced mobile phones
concludes that they reinforce individualism and strengthen interiority in three distinct ways (McVeigh 2003). Phones as artefacts enable students to express their
individuality through choice of colour, functions, ring tones and phone accesso-
ries (such as colourful figurines hung from phone straps). Mobile phones make
it easier to express private feelings, primarily through texting and e-mail. Above
all, mobile phones increase 'personalized individualization' by providing students
with a sense of personal space. In Japan, living areas are often cramped, and there
is a high level of surveillance by employers and educators. Students repeatedly
stressed that their mobile phones enabled them to communicate privately with
friends and create 'their own world' (McVeigh 2003: 47–8). However, there may
be more ambiguity in this outcome than this Western author perhaps acknowledges. Students were expressing themselves as individuals within the strongly
group-conditioned context of being a Tokyo University student.

Sima and Pugsley's study of blogs and bloggers in China (2010) also argues that
the internet enables the showcasing of individuality, and a public process of self-
reflection and self-discovery. They contend that this both reflects and expresses
the greater individualism of China's 'Generation Y', who are growing up at a time
of increasing consumerism and the one-child family rule that encourages a greater
emphasis on the self among the young. However, the internal evidence of their
article suggests that individual voices can sometimes be presented as a collective
voice – that of China's new generation (Sima and Pugsley 2010: 301).

In general, the rise of the internet as a medium of self-communication has
enabled greater self-expression, and probably strengthened the trend towards individualism. This would seem to be the case in the West (Castells 2009), and there
is some evidence that the internet has also reinforced the trend towards greater
individualism in Asia. But communal identities remain strong in many parts of the
world, influencing use of the internet.

Retrospect

Historians of the internet have tended to concentrate on the early, Edenic phase
of Western internet development. This revised history has emphasised, by contrast, the way in which commercialisation subsequently distorted the internet in

the West, while state censorship, in particular, muzzled the internet in the East. Growing corporate influence, the development of online concentration, the introduction of commercial surveillance technology and the strengthening of intellectual property law all entailed the superimposition of a new set of constraints on the internet as a consequence of advancing market influence. Likewise, the introduction of restrictive internet licensing, the outsourcing of state censorship to internet service providers and the adaptation of commercial surveillance technology to monitor dissidence imposed a further set of controls when the internet developed outside its north-western cradle. In brief, the rise of the internet was accompanied by the decline of its freedom.

However, this trend was resisted in both the East and West. The rise of the OS movement, people's continued reluctance to pay for web content and the revival of the user-generated tradition all represented an attempt to arrest the commercial transformation of the internet. Likewise, numerous online dissidents in the Middle East and Asia sought to thwart the extension of state power over the internet. In their different ways, they were part of the same project: they were both seeking to preserve a vision of the internet as belonging to the people.

If one task of rethinking internet history is to take full account of the later period, another task is to narrate the history of the internet as a global rather than Western phenomenon. This preliminary reconnaissance, which necessarily leaves out large parts of the world, concludes that the internet was less effective in destabilising authoritarian regimes than was widely anticipated. The internet also contributed to the advance of women by providing a tool for the organised women's movement and by distributing the sometimes pirated products of Hollywood feminism. More contentiously, internet self-communication seems to have promoted the expression and assertion of the self, though the evidence also points to the way in which strongly communal cultures could result in the internet supporting group identities.

The interaction between the internet and society is complex. This is underscored by this chapter, which indicates that this relationship has varied both in time and space. Yet, even allowing for this complexity, the weight of evidence points to one firm conclusion: society exerts, in general, a greater influence on the internet than the other way around. That is why many of the prophecies about the impact of the internet – surveyed in the first chapter and encountered again in this chapter – have not been fulfilled.

This is not a novel insight into the influence of new communications technology. It is one that dawned on idealistic liberals in Britain after 1880 when they realised that the popular press was not advancing the cause of progress, as they had anticipated (Hampton 2004). Wiser and more sceptical, they stopped capitalising the 'Newspaper Press'. Perhaps we should do the same in relation to the 'Internet'.[9]

Notes

1 My thanks go again to Joanna Redden, to Justin Schlosberg for additional help centred on this chapter and to Colin Lusk for his helpful comments.

2 A notable exception to this uncritical historical tradition is John Naughton (2000 and 2012).
3 Chapter 1, page 4.
4 The estimates for the US film industry exclude DVD sales and TV rights.
5 See Chapter 4, page 132.
6 Microsoft is an exception in that its founder, Bill Gates, allocates enormous funds to admirable charities - an example now followed by Mark Zuckerburg, co-founder of Facebook.
7 Morozov (2011) and Mosco (2005) cite numerous politicians, public officials, journalists and academics who predicted that the rise of the internet would undermine dictatorships. For a more guarded legatee of this tradition, see Howard (2011), who argues that the internet is a key 'ingredient' of the 'recipe' for democratisation.
8 See Chapter 1, page 31.
9 That is why we breach Routledge's house style by referring to the 'internet' throughout this book.

References

Abbate, J. (2000) *Inventing the Internet*, Cambridge, MA: MIT Press.
Alexa (2015a) 'How Popular is Wikipedia.org?' Alexa Traffic Ranks. Online. Available HTTP: <http://www.alexa.com/siteinfo/wikipedia.org> (accessed 12 July 2015).
Alexa (2015b) 'How Popular is Facebook.com?' Alexa.com. Online. Available HTTP: <http://www.alexa.com/siteinfo/facebook.com> (accessed 12 July 2015).
Alexander, A. (2010) 'Leadership and Collective Action in the Egyptian Trade Unions', *Work, Employment and Society*, 24: 241–259.
Alexander, J. (2011) *Performative Revolution in Egypt*, London: Bloomsbury.
Anderson, C. (2006) *The Long Tail*, London: Business Books.
Andrejevic, M. and Gates, K. (2014) 'Big Data Surveillance: Introduction', *Surveillance & Society*, 12 (2): 185–196.
Bachmann, G. (2008a) 'Wunderbar! Nico Nico Douga Goes German – and Some Hesitant Reflections on Japaneseness', London: Goldsmiths Leverhulme Media Research Centre. Online. Available HTTP: <http://www.gold.ac.uk/media-research-centre/project2/project2-outputs/> (accessed 20 June 2011).
Bachmann, G. (2008b) 'The Force of Affirmative Metadata', paper presented at the Force of Metadata Symposium, Goldsmiths, University of London, November.
Baker, C. E. (2007) *Media Concentration and Democracy*, New York: Cambridge University Press.
Banks, M. (2008) *On the Way to the Web*, Berkeley, CA: Apress.
Barro, R. and Lee, J.-W. (2010) 'A New Data Set of Educational Attainment in the World, 1950–2010', NBER Working Paper No. 15902, the National Bureau of Economic Research. Online. Available HTTP: <http://www.nber.org/papers/w15902> (accessed 12 February 2011).
Bauman, Z., Bigo, D., Esteves, P., Guild, E., Jabri, V., Lyon, D. and Walker, R. B. J. (2014) 'After Snowden: Rethinking the Impact of Surveillance', *International Political Sociology*, 8: 121–144.
Beck, U. and Beck-Gernsheim, E. (2001) *Individualization*, London: Sage.
Benkler, Y. (2006) *The Wealth of Nations*, New Haven, CT: Yale University Press.
Benkler, Y. (2011) 'A Free Irresponsible Press: Wikileaks and the Battle over the Soul of the Networked Fourth Estate', *Harvard Civil Rights-Civil Liberties Law Review*, 46: 311–398.

Bergin, T. (2014) 'OECD Unveils Proposals to Curb Corporate Tax Avoidance', Reuters, 16 September. Online. Available HTTP: <www.reuters.com/article/2014/09/16/us-oecd-tax-idUSKBN0HB18V20140916> (accessed 6 July 2015).

Berners-Lee, T. (2000) *Weaving the Web*, London: Orion.

Boies, S. C. (2002) 'University Students' Uses of and Reactions to Online Sexual Information and Entertainment: Links to Online and Offline Sexual Behaviour', *Canadian Journal of Human Sexuality*, 11 (2): 77–89.

Cadwalladr, C. (2013) 'My Week as an Amazon Insider', *Guardian*, 1 December. Online. Available HTTP: <http://www.theguardian.com/technology/2013/dec/01/week-amazon-insider-feature-treatment-employees-work> (accessed 29 June 2015).

Cairncross, F. (1997) *The Death of Distance*, Boston, MA: Harvard Business School Press.

Campante, F. R. and Chor, D. (2011) '"The People Want the Fall of the Regime": Schooling, Political Protest, and the Economy', Faculty Research Working Paper Series. Harvard Kennedy School. Online. Available HTTP: <http://jrnetsolserver.shor ensteincente.netdna-cdn.com/wp-content/uploads/2011/07/RWP11–018_Campante_ Chor.pdf> (accessed 2 July 2011).

Cassidy, J. (2011) 'Prophet Motive', *New Yorker*, 28 February: 32–35.

Castells, M. (2001) *The Internet Galaxy*, Oxford: Oxford University Press.

Castells, M. (2009) *Communication Power*, Oxford: Oxford University Press.

Castells, M. (2015) *Networks of Outrage and Hope*, 2nd edition, Cambridge: Polity Press.

Comer, D. (2007) *The Internet Book*, London: Pearson Education.

Curran, J. (2002) *Media and Power*, London: Routledge.

Curran, J. (2011) *Media and Democracy*, London: Routledge.

Curran, J. and Witschge, T. (2010) 'Liberal Dreams and the Internet', in N. Fenton (ed.) *New Media, Old News: Journalism and Democracy in the Digital Age*, London: Sage.

Curran, J. et al. (2013) 'Internet Revolution Revisited: A Comparative Study'. *Media, Culture and Society*, 35 (7): 880–897.

Dariusz, J. (2014) *Common Knowledge: An Ethnography of Wikipedia*, Palo Alto, CA: Stanford University Press.

Dawisha, A. (2013) *The Second Arab Awakening*, New York: Norton.

Deibert, R., Palfrey, J., Rohozinski, J. and Zittrain, J. (eds) (2008) *Access Denied: The Practice and Policy of Global Internet Filtering*, Cambridge, MA: MIT Press. Online. Available HTTP: <http://opennet.net/accessdenied> (accessed 15 May 2011).

DFC Intelligence (2010) 'Tracking the Growth of Online Game Usage and Distribution', 8 October. Online. Available HTTP: <http://www.dfcint.com/wp/?p=292> (accessed 19 February 2011).

DSG (Dubai School of Government) (2011) *Arab Social Media Report, 2*. Online. Available HTTP: <http://www.dsg.ae/portals/0/ASMR2.pdf> (accessed 25 June 2011).

Durac, V. and Cavatorta, F. (2009) 'Strengthening Authoritarian Rule through Democracy Promotion? Examining the Paradox of the US and EU Security Strategies: The Case of Bin Ali's Tunisia', *British Journal of Middle Eastern Studies*, 36 (1): 3–19.

Edelman, B. (2009) 'Red Light States: Who Buys Online Adult Entertainment?', *Journal of Economic Perspectives*, 23 (1): 209–220.

Edwards, P. (1996) *The Closed World*, Cambridge, MA: MIT Press.

El-Naway, M. (2011) *Sunday Mirror*, 20 February, 8.

European Commission (2013) 'Antitrust: Commission Fines Microsoft for Non-compliance with Browser Choice Commitments', Press Release, 6 March. Online. Available HTTP: <http://europa.eu/rapid/press-release_IP-13-196_en.htm> (accessed 3 July 2015).

European Commission (2015) 'Antitrust: Commission sends Statement of Objections to Google on Comparison Shopping Service; Opens Separate Formal Investigation on Android', Press Release, 15 April. Online. Available HTTP: <http://europa.eu/rapid/press-release_IP-13-196_en.htm> (accessed 3 July 2015).

Evans, M. (2011) 'Egypt Crisis: The Revolution Will Not Be Tweeted', *Sysomos Blog*. Online. Available HTTP: <http://blog.sysomos.com/2011/01/31/egyptian-crisis-twitte/> (accessed 25 June 2011).

Flichy, P. (1999) 'The Construction of New Digital Media', *New Media and Society*, 1 (1): 33–39.

Flichy, P. (2006) 'New Media History', in L. Lievrouw and S. Livingstone (eds) *The Handbook of New Media*, rev. edn, London: Sage.

Flichy, P. (2007) *The Internet Imaginaire*, Cambridge, MA: MIT Press.

Freedom House (2009) 'Freedom on the Net: a Global Assessment of Internet and Digital Media'. Online. Available HTTP: <http://freedomhouse.org/uploads/specialreports/NetFreedom2009/FreedomOnTheNet_FullReport.pdf> (accessed 2 August 2011).

Fukuyama, F. (1993) *The End of History and the Last Man*, Harmondsworth: Penguin.

Gabrys, J. (2013) *Digital Rubbish: A Natural History of Electronics*, Ann Arbor, MI: University of Michigan Press.

George, C. (2005) 'The Internet's Political Impact and the Penetration/Participation Paradox in Malaysia and Singapore', *Media, Culture and Society*, 27 (6): 903–920.

Gandhi, J. and Przeworski, A. (2007) 'Authoritarian Institutions and the Survival of Autocrats', *Comparative Political Studies*, 40 (11): 1279–1301.

Ghannam, J. (2011) 'Social Media in the Arab World: Leading up to the Uprisings of 2011', Centre for International Media Assistance, CIMA: Washington, D.C.

Gillies, J. and Cailliau, R. (2000) *How the Web Was Born*, Oxford: Oxford University Press.

Glanz, J. (2012) 'Power, Pollution and the Internet', *New York Times*, 22 September. Online. Available: <http://www.nytimes.com/2012/09/23/technology/data-centers-waste-vast-amounts-of-energy-belying-industry-image.html?pagewanted=all&_r=0> (accessed 7 July 2015).

Goggin, G. (2000) 'Pay per Browse? The Web's Commercial Future', in D. Gauntlett (ed.) *Web Studies*, London: Arnold.

Golson, J. (2015) 'Apple Under Antitrust Investigation Over Revamping of Beats Streaming Music Service', *TechRepublic*, 10 May. Online. Available HTTP: <http://www.techrepublic.com/article/apple-under-antitrust-investigation-over-revamping-of-beats-streaming-music-service/> (accessed 6 July 2015).

Grant, J. (1871–2) *The Newspaper Press*, 3 vols, London: Tinsley Brothers.

Greenwald, G. (2014) *No Place to Hide: Edward Snowden, the NSA, and the U.S. Surveillance State*, New York: Metropolitan Books.

Groshek, J. (2010) 'A Time-series, Multinational Analysis of Democratic Forecasts and Internet Diffusion', *International Journal of Communication*, 4: 142–174.

Gross, L. (2003) 'The Gay Global Village in Cyberspace', in N. Couldry and J. Curran (eds) *Contesting Media Power*, Boulder, CO: Rowman and Littlefield.

GSMA (2015) 'The Mobile Economy 2015', GSMA. Online. Available HTTP: <http://gsmamobileeconomy.com/global/GSMA_Global_Mobile_Economy_Report_2015.pdf> (accessed 13 July 2015).

Hadj-Moussa, R. (2009) 'Arab Women: Beyond Politics', in P. Essed, D. Goldberg and A. Kobayashi (eds) *A Companion to Gender Studies*, Malden, MA: Blackwell.

Hafner, K. and Lyon, M. (2003) *Where Wizards Stay up Late*, London: Pocket Books.

Hampton, M. (2004) *Visions of the Press in Britain, 1850–1950*, Urbana, IL: University of Illinois Press.

Hamzawy, A. (2009) 'Rising Social Distress: the Case of Morocco, Egypt, and Jordan', *International Economic Bulletin*, Carnegie Endowment for International Peace. Online. Available HTTP: <http://www.carnegieendowment.org/ieb/?fa=view&id=23290> (accessed 15 June 2011).

Harb, Z. (2011) 'Arab Revolutions and the Social Media Effect', *M/C Journal*, 14 (2). Online. Available HTTP: <http://journal.media-culture.org.au/index.php/mcjournal/article/viewArticle/364> (accessed 23 October 2011).

Hauben, M. and Hauben, R. (1997) *Netizens*, New York: Columbia University Press.

Haucap, J. and Heimeshoff, U. (2013) 'Google, Facebook, Amazon, eBay: Is the Internet Driving Competition or Market Monopolization?' *International Economics and Economic Policy*, 11: 49–61.

Hindman, M. (2009) *The Myth of Digital Democracy*, Princeton, NJ: Princeton University Press.

Hinnebusch, R. (2015) 'Introduction: Understanding the Consequences of the Arab Uprisings – Starting Points and Divergent Trajectories', *Democratization*, 22 (2): 205–217.

Howard, P. (2011) *The Digital Origins of Dictatorship and Democracy*, New York: Oxford University Press.

Huang, Y. (2008) 'Consuming *Sex and the City*: Young Taiwanese Women Contesting Sexuality', in Y. Kim (ed.) *Media Consumption and Everyday Life in Asia*, Milton Park: Routledge.

Hufton, O. (1995) *The Prospect Before Her*, London: HarperCollins.

Hunt, F. K. (1850) *The Fourth Estate: Contributions towards a History of Newspapers and the Liberty of the Press*, London: David Bogue.

Internet World Stats (2011a) 'Usage and Population Statistics: China', Miniwatts Marketing Group. Online. Available HTTP: <http://www.internetworldstats.com/asia/cn.htm> (accessed 3 August 2011).

Internet World Stats (2011b) 'Usage and Population Statistics: Mid East', Miniwatts Marketing Group. Online. Available HTTP: <http://www.internetworldstats.com/stats5. htm> (accessed 4 December 2011).

Internet World Stats (2015) 'Internet Usage Statistics: The Internet Big Picture'. Online. Available HTTP: <http://www.internetworldstats.com/stats.htm> (accessed 26 July 2015).

Isaacson, W. (2011) *Steve Jobs*, London: Little, Brown.

Ito, M. (1997) 'Virtually Embodied: The Reality of Fantasy in a Multi-User Dungeon', in D. Porter (ed.) *Internet Culture*, New York: Routledge.

ITU (2010) *Measuring the Information Society,* Geneva: International Telecommunication Union. Online. Available HTTP: <http://www.itu.int/ITU-D/ict/publications/idi/2010/Material/MIS_2010_without_annex_4-e.pdf> (accessed 19 April 2011).

Joshi, S. (2011) 'Reflections on the Arab Revolutions: Order, Democracy and Western Policy', *Rusi Journal*, 156 (2): 60–66.

Juris, J. (2012) 'Reflections on #Occupy Everywhere: Social Media, Public Space, and Emerging Logics of Aggregation', *American Ethnologist*, 39 (2): 259–279.

Kavada, A. (2015) 'Creating the Collective: Social Media, the Occupy Movement and its Constitution as a Collective Actor', *Information, Communication & Society*, 18 (8): 872–886.

Kent, S. K. (1999) *Gender and Power in Britain, 1640–1990*, London: Routledge.

Kim, E. and Hamilton, J. (2006) 'Capitulation to Capital? OhmyNews as Alternative Media', *Media, Culture and Society*, 28 (4): 541–560.

Kim, Y. (2010) 'Female Individualization? Transnational Mobility and Media Consumption of Asian Women', *Media, Culture and Society*, 32: 25–43.

Lametti, D. (2012) 'The Cloud: Boundless Digital Potential or Enclosure 3.0?', *Virginia Journal of Law & Technology*, 17(3): 192–243.

Lessig, L. (1999) *Code and Other Laws of Cyberspace*, New York: Basic Books.

Lessig, L. (2001) *The Future of Ideas*, New York: Random House.

Levy, S. (1994) *Hackers*, London: Penguin.

Loiseau, E. and Nowacka, K. (2015) 'Can Social Media Effectively Include Women's Voices in Decision-Making Processes?' OECD Development Centre, March. Online. Available HTTP: <http://www.empowerwomen.org/en/~/documents/2015/03/17/18/33/can-social-media-effectively-include-womens-voices-in-decision-making-processes> (accessed 13 July 2015).

Lyon, D. (2014) 'Surveillance, Snowden, and Big Data: Capacities, Consequences, Critique', *Big Data & Society*, 1–13.

McChesney, R. (1999) *Rich Media, Poor Democracy*, Urbana, IL: University of Illinois Press.

McVeigh, Brian J. (2003) 'Individualization, Individuality, Interiority, and the Internet: Japanese University Students and E-mail', in N. Gottlieb and M. McLelland (eds) *Japanese Cybercultures*, New York: Routledge.

Magaloni, B. (2008) 'Credible Power-sharing and the Longevity of Authoritarian Rule', *Comparative Political Studies*, 41 (4/5): 715–741.

Mallapragada, M. (2000) 'The Indian Diaspora in the USA and around the World', in D. Gauntlett (ed.) *Web Studies*, London: Arnold.

Miladi, N. (2011) 'Tunisia – a Media Led Revolution', *Aljazeera.net*. Online. Available HTTP: <http://english.aljazeera. net/indepth/opinion/2011/01/2011116142317498666. html> (accessed 24 June 2011).

Miller, D. and Slater, D. (2000) *The Internet*, Oxford: Berg.

Miller, V. (2000) 'Search Engines, Portals and Global Capitalism', in D. Gauntlett (ed.) *Web Studies*, London: Arnold.

Morozov, E. (2011) *The Net Delusion*, London: Allen Lane.

Mosco, V. (2005) *The Digital Sublime*, Cambridge, MA: MIT Press.

Mosco, V. (2014) *To the Cloud: Big Data in a Turbulent World*, Boulder, CO: Paradigm.

Movie Picture Association in America (2013) 'Theatrical Market Statistics 2013'. Online. Available HTTP: <www.mpaa.org/.../MPAA-Theatrical-Market-Statistics-2013_032514-v2> (accessed 28 July 2015).

Mullany, A. (2011) 'Egyptian Uprising Plays out on Social Media Sites Despite Government's Internet Restrictions', *New York Daily News*, 29 January. Online. Available HTTP: <http://articles.nydailynews.com/2011-01-29/news/27738202_1_election-protests-anti-government-protests-social-media> (accessed 20 August 2011).

Myllylahti, M. (2014) 'Newspaper Paywalls – the Hype and the Reality', *Digital Journalism*, 2 (2): 179–194.

Naughton, J. (2000) *A Brief History of the Future*, London: Phoenix.

Naughton, J. (2011) 'Smartphones Could Mean the End of the Web as We Know It', *Observer*, 17 July.

Naughton, J. (2012) *From Gutenberg to Zuckerberg*, London: Quercus.

Negroponte, N. (1996) *Being Digital*, rev. edn, London: Hodder and Stoughton.

Newman, N. and Levy, D. (2014) 'Reuters Institute Digital News Report 2014: Tracking the Future of News', Reuters Institute for the Study of Journalism, University of Oxford. Online. Available HTTP: <https://reutersinstitute.politics.ox.ac.uk/sites/default/files/Reuters%20Institute%20Digital%20News%20Report%202014.pdf> (accessed 10 June 2015).

Newzoo (2013) 'Global Games Market Report'. Online. Available HTTP: <http://www.newzoo.com/infographics/global-games-market-report-infographics/> (accessed 27 July 2015).

Noman, H. (2013) 'Saudi Arabia to Impose Restrictions on Online Content Production, Including on YouTube', OpenNet Initiative.

Norberg, A. and O'Neil, J. (1996) *Transforming Computer Technology*, Baltimore, MD: Johns Hopkins University Press.

Ofcom (2014a) The Communications Market Report, 7 August. Online. Available HTTP: <http://stakeholders.ofcom.org.uk/binaries/research/cmr/cmr14/2014_UK_CMR.pdf> (accessed 13 July 2015).

Ofcom (2014b) 'Context, The Communications Market Report: United Kingdom'. Online. Available HTTP: <http://stakeholders.ofcom.org.uk/market-data-research/market-data/communications-market-reports/cmr14/uk/> (accessed 13 July 2015).

ONS (Office for National Statistics) (2007) 'Consumer Durables', London: Office for National Statistics. Online. Available HTTP: <http://www.statistics.gov.uk/cci/nugget.asp?id=868> (accessed 14 February 2008).

ONS (2008) *Internet Access 2008*, London: Office for National Statistics. Online. Available HTTP: <http://www.statistics.gov.uk/pdfdir/iahi0808.pdf > (accessed 14 February 2009).

ONS (2010) *Internet Access*, London: Office for National Statistics. Online. Available HTTP: <http://www.statistics.gov.uk/cci/nugget.asp?id=8> (accessed 21 August 2011).

OpenNet Initiative (2011) 'Country Profiles', Online. Available HTTP: <http://opennet.net/research> (accessed 19 July 2011).

OpenNet Initiative (2015) 'Country Profiles'. Online. Available HTTP: <https://opennet.net/research/profiles> (accessed 27 July 2015).

Oreskovic, A. (2011) 'Google Inc Launched a Special Service', Reuters. Online. Available HTTP: <http://www.reuters.com/article/2011/02/01/us-egypt-protest-google-idUSTRE71005F20110201> (accessed 25 June 2011).

Ottaway, M. and Hamzawy, A. (2011) 'Protest Movements and Political Change in the Arab world', Carnegie Endowment for International Peace, Policy Outlook. Online. Available HTTP: <http://carnegieendowment.org/files/OttawayHamzawy_Outlook_Jan11_ProtestMovements.pdf> (accessed 20 June 2011).

Pew (2014) 'Mobile Technology Fact Sheet', Pew Research Center. Online. Available HTTP: <http://www.pewinternet.org/fact-sheets/mobile-technology-fact-sheet/> (accessed 13 July 2015).

Poster, M. (1995) *The Second Media Age*, Cambridge: Polity Press.

Rainie, L. and Wellman, B. (2012) *Networked: The New Social Operating System*, Cambridge, MA: MIT Press.

Rheingold, H. (2000) *The Virtual Community,* rev. edn., Cambridge, MA: MIT Press.

Rodan, G. (2004) *Transparency and Authoritarian Rule in Southeast Asia*, London: Routledge Curzon.

Rosenzweig, R. (1998) 'Wizards, Bureaucrats, Warriors, and Hackers: Writing the History of the Internet', *American History Review*, December: 1530–1552.

Rowbotham, S. (1997) *A Century of Women*, London: Viking.

Ryan, J. (2010) *A History of the Internet and the Digital Future*, London: Reaktion Books.

Sakr, N. (ed.) (2004) *Women and Media in the Middle East*, London: I. B. Tauris.

Schechner, S. (2015) 'Facebook Privacy Controls Face Scrutiny in Europe', *The Wall Street Journal*, 2 April. Online. Available HTTP: <http://www.wsj.com/articles/facebook-confronts-european-probes-1427975994> (accessed 3 July 2015).

Schiller, D. (2000) *Digital Capitalism*, Cambridge, MA: MIT Press.

Schiller, D. (2007) *How to Think About Information*, Urbana, IL: University of Illinois Press.

Schlosberg, J. (2013) *Power Beyond Scrutiny*, London: Pluto.

Sharma, R. (2014) 'Social Media as a Formidable Force for Change', *Huffington Post*, 12 November. Online. Available HTTP: <http://www.huffingtonpost.com/ritusharma/power-of-social-media-dem_b_6103222.html> (accessed 29 July 2015).

Shirazi, F. (2011) 'Information and Communication Technology and Women Empowerment in Iran', *Telematics and Informatics* (article in press). Online. Available HTTP: <http://www.mendeley.com/research/information-communication-technology-women-empowerment-iran/> (accessed 20 June 2011).

Sikka, P. (2015) 'No Accounting for Tax Avoidance', *Political Quarterly*, 1–7.

Sima, Y. and Pugsley, P. (2010) 'The Rise of a "Me Culture" in Postsocialist China', *The International Communication Gazette*, 72 (3): 287–306.

Skalli, L. (2006) 'Communicating Gender in the Public Sphere: Women and Information Technologies in the MENA Region', *Journal of Middle East Women's Studies*, 2 (2): 35–59.

Sparks, C. (2000) 'From Dead Trees to Live Wires: the Internet's Challenge to the Traditional Newspaper', in J. Curran and M. Gurevitch (eds) *Mass Media and Society*, 3rd edn., London: Arnold.

Spink, A., Partridge, H. and Jansen, B. (2006) 'Sexual and Pornographic Web Searching: Trends Analysis', *First Monday*, 11 (9). Online. Available HTTP: <http://firstmonday.org/htbin/cgiwrap/bin/ojs/index.php/fm/article/view/1391/1309> (accessed 23 October 2011).

Sreberny, A. and Khiabany, G. (2010) *Blogistan*, London: I. B. Tauris.

Stacher, J. (2015) 'Fragmenting States, New Regimes: Militarized State Violence and Transition in the Middle East', *Democratization*, 22 (2): 259–275.

Statistics Portal (2015) 'Global Games Market Report'. Online. Available HTTP: <http://www.newzoo.com/infographics/global-games-market-report-infographics/> (accessed 27 July 2015).

Streeter, T. (2003) 'Does Capitalism Need Irrational Exuberance? Business Culture and the Internet in the 1990s', in A. Calabrese and C. Sparks (eds) *Toward a Political Economy of Culture*, Boulder, CO: Rowman and Littlefield.

Tavaana (2011) 'Moudawana: A Peaceful Revolution for Moroccan Women'. Online. Available HTTP: <http://www.tavaana.org/nu_upload/Moudawana_En_PDF.pdf> (accessed 21 June 2011).

Taylor, C. (2011) 'Why Not Call It a Facebook Revolution', CNN, 24 February. Online. Available HTTP: <http://articles.cnn.com/2011-02-24/tech/facebook.revolution_1_facebook-wael-ghonim-social-media?_s=PM:TECH> (accessed 2 March 2011).

Tomchak, A-M. (2014) 'BBC trending: How a Million People called to #BringBack OurGirls', BBC News, 6 May. Online. Available HTTP: <http://www.bbc.com/news/blogs-trending-27298696> (accessed 29 July 2015).

Turkle, S. (1995) *Life on the Screen*, New York: Simon and Schuster.

Turner, F. (2006) *From Counterculture to Cyberculture*, Chicago: University of Chicago Press.

Twohig, G. (2015) 'Mobile User Behaviour Statistics 2015', mobiForge, 25 June. Online. Available HTTP: <http://mobiforge.com/research-analysis/mobile-user-behaviour-statistics-2015> (accessed 13 July 2015).

Weber, S. (2004) *The Success of Open Source*, Cambridge, MA: Harvard University Press.

Wellman, B., Quan-Haase, A., Boase, J., Chen, W., Hampton, K., de Diaz, I. and Miyata, K. (2003) 'The Social Affordances of the Internet for Networked Individualism', *Journal of Computer-Mediated Communication*, 8 (3). Online. Available HTTP: <http://onlinelibrary.wiley.com/doi/10.1111/j.1083–6101.2003.tb00216.x/full> (accessed 23 October 2011).

Wheeler, D. (2004) 'Blessings and Curses: Women and the Internet Revolution in the Arab World', in N. Sakr (ed.) *Women and Media in the Middle East*, London: I. B. Tauris.

Wheeler, D. (2007) 'Empowerment Zones? Women, Internet Cafes, and Life Transformations in Egypt', *Information Technologies and International Development*, 4 (2): 89–104.

Wikipedia (2009) 'Wikipedia: About'. Online. Available HTTP: <http://en.wikipedia. org/wiki.wikpedia:About> (accessed 20 February 2009).

Wikipedia (2015) 'History of Wikipedia'. Online. Available HTTP: <http://en.wikipedia. org/wiki/History_of_Wikipedia> (accessed 25 October 2015).

Williams, S. (2002) *Free as in Freedom*, Sebastopol, CA: O'Reilly.

Wright, S. (2008) 'Fixing the Kingdom: Political Evolution and Socio Economic Challenges in Bahrain', *CIRS Occasional Papers*, No. 3, Georgetown University.

Zittrain, J. (2008) *The Future of the Internet and How to Stop It*, London: Allen Lane.

Zook, M. (2007) 'Report on the Location of the Internet Adult Industry', in K. Jacobs, M. Janssen and M. Pasquinelli (eds) *C'lickme: A Netporn Studies Reader*, Amsterdam: Institute of Network Cultures.

Chapter 3

The internet of capital

Concentration and commodification in a world of abundance

Des Freedman

Introduction: a new mode of production?

The world is increasingly shaped by digital prophets – politicians, economists, journalists, academics and tech executives dazzled by the transformative power of the internet. They publish a literature that is premised on the idea that social media, big data and hyperactive algorithms have fundamentally changed the ways in which we socialise, amuse ourselves, learn about the world, act politically and, above all, do business. The internet is no longer merely the backbone of, or the infrastructure for, economic transactions but the very oxygen that allows us to innovate, collaborate, produce, exchange and consume goods and services. It provides the digital DNA of an informational system that is set to be exponentially more dynamic and productive than the analogue system it supersedes.

The most dramatic expression of this potential is said to be related to the internet of things (IoT), a veritable technological earthquake in which internet protocols are applied to what were previously inanimate objects to give them – and us – a new lease of life. Everything from fridges to lightbulbs, assembly lines to energy grids, highways to supermarkets will be connected in a seamless logistical exercise that 'offers the prospect of a sweeping transformation in the way humanity lives on earth, putting us on a course towards a more sustainable and abundant future' (Rifkin 2014: 14). For tech writer Samuel Greengard (2015: xiv), the IoT 'will someday serve as the practical framework for life and business . . . It's as if the rules of earthly physics have been rewritten on the fly'. Business analysts Gartner estimate that there will be some 26 billion internet-connected devices by 2020 (Gartner 2014), presaging a time in which, as MIT professor David Rose puts it, 'enchanted objects' will 'transform the way people use, enjoy, and benefit from the next wave of the Internet' (Rose 2014: 9). According to the chief executive of one IoT start-up, this new architecture 'will help us by functioning autonomously, creating self-aware systems out of our existing real-world objects that will now monitor and improve our environment' (Angelidis 2015).

The cumulative impact of this transformation is set to be a world marked by increased transparency, security, creativity, efficiency and stability – no less than a 'paradigm shift' (Rifkin 2014: 1) from market capitalism to peer production. This has been made possible by the lowering of production and distribution costs due to digital innovations to near zero – or what Chris Anderson, rather more pithily, refers to as 'free' (2009b). Eric Schmidt, Google's executive chairman, echoes this point in his influential assessment of *The New Digital Age* with Jared Cohen (Schmidt and Cohen 2013) in which they characterise the speed, scale and connectedness facilitated by 'modern technology platforms' like Google, Facebook and Amazon as 'a true paradigm shift' (2013: 9). For Mayer-Schonberger and Cukier, these companies' ability to capture such enormous amounts of data suggests that a 'change of scale has led to a change of state' (2013: 6). The quantification of everyday life that is associated with 'big data' means that we can expect transformations in 'everything from businesses and the sciences to healthcare, education, economics, the humanities, and every other aspect of society' (2013: 11). Former US vice-president Al Gore concurs that the internet has spawned novel types of capital flow and consumer markets and that 'we are witnessing the explosive growth of new business models, social organizations and patterns of behaviour that would have been unimaginable before the Internet and computing' (2013: 45).

Yet while the internet is said to be ushering in a radically new epoch, the outcome of these changes – in other words, the identity of the winners and losers – is yet to be decided. Philip Howard (2015) argues that *Pax Americana*, the geopolitical configuration that expressed US hegemony after World War 2, has been replaced by *Pax Technica*, a new information revolution based on the altruism of social media and the sheer pervasiveness of an IoT. *Pax Technica* refers to 'a political, economic and cultural arrangement of institutions and networked devices in which government and industry are tightly bound in mutual defence pacts, design collaborations, standards setting, and data mining' (2015: xx) – an arrangement that promises either to enslave or to emancipate us depending on the extent to which citizens are able to play a controlling role.

The British journalist Paul Mason is firmly committed to the radical democratic potential of distributed technologies that he argues was demonstrated in the Arab Spring and that led him to insist that 'a network can usually defeat a hierarchy' (2012: 77). In his subsequent work (Mason 2015a), he claims that, thanks to a combination of automation, information abundance and collaborative production, we have gone beyond capitalism into a new and extremely dynamic economic paradigm. The key struggle in what he refers to as 'postcapitalism' is that 'between the network and the hierarchy: between old forms of society moulded around capitalism and new forms of society that prefigure what comes next' (2015a: 4). Indeed, the internet has facilitated new prefigurative forms of economy, society and politics (see Milberry 2012) that are further explored, in particular, in Chapter 6.

These digital prophets may have very different political preferences and objectives but they share a view that the internet has fundamentally disrupted traditional business arrangements and impacted on the wider economy: massively lowering transaction costs, stimulating innovation, collapsing barriers between producers and consumers and indeed handing a much more productive and integral role to what were previously seen as rather passive customers. For Jeff Jarvis (2009),

Google provides by far the best role model for *any* company operating in the new digitally enhanced business era: it has changed 'the fundamental architecture of societies and industries the way steel girders and rails changed how cities and nations were built and how they operated' (2009: 27). For Tapscott and Williams (2008), the online encyclopaedia Wikipedia best encapsulates the possibilities and relationships offered by 'new models of production based on community, collaboration, and self-organization rather than on hierarchy and control' (2008: 1). Whatever their respective conceptual starting points and political objectives, these commentators coalesce around the notion that the internet is ushering in a far more productive, smooth, democratic and participatory world. 'A new mode of production is in the making' argue Tapscott and Williams (2008: ix), while Jeremy Rifkin insists that the 'capitalist era is passing . . . not quickly but inevitably. A new economic paradigm – the Collaborative Commons – is rising in its wake that will transform our way of life' (2014: 1).

This chapter examines this literature and explores the claims that the internet has helped to launch, in particular, a media economy based on niches and not mass markets, on flexibility and not on standardisation, on abundance and not scarcity, and on entrepreneurial start-ups and not on the industrial corporations that dominated the 20th century. Digital logic is conceived by theorists such as Chris Anderson (2009a, 2009b), Larry Downes (2009), Philip Howard (2015), Jeff Jarvis (2009, 2014), Charles Leadbeater (2009), Jeremy Rifkin (2014), Eric Schmidt and Jared Cohen (2013), Clay Shirky (2008) and Don Tapscott and Anthony Williams (2008) as adhering to a totally different set of operating principles in which the internet will put an end to the rule of monopolies and inspire more decentralised and customised networks of media flows. We will no longer have media concentration but dispersion where access to niche markets and endless back catalogues will satiate the public's desire for individuality and unlimited choice. Back in 1996 the MIT technologist Nicholas Negroponte predicted that '[w]holly new content will emerge from being digital, as will new players, new economic models, and a likely cottage industry of information and entertainment providers' (1996: 18). A decade later, Chris Anderson, editor of *Wired* magazine, the chronicler of the web revolution, now saw fit to highlight 'the economics of abundance – what happens when the bottlenecks that stand between supply and demand in our culture start to disappear' (2009a: 11).

The chapter assesses the underlying dynamics of a new digital mode of production and interrogates the technological and economic principles on which it is based. Inspired by more critical accounts of the internet's recent history (for example, McChesney 2012; Taylor 2014) and following on from the analysis of the contradictions of social media power (Freedman 2014), it examines the economics of abundance in the light of current trends in online distribution and consumption and considers whether the theorising of a 'niche economy' can account for residual patterns of conglomeration and concentration in the online world. In acknowledging the contradictory trends towards diversification and massification and towards specialisation and generalisation in the emerging online media economy, the chapter attempts to integrate the hugely significant developments of the digital era into an older account of capitalism as a system in which innovation, creativity and, indeed, everyday economic performance are structurally subordinated to the needs of the most powerful interests operating in the marketplace. Given the fact that, at the time of writing, three of the world's five largest companies are intimately associated with the internet, it may be true that the pipes are increasingly digital but the piper is still being paid and looking to make a profit.

The death of the blockbuster economy and other themes

Contemporary proponents of Wikinomics, Collaborative Consumption and Crowdsourcing are the most recent embodiments of an evolving information society discourse that originally sought to theorise the salience of information and knowledge in post-industrial societies (Bell 1973; Machlup 1962; Porat 1977; Toffler 1980; Touraine 1971). These titles focused on the changing economic and occupational structures of late 20th-century capitalism and identified symbolic goods and the service sector as the motors of the economy. Information, not oil or electricity, had become the central ingredient of a post-industrial age; knowledge workers, not coal miners, were its most productive citizens and innovation, not production, its 'axial' principle. In the 1990s, a second generation of writers then attempted to popularise and update these ideas for a world increasingly subject to the twin forces of globalisation and information technology. Notably, a huddle of business correspondents such as Cairncross (1997), Coyle (1997) and Leadbeater (1999) focused on processes of de-territorialisation and de-materialisation that were said to be transforming the foundational principles of Western economies. According to its most passionate political advocate, then British prime minister Tony Blair, this 'new economy' is 'radically different. Service, knowledge, skills and small enterprises are its cornerstones. Most of its output cannot be weighed, touched or measured. Its most valuable assets are knowledge and creativity' (Blair 1998: 8).

Despite many critiques of the 'new economy' (see, for example, Madrick 2001 and Smith 2000) and the uncertainties in relation to the internet following the dotcom crash in 2000 (assessed by Cassidy 2002), many of these ideas remain entrenched in current economic thinking and, indeed, have been adopted by a third generation of digital prophets writing about the huge consumer take-up of digital services in recent years. The success of digital platforms in terms of both revenues and users has led a number of influential commentators to formulate a series of rules, tendencies and predictions in relation to the potential of the internet to democratise production, equalise distribution and liberate labour. These commentators may not share the same political perspectives vis-à-vis the direction, coordination and regulation of the internet but there is a consensus concerning those economic features that have allegedly made it such a revolutionary tool for collaboration and disruption. These features are first summarised and then, in the second part of the chapter, critiqued and contextualised.

The economy of abundance

Thanks to the increasing capacity and falling price of microprocessors and semi-conductors, vast amounts of computing power are now available to consumers for a fraction of the price they once were. Digital technology has not only offered the possibility of abundant provision of healthcare, education, energy and even freedom (Diamandis and Kotler 2012) but it has also solved the problem of limited bandwidth that plagued the analogue universe. Media systems based around a handful of broadcast channels and print titles have now been superseded by communications environments that feature essentially unlimited storage space. Billions of web pages, digital compression technology and low entry costs to production and distribution (for example, a mobile phone and a broadband connection) have massively expanded choice (in quantitative terms) and put an end to the notion that media products are a scarce resource. 'The Internet', as Jarvis so elegantly puts it, 'kills scarcity and creates opportunities in abundance' (2009: 59); 'scarcity', according to Larry Downes (2009: 122), 'has been replaced by abundance'.

The former editor of *Wired* magazine, Chris Anderson, named by *Time* magazine in 2007 as the 12th most influential thinker in the world, has written several books (including Anderson 2009a, 2009b) that reflect on the implications of this economy of abundance and map out the shape of media markets in the digital world. Instead of focusing on the few, lucrative hits that are churned out by giant media corporations, he argues that we should turn our attention from the 'head' to the 'long tail' of media markets where millions upon millions of low-volume transactions are now set to be more lucrative than the increasingly unpredictable number of blockbusters. The power of the Top Ten has been usurped by the economics of the Next Thousand: 'If the twentieth century entertainment industry was about *hits*, the twenty-first will be equally about *niches*' insists Anderson (2009a: 16). Abundant storage space means that online shops can offer an inventory that vastly exceeds their offline competitors and more adequately satisfies the full range of consumer taste, no matter how whimsical or marginal. The long tail, however, is both efficient *and* democratic: 'Bringing niches within reach reveals latent demand for non-commercial content' (2009a: 26) and thus exposes consumers to a far more diverse range of content than the traditional media economy ever did. This changes the balance of power inside decision-making processes in the cultural industries away from hierarchical elites down to 'us', the new gatekeepers of popular (and niche) taste. 'The ants', he states (2009a: 99), 'have megaphones'.

Technologies of abundance have had an impact on media industries in another decisive way: digitisation and the internet's unlimited storage capacity have helped to lower transaction and distribution costs to such an extent (see Downes 2009: 38–40 and Rifkin 2014) that it is now possible to make money by giving things away for free. Google is enormously profitable but provides its search engine to users at no cost; there is no charge to join Facebook or to connect via WhatsApp; craigslist allows users to search its classified ads without paying a penny. Indeed, there are an increasing number of games, songs, news, entertainment and software online, much of which is available for free. This is less about a culture of piracy than, as Chris Anderson puts it (2009b: 12), 'an entirely new economic model': of 'free' in which we now expect *not* to have to part with money to access basic digital services.

> The Web has become the land of the free, not because of ideology but because of economics. Price has fallen to the marginal cost, and the marginal cost of everything online is close enough to zero that it pays to round down.
>
> (2009b: 92)

This is precisely the phenomenon that is proving to be so traumatic for existing record companies, newspapers and magazines which are seeing sales and revenues decline in the face of vicious price competition from their online rivals.

Both Jarvis ('Free is impossible to compete against' [2009: 76]) and Anderson ('Free' refers to 'the hole where the price should be, the void at the till' [2009b: 34]) endow this 'radical' new form of pricing with a mysterious and irrepressible power. They do not claim that 'free' ignores or transcends the rules of free market economics – after all, it is based on lucrative advertising subsidies – but rather that the market will, in the end, simply bow to its allure. 'In the digital realm', Anderson argues (2009b: 241), 'you can try to keep Free at bay with laws and locks, but eventually the force of economic gravity will win'. Indeed, 'free' redistributes value often in a more 'democratic' way than traditional market transactions – benefiting small companies who advertise on Google or the hundreds of thousands of advertisers on craigslist where the 'value in the classifieds was simply transferred from the few to the many' (2009b: 129). The abundant media economy has, therefore, not only carved up the market into a series of interlocking niches but has reconfigured the power relationships within this economy by challenging the ability of the 'old media' to charge exorbitant prices for its products. As Anderson puts it (2009b: 127): 'You can't charge scarcity prices in an abundant market'.

Boulders versus pebbles

If it is true, as Anderson suggests, that a market of niches is replacing the old 'blockbuster economy', then what is likely to happen to the organisations that have traditionally relied on the distribution of hits to mass audiences? 'Big media', the 20th century icons of industrial production, had a significant role to play when attention was abundant but outlets were scarce. They spent millions on production and marketing, developed efficient business models for reaching large numbers of consumers, and dominated the markets in which they participated. In a situation of digital abundance, however, the blockbuster strategy is doomed. According to the influential *Harvard Business Review* blogger Umair Haque (2005: 106), digital markets are structured along principles of 'coordination' and not command, and of 'distributed', not centralised, economies of scale. The 'product strategies' required to profit from niche markets are, therefore, 'openness, intelligence, decentralization and connectedness' (2005: 106), precisely the qualities lacking in the 'old media' with their proprietorial instincts and hierarchical structures. We are set to witness the decline in effectiveness of 'competition-killing strategies' and the emergence of 'a truly competitive market' (Anderson 2009b: 175).

This means that those companies most likely to thrive in a digital cornucopia are those that have understood the implications of abundance and the fact that '[o]wning pipelines, people, products, or even intellectual property is no longer the key to success. Openness is' (Jarvis 2009: 4). For Jarvis, this effectively means Google, which he describes as 'the first post-media company' (2009: 4). By realising that networked power is accrued by those who focus their activities on *linking* rather than *owning*, Google demonstrates by far the best example of a company that understands internet logic. 'If Google thought like an old-media company . . . it would have controlled content, built a wall around it, and tried to keep us inside' (2009: 28). Instead, Google benefits from dominating search traffic on *open* networks in contrast to the proprietorial behaviour of companies like Sony and Apple who have imposed a 'closed architecture' (Tapscott and Williams 2008: 134) on their respective PlayStations and iPads. This mirrors the pre-digital attitudes of the major record labels who, in response to the growth of a fan-led remix culture, have sought to assert their ownership rights and clamped down on the resulting 'mashups'. Google logic would suggest that the labels should instead link these fans together, putting the labels' content at the centre of this relationship, rather than threatening to sue them. 'Customer value, not control', according to Tapscott and Williams (2008: 143), 'is the answer in the digital economy'.

Google's success, together with the decline of the blockbuster economy, demonstrates to many of the latest generation of 'new economy' theorists that the institutional architecture of the media has shifted radically. The old vertically integrated conglomerates have wilted under the pressure of digital abundance and are being challenged by start-ups who are lighter on their feet, less wedded to centralised control and more open to collaborative possibilities. Charles Leadbeater describes this as a 'new organizational landscape' (2009: xxi) in which the mass media 'boulders' that dominated the pre-digital age 'have been drowned by a rising tide of pebbles' (2009: xix) dropped by individual users. The most successful new media companies are those that are able to organise the 'pebbles', whether that is Wikipedia in terms of information, Instagram for photographs, Amazon for books, YouTube for video, Twitter for snippets of conversation or Facebook for social interaction. Google, of course, catalogues the whole beach. Whether you are a 'boulder' or a 'pebble' is not merely a matter of size (Google, after all, is a rather large collection of pebbles) but of composition. 'Boulders' are highly dense and concentrated on the inside while 'pebbles' are light and more transparent. 'There is relatively little inside a pebble compared [to] a boulder. That is why pebbles tend be more outward looking' (2009: xxii) and far more suited to the dynamics of a networked economy. The cottage industry of media organisations that Negroponte predicted in 1996 has, it seems, finally arrived.

The culture of sharing

The 'outward-looking' perspective of digital actors relates to another central feature of the new media economy: that the competitive instinct of the large corporation is being challenged by the collaborative urge of the individual user. The internet, through its vast number of nodes 'connecting people with information, action, and each other' (Jarvis 2009: 28), lends itself to horizontal, peer-to-peer exchanges in a way that previous mass broadcast systems did not. It is stubbornly, or perhaps fundamentally, *social* in its wiring and thus invites its users to aggregate their skills and knowledge in the interests of all. For Leadbeater (2009: 7), the web's 'underlying culture of sharing, decentralization and democracy' has led to a situation he describes as 'We-Think', a revolution in 'how we think, play, work and create, together, *en masse*' (2009: 19). This is not an Orwellian form of 'Groupthink' but an opportunity to use technology to harvest the ideas, creativity and resources of millions of ordinary people. In the pre-digital age, innovation largely took place within the walls of the company and inside the laboratory; the internet allows for collective forms of innovation that originate in garages, bedrooms, studies and living rooms. According to Tapscott and Williams (2008: 15): 'Mass collaboration across borders, disciplines and cultures is at once economical and enjoyable. We can peer produce an operating system [like Linux], an encyclopedia [like Wikipedia], the media, a mutual fund . . . We are becoming an economy unto ourselves'.

The opportunity to collaborate is, of course, at the heart of an emerging 'sharing economy', the re-distribution of spare capacity by ordinary users to meet consumer demand in areas as diverse as accommodation, transport, finance and even chores. With a broadband connection and ownership of an underused resource – for example, a parking space, a house, a drill, a lump sum of cash – individual 'end users' can connect together without the need for a corporate intermediary to provide these services. The sharing economy, according to the CEO of one collaborative venture, is no more than 'the value in redistributing excess to a community, or getting "slack to the pack"' (Stephany 2015: 9). Others insist that the internet has simply extended analogue forms of behaviour such as bartering and neighbourliness into a digital age so that there 'is now an unbounded marketplace for efficient peer-to-peer exchanges between producer and consumer, seller and buyer, lender and borrower, and neighbour and neighbour' (Botsman and Rogers 2011: xiii). Companies such as Zopa (for loans), Airbnb (for property lets), Uber (for taxis), blablacar (for sharing rides) and Peerby (for borrowing household goods) claim that their platforms ensure the efficient mobilisation of spare capacity that remains wholly owned by the users and not the intermediaries. For this reason, even a left-wing economist like Paul Mason is inspired by this model of bottom-up resource distribution and argues that 'if you wanted to re-order the economy to deliver participation and choice alongside social justice, it's the sharing models you would start from' (Mason 2015b).

This new, 'grassroots' economy has a curious dynamic. It is an economy of niches produced by a mass of collaborators; it is highly specialised but organised on collective principles that profit from the 'wisdom of crowds' (Surowiecki 2004). From this perspective, the internet is facilitating a form of mass participation in which immobile 'boulders' with their hierarchical structures and bureaucratic procedures are being outmanoeuvred by 'flatter' and more adaptable institutional structures. 'To be organized', argues Leadbeater (2009: 24), 'we no longer always need an organization, certainly not one with a formal hierarchy'. All you need are some collaborative principles: a commitment to choice, an ability to use spare capacity together with 'belief in the commons and trust between strangers' (Botsman and Rogers 2011: 75). For Tapscott and Williams (2008: 15), there remains a space for 'firms that cultivate nimble, trust-based relationships with external collaborators [who] are positioned to form vibrant business ecosystems that create value more effectively than hierarchically organized businesses.' When society is run according to principles of mutuality and grassroots entrepreneurialism, and when the source of value is the many and not the few – or 'everybody' as opposed to an elite (Shirky 2008) – there are some notable implications both for the structural transformation of the media industries and the democratic possibilities that are said to follow.

First, the flattening of hierarchies and spread of point-to-point communication that has occurred because of the polycentric nature of the internet has shrunk the space in which gatekeepers traditionally used to operate. When the web allows buyers to communicate directly with sellers, fans with bands and readers with writers, there is little need for an intermediary – an estate agent, a record company, a second-hand car dealer or even a newspaper that brings you out-of-date classified advertising. Instead, we have craigslist for classifieds, Bandcamp for music, Rightmove for house sales and Auto Trader for vehicles. This process of disintermediation, or the fact that '[m]iddlemen are doomed' as Jarvis puts it (2009: 73), has long been noted by scholars (see Sparks [2000] in relation to newspapers and Galloway [2004] in relation to digital networks). However, as crowds mobilised by the internet increasingly provide each other with the information and resources necessary to make informed decisions about everyday life, and as the internet facilitates far more direct transactional relationships than previously, gatekeepers are revealed as the 'proprietors of inefficient marketplaces' (Jarvis 2009: 76). How can the traditional ad agency possibly compete with the startling efficiencies of Google's algorithm-based approach to customised advertising?

Second, digital technologies are alleged to have contributed to a huge democratisation of the media production process placing creative tools in the hands of a far greater number of users. Given the increased availability of smartphones, editing software, internet hosting services and broadband subscriptions, content creation is also increasingly in the hands of the 'crowd'. Pew research shows that, for example, some 75% of US teenagers have access to a smartphone, 71% use Facebook, over half turn to Instagram to share photos and videos and 17% read or comment on discussion boards like Reddit and Digg (Pew 2015). An earlier survey shows that 39% of them have their own online journal or blog, 51% remix original content and 59% create or work on their own web page (Purcell,

Buchanan and Friedrich 2013: 72). According to Leadbeater (2009: 211), 'while old-style industrial media consigned us to mainly watching and reading, the web vastly extends the range of people who can join public debate and expands the range of the ideas they can propose'. The upsurge in television commercials produced for top brands by 'amateurs' exemplifies the democratising possibilities of 'crowdsourced' creativity. Instead of hiring expensive ad agencies, user-generated content – the 2014 Doritos 'Crash the Super Bowl' commercial was rumoured to have cost $300 (Petavy 2014) – is seen to be a hallmark of a more collaborative approach to creativity, one that is 'bringing back to life an older, folk culture, which is extinguished by the mass-produced, industrial culture of the record and film industry of the 20th century' (Leadbeater 2009: 56).

This idea of the blurring of distinctions between producers and consumers is finally realising the predictions of Toffler (1980) about the rise of the 'prosumer' and of Fiske (1987) about the emergence of a 'semiotic democracy' engineered by a media-literate 'active audience'. For Tapscott and Williams, however, the rise of 'prosumption' amounts to an *economic* revolution: 'You can participate in the economy as an equal, cocreating value with your peers and favorite companies to meet your very personal needs, to engage in fulfilling communities, to change the world, or just to have fun!' (Tapscott and Williams 2008: 150). Indeed, so revolutionary is the possibility of 'prosumption' that Anderson actually compares the creation of user-generated content today with Marx's vision of unalienated labour in the *German Ideology* where he imagines a communist society in which ordinary people, freed from the constraints of wage labour, would be able to 'hunt in the morning, fish in the afternoon, rear cattle in the evening, criticize after dinner' (quoted in Leadbeater 2009a: 62).

This idea of creative and enjoyable production relates to another significant shift in the social relations of the contemporary world concerning the character of labour in a digital economy. For many of the current 'new economy' theorists, the collaborative principles that are hard-wired into the internet are being carried across into the most far-sighted workplaces. Where labour used to be alienating and where workers were often excluded from decision making, the 'Wiki Workplace (Unleashing the Power of Us)' (Tapscott and Williams 2008: 239–67) is one based on using digital technologies to share knowledge, exchange ideas and co-create. According to its proponents, it now offers meaningful opportunities for employee participation, fulfilling work and, of course, a more efficient use of labour. Tapscott and Williams' book is filled with examples of companies that have blossomed by listening to their customers and employees, by involving them in decision making and by giving them a degree of autonomy that is more likely to stimulate innovative thinking. The result is, they argue (2008: 240), that we are 'shifting from closed and hierarchical workplaces with rigid employment relationships to increasingly self-organized, distributed, and collaborative human capital networks that draw knowledge and resources from inside and outside the firm'.

The best example of this, according to the literature, is Google, the most dynamic and forward-thinking example of a 'wiki workplace'. Employees are fed for free (the chef having a particularly important role to play in many accounts of the company [for example Vise 2008: 192–203), transported on free wi-fi-enabled buses to the Googleplex, provided with a host of 'unusual benefits' like doctors and washing machines (Bock 2015: 22) and, perhaps most famously, given one day off a week to work on their own projects. This '20% rule' provided the time and space from which both Google News and Google Product Search emanated (Vise 2008: 130–40). Google's 'Don't Be Evil' slogan presumably applies as much to its own workplace as to Google products, not because of any intrinsic benevolence on the part of its founders but because 'the costs of evil are starting to outweigh the benefits . . . When people can openly talk with, about, and around you, screwing them is no longer a valid business strategy' (Jarvis 2009: 102). Work, freed from the opacity and isolation of the pre-digital era, can finally be enjoyed as an activity that rewards both the worker and the company.

Disrupting capitalism

In the literature described thus far, the mode of social organisation through which the benefits of the web can best be realised is the free market. There are some rare exceptions. Leadbeater criticises the market fundamentalism of libertarian cheerleaders like Chris Anderson and describes himself (along with Clay Shirky and Yochai Benkler) as a 'communitarian optimist' (2009: xxviii) who is inspired by the non-commercial possibilities of social production and peer networks. Leadbeater condemns the way in which private property has been assumed to be the foundation of all productive activity and argues that the 'spread of the web invites us to look at the future from a different vantage point' (2009: 6) in which proprietorial and non-proprietorial forces co-exist. Leadbeater envisages public and private goods as complementary and calls for a mixed economy where market transactions are tamed by the collaborative spirit and structure of the web. He is explicitly *not* calling to replace market relations with the 'idealistic commune capitalism of open-source and We-Think' (2009: 121) but for the principles of the 'commons' to inform and ameliorate private capitalism. Mason, on the other hand, is committed to the socialisation of digital tools to fully realise their potential and to move towards a form of 'dotcommunism' (Mason 2015b).

In general, however, there is a common assumption that the internet provides the most fantastic opportunities for the renewal and intensification of *private* enterprise. The literature is filled with talk of the efficiencies, cost benefits and strategic possibilities offered by digital technologies. The internet challenges firms to adapt to this new environment or lose out to their competitors: it is the classic case of a 'disruptive' technology that shakes up the status quo and paves the way for a glorious future. This is the approach adopted by legal scholar Larry Downes who argues that the internet, like railroads in the 19th century, are 'disruptive' technologies, forces of Schumpterian 'creative destruction', that 'ultimately demand dramatic transformation' (2009: 3). Instead of looking for a 'killer app' on the internet, Downes (2009: 10) argues that the internet *is* the 'killer app':

'a technological innovation whose introduction disrupts long-standing rules of markets or even whole societies'.

James McQuivey echoes this point when he insists we are facing endemic levels of 'disruptive innovation' in which 'digital disruption happens *to and through* digital things which then accelerate the disruption of physical things (2013: 4). Left to itself, the innate capacity of disruptive technologies, in this case the ability of the internet to expose the inefficiencies of analogue forms of business and to drive down production and transaction costs – McQuivey argues that the internet 'obliterates' barriers to entry (2013: 5) – will force companies increasingly to integrate 'Google logic' into their business plans. Paul Mason claims that the pace of digital disruption is itself disrupted by innovations and that we are seeing the possibility of a more extensive challenge to the current economic order posed by sharing technologies. Reflecting on actions by taxi drivers and hoteliers to defend their livelihoods, Mason argues that 'while the "old" monopoly models of the 2000s [like Amazon, Facebook and eBay] only disrupted dinosaur businesses – such as print publishers or booksellers – the new sharing businesses can actually disrupt society' (Mason 2015b). This is 'the era of Big Bang Disruption' (Downes and Nunes 2014).

Indeed, this continuous process of innovation may be viewed as one of the beauties of a social system in which, from time to time, individuals who are first to identify the benefits of a new technology, and who are not afraid to upset the corporate applecart, burst onto the scene and make us look at the world in a different way. These are what Downes (2009: 220) refers to as 'rebels' and what Jarvis calls 'disruptive capitalists' (2009: 4), people like Sergey Brin and Larry Page of Google, Craig Newmark of craigslist, Jeff Bezos, founder of Amazon, and Steve Jobs of Apple. These are the 'innovators' (Isaacson 2014) who embody the original frontier spirit of 19th-century capitalism. These fearless pioneers take 'decisions that make no sense under old rules of old industries that are now blown apart thanks to these new ways and new thinkers' (Jarvis 2009: 4). They are the outsiders, attacked by entrenched business interests and treated with suspicion by governments.

Of course, this is precisely the image welcomed by the pioneers themselves. For example, when challenged by European and US regulators as well as its more established competitors, Google has repeatedly fallen back on this narrative. 'Every government sort of has some group that's busy trying to figure out what we're up to' argues Google's Eric Schmidt. 'We're quite disruptive, and in the course of that disruption we tend to create enemies' (quoted in Oreskovic 2010). This nurtures a rather romantic image of capitalism in which the rebels take all the risks and in which technology instils social change that, despite the resulting turbulence, uncertainty and opposition, lays the foundation for a more productive future. This latest incarnation, based on the collaborative spirit of internet protocols and digital culture, is ushering in a new era that, if we are to believe Tapscott and Williams (2008: 15), is 'on par with the Italian Renaissance or the rise of Athenian democracy . . . A new economic democracy is emerging in which we all have a lead role'. This is the promise of the digital media economy.

Capitalism bites back

While these eulogies to the transformational power of the internet contain an enormous amount of empirical data, a passionate commitment to the participatory possibilities of the web and a justifiable suspicion of traditional management economics, much of them are nevertheless based on a series of unsubstantiated claims, profound misunderstandings and puzzling absences that render them incapable of providing a rigorous account of the dynamics of the digital environment. In general, they are so steeped in either a market fundamentalist or a technological determinist mode of address that it is hard to read the titles as anything other than paeans to capitalist entrepreneurialism aimed at a particular strata of global CEOs, investors and politicians.

There is an entirely different approach to evaluating claims of a new digital economy: one that is based on a Marxist critique that combines recognition of the revolutionary achievements of capitalism with an analysis of why capitalism is systematically unable to make available the full potential of these achievements to its subjects. Indeed, Marx's tribute to capitalism in the *Communist Manifesto* is almost as glowing as Jarvis' or Anderson's are to Google some 160 years later (although obviously with a sting at the end). Marx famously writes that the capitalist class has played a 'most revolutionary part' in human history: 'It has been the first to show what man's activity can bring about. It has accomplished wonders far surpassing Egyptian pyramids, Roman aqueducts, and Gothic cathedrals' (Marx and Engels 1975 [1848]: 36). It has done this not because of the 'genius' of individual scientists and technologists or the bravery of pioneering entrepreneurs, but because it is a system based on a structural need to innovate and move forward:

> The bourgeoisie cannot exist without constantly revolutionising the instruments of production, and thereby the relations of production, and with them the whole relations of society. Conservation of the old modes of production in unaltered form, was, on the contrary, the first condition of existence for all earlier industrial classes. Constant revolutionising of production, uninterrupted disturbance of all social conditions, everlasting uncertainty and agitation distinguish the bourgeois epoch from all earlier ones.
>
> (Marx and Engels 1975: 36)

Yet, just as Marx was captivated by capitalism's innovations, he was horrified by the means by which it seeks to reproduce itself. First, he notes that, as opposed to earlier societies where any surplus was consumed by the ruling elite, capitalists need to re-invest this surplus to compete more effectively in a market. Capital, understood by Marx as any accumulation of value that acts to increase its own value, 'exists and can only exist as many capitals' (Marx 1973: 414). Competition, as embodied in the modern free market, is the DNA of this new social system and innovation is therefore required to step up productivity, reduce labour costs, identify new markets and increase the rate of profit. Capitalists then become wedded to the further competitive accumulation of capital to be able most effectively to achieve these aims: 'Accumulate, accumulate! That is Moses and the prophets' (Marx 1918: 606). This means that capitalists will do everything they can to extract more value from the production process; that labour, once an essential part of human subjectivity, becomes something over which the labourer has less and less control; that objects that were previously enjoyed for their imme- diate qualities instead become valued mainly for their ability to be exchanged in a market transaction; and finally, that due to the lack of coordination in the economy, there will be a tendency towards crises of overproduction that will wipe out weaker capitals. These processes of exploitation, alienation, commodifica- tion and concentration are, according to Marx, the terrible price to be paid by the majority of people for the wonderful technological advances experienced under capitalism: for the development of railroads, electricity, vaccination programmes, broadcasting and, of course, the internet.

The central issue for this chapter is the extent to which informational goods and processes in particular are subject to these same tendencies and whether, as much of the literature discussed earlier suggests, the internet's privileging of collabora- tion and decentralisation insulates it from these dangers and somehow removes the *digital* economy from the endemic flaws of a crisis-ridden capitalism. One response to this question is to stress, as Larry Downes does (2009: 3), 'the unique properties of information' that render it distinct from other commodity forms: in particular the fact that it is intangible, that it can be consumed simultaneously without degrading it and that it acquires value the more it circulates. This gives an in-built advantage in a networked environment to the 'innovators', as the value of the network increases exponentially the more people join it. Facebook will have limited appeal with 100 users but it becomes extremely desirable if it has 1 billion users; Google's algorithms will be rather clumsy with only a few search requests but extraordinarily powerful with the results of 1.2 *trillion* searches a year to pro- cess. These are the network effects that reward those who move first and who are able to 'capture' customers and thus to mitigate against the possibility of mean- ingful competition (McChesney 2013: 132).

Nicholas Garnham's valuable study of *Capitalism and Communication* (Garnham 1990), although written before the invention of the web, nevertheless helps us to navigate this question of whether a phenomenon subject to network effects is able to escape the tendencies identified by Marx. Reflecting on the spe- cific characteristics of cultural commodities – that they are non-rivalrous, that costs of production vastly outweigh costs of distribution and that they seek nov- elty – Garnham argues that 'it has been difficult to establish the scarcity on which price is based' (1990: 160). However, he shrugs off the idea that cultural, or indeed informational, products are somehow exempt from the rules of the marketplace and identifies the particular strategies that have been applied to media commodi- ties precisely to bring them within the scope of market disciplines. Given that distribution costs are marginal in comparison with production costs, there is first a drive towards securing the largest audiences to maximise profits (1990: 160).

Second, there is a structural need artificially to re-introduce scarcity to regain control over pricing through such means as setting up monopolistic channels of distribution, providing free content as a loss-leader for expensive hardware or other premium services, and turning audiences into commodities to be sold to advertisers (1990: 161). Finally, to deal with the uncertainties of popular taste, there is a tendency to produce not isolated goods but a 'cultural repertoire across which the risks can be spread' (1990: 161).

Some of these approaches appear to be utterly incompatible with the new digital media economy described earlier. Anderson's 'long tail' thesis directly negates the urge to maximise ratings, focus on hits and produce a repertoire, while attempts to introduce scarcity and monopolise distribution channels would seem to be futile in an economy of abundance. The rest of this chapter, therefore, reflects on the extent to which strategies like these are relevant to informational networks in a digital world, and considers Olivier Sylvain's argument that 'the constitutive practices of the "networked information economy" are not actually immune to the undemocratic problems of concentration, centralization, and surveillance. To the contrary, those problems too are constitutive of the new media' (Sylvain 2008: 8).

Commodification in the digital economy

One of the great attractions of the internet is that it consists, to a great extent, of enthusiastic participants who contribute their time and energy – their labour – for no reward other than individual fulfilment and mutual gain. Contributors to, for example, Wikipedia, Linux, Digg, review sites and blogs all play a crucial role in what appears to be a thriving gift economy. Vast areas of the web have no pay-walls, no box office, no subscriptions and no rental fees, none of the price mechanisms that usually apply to the circulation of commodities. There is no immediate point of purchase when a user visits Google, Facebook, Instagram and YouTube. Indeed, Anderson describes the free supply of books, music, software, news, computer games and even the use of bicycles in the digital world as evidence of 'a nonmonetary production economy' (2009b: 189).

There are two immediate problems with Anderson's argument that 'free' is, as the title of his book (Anderson 2009b) puts it, a 'radical price'. First, it is not always clear what is meant by 'free'. Free content online is, of course, dependent on the purchase or rental of a computer or mobile device together with access to the web (neither of which is free) and, for example in the case of news, is simply paid for at a different point in the chain: through advertising, print sales and, in relation to the BBC, a licence fee. Content, in other words, always has to be subsidised whether by the individual user donating their time or the firm wishing to make their services available across different platforms. This is very similar to 'free' admission to London museums which is subsidised by the tax-payer to the tune of £18.06 per visitor to the Victoria & Albert Museum and £13.87 per visitor to the Natural History Museum (*Guardian* 2010: 17). Indeed, just as 'free' is a rather ambiguous concept, Anderson's claim that marginal costs in a digital economy are effectively zero underestimates the costs of marketing and infrastructure that are necessary to offer some goods and services for 'free'. McChesney, for example, talks about the 'serious capital outlays' (2013: 136) that are necessary to pay for the dozens of server farms and data centres that support Google's cloud computing services or Facebook's status updates.

Second, even where content is provided for 'free' at the direct point of contact, there is nevertheless a tendency within a market system to find, wherever possible, a non-zero price. This is what lies behind the very risky decision by the owners of, for example, the *New York Times* and the London *Times* to start charging for content despite the culture and expectation of 'free'. 'Paywalls' may or not work for more generalist audiences (in contrast to specialist business users who have already demonstrated a willingness to pay for premium content), but the fact that leading media moguls like Rupert Murdoch feel they have no choice but to introduce them is indicative of their need to generate revenue despite the resulting uncertainty. For rights holders (though of course not for aggregators who do not have to worry about paying for content), the current structure of 'free' is a particularly difficult concept on which to build a sustainable business. 'I like the competition that markets bring', argues Patience Wheatcroft, former editor-in-chief of the *Wall Street Journal Europe*. 'It's difficult to have a market if you're giving things away. Paid for is something we should aim to keep' (quoted in Armstrong 2009: 5). 'Free', while having obvious benefits for consumers in the short term, is not likely, especially given the competition for advertising revenue, to generate the capital needed to pay journalists, writers, directors and casts that are required to produce original and high-quality content.

Yet whether something is 'free' has little to do with any meaningful understanding of commodification. It is not the fixing of a price (even if that price is zero) that turns a good into a commodity but its general incorporation into a system of market exchange. As Marx puts it, 'objects of utility' become commodities 'only by means of the relations which the act of *exchange* establishes directly between the products, and directly, through them, between the producers' (Marx 1918: 44, emphasis added).

So while we pay nothing to search on Google, to publicise ourselves on LinkedIn or to watch a video on YouTube, others are nevertheless paying for the ability to reach *us*. What is being sold here is our profile, our consumption habits, our search history – our entire data history – in precisely the way that Garnham argued that the main commodity in the cultural industries is the audience as it is sold, over and over again, to advertisers. Far from relationships being 'the one thing you can't commoditize' as Tapscott and Williams claim (2008: 44), Facebook achieves just this objective as 'friendship' becomes the currency that drives the network. Similarly, LinkedIn also functions by transforming professional profiles into objects of exchange to attract advertisers. Relationships do not just 'matter' on LinkedIn but are quantified and monetised as a market of biographies.

Indeed, to the extent that much of the labour online is carried out by highly active 'prosumers' (Tapscott and Williams 2008: 124–50), this makes for an incredibly efficient way of gathering, filtering and analysing data that can be sold on to advertisers. Google and Facebook with their 'instant personalisation' facilities are vast storage containers of personal information that users 'freely' provide. Despite the concerns over safety and privacy that are discussed by writers like Pasquale (2015) and Schneier (2015), this data is then mined for its commercial value, leading Vincent Mosco to argue that digital technologies, far from challenging the logic of commodification, 'are now used to refine the process of delivering audiences of viewers, listeners, readers, movie fans, telephone and computer users, to advertisers' (Mosco 2009: 137). User-generated content, therefore, has a dual character: it is suggestive of a more participatory form of creativity and yet simultaneously very cost-effective as a means of generating free content that helps advertisers and marketers more precisely identify and target desirable audiences.

For writers like Jarvis, this is by no means an unwelcome process. When he writes that 'Google has turned commodification into a business strategy' (Jarvis 2009: 67), he is referring to mainstream economists' understanding of a commodity as a generic good, like sugar, steel or oil. By matching advertisers with consumers on the basis of algorithms rather than reputation, everything becomes commodified, even the mass of niches that makes up the contemporary audience. All Google ads look the same, whatever the marketing budget of the respective company, while users are measured by their 'clicks', not their backgrounds: 'There's little that distinguishes one of us from another – not age, income, gender, education, interest, all the things advertisers historically paid for. Everybody's just like everybody else. We're just users. We might as well be pork bellies' (2009: 68). Jarvis' argument is that, while this may be difficult for traditional brands, it is an efficient and potentially equalising development in the marketplace. But for many people who have no wish for their friendships to be privatised via Facebook or for their personal data to be surveilled and sold on by Google, this is a form of commodification in which their very labour, their own creative self-activity, is repackaged and turned into an object to be exchanged, at a price, on the open market.

This has led to a lively debate among some writers on the left about the conditions of 'digital labour' (Scholz 2013) and the extent to which this labour is a novel form of 'prosumer' activity in which users are formally exploited by capitalists and their labour directly turned into profits. According to Christian Fuchs, internet users freely uploading content to, for example, Facebook 'become productive labourers who produce surplus value and are exploited by capital' (Fuchs 2014: 103) – obviously without direct financial reward. Under conditions of intense globalisation and digitisation, this is set to be an increasingly valuable source of labour for some of the world's largest companies: 'Because capital cannot exist without non-wage labour and exploits the commons that are created by all, society has become a factory' (2014: 111).

Others have challenged this view of the emergence of a 'totalizing or new form of capitalism' (Comor 2015: 13) and argue that there is a significant distinction between commodification and exploitation in the realisation of profits. While the former is certainly rampant in the online world, it is far less clear that prosumption amounts to the kind of 'productive labour' that Marx envisaged lay at the heart of the pursuit of surplus value. 'To, for example, commodify a game that my son and his friends have co-created', argues Comor (2015: 17), 'does not in and of itself mean that my child has been formally exploited'. While it is true that social media companies commodify the data provided to them by users, surplus value is generated through the labour of employees who process this data, as I discuss later in this chapter. Khiabany concurs that there is a danger of overstating the exploitative character of tweeting or uploading a status update and argues that 'new and seasoned political activists in Iran, Tunisia, Turkey and elsewhere . . . might be surprised to learn that, indeed, even in their effort to challenge capitalism and dictatorship, they were being controlled and exploited further' (Khiabany 2015: 267). Hesmondhalgh (2015) focuses on the degree of 'suffering' at the heart of exploitation and doubts that it is legitimate to equate, for example, the experiences of assembly line workers at Foxconn in China with social media users who are free to withdraw their 'labour' without fear of starvation. There are many reasons to criticise social media – including their commodified status (2015: 37) – but exploitation is not one of them.

An additional problem is that the concept of social media exploitation appears to fit only the activities of companies who materially profit from 'digital labour'. If that is the case, what is the status of Wikipedia, Linux, the majority of blogs and those peer-to-peer networks with an explicitly non-commercial character? Does this suggest that the internet is composed of two entirely distinct spheres: a commodified and a non-commodified part, one section that operates like a capitalist marketplace and one that operates as a 'commons' (Benkler 2006; Leadbeater 2009; Lessig 2002)? Zittrain's concern that the internet's earlier 'generativity' – its openness and unpredictability – is becoming tethered and 'appliancized' (2008: 8) and Benkler's worry about the information commons being threatened by increasing online concentration (2006: 240) are further evidence of a bifurcated internet. This leads to the conclusion that we need to protect and nurture the non-commodified zones to fend off the destructive, anti-democratic features of the commercial sector. According to this logic, the open-source environment is the antithesis of proprietary production and constitutes a clear challenge to the principles of private accumulation.

In reality, however, it is becoming increasingly hard to separate the two parts of the internet and, far from one sector being insulated from the other, they are in constant tension. Peer-to-peer and open source may be seen by some as progressive alternatives to market structures and by others, including many rights holders, as mortal threats to profits and investment but capitalism, as we have already identified, is a dynamic and expansive system that attempts to deploy any technological innovation that may increase its profitability and efficiency. Indeed, the whole premise of 'wikinomics' as developed by Tapscott and Williams (2008) is to use the principles of open source to invigorate and renew market institutions. 'Without the commons', they argue (2008: 91), 'there could be no private enterprise'. Their book, along with Anderson (2009b), Downes (2009), Jarvis (2009) and Schmidt and Cohen (2013), is filled with examples of how major corporations, including IBM, Sun and Nokia, have sought to integrate the efficiencies of open source into their own corporate practices. Instead of arguing that open source is a competitive threat to capital accumulation, wikinomics suggests that the 'greatest risk is not that peer production communities will undermine an existing business model, but that a firm will prove unable to respond to the threat in time' (Tapscott and Williams 2008: 96). Companies, in other words, are being encouraged to learn how to apply the collaborative principles of open source to their specific business sector to increase productivity and achieve higher rates of growth.

This is certainly the case for the emerging 'sharing economy' in which collaboration may be freely sought and given but where it also has a price. While barriers to entry are formally low, network effects suggest that the market is going to reward those schemes – whether about recycling cardboard boxes or sharing cars – that are most effectively capitalised, have substantial marketing budgets and that are able to keep costs low. Airbnb may have introduced millions of people to private living rooms away from the grip of overpriced hotel chains, but it is hardly able to escape from corporate logic. Indeed, a report by New York State's Attorney General, Eric Schneiderman, found that commercial landlords accounted for a disproportionate share of short-term rentals on Airbnb and that short-term rentals facilitated by sharing sites took thousands of properties out of the long-term housing market, thus affecting prospects for would-be residents (Schneiderman 2014: 2–3).

Uber, the online taxi service that matches passengers to car owners, is perhaps the most controversial example of the 'sharing economy' – although critics allege that it should not be seen as a form of sharing in the first place (Meelen and Frenken 2015). Uber has flourished in cities across the world by flouting regulations, driving down pay rates, neglecting medical cover and pensions, and incentivising drivers by 'deactivating' those whose ratings are not sufficiently high (Henwood 2015). Most significantly, perhaps, this is a digital platform run on very traditional economic logic. 'You want supply to always be full', argues Travis Kalanick, Uber's CEO, 'and you use price to basically either bring more supply on or get more supply off, or get more demand in the system or get some demand out . . . It's classic Econ101' (quoted in Swisher 2014). Indeed, Kalanick sees Uber as far more than a taxi service and wants to use the sharing platform as a means to perfectly match supply and demand so that Uber may provide access to 'a smoothly functioning instant gratification economy, powered by the smartphone as the remote control for life' (Swisher 2014). The sharing economy is far from homogeneous and consists of both nonmonetary and intensively profit-driven ventures, but Doug Henwood is right to argue that it 'looks like a classically neoliberal response to neoliberalism: individualized and market-driven, it sees us all as micro-entrepreneurs fending for ourselves in a hostile world' (Henwood 2015).

In this situation, capitalism's ability to use, to its own advantage, even those technological developments that appear to challenge its commitment to proprietary principles provides a rebuttal to those who see 'We-Think' (Leadbeater 2009) as an intrinsically non-commodified set of practices. Instead, we should see the relationship between non-commercial and commercial spheres of the web as fundamentally contradictory. This relates to the structural need of capitalism to monetise, and incorporate within a system of market exchange, even those practices – like blogging, commenting, reviewing and sharing – that spring from non-commercial urges. Wikipedia, Linux, Mozilla and even Peerby are crucial in demonstrating the collaborative potential of the internet, but they are also illustrative both of the emancipatory potential of the web *and* its intimate relationship to a corporate logic. Commodification, according to this perspective, is not easily avoided or thrown off like a Weberian 'light cloak', but is a fundamental process through which capitalism is organised and reproduced, online just as much as offline.

Accumulation strategies

We might expect the organising principles of a 'new economy' and a 'digital mode of production' to behave in ways that are different to the competitive strategies adopted by 20th century industrial corporations. This was a model that frowned on collaboration and sought to concentrate all its expertise in-house, that operated as a bureaucracy with strict hierarchies and centralised decision making, and that fiercely protected its own intellectual property. 'New economy' proponents argue that one of the reasons for the success of the most prosperous Web 2.0 companies lies in their determination to avoid a 'command and control' mentality and to instil a more collaborative approach within corporate culture. According to Jarvis (2009: 69):

> In Google's economy, companies will no longer grow to critical mass by borrowing massive capital to make massive acquisitions . . . Instead, they need to learn from Google and grow by building platforms to help others prosper. Indeed, growth will come less from owning assets inside one company and amassing risk there than from enabling others in a network to build their own value.

Success in the digital age, it appears, is more likely to be guaranteed for those companies who eschew proprietorial controls and Fordist accumulation measures and focus on the innovation necessary to make their services and products available to the greatest number of people.

However, even a cursory glance at Google's own history points to a rather different narrative. First, the company was launched on the basis of a $25 million investment in 1999 by two California-based venture capital groups who insisted that the founders, Sergey Brin and Larry Page, hire an experienced CEO 'to help them transform their search engine into a profitable business' (Vise 2008: 67). Although Brin and Page pioneered the technique that allowed them to catalogue billions of web pages, revenues only took off when they adopted the pay-per-click advertising model of a *rival* search engine, GoTo, into its now highly lucrative AdWords system (Battelle 2005: 125). To smooth the way for the transformation of Google into a public company in 2004, it then handed Yahoo, the new owners of GoTo (now called Overture), some 2.7 million shares worth hundreds of millions of dollars to settle its patent dispute with Yahoo out-of-court. Furthermore, although the initial public offering (IPO) was vastly oversubscribed and presented as a model of shareholder democracy, the two owners insisted on a dual class structure in which their operational control of the company would be consolidated and protected. According to Google's IPO document, the executive triumvirate of Brin, Page and CEO Eric Schmidt were to control 37.6% of the company, leaving new investors, in the words of Larry Page, with 'little ability to influence its strategic decisions through their voting rights' (Google 2004). Ironically, while acknowledging that this was unusual for technology companies, Page noted that the New York Times Company, The Washington Post Company and Dow Jones, all of them the most traditional of 'old media' firms, had similar structures that asserted the right of a handful of executives to retain overall strategic control (Google 2004) for the good of the company.

Google has long combined a determination to secure first-mover advantage in new and innovative markets with a rather more old-fashioned commitment to undermining its competitors, in particular Apple and Microsoft (see Vise 2008: 282–91), and to acquire firms that improve both its service and its market share. In its short history it has bought, at the time of writing, some 180 companies – including Blogger, Picasa, the satellite imaging service Keyhole, Doubleclick, Motorola Mobility and, most famously, YouTube – at a total cost of nearly $30 *billion*. Not bad for a company which has *not* had to rely, in Jarvis' words, on making 'massive acquisitions'. Facebook is also no slouch when it comes to acquiring additional expertise, having spent over $21 billion in buying up 55 companies, $19 billion of which was spent on its 2014 purchase of instant messaging service WhatsApp. Both companies have also been heavily reliant on the traditional legal protections given to firms by the state and, far from being amenable to sharing their intellectual property, they recognise that securing its IPO is at the core of their ability to generate revenue. According to Google's 2010 10-K filing to the US Securities and Exchange Commission:

> We rely on a combination of patent, trademark, copyright, and trade secret laws in the U.S. and other jurisdictions as well as confidentiality procedures and contractual provisions to protect our proprietary technology and our brand. We also enter into confidentiality and invention assignment agreements with our employees and consultants . . . and we rigorously control access to proprietary technology.
>
> (Google 2010: 16)

The fact that Google requires its employees to sign confidentiality agreements clashes somewhat with Jarvis' assertion that 'Google rewards – and more and more, we expect – openness' (2009: 236) but, more significantly, it is a stark reminder that there are firm restrictions on the autonomy of labour in a company famous for its free lunches, staff perks and generous conditions. Once again, this can be explained not in terms of Google's exceptionalism but the opposite: its status as a large firm operating in an emerging market. For example, consider Google's celebrated (and now, perhaps, mythical) '20% rule' which stipulates that its software programmers should spend at least one day a week on their own projects. This is, as Tapscott and Williams put it (2008: 260), evidence of the company's belief in 'collaboration and encouraging self-organization'. It has also been highly productive: Google News, the product search engine Froogle and social networking service Orkut all originated from this seemingly enlightened corporate policy. Yet should this be seen as 'time off' or as an effective incentive for research and development, the results of which are wholly appropriated by Google and not by the employee? Similarly, the provision by the company of high-quality free lunches was a 'perk with a purpose. It would keep people near one another and their desks; prevent them from developing poor eating habits that would diminish productivity; eliminate the time they would otherwise spend going out to lunch . . . and create a sense of togetherness' (Vise 2008: 194). Even the company's supply of wi-fi-enabled buses to take employees to and from its Mountain View headquarters is an effective way of lengthening the working day for staff, virtually all of whom would have laptops – to say nothing about the impact of this form of private transport on the gentrification of San Francisco (Berniker and Lipton 2014).

None of these strategies for maximising the exploitation of staff and accumulation of capital should come as a surprise when reflecting on a public company with a market valuation of approximately $438 billion and annual revenues of over $66 billion. Google is simply following in the path of many previous market leaders by making shrewd acquisitions that enhance and make more efficient its offer, by thinking creatively about the ways in which it can extract full value from a highly skilled workforce, and by constantly innovating to remain one step ahead of its rivals (should it not be able to buy them). Google's offices may be open plan but, as a company, it is hardly open source; indeed the company is not structured horizontally but, as we have seen, with operational power and strategic control concentrated at the top. 'Openness' and 'connectedness' are not the principles on which it is organised so much as the products it sells. Indeed this is precisely what Google's CEO, Eric Schmidt, admitted in a 2005 speech to Wall Street financial analysts:

> We are not quite as unconventional as we actually say all the time. The things that we do are unique in the way that products are created, but much of the rest of the business is run in all the normal ways and very much at the state-of-the-art but in a traditional way. We actually do care about objectives. Every quarter we go through, 'How are we doing?'
>
> (Quoted in Vise 2008: 256)

The digital economy depends, therefore, on the exploitation of paid creative labour and, in the context of uncertain business models and a highly unstable economy, we can expect an intensification of this exploitation. Consider, for example, the highly controversial decision in 2010 by leading consumer magazine publisher Bauer – whose music titles include *Kerrang*, *Q* and *Mojo* – to impose an 'all rights' contract which secures its ownership of freelance content across all platforms but makes the freelancer 'liable for all damages and costs in the event of legal action' (Armstrong 2010). Exploitation is rife in the digital economy where companies increasingly foster relationships with 'independent contractors' to avoid paying for the benefits, holidays and even lunch breaks that would be owed to permanent employees. 'Sharing economy companies like Uber, Airbnb, TaskRabbit, Postmates and Homejoy claim they are liberating workers to become independent – "their own CEOs" – in reality, workers are forced to take ever-smaller jobs (gigs sand micro-gigs) and wages while the companies profit handsomely' (Hill 2015).

The digital media economy, in particular, profits from the increasing amount of unpaid labour, otherwise known as 'user-generated content', facilitated by the falling costs of smartphones and cameras. As we have already noted, user-generated content has a contradictory character: expressive of the generative possibilities of the internet but all too easily used as 'free' content by media and information companies who, in previous years, would have expected to pay for such content. So while newspapers eagerly reproduce Twitter feeds about election debates and TV news bulletins gratefully broadcast 'witness videos' of bomb blasts and train crashes, user-generated content is actively sought by a range of companies wishing to reduce marketing costs and to associate themselves with the 'semiotic democracy' of consumer-made content. The 'new economy' literature is filled with examples of this 'participant consumerism' (Leadbeater 2009: 105): from the Canadian music label that organised a remix contest in which hundreds of DJs willingly sent in their entries (Tapscott and Williams 2008: 280) and saved the company tens of thousands of dollars, to the interactive web ads made for Chevrolet (Anderson 2009a: 226), and the celebrated case of the home-produced television commercials for Doritos that continue to be transmitted during the hugely expensive ad breaks in the Superbowl (Leadbeater 2009: 105).

Tapscott and Williams et al. argue that this kind of co-creation, enabled by the decentralised and interactive features of the internet, has resulted in a more engaged and active citizenry and the phenomenon of the 'prosumer' revolution. Yet, far from signalling a democratisation of media production and distribution, 'prosumption' is all too often incorporated within a system of commodity exchange controlled by existing elites who either *call* for user-generated material or *cull* material from already existing sites. In both cases, the imaginative labour of ordinary people is appropriated for the benefits it accrues to social media companies who hope to sell the personalised content generated by users to advertisers and marketers. It is a further example of the commodification and drive to accumulation that lies at the heart of the market economy, whether it is one based on Fordist assembly lines or digital networks.

Concentration in the digital media economy

Back in the heady days before the millennium when the web was expanding rapidly and when fresh new upstarts were challenging traditional IT and media companies for hegemony over the internet, Oxford economist Andrew Graham (1998) pursued a rather unfashionable argument. He argued that, despite the capacity of the internet to operate on near zero marginal costs, a digital media economy still required significant resources for the production and marketing of high-quality content. He predicted, therefore, an intensification of economies of both scale (to offset costs) and scope (due to convergence and cross-promotion) and the emergence of new types of scarcity (not of spectrum but of talent) and further concentration (as opposed to a 'world of free competition') because of the economic benefits of being in a network (1998: 33). Over 15 years later, to what extent have Graham's predictions of the consequences of 'network effects' been proved right – or are we seeing an environment dominated by a plethora of information-age 'pebbles' rather than a concentration of corporate 'boulders'?

Headline figures certainly appear to support Graham's analysis and to challenge the notion that bottlenecks are disappearing in crucial areas of the digital economy like search, advertising and entertainment. For example, figures from the statistics portal statista (www.statista.com) reveal that Google dominates just under 90% of total worldwide searches, with more than 96% in Brazil, nearly 95% in Germany and nearly 90% in the UK. Clear patterns of concentration are also visible in search advertising where, in 2014, the top four companies (Google, Baidu, Microsoft and Yahoo!) attracted 70% of gross revenue across the globe with Google alone accounting for some 55% of the total $70 billion market (*eMarketer* 2015). Online display may be the fastest-growing sector of the world advertising market but the proceeds are hardly equally shared with the top two firms (Google and Facebook), accounting for nearly 40% of revenue (*eMarketer* 2014). Internet advertising, according to McChesney (2013: 148), 'is on an explosive trajectory to gobble up an ever increasing portion of all advertising expenditures for the foreseeable future' – a development that is likely to have very serious implications for privacy given the intimate relationship between online advertising and extensive data surveillance (Turow 2011).

Far from digital networks leading to a dissolution of monopolistic behaviour, we are looking at some highly concentrated market sectors, particularly in the US where iTunes controls 64% of the music download market and YouTube 71.5% of online video, while Facebook accounts for 38% of all social networking traffic (www.statista.com). Globally, four of the five most popular apps are owned by a single company, Facebook, while consumers in the UK and the US spend 80% of their time on just five apps including Facebook, YouTube and Gmail (Tode 2015). Indeed, online attention in the UK is overwhelmingly concentrated on just Facebook and Google sites which, between them, account for some 35% of *total* time spent online (comScore 2015). While these figures are likely to fluctuate over the next few years, they are nevertheless comparable to those same 'old media' markets that were held to be examples of the lack of competition that the web would supersede. It is hardly surprising, therefore, that the European Commission has announced an antitrust investigation into Google's activities.

The point is that although the internet is facilitating an enormous increase in content as well as the means of distributing this content, it is doing so on the basis of economic and consumer trends that are not so dissimilar to those of the past. As Tim Wu puts it, '[f]or all its supposed singularity, the Internet shows itself, like any network, to be subject to network economics, with efficiencies naturally arising from central control. Economies of scale, a leading story of the twentieth century, is playing out in this century already' (2010: 318). In fact, dig deeper behind the rhetorical flourishes of the digital prophets and you will find some internet analysts who accept this line of argument. For example, PayPal founder Peter Thiel insists that monopoly is effectively the economic prerequisite for success in a field, and refers to the situation in which one firm has (legally) outwitted all its rivals through the sheer quality and distinctiveness of its product. Google may pretend that it is not a monopolist, that it is 'just another tech company', but this is simply so that it may 'escape all sorts of unwanted attention' (Thiel 2015). In fact, monopoly provides the basis for both strategic thinking *and* ongoing innovation given that the monopolist can afford to plan ahead while its rivals are constantly obsessed with short-term survival. Monopoly, according to Thiel (2015), is therefore 'not a pathology or an exception. Monopoly is the condition of every successful business'.

Of course, just as monopoly in the sphere of news and information suggests a potential democratic deficit in terms of the domination of a single powerful voice, digital monopolies like Google and Facebook are neither intrinsically more benevolent nor more public-minded, and have amassed staggering degrees of political, economic and cultural power. Despite Thiel's libertarian zeal for monopoly profits, it is worth repeating the fact that monopolies are not organic features of a digital environment but the beneficiaries of venture capital investment, lax regulation and sympathetic tax regimes. 'None of these monopolies would have been possible without supportive and enabling government policies on a range of issues, as well as considerable previous investments by the government, a point lost in Thiel's self-congratulatory paean' (McChesney 2013: 142). Even the free market *Economist* magazine is suspicious of the extent to which digital monopolies can be relied upon to act honourably over time. 'As the first flush of heady growth wears off and the technological or business edge that made it possible gets copied or ground down, the need to keep satisfying market expectations get stronger and once insurgent, even idealistic cultures turn more corporate' (*Economist* 2014: 23).

In relation to digital media, there remains therefore not simply a pattern of monopolistic (and sometimes oligopolistic) markets but an incentive for companies to produce 'blockbusters' and an apparent willingness on the part of audiences to consume them. In an empirical investigation of Anderson's 'long tail' thesis, the guiding principle of a digital media economy, Harvard Business School professor Anita Elberse found that the top 10% of songs on the digital download service Rhapsody accounted for 78% of all plays and that the top 1% account for nearly one third of all plays: a result that demonstrates 'a high level of concentration' (2008: 2). The 'tail' is certainly getting longer, i.e. there is now a vast amount of content that is accessible even if there is no demonstrable mass market for it, but it is also getting flatter and is, in general, 'a diversion for consumers whose appetite for true blockbusters continues to grow' (2008: 9). If this is correct, then Anderson's 'long tail' thesis is evidence not so much of an equalisation of power in the cultural marketplace, but of the internet's capacity to act as a much more efficient and expansive storage system.

The recent trajectory of Netflix appears to bear this out. While it started out as a DVD rental service with a very big back catalogue – the epitome of a 'long tail' provider – it has more recently discovered the value of blockbusters in attracting and then maintaining mass audiences. Far from concentrating on exploiting its potentially unlimited digital shelf space, it has now started to produce high-quality and very expensive original 'television' programmes like *House of Cards* and *Orange is the New Black*. According to its chief content officer, Ted Sarandos:

> What we're seeing is the dollars invested in our original programming are more efficient in that for every dollar spent, we get more bang for buck in terms of hours viewed. And hours viewed leads to higher retention, more word of mouth and more brand halo.
>
> (Quoted in Fox 2015)

Sarandos further claims that another source of profit for Netflix has been its decision to stream *Friends* – hardly the epitome of the obscure title hidden away in the archives that was supposed to be the hallmark of the long tail. 'Today's Netflix and its "brand halo"', argues one critic, 'seem to have a lot more in common with existing TV channels, most obviously HBO, than the back-catalog specialist that it was back in 2006' (Fox 2015).

Netflix's direction of travel supports Elberse's conclusion that the companies that are set to gain most from the digital economy are not those who supply the 'tail' but those who are 'most capable of capitalizing on individual best sellers' (2008: 9) and a clear riposte to those who emphasise the power of niche culture over the blockbuster economy. These theorists insist that as the old 'mass market' fragments, we will inevitably see the 'shattering of the mainstream into a zillion different cultural shards' (Anderson 2009a: 5) and the emergence of a de-massified market. This is partly an empirical matter. There may be 'zillions' of tweets, blogs and uploaded pictures and videos, but there is little evidence to suggest that they are likely either to replace traditional content providers or to escape traditional economic imperatives that reward scale and scope.

Even if it was true that there was no demand or incentive to produce blockbuster goods, there is little evidence that the circulation of niche goods is predicated on a *different* market logic, one that is *not* based on the tendency towards concentration and the need for accumulation. When Jarvis argues, in a section headed 'The mass market is dead – long live the mass of niches' (2009: 63), that 'Google figured out how to navigate the universe of niches and profit from it' (2009: 66), all he is doing is correctly identifying the extent to which even the smallest demographic may be commodified and used as a source of value.

But Anderson and Jarvis' belief in the democratic benefits of a niche economy also appears to be based on a misunderstanding of the relationship between the 'mass' and 'niche', where the former is seen as an outmoded form of top-down control and the latter as a rather romantic expression of individuality. Both cite the celebrated aphorism of Marxist sociologist Raymond Williams, that '[t]here are no masses; there are only ways of seeing people as masses' (quoted in Anderson 2009a: 185; Jarvis 2009: 63), as proof of the welcome decline of the mass market. But Williams was saying no such thing: he was instead commenting on the power of elite institutions to organise the representation of ordinary people as an unruly 'mob' to better regulate them. He was condemning not the ability of citizens to act collectively but the use of the word 'masses' by industry leaders and politicians to commodify large groups of people. 'This is the trouble with phrases like "the masses" and "the great British people", which lead us to think not of actual people, living and growing in different ways, but of some large, many-headed thing with fixed habits' (Williams 1968: 93). Just as there ought to be nothing intrinsically threatening about 'masses', there is nothing automatically democratic about 'niches'.

Ironically, the growth of niches has contributed to another area of concentrated activity: the need for 'gatekeepers' to structure access to increasingly populated and complex markets. Consider the case of online advertising which is dominated by a single company, Google, that is increasingly able to deal directly with clients without the need for dedicated ad agencies. 'Google is an incredibly efficient system for placing ads', writes Michael Wolff (2012). 'In a disintermediated advertising market, the company has turned itself into the last and ultimate middleman'. Given the monopolistic structure of other emerging digital media markets where large companies continue to interject themselves between the buyer and the seller – for example, Apple in relation to apps and music downloads and Amazon in relation to e-publishing – and to assume a prominent gatekeeping role, power may be shifting but it appears to be displacing previously dominant distributors (like book publishers or music companies) in favour of new digital intermediaries who may be reluctant to cater equally to all niches. It is a reminder that traditional mechanisms for ensuring the viability of cultural commodities in a capitalist market – of monopolies, bottlenecks and manufactured scarcity – are especially relevant to the new digital economy. The logic is straightforward: 'A variety of economic effects reward first movers, penalize latecomer competitors, entice people to join the largest networks, and make it hard for them to switch to a competing system. The result is that these new middlemen have more power than those they replaced' (Schneier 2015: 57).

Conclusion

The accounts of the collaborative possibilities of the digital world provided by Anderson, Downes, Jarvis, Schmidt and Cohen and Tapscott and Williams are powerful reminders of the tremendous impact that the internet has had on many areas of creative and cultural life. Yet, for all their insider knowledge and cutting-edge perspectives, these books articulate a deterministic vision of a frictionless capitalism in which questions of property have been sidelined, profit-making naturalised and exploitation minimised. The dynamics of the free market have been abstracted from their daily iteration and replaced with a technologically induced vision of an economic system based on an innate tendency to equalise and make transparent the social relations on which capitalism rests.

The problem is that even a digital capitalism is still subject to the same episodic crises of supply and demand and the same periods of speculation that affect other varieties of capitalism. Google may not have been as badly damaged by the recession as, for example, house-builders and steel-makers, but it was nevertheless still affected by a decline in overall economic activity. 'Despite claims to the contrary', argues Mike Wayne (2003: 59), 'there is no new paradigm by which the economics of capitalism transcends its absolutely fundamental tendency towards overproduction and hence crisis'. Many of the factors that were symptomatic of the 'mass' media economy – especially its propensity towards monopolisation, commodification and accumulation – are central to the dynamics of a new media economy shaped by the contradictory forces of the internet that promise dispersion but reward concentration and that fetishise openness but encourage proprietary behaviour. The digital sphere is not a parallel economy but one that accentuates the tensions between the creativity and collaboration of a generative system and the hierarchies and polarisation prioritised by a system that rests, above all else, on the pursuit of profit.

References

Anderson, C. (2009a [2006]) *The Longer Long Tail: How Endless Choice Is Creating Unlimited Demand* (first published in the US as *The Long Tail*), London: Random House Business Books.

Anderson, C. (2009b) *Free: The Future of a Radical Price*, London: Random House Business Books.

Angelidis, E. (2015) 'The internet of things is as important as the world wide web', *Guardian*, 9 January. Online. Available HTTP: <http://www.theguardian.com/media-network/2015/jan/09/internet-of-things-important-world-wide-web> (accessed 28 July 2015).

Armstrong, S. (2009) 'It's Very Dangerous To Go Free', *Media Guardian*, 16 November.

Armstrong, S. (2010) 'Bauer's Freelancers up in Arms over New Contracts', *Guardian*. 19 April. Online. Available HTTP: <http://www.theguardian.com/media/2010/apr/19/bauer-freelance-contracts-row> (accessed 28 July 2015).

Battelle, J. (2005) *The Search: How Google and Its Rivals Rewrote the Rules of Business and Transformed Our Culture*, London: Nicholas Brealey.

Bell, D. (1973) *The Coming of Post-industrial Society: A Venture in Social Forecasting*, New York: Basic Books.

Benkler, Y. (2006) *The Wealth of Networks: How Social Production Transforms Markets and Freedom*, New Haven, CT: Yale University Press.

Berniker, M. and Lipton, J. (2014) 'Atmosphere tense at a Google bus stop in San Francisco', CNBC, 13 February. Online. Available HTTP: <http://www.cnbc.com/2014/02/13/atmosphere-at-a-google-bus-stop-in-san-francisco.html> (accessed 28 July 2015).

Blair, T. (1998) *The Third Way: New Politics for the New Century*, Fabian Pamphlet 588, London: Fabian Society.

Bock, L. (2015) *Work Rules: Insights from Inside Google that will Transform How You Live and Lead*, New York: Hachette.

Botrsman, R. and Rogers, R. (2011) *What's Mine is Yours: How Collaborative Consumption is Changing the Way We Live*, London: Collins.

Cairncross, F. (1997) *The Death of Distance: How the Communications Revolution Will Change Our Lives*, London: Orion.

Cassidy, J. (2002) *dot.con*, London: Allen Lane.

Comor, E. (2015) 'Revisiting Marx's Value Theory: A Critical Response to Analyses of Digital Prosumption', *The Information Society*, 31 (13): 13–19.

comScore (2015) *UK Digital Market Overview*, April. Online. Available HTTP: <http://www.comscore.com/Insights/Presentations-and-Whitepapers/2015/UK-Digital-Market-Overview-April-2015> (accessed 28 July 2015).

Coyle, D. (1997) *The Weightless World: Strategies for Managing the Digital Economy*, Oxford: Capstone.

Diamandis, P. and Kotler, S. (2012) *Abundance: The Future is Better than You Think*, New York: Free Press.

Downes, L. (2009) *The Laws of Disruption: Harnessing the New Forces that Govern Life and Business in the Digital Age*, New York: Basic Books.

Downes, L. and Nunes, P. (2014) *Big Bang Disruption: Strategy in the Age of Devastating Innovation*, New York: Penguin.

Economist (2014) 'Everyone wants to rule the world', *Economist*, 29 November, 21–24.

Elberse, A. (2008) 'Should You Invest in the Long Tail?', *Harvard Business Review*, July–August, 1–11.

eMarketer (2014) 'Microsoft to Surpass Yahoo in Global Digital Ad Market Share This Year', *eMarketer*, 15 July. Online. Available HTTP: <http://www.emarketer.com/Article/Microsoft-Surpass-Yahoo-Global-Digital-Ad-Market-Share-This-Year/1011012> (accessed 28 July 2015).

eMarketer (2015) 'Google Will Take 55% of Search Ad Dollars Globally in 2015', *emarketer*, 31 March. Online. Available HTTP: <http://www.emarketer.com/Article/Google-Will-Take-55-of-Search-Ad-Dollars-Globally-2015/1012294> (accessed 28 July 2015).

Fiske, J. (1987) *Television Culture*, London: Methuen.

Fox, J. (2015) 'Netflix Wags Its Short Tail', *Bloomberg View*, 17 April. Online. Available HTTP: <http://www.bloombergview.com/articles/2015-04-17/former-long-tail-exemplar-netflix-goes-hollywood> (accessed 28 July 2015).

Freedman, D. (2014) *The Contradictions of Media Power*, London: Bloomsbury.

Fuchs, C. (2014) *Digital Labour and Karl Marx*, New York: Routledge.

Galloway, A. (2004) *Protocol: How Control Exists After Decentralization*, Boston: MIT Press.

Garnham, N. (1990) *Capitalism and Communication*, London: Sage.

Gartner (2014) 'Gartner Says the Internet of Things Will Transform the Data Centre', press release, 19 March. Online. Available HTTP: <http://www.gartner.com/newsroom/id/2684616> (accessed 28 July 2015).

Google (2004) *2004 Founders' IPO Letter*. Online. Available HTTP: <http://investor.google.com/corporate/2004/ipo-founders-letter.html> (accessed 24 October 2011).

Google (2010) *10-K Report*. Online. Available HTTP: <http://investor.google.com/documents/20101231_google_10K. html> (accessed 24 October 2011).

Gore, A. (2013) *The Future: Six Drivers of Global Change*, New York: Random House.

Graham, A. (1998) 'Broadcasting Policy and the Digital Revolution', *Political Quarterly*, 69 (B): 30–42.

Greengard, S. (2015) *The Internet of Things*, Cambridge, MA: MIT Press.

Guardian (2010) 'Factfile UK: Education, Sport and Culture', *Guardian*, 27 April.

Haque, U. (2005) 'The New Economics of Media', www.bubblegeneration.com. Online. Available HTTP: <http://www. scribd. com/doc/12177741/Media-Economics-The-New-Economics-of-Media-Umair-Haque> (accessed 20 April 2010).

Henwood, D. (2015) 'What the Sharing Economy Takes', *The Nation*, 27 January. Online. Available HTTP: <http://www.thenation.com/article/what-sharing-economy-takes/> (accessed 28 July 2015).

Hesmondhalgh, D. (2015) 'Exploitation and Media Labour', in R. Maxwell (ed.) *The Routledge Companion to Labor and Media*, New York: Routledge, 30–39.

Hill, S. (2015) 'The Future of Work in the Uber Economy', *Boston Review*, 22 July. Online. Available HTTP: <http://www.thenation.com/article/what-sharing-economy-takes/> (accessed 28 July 2015).

Howard, P. (2015) *Pax Technica: How the Internet of Things May Set Us Free or Lock Us Up*, New Haven, CT: Yale University Press.

Isaacson, W. (2014) *The Innovators: How A Group of Hackers, Geniuses, and Geeks Created the Digital Revolution*, New York: Simon and Schuster.

Jarvis, J. (2009) *What Would Google Do?*, New York: Collins Business.

Jarvis, J. (2014) *Geeks Bearing Gifts: Imagining New Futures for News*, New York: CUNY Journalism Press.

Khiabany, G. (2015) 'Uneven and Combined Independence of Social Media in the Middle East: Technology, Symbolic Production and Unproductive Labour' in J. Rodgers and N. Strange (eds) *Media Independence: Working with Freedom or Working for Free?* London: Routledge, 261–280.

Leadbeater, C. (1999) *Living on Thin Air*, London: Viking.

Leadbeater, C. (2009) *We-Think*, London: Profile Books.

Lessig, L. (2002) *The Future of Ideas: The Fate of the Commons in a Connected World*, New York: Vintage.

Machlup, F. (1962) *The Production and Distribution of Knowledge in the United States*, Princeton, NJ: Princeton University Press.

Madrick, J. (2001) 'The Business Media and the New Economy', Research Paper R-24, Harvard University, John F. Kennedy School of Government.

Marx, K. (1918) *Capital: A Critical Analysis of Capitalist Production, Volume One*, London: William Glaisher.

Marx, K. (1973) *Grundrisse: Foundations of the Critique of Political Economy*, New York: Vintage.

Marx, K. and Engels, F. (1975 [1848]) *Manifesto of the Communist Party*, Peking: Foreign Languages Press.

Mason, P. (2012) *Why It's Kicking Off Everywhere: The New Global Revolutions*, London: Verso.

Mason, P. (2015a) 'Welcome to a new way of living', *Guardian Review*, 18 July, 2–4.

Mason, P. (2015b) 'Airbnb and Uber's sharing economy is one route to dotcommunism', *Guardian G2*, 22 June, 5.

Mayer-Schonberger, V. and Cukier, K. (2013) *Big Data: A Revolution That Will Transform How We Live, Work and Think*, Boston: Houghton Mifflin Harcourt.

McChesney, R. (2013) *Digital Disconnect: How Capitalism is Turning the Internet Against Democracy*, New York: The New Press.

McQuivey, J. (2013) *Digital Disruption: Unleashing the Next Wave of Innovation*, Cambridge, MA: Forrester Research.

Meelen, T. and Frenken, K. (2015) 'Stop Saying Uber Is Part Of The Sharing Economy', *Fastcoexist*, 14 January. Online. Available HTTP: <http://www.fastcoexist.com/ 3040863/stop-saying-uber-is-part-of-the-sharing-economy> (accessed 28 July 2015).

Milberry, K. (2012) 'Hacking for Social Justice: The Politics of Prefigurative Technology', in A. Fennberg and N. Friesen (eds) *(Re)Inventing the Internet: Critical Case Studies*, Rotterdam: Sense Publishers, 109–130.

Mosco, V. (2009) *The Political Economy of Communication*, 2nd edn, London: Sage.

Negroponte, N. (1996) *Being Digital*, London: Coronet.

Oreskovic, A. (2010) 'Google CEO Says Company Tends to Create Enemies', Reuters. com, 13 April. Online. Available HTTP: <http://uk.reuters.com/article/idUK TRE63C0 AM20100413> (accessed 7 May 2010).

Pasquale, F. (2015) *The Black Box Society: The Secret Algorithms That Control Money and Information*, Cambridge, MA: Harvard University Press.

Petavy, F. (2014) 'My Top 10 Global Crowdsourced Campaigns of 2014', *Advertising Age*, 18 December. Online. Available HTTP: <http://adage.com/article/digitalnext/top-10-global-crowdsourced-campaigns-2014/296224/> (accessed 28 July 2015).

Pew (2015) *Teens, Social Media & Technology Overview 2015*. Pew Research Centre, 9 April. Online. Available HTTP: <http://www.pewinternet.org/2015/04/09/teens-social-media-technology-2015/> (accessed 28 July 2015).

Porat, M. (1977) *The Information Economy*, Ann Arbor, MI: University Microfilms.

Purcell, K., Buchanan, J. and Friedrich, L. (2013) *The Impact of Digital Tools on Student Writing and How Writing is Taught in Schools*. Pew Research Center, 16 July. Online. Available HTTP: <http://www.pewinternet.org/files/old-media//Files/Reports/2013/ PIP_NWP%20Writing%20and%20Tech.pdf> (accessed 28 July 2015).

Rifkin, J. (2014) *The Zero Marginal Cost Society: The Internet of Things, The Collaborative Commons and the Eclipse of Capitalism*, New York: Palgrave Macmillan.

Rose, D. (2014) *Enchanted Objects: Design, Human Desire and the Internet of Things*, New York: Scribner.

Schmidt, E. and Cohen, J. (2013) *The New Digital Age: Reshaping the Future of People, Nations and Businesses*, London: John Murray.

Schneiderman, E. (2014) *Airbnb in the City*. Office of New York State Attorney General. October. Online. Available HTTP: <http://www.ag.ny.gov/pdfs/Airbnb%20report.pdf> (accessed 28 July 2015).

Schneier, B. (2015) *Data and Goliath: The Hidden Battles to Collect Your Data and Control Your World*, New York: W.W. Norton.

Scholz, T. (ed). (2013) *Digital Labour: The Internet as Playground and Factory*, New York: Routledge.

Shirky, C. (2008) *Here Comes Everybody: the Power of Organizations without Organization*, London: Allen Lane.

Smith, T. (2000) *Technology and Capital in the Age of Lean Production*, Albany, NY: SUNY Press.

Sparks, C. (2000) 'From Dead Trees to Live Wires: The Internet's Challenge to the Traditional Newspaper', in J. Curran and M. Gurevitch (eds) *Mass Media and Society*, 3rd edn, London: Arnold, 268–292.

Stephany, A. (2015) *The Business of Sharing: Making it in the New Sharing Economy*, Houndmills: Palgrave Macmillan.

Surowiecki, J. (2004) *The Wisdom of Crowds*, New York: Doubleday.

Swisher, K. (2014) 'Man and Uberman', *Vanity Fair*, December. Online. Available HTTP: <http://www.vanityfair.com/news/2014/12/uber-travis-kalanick-controversy> (accessed 28 July 2015).

Sylvain, O. (2008) 'Contingency and the "Networked Information Economy": A Critique of *The Wealth of Networks*', *International Journal of Technology, Knowledge, and Society*, 4 (3): 203–210.

Tapscott, D. and Williams, A. (2008) *Wikinomics: How Mass Collaboration Changes Everything*, London: Atlantic Books.

Taylor, A. (2014) *The People's Platform: Taking Back Power and Culture in the Digital Age*, London: Fourth Estate.

Thiel, P. (2015) 'Competition Is For Losers', *Wall Street Journal*, 12 September. Online. Available HTTP: <http://www.wsj.com/articles/peter-thiel-competition-is-for-losers-1410535536> (accessed 28 July 2015).

Tode, C. (2015) '80pc of time spent in just five apps: Forrester', *Mobile Marketer*, 2 February. Online. Available HTTP: <http://www.mobilemarketer.com/cms/news/research/19673.html> (accessed 28 July 2015).

Toffler, A. (1980) *The Third Wave*, London: Pan Books.

Touraine, A. (1971) *The Post-industrial Society: Classes, Conflicts and Culture in the Programmed Society*, London: Wildwood House.

Turow, J. (2011) *The Daily You: How the New Advertising Industry Is Defining Your Identity and Your Worth*, New Haven, CT: Yale University Press.

Vise, D. (2008) *The Google Story*, London: Pan Books.

Wayne, M. (2003) *Marxism and Media Studies*, London: Pluto Press.

Williams, R. (1968 [1962]) *Communications*, Harmondsworth: Penguin.

Wolff, M. (2012) 'The Facebook Fallacy', *MIT Technology Review*, 22 May. Online. Available HTTP: <http://www.technologyreview.com/news/427972/the-facebook-fallacy/> (accessed 28 July 2015).

Wu, T. (2010) *The Master Switch: The Rise and Fall of Information Empires*, London: Atlantic.

Zittrain, J. (2008) *The Future of the Internet*, London: Penguin.

Chapter 4

The internet of rules

Critical approaches to online regulation and governance

Des Freedman

Introduction: leave us alone

On 8 February 1996, President Bill Clinton signed into law a major piece of legislation, the Telecommunications Act, the first comprehensive overhaul of US communications since the 1934 Communications Act. Broadly deregulatory in spirit, it contained within it one especially controversial section, the Communications Decency Act (CDA), which sought to regulate indecency and obscenity on a relatively new part of the world's communications infrastructure, the internet, and to criminalise the circulation of pornographic content to people under 18 years of age. Later that day, many thousands of miles away on a mountaintop in Switzerland, the former Grateful Dead lyricist and internet freedom activist John Perry Barlow published a call to arms that combined righteous indignation with libertarian passion. Barlow argued that the CDA 'attempts to place more restrictive constraints on the conversation in Cyberspace than presently exist in the Senate cafeteria, where I have dined and heard colorful indecencies spoken by United States senators on every occasion I did' (Barlow 1996). His considered reaction: 'Well, fuck them'.

There then followed a manifesto for an open and unregulated internet that resonates in the online world to this day.

> Governments of the Industrial World, you weary giants of flesh and steel, I come from Cyberspace, the new home of Mind. On behalf of the future, I ask you of the past to leave us alone. You are not welcome among us. You have no sovereignty where we gather. We have no elected government, nor are we likely to have one, so I address you with no greater authority than that with which liberty itself always speaks. I declare the global social space we are building to be naturally independent of the tyrannies you seek to impose on us. You have no moral right to rule us nor do you possess any methods of enforcement we have true reason to fear.
>
> (Barlow 1996)

Interestingly, Barlow published his declaration from Davos, home of the World Economic Forum, the annual summit of business and political leaders who spend one week each year strategising and brainstorming about how best to preserve the spirit of the free market and to minimise government interference in the running of industry. Not for the first (or the last) time, a fierce declaration of support for the independence of the internet coincided with an equally robust defence of the principles of an unfettered capitalism.

Barlow's homage to the liberal principles of the US Constitution and the freedom of cyberspace were echoed by many internet activists. Nicholas Negroponte, the founder of MIT's Media Lab, wrote in his celebrated guide to the online world, *Being Digital* (Negroponte 1996), of the difference, in relation to regulation, between analogue atoms and digital 'bits'. 'Most laws were conceived in and for a world of atoms, not bits. I think the law is an early-warning system telling us "This is a big one." National law has no place in cyberlaw' (1996: 237). Negroponte's argument was twofold. First, he insisted, following much contemporary globalisation theory (see, for example, Ohmae 1995), that the traditional nation-state had lost its privileged position as the repository of symbolic and political power. Nations are 'not small enough to be local and they are not large enough to be global' (Negroponte 1996: 238). Second, he highlighted what he saw as an inevitable restructuring of the media world, away from the domination of large bureaucracies and towards the emergence of a new, decentralised layer of 'cottage industries'. The consequence for Negroponte is that just as 'media have gotten bigger and smaller at the same time, so must world governance' (1996: 239).

For many influential enthusiasts of the new internet environment, this translated into a consensus that government intervention would only stifle the creativity and innovation that was a hallmark of cyberspace. The people best placed to shape the development of the internet were not public policy experts, let alone meddling bureaucrats, but the engineers and programmers who designed the internet in the first place as a series of networks that were intrinsically hostile to outside interference: as reflected in its military origins, 'the Net interprets censorship as damage and routes around it' (Gilmore 1993). According to Kevin Kelly, former executive editor of *Wired*, the in-house magazine of the online world, the result of this was that:

> No one controls the Net, no one is in charge. The U.S. government, which indirectly subsidizes the Net, woke up one day to find that a Net had spun itself, without much administration or oversight, among the terminals of the techno-elite. The Internet is, as its users are proud to boast, the largest functioning anarchy in the world.
>
> (Kelly 1995: 598)

For Esther Dyson, the founding chair of the domain-naming organisation the Internet Corporation for Assigned Names and Numbers (ICANN), government's role in relation to the internet was, necessarily, extremely limited. 'The question is how to focus the public's imagination on a better solution – not government regulation or even industry self-regulation, but an environment where consumers themselves can exercise their power and control their own information' (Dyson 1998: 6).

It is important to stress that these were voices reflecting a particular form of US libertarianism that is not necessarily illustrative of all political cultures but, nevertheless, they were (indeed, *are*) not marginal figures but individuals playing a decisive role in the popularisation of the internet across the globe. They reflected a passionately held view that, finally, here was a communication medium that could circumvent and potentially usurp the power of traditional gatekeepers – notably, 'old' media giants and all forms of government – and restore power to ordinary users. Despite the actual history of the internet, explored in Chapter 2 of this book, state power in its current form was viewed, not without reason, as we shall later see, as inimical to the free (in both monetary and political terms) and open development of networks that were characterised by principles of non-discrimination, decentralisation and connectivity.

This is hardly ancient history, but, given the developments on which this chapter focuses, it does appear that such libertarian narratives are emblematic of a very different period: when the internet was in its 'infancy', as opposed to the rather more mature stage of development in which it finds itself today. There is now a broad acceptance that, as with any large-scale communication medium with such vital economic and social significance, there needs to be at least a minimal system of rules to ensure its smooth functioning, safety and security. Of course, there is far less agreement concerning the forms that this regulation will take, together with the staffing, control and direction of the governance process in different countries. The situation is made massively more complicated by the ways in which the internet itself, as a technology predicated on facilitating abundance, interoperability and a lack of respect for national borders, has problematised and undermined traditional structures of regulation. As legal scholars Johnson and Post argued in a celebrated article concerning the inadequacy of existing legal regimes, the internet 'radically subverts a system of rule-making based on borders between physical spaces, at least with respect to the claim that cyberspace should naturally be governed by territorially defined rules' (Johnson and Post 1996: 1368).

This chapter, therefore, attempts to address key dynamics of the regulatory process as it has developed over the last two decades. Instead of simply trying to describe and list the various locations in and mechanisms through which this regulation takes place, it focuses on the most significant literature and mobilising ideas that have helped to shape what we now understand as 'internet regulation'. It highlights the turn towards 'governance' and code-based regulation, but also discusses the continuities between 'networked' and more established forms of communication regulation and, in particular, considers the central role of the state in presiding over network infrastructure. The chapter also considers how, despite different inflections in different countries, the internet is implicated in a fundamental neoliberal transformation of the power relations inside the regulatory process, and poses the question: who are the regulators now? In asking this question, it suggests that if we are to secure and extend the internet's public good characteristics, we need to challenge the current direction of travel and, instead, to devise regulatory systems that are independent from both commercial *and* governmental interests. The internet is itself a creature of public policy and it is entirely legitimate to propose that fully democratic states – and not outsourced private interests, repressive surveillance regimes, partisan administrations, authoritarian governments or opaque supranational bodies – should regulate the internet as a public utility that is accessible and accountable to all their citizens.

The non-governmentalisation of internet regulation

The anti-statist ideas that dominated the thinking of many internet advocates in the 1990s have morphed into a new consensus that the internet is best governed, wherever possible, by users and experts rather than politicians and governments. Thomas Friedman, in his best-selling account of the possibilities unleashed by capitalist globalisation, *The Lexus and the Olive Tree* (Friedman 2000), makes an explicit distinction between what he sees as desirable 'governance' and undesirable 'government', where the latter is viewed as a 'global cop'. Coercion, for Friedman, is generally more of a last resort in the pursuit of democracy and free markets: 'when you are the shaper of a coalition in support of a certain human value, you would be amazed at what you can do without global government to create better global governance' (2000: 206). In relation to a technological innovation that relies on open standards, coercive forms of control will be at best counter-productive and at worst destructive. Indeed, the reason why the internet is so dynamic, according to Friedman, is precisely because of an openness in which the 'best solutions win out quickly and the dead are removed from the battlefield quickly' (2000: 226).

Governance, unlike more top-down forms of government-induced regulation, refers to a dispersed and flexible form of organisation and is seen 'to imply a network form of control, to refer primarily to a process and to have associated with it diverse agents' (Daly 2003: 115–16). Laura DeNardis describes it as a form of 'bricolage', a system shaped by diverse actors (2014: 11), while for internet governance theorist Milton Mueller, 'it denotes the coordination and regulation of interdependent actors in the *absence* of an overarching political authority' (2010: 8). According to the UN Working Group on Internet Governance (WGIG), 'governance is the development and application by Governments, the private sector and civil society, in their respective roles, of shared principles, norms, rules, decision-making procedures and programmes that shape the evolution and use of the Internet' (quoted in de Bossey 2005: 4). Governance is, therefore, a more expansive and fluid concept than government, which 'refers not only to formal and binding rules, but also to numerous informal mechanisms, internal and external to the media, by which they are "steered" towards multiple (and often inconsistent) objectives' (McQuail 2005: 234). Rules are designed and protocols agreed on less by national governments operating in isolation than by specialist standards-setting organisations, like the Internet Engineering Task Force (IETF), the Internet Society and the World Wide Web Consortium (W3C), which have a normative, rather than a legal, power (Benkler 2006: 394). In a similar vein, the allocation of domain names is not a statutory exercise but one enforced by a private, non-profit company, ICANN, which has taken over duties previously carried out by the US government.

These organisations are emblematic of what supporters view as a more independent and meritocratic approach to regulation that mirrors directly the decentralised structure and participatory potential of the internet. For A. Michael Froomkin (2003), a standards-setting body like the IETF is perhaps the best institutional expression of a Habermasian commitment to discourse ethics and an operational public sphere. Froomkin argues that the IETF exhibits a 'high degree of openness and transparency' as well as 'a surprising degree of self-consciousness, or reflexivity, in that IETF participants have a common story that explains how the IETF came to be and why its outputs are legitimate' (2003: 799). Indeed, it is the commitment on behalf of IETF participants to the 'emancipatory potential of communication' that ends up being of 'instrumental value in enhancing both democracy and commerce' (2003: 810). Yes, it is highly specialist, male dominated and monolingual (meetings are conducted in English), but in its single-minded purpose to preserve open standards it is 'inherently communitarian' (2003: 816) and the best inspiration we have with which to pursue common agreement about the infrastructure of the internet.

Even ICANN, which has generated an enormous amount of criticism for failing to act in a transparent or democratic fashion, was initially greeted by some commentators as a potential harbinger of 'good' governance. According to Manuel Castells, writing in 2001, 'its by-laws embody the spirit of openness . . . decentralization, consensus-building and autonomy that characterized the *ad hoc* governance of the Internet over thirty years' (Castells 2001: 31). Whatever its actual shortcomings, Castells insisted that it was nevertheless very revealing that, to gain legitimacy, new bodies with oversight of the internet, such as ICANN, had to be set up 'on the tradition of meritocratic consensus-building that characterized the origins of the Internet' (2001: 33).

There has been a similar development at the international level. As a direct response to the internet's reluctance passively to yield to fixed, geographic borders, we have seen the emergence of a supranational governance regime that cannot be contained within traditional national systems of regulation. This includes both state-based supranational bodies like the World Trade Organization (WTO) and the World International Property Organization (WIPO), as well as ones with more civil society involvement like the World Summit on the Information Society, which met in 2003 and 2005 to discuss how best to overcome the digital divide, and the subsequent Internet Governance Forum which continues to meet annually. The internet has contributed, therefore, to the rise of a network of organisations that has led theorists to pronounce the emergence of a system of 'global governance' (see Ó Siochrú et al. 2002 in relation to the media and Radu, Chenou and

Weber 2014 in relation to the internet) composed primarily, but not exclusively, of intergovernmental agencies organised around the United Nations. According to Franklin, this is evidence of a decline in the power of nation-based policy structures and the re-spatialisation of ICT regulation: 'Translocal, transnational and supraterritorial trajectories and alliances overlay domestic–international demarcation lines as multilateral institutions broker "multi-stakeholder" meetings' (Franklin 2009: 223). A range of non-state actors from both the private sector and civil society are now central to the development and enforcement of contemporary information policies.

Governments and other stakeholders, however, are not only reaching up to a supranational level but also reaching down to establish independent or quasi-autonomous regulatory agencies within their national jurisdiction. This points to a willingness to part with a range of responsibilities that were previously carried out by the state but that have now been handed over to non-state organisations. The monitoring of content, allocation of domain names and the protection of privacy are all areas where the state (at least in some countries) has relinquished its role as sole arbiter of what is permissible or not. The preferred mechanisms of contemporary governance regimes are increasingly self-regulation, where industry modifies its behaviour in response to a set of agreed codes, and co-regulation, where industry works in partnership with the state to design and enforce adherence to rules (see Tambini et al. 2007 for an extensive discussion of modes of self-regulation of the internet). The European Commission's Audiovisual Media Services Directive, for example, explicitly advocates the use of self- and co-regulation to help deliver public policy objectives (EC 2010: 5).

Why should this be the case? Freedman (2008: 126) argues that the increasing appeal of self-regulation *across* the communications industry is a result, at least in part, of the desire by neoliberal actors to secure a more lightly regulated environment to pursue their own aims. However, there is little doubt that it is the characteristics of the internet itself that have galvanised the drive to self-regulation over statutory methods. For Ang (2008: 309–10), self-regulation can claim to be more appropriate for the online world, first because in the context of such a dynamic system, *informal* processes will be more adaptable to change and less likely to inhibit innovation and, second, because those in the best position to understand and then enforce any rules are unlikely to be judges or politicians, but entrepreneurs and software engineers. But there is another reason for the confluence of self-regulation with the online world. As Thomas Friedman puts it (2000: 471), 'precisely because the Internet is such a neutral, free, open and unregulated vehicle for commerce, education and communication, personal judgment and responsibility are critical when using this technology'. Self-regulation, in other words, appears to fit an environment in which content is freely extracted by the consumer and is not imposed by the broadcaster; it is suitable not only technologically but also culturally, as the individual user is credited with more agency than in analogue forms of media consumption. Self-regulation, to misquote Stanley Baldwin, aims to give the consumer both power *and* responsibility.

For example, illegal internet content in the UK is overseen not by a government department but by an industry-funded body, the Internet Watch Foundation (IWF), set up by a group of internet service providers (ISPs) in 1996. The IWF argues that, as most illegal material, for example images of child sexual abuse and violent pornography, is hosted outside the UK and thus not accountable to UK obscenity or child protection laws, a new approach is needed. While it presses similar bodies in other countries to warn authorities about the existence of this material, it focuses its activity on passing on individual complaints to UK ISPs concerning the existence of illegal content on their networks and encourages them to remove it as quickly as possible: the policy of 'notice and takedown'. According to Peter Robbins, former chief executive of the IWF, the system works on 'consensus': 'It's a corporate social responsibility of many of the companies that fund us to try and do something to make a difference to the type of content that we deal with' (Robbins 2009: 9). By providing a hotline service and working closely with both the police and ISPs, the IWF claims that the amount of UK-hosted child pornography has declined to less than 1% of the total and that this material is often taken down within one hour. Self-regulation, claims Susie Hargreaves, the current CEO, 'ensures that the IWF model remains relevant as it is able to react to changes in the online environment much faster than it would if the IWF was bound by statute' (quoted in Hulin and Stone 2013: 55).

UK law, in accordance with European e-commerce regulations, exempts ISPs and other online intermediaries from any liability for content where they can establish their status as 'mere conduits'; in other words, where they can demonstrate that they have not knowingly circulated illegal material. Liability in this case rests with the original author or poster of the material. While early case law in the UK tended to rule against such 'innocent distribution' defences, recent cases have been more sympathetic to ISPs, proving perhaps the increasing effectiveness of self-regulation. Indeed, Zittrain (2009) argues that the 'notice and takedown' approach is a useful balance between copyright protection and amateur expression that operates on a reactive, rather than a proactive, model that better suits the permissive environment of the internet: 'a preemptive intervention to preclude some particular behaviour actually disempowers the people who might complain about it to decide that they are willing, after all, to tolerate it' (2009: 120). For Zittrain, this reflects the 'generative' nature of a technology where accessibility, unpredictability and 'unanticipated change' are at the heart of its appeal (2009: 70) and, therefore, where 'top-down' regulation is best minimised.

The growing tension between the 'generative' and the 'non-generative' in relation to regulation is most powerfully expressed by Yochai Benkler, who argues in *The Wealth of Networks* (Benkler 2006) that new, commons-based forms of information production are challenging incumbent, centralised and hierarchical information flows. Nowhere is this battle between the old and the new more visible than in the sphere of law and regulation, where battles over, for example, copyright, patents and the shape of social production are constantly being waged. For Benkler, this suggests a 21st century 'clash of civilizations' where 'political and judicial pressures to form an institutional ecology that is decidedly in favor of proprietary business models are running headlong into the emerging social practices described throughout this book' (2006: 470). Regulation, however, does not appear to constitute a neutral process in the midst of this battle. Given how often the law has been used in a 'reactive and reactionary' (2006: 393) fashion to protect the interests of industrial actors and to contain the possibilities of the emerging social sharing media, regulation, for Benkler, seems to be expressive of an outdated information ecology. While he acknowledges that intervention may be necessary in limited circumstances, for example to open up a market using antitrust measures, what the 'emerging networked information economy therefore needs, in almost all cases, is not regulatory protection, but regulatory abstinence' (2006: 393).

The governmentalisation of internet regulation

Yet there is an alternative history to the formation of an idiosyncratic governance regime for the internet, perhaps best expressed by Mueller's rather understated comment that, referring to the classic statement of cyber-libertarianism, 'Barlow's declaration hasn't aged well' (Mueller 2002: 266). There is instead another narrative that stresses that, despite globalisation processes, national governments and legal authorities continue to play key roles in shaping, populating and enforcing the various agencies and mechanisms involved in the regulation of online networks. From the US Digital Millennium Copyright Act of 1998, which sought to impose a heavily proprietorial intellectual property regime on the new digital environment through the mandating of anti-circumvention devices (Benkler 2006: 413–18), to the UK's Digital Economy Act of 2010, which sanctions the disconnection of users persistently engaging in unlicensed downloads (see Doctorow 2010 for a critical view); from the Clinton administration's critical role in setting up ICANN in 1998 to the Chinese government's continuing control of access to the internet; from state support for the extension of copyright in both Europe and the US to increasing state surveillance of personal data across the world; and from US court rulings on net neutrality to the European Court's ruling on the 'right to be forgotten' (European Commission 2014) – the imprint of law and government is rarely absent from internet governance schemes. Indeed, to the extent that the state power over the internet *had* started to slip with the emergence of multilateral bodies and self-regulatory agencies, Mueller (2010: 4) asserts that states have more recently fought back in what he describes as a 'counter-revolution'. While there will be different inflections of regulatory intervention in different countries, state coordination and oversight of the internet is increasingly significant.

The most celebrated account of and justification for the continuing role of nation-state-based regulation of the internet was developed by Goldsmith and Wu (2006) in their book subtitled 'Illusions of a Borderless World'. Goldsmith and Wu argue that not only are national borders and territorial governments still meaningful in a globalised world, but governments, at least the representative ones, are actually best placed to protect democratic institutions and spaces: 'With an open and free press, regular elections and an independent judiciary, democratic governments are the best system that human beings have ever devised for aggregating the varied interests and desires of a sovereign people into a workable governing order' (2006: 142). Supranational or hyperlocal assemblies may serve a purpose, but ultimately, while one can 'criticize traditional territorial government and bemoan its many failures, there is no reasonable prospect of any better system of governmental organization' (2006: 153).

Drawing on a traditional Weberian conception of states in relation to their monopoly of coercive power, Goldsmith and Wu insist that those people who thought the internet was outside the jurisdiction of nation-state-based forms of law were, quite simply, wrong: 'the last ten years have shown that national governments have an array of techniques for controlling offshore Internet communications, and thus enforcing their laws, by exercising coercion within their borders' (2006: viii). Even Schmidt and Cohen, who admit to describing the internet 'as a "lawless" space, ungoverned and ungovernable by design', note that 'states have an enormous amount of power over the *mechanics* of the Internet in their own countries' (2013: 82) and devote a whole chapter of their book to considering the relationship between the internet and state power. Manuel Castells argues that the need for the regulation of online spaces started to be taken seriously in 2000, when governments first started to wake up to the threat posed by cybercrime (2001: 177). In an attempt to restore order and win back control of the regulatory arena, 'it became necessary for the most important governments to act together, creating a new global space of policing . . . a network of regulatory and policing agencies' (2001: 178). Castells identifies the emergence of a new architecture, built on commercialisation and surveillance, that becomes 'the fundamental tool of control, making it possible to exercise regulation and policing by traditional forms of state power' (2001: 179).

This policing was dramatically illustrated by the reaction to the publication in 2010 of some 250,000 US embassy cables by the whistle-blowing website WikiLeaks (Leigh and Harding 2013). The cables revealed embarrassing details of diplomatic missives concerning the international community, including Anglo-American doubts about the security of the Pakistani nuclear industry, allegations of corruption involving the US-backed Afghan government and evidence of the Saudi regime's call to bomb Iran. Many countries adopted a distinctly non-libertarian stance to the circulation of the cables: China, Pakistan, Thailand (and the US Air Force) blocked access to some or all of the material, while the US Army and the White House warned employees against accessing classified material (IFEX 2010). The US Department of Justice then issued a subpoena demanding that Twitter hand over details of its users in relation to an ongoing investigation of the leaks, while Mastercard, Visa and PayPal all severed links with WikiLeaks after pressure from senior figures in Washington, D.C. (Hals 2010). WikiLeaks itself leaked an intelligence report by the Cyber Counterintelligence Assessments Branch on the dangers posed by the organisation that contained the following threat: 'The identification, exposure, or termination of employment of or legal actions against current or former insiders, leakers, or whistleblowers could damage or destroy this center of gravity and deter others from using Wikileaks.org to make such information public' (Army Counterintelligence Center 2008: 3).

Further evidence of the state's policing of the digital realm was provided by former US National Security Agency (NSA) operative Edward Snowden in 2013 when he leaked documents that revealed the existence of widespread government surveillance of the communications of ordinary citizens. Programmes like PRISM in the US and Tempora in the UK are vast, sophisticated and centralised systems for acquiring the metadata of telephone conversations, e-mails and social media activity for intelligence purposes. Snowden showed how the security services were working covertly with tech companies to collect – indiscriminately – raw data from citizens without their consent or knowledge on a mass scale.

> The U.S. government, in conspiracy with client states, chiefest among them the Five Eyes – the United Kingdom, Canada, Australia and New Zealand – have inflicted upon the world a system of secret, pervasive surveillance from which there is no refuge. They protect their domestic systems from the oversight of citizens through classification and lies, and shield themselves from outrage in the event of leaks by overemphasizing limited protections they choose to grant the governed.'
>
> (Quoted in Greenwald 2014)

Snowden's revelations caused shockwaves, especially in the US, and helped to start a conversation about rights to privacy and confidentiality that culminated in June 2015 with the replacement of the Patriot Act with the USA Freedom Act. Although this involves a slightly more restrictive legislative framework for bulk collection of communications data (Yuhas 2015), public pressure was not sufficient to get President Obama to issue a pardon to Snowden himself (Siddiqui 2015). The response to such a brazenly illiberal use of the state to monitor its citizens was rather more muted in the UK and the government is still determined to introduce a Communications Data Bill – otherwise known as a 'Snooper's Charter' – that would permit communications companies to retain personal data for up to a year for inspection by security personnel (Boffey 2015).

From a neoliberal perspective, state power is required to correct the 'increasingly Hobbesian' (Lewis 2010: 63) nature of the internet, to treat the online world as a 'failed state', much in the same way that military intervention has been justified to restore US-style democracy to physical territories such as Iraq and Afghanistan. James Lewis of the Center for Strategic and International Studies argues that while self-regulation has deep roots in an American political culture that has privileged scientific approaches and a discourse of 'engineering efficiency' (2010: 61), a hands-off approach is no longer sufficient to allow the state to maintain control. The idea that a functioning rule of law would spontaneously emerge to preside over the internet has been disproved and, instead, 'passive sovereignty is evolving into a more active assertion of the rights of national governments to exert their control' (2010: 63). This is a particularly urgent task for the US government because it is already being challenged by other regions and sovereign states, most notably China, which are starting to assert their own power over the internet. 'In this new phase of administering and securing the internet', Lewis concludes, 'governments will lead, not private actors' (2010: 64).

Such a statement, however, implies a false dichotomy between government and the private sector, given the fact that the US government (and it is by no means the only one) has long adopted a pro-business approach to the internet and is well aware of the importance of the internet for economic development. This is best described by Ira Magaziner, President Clinton's adviser on technology matters and a key individual in the Clinton administration's team that sought to build up the internet sector in the heady days of the 1990s. It is worth quoting him at length, not least because of his remarks' contemporary relevance, as he confirms the US government's commitment to a:

> market-driven approach to the development of the internet. We felt that it was a bottom up kind of medium that should not be over-regulated, and we felt that we wanted to preserve the organic nature of the internet, but to set in motion a series of predictable rules that would allow commerce to take place because commerce requires a certain amount of predictability. So we advocated creation of uniform commercial code to govern transactions, market oriented approach to digital signatures; we opposed censorship of the internet, felt that that should be free content on the internet, that you wanted to evolve the government's mechanism to one that would gain global acceptance but that would still be market-driven and not heavy regulation. We advocated not having taxes on the internet, getting agreement for internet commerce to be free of tariffs across borders, and also to avoid internet taxation. At that time there were proposals floating around to tax bits. We proposed leaving, not having the FCC or ITU regulate the internet the way they did telecom, to keep the packet-switch networks out of FCC regulation.
>
> (quoted in Lewis 2010: 65)

Far from governments retreating from the desire to control their online environments, Magaziner's comments make it clear how governments have sought to micro-manage the evolution of the internet and to secure an online space that is safe for business, reliable for consumers, acceptable to government and accessible by intelligence agencies. They may call this 'light-touch' regulation, but it is circumscribed by a more coercive element that suggests that underlying the 'velvet glove' remains an 'iron fist'.

The codification of internet regulation

Yet the debate on internet regulation remains mired in a conceptual impasse between claims that cyberspace can or cannot easily be regulated, that any regulation that does occur should be subject to statutory or voluntary oversight, that regulation should be supervised by national or supranational regimes. Perhaps the most effective answer to this conundrum is provided by Stanford law professor Lawrence Lessig, who rejects the notion that regulation is somehow external to or imposed on technological systems like the internet. Instead he argues in his celebrated account of the internet that 'cyberspace is regulated by its code' (Lessig 2006: 79). The programmes, protocols and platforms that make up the internet are not separate from but the very stuff *of* regulation. Software and hardware constitute the architectural foundation of cyberspace – its code – and this is what essentially structures online spaces. Code, according to Lessig, refers to 'the instructions embedded in the software or hardware that make cyberspace what it is. This code is the "built environment" of social life in cyberspace. It is its "architecture"' (2006: 121), which then embeds particular values into the technology and facilitates certain possibilities or, of course, presents certain constraints for the user. So just as open networks allow for unfiltered conversations, paywalls are designed to shut people out; while open-source software encourages experimentation and remediation, 'tethered' devices like the iPad and iTouch try to stop you from leaving their space. So it is not enough to say that the internet is regulated by external forces, as networks themselves act to regulate their own environments, to induce certain forms of behaviour and to clamp down on others.

Crucially, Lessig works with a very expansive notion of regulation that goes way beyond the mere implementation of particular legal provisions or guiding principles. Regulation is 'produced' by the interaction of four 'modalities': the law, social norms, the market and architecture (2006: 123). The first three are not so contentious: we control our behaviour in the face of what the law may throw at us, with a regard to what is seen as 'acceptable' or not and also in the context of what the market makes available. Indeed, we have also long been regulated by physical architecture – witness Foucault's analysis of the self-regulatory impact of the Panopticon (Foucault 1977) – but, in the intersection of these four 'modalities', power in and over the online world is rapidly shifting towards those who design the hardware or who write the software. According to Lessig, 'code writers are increasingly lawmakers. They determine what the defaults of the Internet will be; whether privacy will be protected; the degree to which anonymity will be allowed; the extent to which access will be guaranteed' (2006: 79). DeNardis concurs: in relation to internet governance, 'arrangements of technical architecture are also arrangements of power' (2014: 9).

Lessig actually distinguishes between two types of code. 'Open code', such as that which drives peer-to-peer networks and free software, fosters a kind of transparency in networked behaviour (2006: 153); 'closed code', on the other hand, is designed, above all, for proprietorial purposes and, while being far more opaque, now plays a central role in a market-driven internet space. After a period of collaboration and experimentation, commercial interests are increasingly defining the architecture of the online world: code becomes a vital commodity and, as such, enters the orbit of government's desire to foster a rule-bound and lucrative market for code-based services and products. According to Lessig, 'as code writing becomes commercial – as it becomes the product of a smaller number of companies – the government's ability to regulate it increases' (2006: 71), to the detriment of the 'open code' that has a far more democratic and inclusive flavour.

Lessig's account of code as regulation may smack of determinism – in the sense that code seems intrinsically to prescribe certain forms of behaviour – and it is certainly open to co-option by pro-state forces who recognise the power of internet architectures. Regulation by code, according to Goldsmith and Wu, for example, is essential and part of 'an underlying system of territorial government and physical coercion' (2006: 181), while for Lewis (2010: 63), 'those who set the standards, manufacture the hardware and write the code have a deep degree of control'. Lessig's point, however, is actually quite different. He is keen to stress that the internet, like any built environment, is always open to intervention and re-coding. As Zittrain (2009: 197) warns, 'code is law, and commerce and government can work together to change the code'. Although everyday regulation of the internet may occur through small-scale actions – Lessig deploys the notion of 'bovinity', where '[t]iny controls, consistently enforced, are enough to direct very large animals' (2006: 73) – he is scathing about those who fail to see the bigger picture and who refuse to act to stop the imminent enclosure of the internet by commercial code. The failure to act, he argues, 'will produce not no regulation at all, but regulation by the most powerful of special interests' (2006: 337–8). The struggle for open code is no less than a struggle for democracy and against the potential abuse of state power: 'open code is a foundation for an open society' (2006: 153).

Libertarian ideas have not disappeared off the face of the Earth

Lessig describes the complacency of those who continue to sit back in the face of the increasing circulation of 'closed code' as evidence of 'libertarian failure' (2006: 337). But surely, given the emergence of the governance regimes described in previous sections, libertarianism – the belief that individual freedom is best guaranteed by a lack of state intrusion into private matters – poses little threat in contrast to government or market failure. It is true that the passionate conviction of Barlow, Negroponte and others in the 1990s, that the internet is fundamentally hostile to and distorted by formal regulation, has been superseded by events. There remains, however, a powerful libertarian undercurrent in arguments that propose, if not the complete abolition of any kind of public oversight of the internet, only *minimal* levels of interference into the operation of a self-correcting organism such as the internet that is, according to this perspective, best served by market competition.

One factor that underpins the continuing attraction of libertarian ideas is the resilience of technologically determinist approaches to the internet, including the notion that the internet is, due to its DNA, fundamentally dealigned from existing systems of regulation. While there have been powerful critiques of determinism in the social sciences more broadly (see, for example, Williams 1974 and Webster

2006), Sonia Livingstone is right to suggest that 'it remains the assumption behind much public policy associated with social uses of the internet' (Livingstone 2010: 125). We can see this in the notion that digitalisation, simply by facilitating duplication, increasing scale and lowering costs of entry, is said to undermine traditional approaches to the enforcement of copyright, the protection of minors and the regulation of content. According to Emily Bell in an opinion piece for the *Guardian* (headed 'Digital media cannot be contained by the analogue rulebook'), 'once something is digitized, the ability over time to control it, charge for it, regulate it or contain it exponentially decreases' (Bell 2009: 4). This is very different to Lessig's proposition that, while code may enhance or constrain specific forms of online behaviour, it is not at all the case that code makes regulation impossible.

Second, we have the continuing hegemony of neoliberalism in which a combination of anti-state triumphalism and market economics 'permeates substantive broadband policymaking' (Sylvain 2010: 250). For Sylvain, the rather romantic libertarian ideas of 1990s internet pioneers, based on what he describes as 'engineering' principles of decentralisation, interoperability and consumer sovereignty, continue to motivate many in the policy community although, in practice, these ideas 'amount to little more than a policy of administrative deference to engineers, programmers, and entrepreneurs – not positive law per se' (2010: 224). In 2002, for example, Vint Cerf, one of the founders of the internet and chairman of ICANN, declared in a much-quoted statement for the Internet Society that the 'Internet is for everyone – but it won't be if Governments restrict access to it, so we must dedicate ourselves to keeping the network unrestricted, unfettered and unregulated' (Cerf 2002). The chairman of Google, Eric Schmidt, made precisely the same point some years later when he bemoaned the impact of state intervention into the online world and, in particular, threats to regulate Google itself: 'When markets get regulated, creative innovation is slowed . . . A much better outcome is for us to use good judgement. We take what we see as the consumer interest as our guiding principle' (quoted in Palmer 2009).

The association of deregulation with dynamism, and of intervention with illiberalism, is present in many key internet policy debates. When European politicians discussed whether to incorporate new 'non-linear' services into the European Union's Television without Frontiers Directive in 2006, Shaun Woodward, then UK communications minister, warned that 'the extension of scope will create huge new regulatory burdens, expensive and impossible to enforce . . . We shouldn't put restrictions in place to inhibit growth and innovation' (quoted in Freedman 2008: 126). This was only a mild version of comments made by James Murdoch, the former CEO of BSkyB, who in the previous year had argued that a 'totally new approach which recognizes the new on-demand world we live in is badly needed . . . there is a long way to go before consumers enjoy the sovereignty that is their right. We don't need more controls to achieve that. We need a bonfire of controls' (quoted in Freedman 2008: 127). In the end, the revised Directive (EC 2010) accepted many of these arguments and recommended a far more deregulatory approach to on-demand services than those still maintained on broadcast outlets.

We find similar arguments being proposed in relation to the vexed question of net neutrality, the regulatory response to the ability of certain providers to restrict or segregate the distribution of content online. Indeed many commentators have insisted that formal government protection of neutrality is an affront to the very principles of openness, consumer sovereignty and decentralisation that characterise the internet's appeal. Larry Downes (2009: 128–37), for example, argues that net neutrality legislation will be both hard to police and counter-productive because the internet's architecture is already based on a concept of neutrality that is intrinsic to, not imposed on, its networks. Furthermore, laws that have been passed in relation to the internet are, for the most part, 'ignored, thanks to the Internet's ability to treat regulation as a network failure and reroute around the problem' (2009: 137). One lobby group with ties to the conservative Koch brothers describes net neutrality as 'Marxist', 'one of the biggest attacks on our free-market economy' and 'the first step in the fight to destroy American capitalism altogether' (Koebler 2014). These comments exemplify what Victor Pickard has called 'corporate libertarianism', a perspective that 'conflates corporate privilege with First Amendment freedoms' (Pickard 2015: 190) and seems to resonate closely with many of the telecoms interests in net neutrality debates.

In the op-ed pages of the *New York Times*, a group of prominent neoliberal economists even went so far as to praise the European approach to net neutrality as a model example of negative policy: 'Perhaps the most noteworthy things about the European regulations is what they do not do. They do not prescribe business or pricing models for European telecommunications companies' (Mayo et al. 2010). Forcing 'heavy-handed rules' on such a dynamic system will, from this perspective, only squash innovation and distort competition. 'Official' contributions to European net neutrality debates have tended to rely heavily on legal and economic arguments that lack a focus on broader theories of the public interest, citizenship or, in particular, democracy. By reducing it to a mere 'traffic management' issue (Ofcom 2010), European policymakers have sought to limit what should be a discussion about how best we should make available information, media and culture to online audiences, to a much narrower preoccupation with ill-defined notions of 'transparency', 'competition' and 'openness' that sit happily with libertarian approaches. In the UK, communications minister Ed Vaizey has challenged the need for neutrality regulations on the basis that the country already has a competitive broadband market and that a lightly regulated internet is 'good for business, good for the economy and good for people' (quoted in Halliday 2010). When forced to clarify his comments, Vaizey declared that he was not ruling out intervention in the future but that he was indeed against 'heavy-handed' regulation and was not prepared 'to put regulatory hurdles in the way – the last 20 years have told us not to do that' (quoted in Warman 2010). Not surprisingly, therefore, the European Commission announced in spring 2015 that they had reached an agreement that would both protect net neutrality *and* allow for 'specialised services of higher quality' to 'make sure that all needs are served, that all opportunities can be seized and that no one is forced to pay for a service that is not needed' (quoted in Lapowsky 2015). It was widely greeted by digital activists as sanctioning a two-tier internet.

In the US, however, a grassroots campaign for net neutrality caught the imagination of millions of Americans and eventually forced the Federal Communications Commission in early 2015 to reclassify broadband internet as a 'common carrier' telecommunications service. New rules were introduced, in spite of a powerful lobby led by cable companies, to prevent broadband providers from slowing down or discriminating against internet traffic, no matter its origin. According to Tim Berners-Lee, the founder of the web, this was a significant victory both for ordinary citizens and for an open internet: net neutrality is 'about consumer rights, it's about free speech, it's about democracy' (quoted in Rushe 2015).

To what extent does the fact that the Federal Communications Commission (FCC) was able to introduce net neutrality rules suggest that it is perhaps possible to overstate the influence of libertarian ideas in the regulatory environment? It is certainly true that the net neutrality campaign in the US was a decisive blow to the vested interests of the dominant telecoms and cable companies and that the FCC rules demonstrate the potential application of regulation in the public interest. Milton Mueller, however, argues that while it is right to see net neutrality in terms of the neutralising of dominant players and the protection of a 'commons', net neutrality itself is actually a balancing act between commons-based and proprietorial interests and is thus far from a rejection of market forces. 'Progressive intellectuals should not be seduced by the warm and fuzzy communitarian overtones of the common ideal' just as 'pro-market liberals need to overcome their association of commons with "communism" and heavy-handed regulation' (2012: 42). Indeed, President Obama warmly greeted the FCC ruling on the basis that the rules were needed to secure the long-term strategic interests of US capital in this area: an 'open Internet is essential to the American economy, and increasingly to our very way of life . . . We cannot allow Internet service providers (ISPs) to restrict the best access or to pick winners and losers in the online marketplace for services and ideas' (Obama 2015).

We should also not forget that net neutrality's opponents have not given up and that the determination of the Republicans, together with some major industry figures, to overturn the rules demonstrates the continuing presence of pro-market, anti-state ideologies. The fact that several major industry lobbies including the Cellular Telecommunications Industry Association, the National Cable & Telecommunications Association and USTelecom all announced lawsuits against the FCC for over-reaching its authority immediately after the new rules were passed (Thielman 2015) is further evidence that libertarian ideas are likely to play a significant role in future internet regulation debates.

Limitations of governance regimes

Libertarian or not, one issue on which many commentators continue to agree is the desirability of self-regulation and, particularly following the Snowden disclosures, the use of non-state institutions for internet governance. This argument is made not just by free-market enthusiasts with a natural hostility to state intervention but also by activists who are keen to extend the principles of content-sharing networks and non-proprietorial practices into the regulatory layer of the internet. The success of Wikipedia, the widespread use of open-source software and the popularity of peer-to-peer sites all suggest, as we have already discussed, that there is a need to move away from traditional top-down forms of regulatory authority and towards more consensual governance spaces like the Internet Governance Forum (IGF) and more flexible practices of self-regulation and self-governance.

Critics, however, point to a significant problem: that such practices have not led to an internet free from viruses, spam, illegal content and security risks or, of course, to an online environment independent of either corporate control or state influence. Jonathan Zittrain, for example, argues that the internet's 'generative' nature, its openness and unpredictability, are precisely the qualities that allow worms, viruses and malware increasingly to suffuse its networks. Indeed, as the internet has become further institutionalised and commercialised, a business model for 'bad code' (Zittrain 2009: 45) has emerged in which the threat to launch a cyberattack has serious financial consequences. 'The economics', argues Zittrain (2009: 47), 'is implacable: viruses are now valuable properties, and that makes for a burgeoning industry in virus making where volume matters'. Furthermore, the US, with its established systems of self-regulation, is at, or near, the top of the rankings when it comes to instances of malicious activity (2009: 49).

Others are critical of the viability of specific regimes of self-regulation. According to Peng Hwa Ang (2008), attempts to protect online privacy or to develop workable and popular content labelling and filtering systems have been generally disappointing. This is partly because there are few effective enforcement mechanisms and partly because internet users constitute such a diverse and diffuse group. 'The easiest solution to heterogeneity is to set the lowest standard. But that undermines the confidence of users in the self-regulatory regime. All things considered, therefore', Ang concludes (2008: 311), 'the conditions for self-regulation of the Internet are absent'. In relation to the UK in particular, Richard Collins challenges the myth 'that network governance and self-regulation is both pervasive and dominant' (2009: 51). Instead, Collins identifies a system in which hierarchical and horizontal forms of governance coexist and in which self-regulation offers only an unstable support for the system as a whole. Given that most industry players view each other as rivals rather than collaborators, and given the power of the largest firms to shape the self-regulatory agenda, Collins argues that the UK's 'self-regulatory governance structures may not be well adapted to securing long-term public interest objectives' (2009: 57). Largely unaccountable, reactive and susceptible to or driven by industry interests, self-regulation has proved to be an inconsistent advocate for a robust, competitive and equitable system.

Olivier Sylvain presents a more sustained critique of self-regulation in which he relates the 'delegation of rulemaking to nongovernmental bodies' directly to the neoliberal belief that 'unimpeded market competition is generally the most efficient and objective adjudicator of contests between market actors' (2010: 233). Governance schemes are, according to Sylvain, all too often based on engineering principles like decentralisation, user empowerment and interoperability that, while powerful in a technical sense, are not necessarily adequate for developing a public-minded communications policy. When Lessig argues that 'open code' ought to preclude the need for government intervention or when Froomkin claims that a private self-regulatory organisation like the IETF is based on a high level of discourse ethics, Sylvain replies that this kind of technological approach to governance is 'untenable' (2010: 231), for two main reasons. First, because not everyone in the internet community is sympathetic to social production and collaborative methods, and second, because the power to select or enforce common standards is distributed extremely unequally (2010: 232).

This is borne out by analysis of the emergence of one of the most important regulatory bodies, ICANN. While ICANN, as we saw earlier, was created with particular emphasis on its self-governance and autonomy, Milton Mueller (1999) claims that this was merely a rhetorical device designed to obscure key issues concerning the US government's determination to maintain oversight over the domain-naming process. Industry self-regulation, he argues, 'was an appealing label for a process that could be more accurately described as the US government brokering a behind-the-scenes deal among what it perceived as the major players – both private and governmental' (1999: 504). Outsiders, however, were more positive, reading self-regulation as 'an open invitation for the internet community to set aside their differences and come together to forge a new consensus' (1999: 506). This led to a twin-track process: one open, democratic and discursive, the other closed and opaque and led by private organisations like the Internet Assigned Numbers Authority (IANA) and IBM (1999: 506). According to Mueller, this has produced a clear contradiction between principles of self-organisation and the unaccountable lobbying that took place, as a result of which the 'Commerce Dept basically devolved global state power to ICANN' (1999: 516). In conclusion, the setting up of ICANN was 'part of the process by which established economic players and arrangements assimilate internetworking' (Mueller 2002: 267) and attempt to take control of the 'root', the internet's address system. Far from reflecting new forms of consensual politics, it owes its allegiance to old corporatist, hierarchical structures and deferential forms of behaviour.

At the supranational level, there are far more sympathetic critiques (for example Mathiason 2009; Raboy, Landry and Shtern 2010) of fora like WSIS and the IGF in which civil society and social movements can claim to have forced issues concerning the digital divide, universal access and democratic governance onto the agenda. Franklin (in press) writes persuasively about the drawing up of the Charter of Human Rights and Principles for the Internet, a document that 'articulates the past, present and future of the internet from a rights-based sensibility, and [which] does so in substantive moral, legal and political terms'. Yet, despite the reforms that activists can point to as a result of sustained civil society engagement, Mueller argues that, at its core, multistakeholderism is process, more than ends, driven: 'While it does address the problem of democracy and participation, it mostly evades the key axes of national sovereignty and hierarchical power' (2010: 264). Zittrain echoes this point, arguing that dialogues at gatherings like WSIS 'end either in bland consensus pronouncements or in final documents that are agreed upon only because the range of participants has been narrowed' (2009: 242). According to Castells (2009: 115), the value of WSIS and IGF is undermined, as 'they are not directed towards specific corporations or organizations but at the user community at large'. They are weak precisely because they are unable to combat the unequal agenda-setting power of the most influential players and therefore continue to submit to 'relentless pressure from two essential sources of domination that still loom over our existence: capital and the state' (2009: 116).

Indeed, pro-state commentators tend to illustrate the argument that the state has not at all withdrawn from the governance sphere simply by facilitating new self-governance arrangements at a domestic and international level. Goldsmith and Wu, for example, describe how the US government achieved its aim to develop an internet system fit for purpose through outsourcing many operations. 'The United States, while talking about things like "bottom up governance" and "the Internet community" never actually ceded control over either ICANN or the root' (2006: 169). According to James Lewis, a proponent of the state's role in regulating the internet in response to the challenge of international competition, multistakeholder governance structures afford much-needed legitimacy to state institutions. 'Countries are beginning to assert sovereign control over their national cyberspace. The next steps will be to deploy technologies to let them enforce control *and to create multilateral governance structures to legitimize these actions*' (2010: 63, emphasis added).

The idea that such structures have been created, in part, to lend democratic legitimacy to processes that have at their heart the re-establishment of state oversight over the internet should not imply that self-governance *cannot* make a contribution to more participatory forms of regulation. But until multistakeholder bodies combine an interest in procedural matters with a willingness to campaign independently at the national and supranational level for an *alternative* agenda to those of the most powerful states and companies, they will continue to be marginalised. Indeed, tensions between state and civil society groups as well as between civil society groups themselves have long been in evidence inside spaces like WSIS and the IGF. For example, activists have now set up an Internet Ungovernance Forum 'to expose the areas of discussion not up for debate at the IGF and [to] question the fundamental ideas of governance on which it rests' (Hintz 2014). Echoing the point made by Lewis above, Hintz suggests that the multistakeholder process has been captured by powerful groups and that 'civil society may not be in a position to significantly make its mark on an agenda dominated by others with diametrically opposed interests, instead only lending it a legitimacy it doesn't deserve' (Hintz 2014). Multistakeholder governance, it seems, has not proved to be a viable solution to the problems posed by entrenched state and corporate power.

The privatisation of internet regulation?

The claim that the internet is either 'regulated' or 'unregulated' is an unhelpful binary, not simply because it is outdated (indeed, it was never an adequate way of talking about the evolution of the internet) but also because it misses out on the complex nature of governance systems that combine market liberalism, state control and a nod towards consensual decision making. We have therefore moved from a redundant polarisation between 'non-regulability' and 'regulability' to a set of more subtle distinctions between different forms of regulation: statutory/ voluntary, formal/informal, national/supranational, hierarchical/diffuse. In doing this, we are reminded, first, of the blurred boundaries between 'governmental' and 'nongovernmental' approaches and, second, of certain continuities of new forms of governance with traditional forms of communications regulation.

For example, Cass Sunstein, whose plea in *Republic.com* (Sunstein 2002) for tighter regulation of online spaces to balance out political partisanship caused outrage among libertarians, had, by 2007, totally changed his tune. In an interview with Salon.com, he insisted that fresh laws were unnecessary, as the internet was already heavily regulated through existing legal frameworks: 'The equivalent of trespass is forbidden. You can't libel people on the Internet, you can't commit fraud over the Internet. So that's good' (quoted in Van Heuvelen 2007). The British legal scholar Jacob Rowbottom identifies an ongoing hierarchy in online expression and argues that while small-scale 'associative' activity should not be regulated, 'a small number of speakers, often with substantial economic resources behind them, will consistently command a mass audience. Consequently, there will be certain types of online speaker that are appropriate targets for mass media regulations' (2006: 501). Richard Collins (2009) argues that much regulatory literature makes the mistake of treating the internet as a completely novel technological environment, immune to all previous pressures, 'bounded and different from all other electronic media' (2009: 53). Instead, he stresses the 'interdependence' of internet and legacy media and, reflecting on various layers of internet regulation, writes that the '"shadow" of hierarchy always lies over market and network governance systems and often shapes the behaviour of such agents in such systems of governance' (2009: 61).

Zittrain, Benkler and Lessig all describe in some detail how this 'shadow' of hierarchy has been implicated in moves to re-regulate the communications environment on behalf of corporate interests seeking to 'gain and assert exclusivity in core resources necessary for information production and exchange' (Benkler 2006: 384). Statutory instruments, like the 1996 Telecoms Act in the US and the 2010 Digital Economy Act in the UK – together with those that were successfully opposed like the Stop Online Piracy Act (SOPA) and the Protect IP Act (PIPA) in the US and the Anti-Counterfeiting Trade Agreement (ACTA) in Europe – were designed to update regulations for the digital age but, above all, to normalise the enclosure of the internet in the interests of the state and its allies. According to Benkler, these shifts in the regulatory climate 'are skewing the institutional ecology in favor of business models and production practices that are based on exclusive proprietary claims; they are lobbied for by firms that collect large rents if these laws are expanded, followed, and enforced' (2006: 470). This is borne out by research produced by the Sunlight Foundation which found that anti-net neutrality lobbyists spent five times as much as their opponents between 2005 and 2013 and produced three times as many reports, with the top five most active companies *all* opposing net neutrality (Drutman and Furnas 2014).

The internet, as Lessig (2006) reminds us, has facilitated a re-thinking of the origins and scope of regulatory power. Alongside the impact of code-based regulation, governments are not only re-regulating on behalf of powerful corporate actors but actually delegating regulatory responsibility and initiative to private companies themselves. 'Delegated censorship, delegated surveillance, delegated copyright enforcement, and delegated law enforcement have shifted governance – for better or worse – to private intermediaries' (DeNardis 2014: 13). The neoliberal state is not evacuating the regulatory field so much as launching joint ventures in which it finds itself as the junior partner in what it describes as a process of 'networked governance'. For example, the state 'is no longer the monopolistic provider of the means of enforcement. Public-private partnerships characterize an increasing number of functions related to the provision of public order' (Brousseau et al. 2012: 5). While countries like the US and UK remain preoccupied with monitoring internet traffic to address 'security risks', it may be that the state is willing to retreat 'from its core "regal" functions' (2012: 5) and to hand over certain tasks to security companies, ISPs and social media platforms.

Indeed the 'policing' of digital networks is hardly an approach with which 'liberal' governments will want to be associated. While surveillance operations are far more likely to remain covert, governments are rather more keen to 'incentivise' digital intermediaries like search engines, ISPs and social media platforms to regulate access and content through the creation of co-regulatory schemes. This achieves, in the words of Goldsmith and Wu, 'extraterritorial control through local intermediaries' (2006: 68). Co-regulation, in this context, suggests not the autonomous or peer-dominated process that we discussed earlier in this chapter in relation to self-regulation but one in which both agenda-setting as well as 'backstop' (enforcement) power rests largely with the state.

For example, a workshop organised by the Organisation for Economic Co-operation and Development (OECD) on the 'role of Internet intermediaries in advancing public policy objectives' agreed that, while restricting the liability of intermediaries had helped the internet to grow, there is nevertheless 'increasing national and international pressure from governments, intellectual property rights-holders, and some consumer groups, to enlist the help of Internet intermediaries to control copyright infringement, child pornography, improve cyber security etc.' (OECD 2010: 3). In other words, intermediaries are seen to offer a more effective regulatory mechanism to establish secure and operable networks than direct, coercive action. The objective for government is to find the right regulatory balance between stimulating economically desirable activities and protecting individual rights to privacy and safety (in the knowledge, of course, that intelligence agencies will still hold the keys to masses of data). Indeed, the US ambassador to the OECD gave the opening keynote to the workshop, in which she highlighted 'the increasing challenges for policy makers to maintain such "hands-off" policies in a rapidly changing environment characterized by increasing data flows across borders, heightened censorship and privacy concerns' (2010: 7). Intermediaries, in other words, are the most important institutions through which governments are increasingly likely to maintain overall strategic oversight of the internet environment while delegating day-to-day operational control to private operators 'in the field'.

According to Mueller (2010: 7), this type of governance refers to a situation in which internet companies are permitted to 'establish their own policies and negotiate among themselves what is blocked and what is passed, what is authenticated and what is not'. It also suggests a new dynamic of regulatory power in which it becomes increasingly difficult to distinguish both between public and private sources of regulation and between self- and co-regulation. If we think of regulation in terms of the ability to structure access to and shape content on the internet, then powerful new regulators appear: not simply Comcast, Verizon and AT&T but Facebook, Amazon and, of course, Google. Reflecting on the importance of online gatekeepers, Jeffrey Rosen argues that it is private actors like Google who 'arguably have more influence over the contours of online expression than anyone else on the planet' (Rosen 2008). The fact that a small legal team takes the final decision on what content is suitable to be circulated on Google's search engines or on YouTube suggests that a fairly rigid form of hierarchical governance is in place. Indeed, for Rosen, '[v]oluntary self-regulation means that, for the foreseeable future, [then deputy general counsel of Google, Nicole] Wong and her colleagues will continue to exercise extraordinary power over global speech online' (Rosen 2008). Franklin argues that this kind of gatekeeping power makes it more and more difficult to distinguish between public and private forms of regulation. 'Google administers or controls increasingly large parts of this [online] space where a growing percentage of global internet users' activities happens. Corporate actors' increasing power and influence in everyday cyberspaces most of us occupy is, arguably, government-like' (Franklin 2010: 77).

Regulation, therefore, has not simply been subcontracted to private companies but embedded in 'regulating' technologies. Jonathan Zittrain argues that the most immediate danger to creative expression online may not be overt government censorship and surveillance but the ways in which 'non-generative' devices and spaces (like the Apple Watch and the iPhone) restrict the range of uses and connections and thus constrain our behaviour (2009: 106). The increasing popularity of 'walled gardens' like the Apple Watch or apps for the iPhone which do not permit any modification signal further evidence the enclosure of the online environment and its potential 'lockdown'. As Zittrain puts it: 'The prospect of tethered appliances and software as service permits major regulatory intrusions to be implemented as minor technical adjustments of code or requests to service providers' (2009: 125). Even small technical decisions – an upgrade here, a copy-protection scheme there – can have profound regulatory consequences.

There remain many who put their faith in the power of social media, collaborative platforms or, as Zittrain does, in the 'generosity of spirit [which] is a society's powerful first line of moderation' (2009: 246) somehow to beat this threat of a 'lockdown'. They are, however, perhaps underestimating the power of corporations – whether traditional or emerging, 'bureaucratic' or 'innovative', software- or hardware-related – either to neutralise the threat of commons-based media or to assimilate their distinctive features into for-profit models (usually both). As we have seen from the last chapter, while the internet has thrown up a fast-changing array of sites destined to be 'the next big thing' – from Compuserve and America Online to MySpace and Bebo and, more recently, to Google and Facebook – one thing that has remained constant is the structure of a 'winner takes all' market which systematises the need for huge concentrations of online and offline capital. A key consequence of this, and perhaps this is genuinely novel, is that the internet has facilitated an era, partly because of technological characteristics but also partly because of the global roll-out of neoliberalism, in which it is not simply politicians or programmers but, increasingly, *capital* that regulates.

Conclusion

The internet is not the first technological system to serve both public and private interests – the ability of broadcasting and the press to facilitate significant public conversations has also been fully exploited by the market. Yet the internet is particularly susceptible to competing pressures, as, while it was established by public bodies and continues to operate on open protocols, its backbone and most of its access points are privately owned and operated. One response to this dichotomy is to accept that tensions between public and private (or between proprietorial and non-proprietorial) will be played out following a predetermined technological logic: that all information-based innovations go from being 'somebody's hobby to somebody's industry; from jury-rigged contraption to slick production marvel; from a freely accessible channel to one strictly controlled by a single corporation or cartel – from open to closed system. It is a progression so common as to seem inevitable' (Wu 2010: 7–8). Wu describes this as the 'Cycle' in much the same way that Chris Anderson talks about a 'natural path of industrialisation: invention, propagation, adoption, control' (Anderson 2010: 126). Deborah Spar cites four inevitable phases of technological development: innovation, commercialisation, 'creative anarchy' and finally the imposition of rules (Spar 2001: 11). Technologies start out messy but end up tamed.

There is a danger in this deterministic reading of technological evolution that regulation, far from being an activity that seeks *actively* to shape and respond to concrete developments on the internet on the basis of particular views and beliefs, becomes a *fait accompli* followed by a shrug of the shoulders. According to this perspective, we would 'treat code-based environmental disasters – like the loss of privacy, like the censorship of censorware filters, like the disappearance of an intellectual commons – as if they were produced by gods, not by Man' (Lessig 2006: 338). But there is little need for this kind of fatalism: the internet is not a spiritual or transcendent object but a built environment based on the visions and actions of a range of architects. Mueller is quite right to emphasise that the history of the internet has not been predetermined and that its future is something to be contested: 'Those who projected that the state will automatically wither away in this sphere were clearly wrong. Those who rationalize as inevitable a reversion to a bordered and controlled Internet dominated by states are also wrong. Nothing is inevitable. Whatever happens, we will make happen' (Mueller 2010: 254).

To preserve and build on the democratic possibilities of the internet, we need therefore to have a robust notion of regulation for the public good that aims to halt the increasing enclosure of online spaces. Not all regulation is necessarily about banning content, spying on users or enforcing proprietary relations, although that is certainly the direction of travel we currently face. It is interesting that when the internet's underlying principles of openness and decentralisation are severely threatened, many commentators, including those traditionally reluctant to involve government, turn to the state for support and action. Zittrain argues, for example, that traditional regulators may be required 'when mere generosity of spirit among people of goodwill cannot resolve conflict' (2009: 246), while Tim Berners-Lee insists that net neutrality is essential to preserve a dynamic, innovative and egalitarian internet when these principles are threatened by the 'walled gardens' and 'closed silos' of social networks, proprietary programmes and insulated apps (Berners-Lee 2010).

Given the degree of online concentration that has developed, the weakness and fragility of new journalism start-ups, and the way that Google and other online aggregators give prominence to their own content and hegemonic sources, there remains a strong case for positive interventions that are aimed firmly at protecting the public interest. This requires an understanding of and a commitment to forms of regulation that are *not* subservient to intelligence gathering, corporate bottom lines and government priorities but, indeed, regulatory actions that are required precisely to fend off the distortion of the public good by special interests. And what else, other than a democratically accountable and fully representative state, would be capable of providing this? This is not the state we have and therefore not the regulation to which we are currently exposed, but it is certainly the one to which we should aspire.

References

Anderson, C. (2010) 'The Web Is Dead: Long Live the Internet', *Wired*, September.
Ang, P. H. (2008) 'International Regulation of Internet Content: Possibilities and Limits', in W. Drake and E. Wilson III (eds) *Governing Global Electronic Networks: International Perspectives on Policy and Power*, Cambridge, MA: MIT Press, 305–330.
Army Counterintelligence Center (2008) 'Wikileaks.org – An Online Reference to Foreign Intelligence Services, Insurgents, or Terrorist Groups?', 18 March. Online. Available

HTTP: <http://www.wired.com/images_blogs/threatlevel/2010/03/wikithreat.pdf> (accessed 28 July 2015).

Barlow, J. P. (1996) *A Cyberspace Independence Declaration*, 9 February. Online. Available HTTP:<http://w2.eff.org/Censorship/Internet_censorship_bills/barlow_0296.declaration> (accessed 28 July 2015).

Bell, E. (2009) 'Digital Media Cannot Be Contained by the Analogue Rulebook', *Media Guardian*, 23 March. Online. Available HTTP: <http://www.theguardian.com/media/2009/mar/23/regulating-digital-media> (accessed 28 July 2015).

Benkler, Y. (2006) *The Wealth of Networks: How Social Production Transforms Markets and Freedom*, New Haven, CT: Yale University Press.

Berners-Lee, T. (2010) 'Long Live the Web: A Call for Continued Open Standards and Neutrality', *Scientific American*, 22 November. Online. Available HTTP: <http://www.scientificamerican.com/article/long-live-the-web/> (accessed 28 July 2015).

Boffey, D. (2015) 'Theresa May keeps snooper's charter secret', *Guardian*, 13 June. Online. Available HTTP: <http://www.theguardian.com/politics/2015/jun/13/snoopers-charter-theresa-may-refuse-to-share> (accessed 28 July 2015).

Brousseau, E., Marzouki, M. and Méadel, C. (2014) 'Governance, networks and digital technologies: societal, political and organizational innovations', in E. Brousseau, M. Marzouki and C. Méadel (eds) *Governance, Regulation and Powers on the Internet*, New York: Cambridge University Press, 3–38.

Castells, M. (2001) *The Internet Galaxy: Reflections on the Internet, Business and Society*, Oxford: Oxford University Press.

Castells, M. (2009) *Communication Power*, Oxford: Oxford University Press.

Cerf, V. (2002) 'The Internet Is for Everyone', *Internet Society*, April. Online. Available HTTP: <http://www.ietf.org/rfc/rfc3271.txt> (accessed 28 July 2015).

Collins, R. (2009) *Three Myths of Internet Governance: Making Sense of Networks, Governance and Regulation*, London: Intellect.

Daly, M. (2003) 'Governance and Social Policy', *Journal of Social Policy*, 32 (1): 113–128.

de Bossey, C. (2005) 'Report of the Working Group on Internet Governance', June, 05.41622. Online. Available HTTP: <www.wgig.org/docs/WGIGREPORT.pdf> (accessed 28 July 2015).

DeNardis, L. (2014) *The Global War for Internet Governance*. New Haven, CT: Yale University Press.

Doctorow, C. (2010) 'Digital Economy Act: This Means War', guardian.co.uk, 16 April. Online. Available HTTP: <http://www.guardian.co.uk/technology/2010/apr/16/digital-economy-act-cory-doctorow?intcmp=239> (accessed 28 July 2015).

Downes, L. (2009) *The Laws of Disruption: Harnessing the New Forces that Govern Life and Business in the Digital Age*, New York: Basic Books.

Drutman, L. and Furnas, Z. (2014) 'Who's putting the most money against net neutrality?' *dailydot.com*, 9 September. Online. Available HTTP: <http://www.dailydot.com/politics/lobbyists-net-neutrality-fcc/> (accessed 28 July 2015).

Dyson, E. (1998) *Release 2.1: A Design for Living in the Digital Age*, London: Penguin.

European Commission (2010) 'Audiovisual Media Services Directive (2010/13/EU)', Official *Journal of the European Union,* 15 April, Brussels: European Commission.

European Commission (2014) *Factsheet on the 'Right to be Forgotten' Ruling*, C-131/12. Online. Available HTTP: <http://ec.europa.eu/justice/data-protection/files/factsheets/factsheet_data_protection_en.pdf> (accessed 28 July 2015).

Foucault, M. (1977) *Discipline and Punish*, London: Allen Lane.

Franklin, M. I. (2009) 'Who's Who in the "Internet Governance Wars": Hail the "Phantom Menace"?' *International Studies Review*, 11: 221–226.

Franklin, M. I. (2010) 'Digital Dilemmas: Transnational Politics in the Twenty-First Century', *Brown Journal of World Affairs*, 16 (2), Spring/Summer: 67–85.

Franklin, M. I. (in press) 'Mobilizing for Net Rights: The Charter of Human Rights and Principles for the Internet', in D. Freedman, J. Obar, C. Martens and R. McChesney (eds) *Strategies for Media Reform: International Perspectives*, Fordham: Fordham University Press.

Freedman, D. (2008) *The Politics of Media Policy*, Cambridge: Polity Press.

Friedman, T. (2000) *The Lexus and the Olive Tree*, London: Harper Collins.

Froomkin, A. M. (2003) 'Habermas@Discourse.Net: Towards a Critical Theory of Cyberspace', *Harvard Law Review*, 116 (3), January: 749–873.

Gilmore, J. (1993) John Gilmore's home page. Online. Available HTTP: <http://www.toad.com/gnu/> (accessed 28 July 2015).

Goldsmith, J. and Wu, T. (2006) *Who Controls the Internet? Illusions of a Borderless World*, Oxford: Oxford University Press.

Greenwald, G. (2014) *No Place to Hide: Edward Snowden, the NSA & The Surveillance State*, London: Penguin.

Halliday, J. (2010) 'ISPs Should Be Free to Abandon Net Neutrality, Says Ed Vaizey', guardian.co.uk, 17 November. Online. Available HTTP: <http://www.theguardian.com/technology/2010/nov/17/net-neutrality-ed-vaizey> (accessed 28 July 2015).

Hals, T. (2010) 'WikiLeaks Shows Reach and Limits of Internet Speech', Reuters, 9 December. Online. Available HTTP: <http://www.reuters.com/article/idUS TRE6B85 I420101209> (accessed 28 July 2015).

Hintz, A. (2014) 'Forums on internet governance reveal tensions over how the web should be regulated', *The Conversation*, 11 September. Online. Available HTTP: <http://theconversation.com/forums-on-internet-governance-reveal-tensions-over-how-the-web-should-be-regulated-31536> (accessed 28 July 2015).

Hulin, A. and Stone, M. (eds) (2013) *The Online Media Self-Regulation Guidebook*, Vienna: OSCE.

IFEX (2010) 'News Media and Websites Censored and Blocked for Carrying Leaked Cables', 20 December. Online. Available HTTP: <http://www.ifex.org/international/2010/12/20/news_websites_censored/> (accessed 28 July 2015).

Johnson, D. R. and Post, D. G. (1996) 'Law and Borders: The Rise of Law in Cyberspace', *Stanford Law Review*, 48 (5): 1367–1402.

Kelly, K. (1995) *Out of Control: The New Biology of Machines*, London: Fourth Estate.

Koebler, J. (2014) 'Net Neutrality Is "Marxist," According to This Koch-Backed Astroturf Group', *Vice Motherboard*, 25 August. Online. Available HTTP: <http://motherboard.vice.com/read/net-neutrality-is-marxist-according-to-this-koch-backed-astroturf-group> (accessed 28 July 2015).

Lapowsky, I. (2015) 'The EU Could Kill Net Neutrality With A Loophole', *Wired*, 30 June. Online. Available HTTP: <http://www.wired.com/2015/06/eu-net-neutrality-loophole/> (accessed 28 July 2015).

Leigh, D. and Harding, L. (2013) *Wikileaks: Inside Julian Assange's War on Secrecy*, London: Guardian Books.

Lessig, L. (2006) *Code 2.0*, New York: Basic Books.

Lewis, J. (2010) 'Sovereignty and the Role of Government in Cyberspace', *Brown Journal of World Affairs*, 16 (2), Spring/Summer: 55–65.

Livingstone, S. (2010) 'Interactive, Engaging but Unequal: Critical Conclusions from Internet Studies', in J. Curran (ed.) *Mass Media and Society*, London: Bloomsbury, 122–142.

McQuail, D. (2005) *Mass Communication Theory*, 5th edn, London: Sage.

Mathiason, J. (2009) *Internet Governance: The New Frontier of Global Institutions*, New York: Routledge.

Mayo, J. et al. (2010) 'How to Regulate the Internet Tap', *New York Times*, 21 April. Online. Available HTTP: <www.nytimes.com/2010/04/21/opinion/21mayo.html> (accessed 28 July 2015).

Mueller, M. (1999) 'ICANN and Internet Governance: Sorting through the Debris of "Self-regulation"', *Info: The Journal of Policy, Regulation and Strategy for Telecommunications, Information and Media*, 1 (6), December: 497–520.

Mueller, M. (2002) *Ruling the Root: Internet Governance and the Taming of Cyberspace*, Cambridge, MA: MIT Press.

Mueller, M. (2010) *Networks and States: The Global Politics of Internet Governance*, Cambridge, MA: MIT Press.

Mueller, M. (2012) 'The interconnection regime: property and commons: learning from the telecommunication industry privatization process', in E. Brousseau, M. Marzouki and C. Meadel (eds) *Governance, Regulation and Powers on the Internet*, New York: Cambridge University Press, 39–62.

Negroponte, N. (1996) *Being Digital*, London: Coronet.

Obama, B. (2015) 'President Obama's Plan For a Free and Open Internet', 26 February. Online. Available HTTP: <https://m.whitehouse.gov/net-neutrality> (accessed 28 July 2015).

OECD (2010) 'The Role of Internet Intermediaries in Advancing Public Policy Objectives', 16 June. Online. Available HTTP: <www.oecd.org/sti/ict/intermediaries> (accessed 28 July 2015).

Ofcom (2010) *Traffic Management and 'Net Neutrality'*, discussion document, 24 June, London: Ofcom.

Ohmae, K. (1995) *The End of the Nation State*, London: Harper Collins.

Ó Siochrú, S., Girard, B. and Mahan, A. (2002) *Global Media Governance: A Beginner's Guide*, Lanham, MD: Rowman & Littlefield.

Palmer, M. (2009) 'Google Tries to Avoid the Regulatory Noose', FT.com, 21 May. Online. Available HTTP: <http://www.ft.com/cms/s/0/cd5cf33c-452b-11de-b6c8-00144feabdc0.html#axzz3hJDR3sGn> (accessed 28 July 2015).

Pickard, V. (2015) *America's Battle for Media Democracy: The Triumph of Corporate Liberarianism and the Future of Media Reform*, New York: Cambridge University Press.

Raboy, M., Landry, N. and Shtern, J. (2010) *Digital Solidarities, Communication Policy and Multi-stakeholder Global Governance: The Legacy of the World Summit on the Information Society*, New York: Peter Lang.

Radu, R., Chenou, J.-M. and Weber, R. (eds) (2014) *The Evolution of Global Internet Governance*, New York: Springer.

Robbins, P. (2009) Comments to the Westminster eForum, 'Taming the Wild Web?' – Online Content Regulation, 11 February. London: Westminster eForum.

Rosen, J. (2008) 'Google's Gatekeepers', *New York Times*, 30 November. Online. Available HTTP: <http://www.nytimes.com/2008/11/30/magazine/30google-t.html> (accessed 28 July 2015).

Rowbottom, J. (2006) 'Media Freedom and Political Debate in the Digital Era', *Modern Law Review*, 69 (4), July: 489–513.

Rushe, D. (2015) 'Net neutrality activists score landmark victory in fight to govern the internet', *Guardian*, 26 February. Online. Available HTTP: <http://www.theguardian.com/technology/2015/feb/26/net-neutrality-activists-landmark-victory-fcc> (accessed 28 July 2015).

Schmidt, E. and Cohen, J. (2013) *The New Digital Age: Reshaping the Future of People, Nations and Business*, London: John Murray.

Siddiqui, S. (2015) 'Petition to pardon Edward Snowden rejected by Obama administration', *Guardian*, 28 July. Online. Available HTTP: <http://www.theguardian.com/us-news/2015/jul/28/edward-snowden-petition-rejected-obama-administration> (accessed 28 July 2015).

Spar, D. (2001) *Ruling the Waves: Cycles of Discovery, Chaos, and Wealth from the Compass to the Internet*, New York: Harcourt.

Sunstein, C. (2002) *Republic.com*, Princeton, NJ: Princeton University Press.

Sylvain, O. (2010) 'Internet Governance and Democratic Legitimacy', *Federal Communications Law Journal*, 62 (2): 205–273.

Tambini, D., Leonardi, D. and Marsden, C. (2007) *Codifying Cyberspace: Communications Self-regulation in the Age of Internet Convergence*, New York: Routledge.

Thielman, S. (2015) 'FCC's net neutrality rules challenged in lobbyist lawsuit', *Guardian*, 14 April. Online. Available HTTP: <http://www.theguardian.com/technology/2015/apr/14/fcc-lobbyists-net-neutrality-internet> (accessed 28 July 2015).

Van Heuvelen, B. (2007) 'The Internet is Making Us Stupid', salon.com, 7 November. Online. Available HTTP: <http://www.salon.com/news/feature/2007/11/07/sunstein> (accessed 28 July 2015).

Warman, M. (2010) 'Ed Vaizey: My Overriding Priority Is An Open Internet', telegraph.co.uk, 20 November. Online. Available HTTP: <http://www.telegraph.co.uk/technology/internet/8147661/Ed-Vaizey-My-overriding-priority-is-an-open-internet.html> (accessed 28 July 2015).

Webster, F. (2006) *Theories of the Information Society*, 3rd edn, London: Routledge.

Williams, R. (1974) *Television: Technology and Cultural Form*, London: Fontana.

Wu, T. (2010) *The Master Switch: The Rise and Fall of Information Empires*, New York: Knopf.

Yuhas, A. (2015) 'NSA reform: USA Freedom Act passes first surveillance reform in decade – as it happened', *Guardian*, 2 June. Online. Available HTTP: <http://www.theguardian.com/us-news/live/2015/jun/02/senate-nsa-surveillance-usa-freedom-act-congress-live> (accessed 28 July 2015).

Zittrain, J. (2009) *The Future of the Internet*, London: Penguin.

Chapter 5

The internet of me (and my 'friends')

Natalie Fenton

Introduction: social media

The growth in social networking sites and their usage has been phenomenal. In May 2015 Facebook was second only to Google as the world's most popular website (http://www.alexa.com/topsites) and it gained this status in a remarkably short time from the date of its inception in 2004. In March 2015 it had an average of 936 million daily active users (http://newsroom.fb.com/company-info/) compared to 250 million in 2010, with an average of 12.58 daily unique page views per visitor for an average of 19.37 minutes per day (www.alexa.com/siteinfo/face-book.com). Alexa also ranks YouTube as the third most popular website globally. Nielsen research (2010, 2012) shows that in 2012 people spent 20% of their total time online via their personal computer on social media and 30% via mobile devices. In the UK, Ofcom (2015) note that 72% of internet users now have at least one social media profile compared to 22% in 2007 and of these 81% say they visit social media sites at least once a day compared to 30% in 2005. Other research (http://www.adweek.com/socialtimes/time-spent-online/613474) shows that the average global daily time spent on social media sites has risen from 1.66 hours per day in 2013 to 1.72 hours per day in 2014. Put simply, social media has experienced massive growth over the last decade and is now a staple ingredient of the majority of internet users' daily media diet.

Social networking is an activity that is more popular with the young: the Pew Research Center (Lenhart 2015) report that in the US 24% of teens go online 'almost constantly' with 92% reporting they go online daily. The popularity of and time spent on these sites have brought about new rituals of communication and prompted media theorists to reconsider the traditional contexts of mass communication and the traditional (and previously often separate) concerns of production, text and reception. In this newly communicative context, the audience is described as 'prod-users' (Bruns 2008) or 'pro-sumers' (Tapscott and Williams 2008: 124–50), to account for the creative and interactive nature of much online activity.

Digital media, and the internet in particular, are transforming our means of gathering information, communicating with each other and contributing to both these practices through creative production. In informational terms, use of the internet clearly has the *potential* to influence the capacity of 'ordinary' citizens and resource-poor social or political groups to gain information and expertise through vastly increasing the range of information that is freely available to any internet user, on virtually any subject imaginable (Bimber 2002). In communicational terms, sites like Facebook, YouTube (the video-sharing website) or Weibo (a Chinese social networking site) have acquired billions of users in a very short space of time, largely by 'word of mouth' – or, at least, via millions of communications carried out through online social contacts – connecting with others, sharing thoughts and discussing concerns, forming groups and joining forces with others in mutual interests and activities. Twitter – the microblogging site that allows people to connect to others and follow their stream of thought through linked communications no more than 140 characters long – currently (April 2015) has over 302 million active monthly users, with over 500 million tweets being sent every day attempting to prompt a particular ordering of information and the prioritising of certain subject matters (https://about.twitter.com/company).

These social networking sites are also claimed to break down the barriers between traditionally public and private spheres of communication, putting power into the hands of the user and thereby giving the details of our private concerns a public presence, and enabling the public domain of the official political and institutional realm to be more easily monitored by the private citizen (Papacharissi 2009). Hence, social networking is said to bring forth a means of communication that is for the public, by the public (e.g. Rheingold 2002; Gillmor 2004; Beckett 2008; Shirky 2008). These theorists proffer positive interpretations that refer to social networking sites or person-to-person media or mass self-communication (Castells 2009) as both supporting the maintenance of pre-existing social networks while also helping strangers to connect on the basis of shared interests, political views or activities. In this manner, social networking sites are heralded as novel, pervasive and conferring agency.

On the other hand, there are those who propose a more critical assessment, viewing the form and nature of communication on display as no more than an incessant version of a 'daily me' (Sunstein 2007) that personalises and depoliticises public issues and simply re-emphasises old inequalities while feeding corporations the necessary data for online marketing, business promotion and the exploitation of private affairs – a specifically anti-democratic turn leading to civic privatism. This approach emphasises political economic concerns, reminding us that the internet does not transcend global capitalism but is deeply involved with it by virtue of the corporate interests it supports and the discourses of capitalism and neoliberalism in which the people who use it are drenched (see Chapter 4).

In 2014, Facebook had an annual turnover of $12.466 billion and a quarterly advertising revenue of $3.594 billion (representing a 7.6% share of the US digital advertising market), while Twitter had an annual turnover of $1.403 billion and a quarterly advertising revenue of $432 million. In this manner, social networking is claimed to further promote forms of mediation that are deeply commodified while also being conducive to sociality. The sociality inscribed within these platforms is argued not only to enable corporations to extract value from our personal data, but also to encourage a form of sociality that foregrounds the self and self-promotion. In other words, in developed Western democracies, where social media exist within social and political contexts that foreground individualisation, embedded in technological developments that encourage pervasive communication and an ever-connected online presence, social networking sites are seen as extending neoliberal ideology rather than contesting it.

Situating a discussion in a sterile binary framework, with the optimists on one side and the pessimists on the other, is often how debates on new technologies begin (whether referring to the radio, television or the computer). But both approaches in isolation are reductive (either in relation to technology or in relation to largely political economic factors) and can never fully appreciate the form of communication they are commenting upon. As a result, each approach misunderstands the nature and impact of the media (in this case, of digital social media) on the social and political contours of contemporary life and the complexity of power therein. Part of this misunderstanding comes from a media centrism that resists a deep and critical contextualisation of social and political life. As Couldry (2003) has suggested, once the media (in any form) presents itself as the centre of society and we organise our lives and orient our daily rituals and practice towards it, we run the risk of falling prey to 'the myth of the mediated centre' (2003: 47). Media rituals not only stress the significance of media but also allude to the importance of being 'in the media' and of being able to communicate your message to others – whether this is for financial, political or social gain. The more powerful and influential you are, the better placed you are to get your message across. The internet and social networking push this argument one step further. The millions of people who use social networking sites inhabit a mediated world that offers the possibility of more control than mainstream media, that is mobile, interactive and holds endless creative potential, but is nonetheless mythic. The claimed ubiquity of the internet and social media stresses the significance of always being tuned in and online. The seductive power of this mythic centre circulates around social life and serves to obscure the reproduction of the dominant values of neoliberal society.

Once this is appreciated, it has ramifications for media theory – particularly in situating the destabilisation of the old producer/consumer divide in a broader and deeper context that can recognise and take account of communicational life without fetishising the media forms that may enable it. In resisting a fetishised media centrism, we are also encouraged to rethink the relationship between structure and agency, between political economic approaches and their relationship to those that emphasise the constructive ability of individuals, the importance of subjectivities and the relevance of identity. It is in this critical contextual frame that we need to understand mediation and its relationship to our social and cultural practices. In the rest of this chapter I offer a critical consideration of the four main arguments that seek to place the internet and social networking at the centre of this mythology.

Social media are communication led rather than information driven

Social networking sites operate through organic networks. Each user sends an invitation to join a particular community, whether to an individual or an entire group, who are then encouraged to pass it on to their own network of friends. In this manner the networks can expand extremely quickly (e.g. Haythornthwaite 2005). As Papacharissi (2010a) notes, social media have been invested with the ability to facilitate the development of strong relations with family members and friends and weaker relations with a range of acquaintances (Ellison et al. 2007). There is no doubt that the act of digital self-communication has become part of many people's everyday rituals. The daily rhythms and activities of life are informed by, punctuated by and inhabited by social media. As we post our photographs on Instagram, discuss the latest film on Facebook, share a joke on WhatsApp (owned by Facebook), alert people to a nugget of information on Twitter, we have a sense that we are participating in something that is going on out there; that rather than being told what to do or what to think through the linear provision of information, we can join in the telling through a pulsating network of digital social communication.

This is neither straightforward interactivity nor simple participation in a network, but participation in a communicative act for a complex range of purposes that may be personal or public, social, political or cultural; or any or all of these at once (Papacharissi 2010a). Social networking sites such as Facebook are only one aspect of the multi-faceted phenomena of social media that allow a click and link process to a news site, to a YouTube video, to a blog, to Twitter, sending links, photographs and messages directly from your internet-enabled phone, through your social network site, in a thoroughly converged mediated experience. It is a form of communicative experience based on a sense of participation that is claimed to offer a sense of ownership that incurs emotional involvement (Donath 2007), through a commonly shared understanding of protocol and conduct that frames the network and speaks to identities that are reflexive, mobile and performative. Communicative involvement is the primary motivation and its aim is to perform the self anywhere at any time, on whatever mode the sender decrees. Clearly, communication is never just about the act of communicating, and communicational desires and informational requirements often overlap. But in social networking the need to be linked in, to feel at once connected and in control of your forms of interaction and means of self-expression and, ultimately, the creative promotion of self, is argued to gain in importance.

This resonates with many people's knowledge and practice of social media and brings to the fore the affective dimension of communication that is critical to our understanding of contemporary mediated experiences. A form of media that is communication led rather than content driven highlights the psychological and personal incentives of interaction and participation over and above the politics of media content for public consumption. Social media is a form of communication that is, above all, connective, and this has tended to dominate much of the early writing on it. Because it is social and is felt to begin with the individual user choosing to communicate with whomsoever they desire, it also confers a high degree of autonomy to the communicator. This increased sociality is said to bring new understandings, as we are increasingly subjected to a wider range of viewpoints and encouraged to deliberate freely within a variety of networks. The enhanced autonomy is said to bring improved levels of power and control to the user. We should, however, remember that people rarely have democratic enhancement at the top of their agendas and use the internet far more for entertainment purposes than for informational gain (Althaus and Tewksbury 2000; Shah et al. 2001; Blank and Groselj 2014). Neither should acknowledgement of the communicational intensity of social media devalue the importance of the political and the economic context in which this increased sociality takes place.

Put another way, in emphasising communicational desires and motivations – the need to connect and relate to others (which we should acknowledge as a major facet of social networking and part of its vast success) – we should not fall into the trap of diminishing the importance of who is communicating what to whom. A consideration of *who* is communicating is a sobering exercise. Usage of social media is highly uneven among participants and much content is dominated by a small percentage of people. A survey by the Harvard Business School (Heil and Piskorski 2009) found that 10% of Twitter users generate more than 90% of the content and most people have only tweeted once. The top 10% are dominated by celebrities or mainstream media corporations such as CNN. Other recent studies (Bruner 2013) show that 60% of twitter users have fewer than 100 followers, while those with over 1,000 are in the 97th percentile, with the likes of the popstar Katy Perry topping the global Twitter charts, attracting 70.3 million followers (http://twittercounter.com/pages/100). Participation, it seems, is still the preserve of a privileged few.

Furthermore, fake accounts operated by automated software (bots) are also on the rise, with some estimates putting them at one in 20 active accounts. Social bots are hard to spot. They are programmed to tweet and retweet; they have social quirks and create their own online histories; they can infiltrate popular discussions and generate content; they operate on sleep-wake patterns to make them more convincing (Ferrara et al. 2015). These robots can inflate followers, influence the stock market and sway political discourse as well as massively enhance marketing campaigns. A study on Weibo (Xie 2014), a social networking platform in China, found 4.7 million accounts that were involved in campaigns to manufacture support for particular products. Another study (Gupta et al. 2013) that analysed Twitter posts around the Boston marathon bombing also reported how automated tweets resulted in the wide circulation of false accusations in the aftermath of the attack mostly as a result of bots automatically retweeting unverified information. Astroturfing is also common practice on social networks. Just like artificial grass made to appear real, astroturfing online uses software to disguise the sponsors of messages to make it seem as if they have come from the general public and so give the impression of widespread support for a particular idea or product. It would seem, then, that identifying *who* is communicating on social media is not as simple as it first seems, with social media traffic weighted heavily in favour of corporate players and commercial agendas.

A consideration of *what* social networks are communicating is no more encouraging. Leaving aside the bots and the astroturfing, research shows that the means to self-expression have also been found to be carefully controlled impressions of the self, structured around class affiliation (Papacharissi 2002a; 2002b; 2009) and cultures of taste (Liu 2007). This research suggests that, far from broadening our communicational horizons and deliberative understandings, social media work to reinforce already existing social hierarchies and further strengthen close(d) communities. This funnelling and fragmentation of our communications is further exacerbated by the move from link to like. In April 2010 Facebook introduced the 'Like' device as a means of indicating preference and signalling recommendations. 'Liking' rather than linking marks a move from search to ever-increasing self-referentiality (Lovink 2012). With a knowing wink, it states 'see how many of us think alike' – reinforcing already established communities. Furthermore, it has also been argued that social networking sites predetermine content in a manner that prioritises consumption over friendship and community building; and the more prolific the bots become, the more exaggerated the consumer ethic. As Marwick (2005) points out:

> First, the rigid profile structure encourages the user to present him or herself in a way that is partly constructed by the application, not the user. . . . Second, the way that profiles are structured is not neutral; rather, power is embedded throughout the applications in a variety of ways. Generally, the user is portrayed not as a citizen, but as a consumer . . . applications encourage people to define themselves through the entertainment products they consume: music, movies, books, and television shows. . . . Not only are users treated as consumers, they are encouraged to consume others in a concept of networking that privileges social capital over friendship or community building. 'Networking', in business terms, is a goal-oriented process in which one's social circle is constantly expanded in order to connect with as many people as possible, in order to gain business advantages. . . . Third, SNSs [social networking sites] inherently exclude certain segments of the world population. For instance, the majority of sites are American applications that attract primarily US users.
>
> (Marwick 2005: 9–11)

For Castells (2009), the internet is shaped by a conflict between the global multimedia business networks that try to commodify it and the 'creative audience' that tries to establish a degree of citizen control over it and to declare its right to communicative freedom without corporate control or interference. He describes how all the corporate giants are:

trying to figure out how to re-commodify Internet-based autonomous mass self-communication. They are experimenting with ad-supported sites, pay sites, free streaming video portals, and pay portals. . . . Web 2.0 technologies empowered consumers to produce and distribute their own content. The viral success of these technologies propelled media organizations to harness the production power of traditional consumers.

(Castells 2009: 97)

Although critical of the global media corporations that dominate our online worlds, Castells still invests a great deal of faith in the capacity for social media to bring into existence multiple and diverse voices with an apparent unprecedented autonomy in the modes of communication. This is a claim that is frequently said to be a central facet of the productive creativity of the prod-user in a social media habitat. But all of our online comings and goings leave digital footprints that can be tracked, analysed and commodified. Social media applications attempt to extract value from our every online move: the choices we make, the sites we visit, who we talk to and who we follow all create data that is mined and sold to third parties for profit.

Geveran (2009) notes how social marketing emerged on the internet. Using online social networks such as Facebook or MySpace, marketers send person-alised promotional messages featuring an ordinary customer to that customer's friends. Because they reveal a customer's browsing and buying patterns, and because they feature implied endorsements, the messages raise significant con-cerns about disclosure of personal matters, information quality and individuals' ability to control the commercial exploitation of their identity.

Furthermore, McChesney (2014) points out how the global power of new digital distributors has created the greatest monopolies in economic history with new digital industries moving from competitive to oligopolistic to monopolistic at a furious pace until the internet has rested in the hands of a very few giant global corporations. McChesney argues that the hyper commercialism, adver-tising and monopoly markets we now find online enhance rather than disrupt the contours of capitalism and lead to rampant depoliticisation and undemo-cratic, commercial media policy, as the point of government regulation pivots on helping corporate media maximise their profits rather than advancing the public interest (see Chapter 4). Freedman (2014: 101) also challenges the view that digital networks have shifted power from 'the centre to the periphery and from elites to ordinary users and creators', outlining how they have privileged 'accumulation strategies that are designed to reward corporate interests more than to empower individual actors' (ibid). He goes on to note that the power imbalance between states and those who oppose them remains vast, and when it comes to digital surveillance, states are complicit with the world's largest com-munications providers. In this context, it is hard to see how Castells' 'creative audience' engaged in 'autonomous mass self-communication' can bring about the progressive social changes he claims.

It is also worth reminding ourselves that the concept of autonomy has a long history and is frequently connected to acts of resistance and the ability to rise above dominant ideologies and 'be yourself'. It is useful to draw on Castoriadis' (1991) distinction between individualistic autonomy, social autonomy (through equality of participation) and autonomy as political subjectivity (that liberates the imagination). In this critique of autonomy, Castoriadis confronts autonomy within the system of neoliberal capitalism (individualist), as opposed to autonomy that seeks to challenge the system (social) or transcend the system (through political subjectivity). Of course, while these theoretical distinctions are useful in enabling us to interrogate the term, in daily life, facilitated by converged media, we may well engage in all three forms of autonomy at once. So I may go on to my social networking site and comment on the latest celebrity gossip story, then click and link my way to a petition on ending child poverty while updating my blog that tells everyone what I've just done and how I think the world could be a better place. These activities traverse private autonomy and public autonomy with each influencing the other. In other words, autonomy is always situated in particular social and political contexts and we will only ever understand the various manifestations of it if we appreciate the context fully. In a consumerist society, autonomy enacted through communication-led media may in fact amount to little more than an active endorsement of individualisation and an extension of a neoliberal approach that prioritises the self, seeking to market the self and reproduce the self in myriad ways for the sole advantage of the self, while constantly leaving behind a trail of data that can be monetised by the likes of Google through the sale of data imprints of ourselves to others who then sell stuff back to us.

Digital citizens are far from being autonomous from capital. We not only constitute what Dallas Smythe once called an 'audience commodity' (Smythe 1994) that is sold to advertisers; we also actively engage in self-commodification. The difference between the audience commodity of traditional mass media and of the internet is that on the internet the users are also content producers. 'User-generated content' is a catch-all description of the endless creative activity, communication and content production online. But this still does not escape the fact that this user activity is commodified in precisely the way we argued in Chapter 4. In fact, we are excessively and ever more deeply commodified as so much more of our daily habits and rituals take an IT form. Lovink (2012: 34) refers to social media use as 'hyped-up individualization that results . . . in the algorithmic outsourcing of the self'. The audience-turned-producer does not, in this context, signify a democratisation of the media towards a truly participatory system. It certainly does not confer autonomy from capital but, rather, the profound and subcybernetic commodification of online human creativity. Seen from this angle, the participation and autonomy that have been heralded as revolutionary amount to no more than the automatic co-creation of consumer profiles (e.g. Hamelink 2000; Turrow 2001). As Nancy Baym (2015) argues, the term 'social media happened when companies figured out how to harness what people were already doing, make (some of it) a bit easier, call it "content" and funnel our practices into their revenue streams'.

Social media allow or encourage deliberation and dissent through multiplicity and polycentrality

An emphasis on communication and the multiple ways in which this can now take place with a variety of people through social media is suggestive of the pluralisation of social relationships, as discussed above. But social media are also claimed to aid democracy through an increase in the sheer number of spaces available for deliberation and dissent. This is an argument for information abundance freed from the shackles of a mass communication system that broadcasts from one to many.

Within online discussion research, some scholars argue that internet communication expands our horizons and broadens our understandings by offering a multitude of sites for debate among persons of varied opinions and beliefs. Holt (2004) states that the ability of the internet to unite those of disparate backgrounds has great potential for fostering debate and discussion of issues in the civic arena. Furthermore, research has shown that online political discussion serves to expose participants to non-likeminded partners (Brundidge 2006). Yet, despite the potential of the internet to bring opposing camps together in a common space and provide exposure to different ideas, other evidence suggests that, looked at from a different vantage point, this may not necessarily be occurring.

The structure of the internet has been found to offer conditions particularly conducive to selective exposure to media content (Bimber and Davis 2003). For example, on Friendster and MySpace particular cultural tastes and reference points were found to be carefully displayed and managed to indicate a clear sense of relation to particular cultures and allegiance to certain groups (Liu 2007). Some evidence indicates that selective exposure also occurs in online political discussion arenas, which may lead to political polarisation. For example, scholars have noted that virtual communities are fairly homogeneous in terms of values and viewpoints (Dahlberg and Siapera 2007), and that participants in an online discussion often hold comparable political perspectives (Wilhelm 1999). Schlozman et al. (2010: 487) describe the internet as 'the weapon of the strong', referring to its usage for political protest by a largely highly educated middle class. Similarly, work by Blank and Groselj (2014) at the Oxford Internet Institute shows how the varying forms of political participation online correlate almost exactly to indicators of social class and educational achievement. In other words, although half of the world may now be online, those using the internet for political purposes are still largely middle class and well educated.

Multiplicity, or the sheer abundance of information available to us, has also been argued to breed misinformation and a lack of understanding (Patterson 2010) because the daily habits and rituals of news have changed. People are no longer required to sit in front of the television for a set period of time each day or to read the newspaper over breakfast. Instead we do news snacking. But there are so many other more tempting treats on offer that 'healthy' news snacking is rapidly replaced by the more immediately gratifying tasty titbits of entertainment. Even more worryingly, Patterson identifies a pattern whereby, in a high-choice media environment, the less well informed are more inclined to opt for entertainment while the better informed include the news junkies, leading to increasing inequality of knowledge between the more informed and the less informed. Patterson (2010: 20) also argues that speed 'increases sensation but decreases learning', noting that about 60% of those who regularly read a daily newspaper spend at least half an hour doing so, compared to only 40% of those who read an online daily newspaper.

This raises important issues for news and information in a world of social media where genre categories are also blurred and often difficult to tell apart. How do you distinguish between the facts – albeit contextualised and problematised – and the noise that builds with the increasing and ever-expanding volume of comment, opinion and propaganda? In Alexander Wolfe's column on InformationWeek, he addresses the issues and overwhelming impact of real-time live-citizen journalism:

> Indeed, the sheer volume of 'Mumbai' tweets would seem to militate against the notion that there's anything of value easily accessible within. Since going through the first 100 pages of tweets only takes you back several hours, I did random searches on postings from Wed., Nov. 25; Thurs., Nov. 27, and Friday, Nov. 28, and couldn't come up with much hard information.

Another argument is the same in reverse – that there is so much audience content online that it enables journalists to see a broader world and connect with a wider range of news sources that will ultimately democratise the news product itself. But Örnebring (2008: 783) finds that even when audience content gained from sources such as social media is used as a means of generating news stories, it is usually in a very restricted range of areas: 'the overall impression is that users are mostly empowered to create popular culture-oriented content and personal/ everyday life-oriented content rather than news/informational content'. In a study of 24-hour television news, Wardle et al. (2014) found that user-generated content was only used when there were no other pictures available and usually as a stop-gap before news agency pictures emerged.

Further research in the UK by the Carnegie Trust (2010) found evidence of diminishing arenas for public deliberation, along with the marginalisation of dissent, especially in relation to those who lack power or confidence to voice their concerns or those who have non-mainstream views. This narrowing of the public sphere appears to be happening despite the expansion of mediated space and a multiplicity of media platforms and claims regarding interactivity, speed and the international reach of online communications.

Polycentrality, the notion that power is spread more widely in an environment where anyone can set up a website, can also be challenged on the grounds that social and political elites have greater cultural and economic capital at their disposal to harness the power of social media to their advantage. It is inevitable that as soon as a form of technology is seen to be a useful means of relaying information and connecting with people, particularly people who may otherwise not engage with their message, then political elites will try to find ways of exploiting it to their advantage. So political leaders post video blogs on YouTube, while senior politicians apparently Twitter their way through their days while attempting to perform their political duties. On 30 December 2008 Twitter was used as a real-time news conference podium by the Consulate General of Israel in New York and featured on the news and commentary blog Israel Politik. David Saranga, Israel Consul of Media and Public Affairs in New York, answered questions regarding the situation in the Middle East in relation to Israel and Gaza and all parties involved. Questions were submitted to its Twitter account, @IsraelConsulate, and attempts were made to respond to the questions through the 140-character limit, with those requiring lengthy answers being posted on the Israel Politik blog. When asked why it chose to go on Twitter, the Israeli consulate said that it saw debate on Twitter and saw people who had unreliable information. It felt, in response, that Twitter would be a good way to put an official voice out there. This is now common practice.

Barack Obama's Twitter account was one of the first presidential candidates to bring up-to-the-minute information on the US President elect's life and activities before and after the election. Other presidential candidates soon jumped on the social media bandwagon, and continue to use blogs and Twitter, along with other microblogging tools, to get their messages out to the public, creating the next generation of 'transparent' politicians. Similarly, as a mass medium that is often working directly alongside other converged media, the internet is also claimed to replicate the same types of control and function, with the same types of commercial concerns, as any other medium (Margolis et al. 1997; McChesney 1996), thereby reproducing homogeneity of content rather than challenging existing structures. Research in this vein (e.g. Agre 2002; Hindman 2009) indicates that social media do not deliver the liberatory potential through multiplicity and polycentrality that they are said to possess. Rather, romanticised retrospectives of past and future civic engagement frequently impose language and expectations that misrepresent what actually happens in the mediations of the present. More pointedly, Andrejevic (2008: 612) argues that 'the trumpeting of the subversive power of interactivity contributes to the deployment of what might be described as "the mass society repressive hypothesis" which pays lip service to revolution even as it stimulates the productivity of consumer labor'.

Of course, this should not undermine the ability of social media as a potential route to counter-expression in authoritarian regimes or developing democracies. But the need to take control of one's own life in developed capitalist neoliberal democracies is quite different from the need to claim control in oppressive regimes where it is difficult to get information out and dangerous to express political subjectivity. In such countries, the use of social media has undoubtedly enabled otherwise repressed voices to be heard. In February 2005, the Nepalese government shut down all international internet connections after the king imposed martial law, though they were only down for a short time. During that time, many technologically creative people were able to get some information out via social media channels. The government shutdown of internet connections inside and outside Burma (Myanmar) in 2007 led to overwhelming support from outside of the country to get news and information to the world through social media tools, especially blogs, Twitter and Flickr, creating a form of underground network for internet communications and social media (see Chapter 6). Similarly, in Egypt in 2011, protesters used social media like Facebook and Twitter to garner momentum for attendance at demonstrations and spread news of the revolution to the rest of the world. Even when Egyptian authorities shut off internet access, speak-2tweet enabled people to call through their messages, which were recorded and put out instantly on Twitter using the hashtag #Egypt (see Chapter 2). The birth of the Indignados/15M social movement in 2011 in Spain also emerged partly in response to an online call for political action by a site called 'Democracia Real Ya!' (Real Democracy Now). Consequently, on 15 May, 20,000–50,000 protested on the streets in many cities across Spain (see Chapter 6). They were met with police brutality that was quickly relayed online via Twitter, Facebook and SMS with a call to occupy the main squares of Spanish cities (Sloam 2014). The 15M movement brought campaigns against cuts and spurned many associated protest movements (known as tides) against evictions and home repossessions, the privatisation of healthcare, cuts in education, wage cuts and attacks on working conditions, among others. 15M relied heavily on social media to communicate with supporters in Spain and around the world, and was said to be the inspiration for the protest movement Occupy Wall Street that began on 17 September 2011 in response to social and economic inequality and the undue influence on government by corporations and financial agencies.

Social media are predicated on self-communication to a mass audience

For Castells, a novel quality of communication in contemporary society is mass self-communication. This builds on the positive proclamations of multiplicity and polycentrality but centres more directly on the enhanced power of the individual:

> It is mass communication because it can potentially reach a global audience, as in the posting of a video on YouTube, a blog with RSS links to a number of web sources, or a message to a massive e-mail list. At the same time, it is self-communication because the production of the message is self-generated, the definition of the potential receiver(s) is self-directed, and the retrieval of specific messages or content from the World Wide Web and electronic networks is self-selected. The three forms of communication (interpersonal, mass communication, and mass self communication) coexist, interact, and complement each other rather than substituting for one another. What is historically novel, with considerable consequences for social organization and cultural change, is the articulation of all forms of communication into a composite, interactive, digital hypertext that includes, mixes, and recombines in their diversity the whole range of cultural expressions conveyed by human interaction.
>
> (Castells 2009: 55)

The personalised content provided by social media, the ability to be publicly private and privately public (Papacharissi 2009), retains an emphasis on the self and on personhood rather than citizenship. In their private sphere (as defined by themselves) people connect with others on the basis of shared social, political and cultural agendas. Here, importantly, they experience mutuality, closeness and empathy (Coleman 2005) that may be lacking elsewhere in advanced capitalist societies. The spaces afforded by social media are mobile – they could be in train stations, cafés, the workplace or on the bus – but they allow for acts of association that bring with them notions of being in control, having autonomy and expressing the self. They frequently serve as alternatives to face-to-face interaction within or across networks, locally, nationally or globally, and have been linked to the generation of social capital (Hampton and Wellman 2001, 2003). An increase in emphasis of the values of self-expression certainly seems to point to the development on new social habits. And if we accept that the public and private spheres are ever overlapping and interlinked in an online world, then they are also likely to have political consequences too.

Castells sees mass self-communication as the 'interactive production of meaning' (2009: 132) through 'the creative audience' (2009: 127) whereby the self is realised through the creative process. He argues that in mass self-communication traditional forms of access control do not apply. Anyone can upload a video to the internet, write a blog, start a chat forum or create an e-mail list. Access in this case is the norm and blocking internet access is the exception (Castells 2009: 204). This may be true, but although in principle everyone can produce and distribute information easily with the help of the internet, not all information is visible to the same degree and gets the same attention. Even accepting that social media engender a form of self-communication that is expressive and creative, self-communication to a mass audience is still the individual trying to be heard above the organisation, still the small organisation trying to shout louder than the large organisation. Social media cannot escape, and indeed are part of, the stratified online eyeball economy. And in this economy the traditional and the mainstream are still dominant.

Mainstream news and information sites remain the main source of news, just as certain celebrities and elites generate the largest networks. Despite the abundance of information available online, the mainstream established news outlets still dominate our news consumption across all platforms with increasingly homogenous content. In a nine-country study of news websites Curran et al. (2013) note that 'leading websites around the world reproduce the same kind of news as legacy media. These websites favour the voices of authority and expertise over those of campaigning organizations and the ordinary citizen' (2013: 887). In 2014, the Reuters Institute Digital News Report, covering digital news consumption in 10 countries, showed that people still consume the majority of their online news from familiar and trusted brands although they may reach that content via intermediaries such as Google, Facebook and Twitter. In the UK, Twitter has become an important network for finding, sharing and discussing news, but still only 12% of news consumers view it as a news source. Of this 12%, 48% follow a journalist with the five most popular journalist accounts all originating from large main-stream news organisations. Furthermore, using Twitter to spread entertainment news massively outstrips hard news. The Reuters Institute study (2014) shows that there were 11,559 Twitter accounts tweeting about the Oscars but only 1,500 tweeting about the opposition leader's speech on the European Referendum. The dominance of the same old familiar, trusted news corporations remains even in the Twittersphere. And while news organisations obsessively monitor traffic on all online sites to see which stories are trending as a means of ensuring audience reach for advertisers, so the push to the popular becomes ever harder to resist. So, 'mass self-communication' via social media is clearly present and forms an important source of additional and often experiential insight, but when it comes to information provision, this is framed by and subsumed under the influence of established powerful media actors that have found a way to capitalise on the strength of their market position. The power of multinational media corporations is not dispersed in the age of new media; rather, new forms of and routes to media capital come to the fore.

Mass self-communication must also be understood through the social and political context of which it is a part. In advanced capitalist societies in the West, such as the US or the UK, where a politics of individualism is prevalent as part of a neoliberal approach, mass self-communication through social media is more likely to be largely self-referential and motivated by personal fulfilment (Kaye 2007; Papacharissi 2007, 2010a, 2010b, 2015) that is resonant of a materialis-tic and market-dominated culture (Scammell 2000; Gilbert, 2014). Indeed, social media in these contexts lend themselves very neatly to what could be termed the neoliberal production of self wherein, as Margaret Thatcher once famously stated, 'there is no such thing as society, there are only individuals' – albeit a mass of individuals networked to each other. This self-expressive, thoroughly networked individual may be alone, but they are not lonely or isolated, at least not while they have their social media 'friends'. The network, the notion of unlimited, myriad connections to others, is based on the individual as a self-communicator but can also work to deny the deeper structures of inequality online. Similarly, Miller (2008: 399) states that:

> In the drift from blogging, to social networking, to microblogging we see a shift from dialogue and communication between actors in a network, where the point of the network was to facilitate an exchange of substantive con-tent, to a situation where the maintenance of a network itself has become the primary focus. Here communication has been subordinated to the role of the simple maintenance of ever expanding networks and the notion of a connected presence . . . The movement from blogging, to social network-ing, to microblogging demonstrates the simultaneous movements away from communities, narratives, substantive communication, and towards networks, databases and phatic communion.

Phatic communications focus purely on social (networking) and not on informational or dialogic intents. As such, self-expression may well offer moments of individual control and a freeing of the creative imaginary, but it can also be fragmentary and disconnected from institutions of power. As Castells (2009) notes, we are indeed living through a paradigmatic shift in the articulation of all forms of communication that mixes and recombines forms of cultural expression while expanding the possibility for voices and their potential reach. But the self that is given enhanced prominence in social media must not be reduced to the technological capacity of the form of communication under consideration; rather, it must be firmly understood in relation to the sociostructural context from which the means of expression is given voice and volume. If the sociocultural context consists of the consumerist and individualistic ideology of neoliberalism, then any claims to the liberatory potential of the expansion of the means to self-expression should be treated with extreme caution.

Social media offer a new form of social telling

If traditional news media have been claimed to function as a fourth estate holding the institutions of the state to account, Dutton (2007) argues that new media bring forth a new 'pro-social' dimension that exceeds the limitations of traditional media, leading to a 'Fifth Estate' that reaches beyond and moves across the boundaries of existing institutions, becoming an alternative source of news as well as a citizen-check on public life and private enterprise. In this manner, they proffer a new form of social telling.

This has also been closely linked to the concept of monitorial democracy (Keane 2009), a variety of 'post representative politics' defined by the rapid growth of many different kinds of extra-parliamentary, power-scrutinising mechanisms that keep politicians, governments and political parties on their toes. Keane (2009: 15) describes monitorial democracy as being indelibly linked to a digital age of multimedia-saturated societies: 'societies whose structures of power are continuously "bitten" by monitory institutions operating within a new galaxy of media defined by the ethos of communicative abundance'. Social media present a certain form of publicly private monitorial endeavour. Indeed, there are several examples of instances where a wave of twittering has caused an issue to go viral and forced a rethink by either mainstream news media, corporate business or political powers that be.

When the circumstances of the death of the gay popstar Stephen Gately, of the boy band Boyzone, were claimed by a UK *Daily Mail* tabloid newspaper columnist to be linked to his sexuality, it produced a storm of protest on Twitter, led by the celebrities Stephen Fry and Derren Brown. Fry wrote: 'I gather a repulsive nobody writing in a paper no-one with any decency would be seen dead with has written something loathsome and inhumane. Disgusted with Daily Mail's Jan Moir? Complain where it matters. She breaches 1, 3, 5 and 12 of the code' (cited by Booth, *Guardian*, 17.10.09: 2). Complaints poured in to the Press Complaints Commission at the fastest rate in its history, causing its website to crash. Several mainstream newspapers reported the response and it was a point of discussion on the main BBC1 political discussion programme *Question Time*. Although it is unknown whether Jan Moir or the *Daily Mail* suffered as a consequence of this outpouring of anti-homophobic sentiment, the incident is indicative of the way in which a buzz can be created around a particular issue within a very short space of time and certain (undesirable) discourses can be subject to widespread criticism in a social media world.

In a similar demonstration of social media acting for democratic gain, an attempt to prevent the *Guardian* newspaper writing about a report on toxic waste being dumped off the Ivory Coast by the oil-trading company Trafigura, through the issuing of an injunction to keep it secret, was foiled by a combination of web users and Parliament. The *Guardian* had been embroiled in a five-week legal battle to reveal the details of the damning Minton Report, but an MP tabled a parliamentary question revealing the existence of the injunction. The lawyers operating for the oil firm, Carter-Ruck, immediately warned the newspaper that it would be in contempt of court if it published the information discussed in Parliament. The *Guardian* then ran a story on the fact that it had been prevented from publishing the proceedings of Parliament and within 12 hours bloggers had discovered the banned information (many through the WikiLeaks website – often used by whistle-blowers to publish information banned by the courts in a particular country), millions of people knew of the report and Trafigura had become one of the most searched-for internet terms. The use of social media platforms for disclosing secret information either from private corporations or from governments is now common practice and offers a relatively easy means to disrupt and unsettle traditional institutions and to engender debate.

Both of the above examples, notably, originated with the mainstream news media. But the novelty in this way of telling is the speed at which someone or something can be 'found out' through the search facilities of the internet as archive and library; the fact that anyone with access to a computer connected to the internet can contribute to the telling; and that the manner of being told can create an atmosphere around a particular issue or concern provoking mainstream publicity and political response. Twitter's greatest strength is its ability to provide a snapshot of what anyone is discussing, anywhere in the world, right at the time of asking. For example, in October 2009 Nick Griffin, leader of the British National Party (a far-right neo-fascist political party in the UK), made a controversial appearance on the BBC1 television discussion panel *Question Time*. At the time, a quick Google search for 'Nick Griffin' revealed some interesting results, including a profile on the BBC website and an editorial from the *Guardian* newspaper. But searching Twitter for the same term produced a detailed and compelling insight into the views of tens of thousands of people about the whole issue.

Twitter's ambition to be the pulse of the planet, allowing us to participate in a global conversation among the web community, is seductive, but this particular regime of attention is also still structured by the privileged few (Heil and Piskorski 2009). The Pew Internet and American Life Project (Smith 2010) found that the more educated you are, the more likely you are to be on Twitter. And as noted above, the use of social media for political participation in particular also correlates with measures of social class and educational attainment – the more educated and the more middle class you are, then the more politically active you are online (Blank and Groselj 2014). Cellan-Jones (2009) also noted how, at the G20 protests in London, Twitter was mainly used in broadcast mode to relay messages from the mainstream media. The popularity of Twitter can then also be argued to represent a concentration of power over communication, rather than the radical explosion of a two-way, peer-to-peer communication network, as has been claimed.

In October 2009 Twitter signed a deal with both Google and Microsoft to allow each company to include 'tweets' in its respective search engines as soon as they are posted, allowing real-time searching and increasing the competition between the two search engine rivals. Partnering with Twitter allows both sites to leverage data from the site's millions of active users, providing a ready-made package of real-time views and opinions at the click of a mouse. Both companies use their algorithms to try to identify the sorts of messages that users are likely to find most relevant, not just those that are posted most recently, as Twitter does with its own search service. And therein lies the rub. How do Google and Microsoft prioritise certain tweets over others? Do they have democratic intent as their ambition, or profit from advertising as their purpose?

So, do social media offer a new form of telling? Again, we have to come back to who is telling what to whom. Who is doing the telling is still dominated by a few, well-educated people who can occasionally set the news agenda but more often than not respond to the news agenda already set; rarely do they shift the framework of news. What are they telling? Are they telling tales or telling the truth? In an environment where speed is of the essence, fact checking is bound to be a casualty.

In this new form of social telling, where many voices contribute to the cacophony of online noise, digital presence is delineated both by market power and social power. Paradoxically, it is often hard to speak in a whisper and not be overheard. The ability to trace and track information, and therefore the individuals that send it, also 'tells' the authorities and the institutions of policing and control precisely what is being said and by whom. This was thrust into the public realm when Edward Snowden, a former contractor for the CIA, exposed extensive global internet and phone surveillance by the US National Security Agency (NSA) with more than 61,000 hacking operations worldwide. GCHQ in the UK was also revealed as having the capacity to engage in electronic eavesdropping that could cover up to 600 million communications every day (see Chapter 4). So, social media may provide a new way of telling, but in doing so they also aid surveillance and censorship – a case of us watching them watching us watching them. Social media have been incorporated into police control and surveillance techniques for identifying deviants, criminals and terrorists. Rhoads and Chao (2009) discuss how the Iranian government is using social media to survey its citizens, to anticipate their plans, to identify dissidents and to counter them. They argue that when Iran keeps the internet open it does so to provide it with much richer information to spy on its citizens. Freedom House's 2011 report on *Freedom on the Net* documents the increase in the extent and diversity of internet restrictions around the world. Calingaert (2012: 159) reports that these include 'bans on social media applications, denial of internet access, intermediary liability for service providers, online surveillance and digital attacks'. Deibert and Rohozinski (2012) note that 'malware' (malicious software that can effect control of an unsuspecting user's computer for the purposes of crime, surveillance or sabotage) is now estimated to exceed that of legitimate software (Diamond 2012).

The above debates bring the issue of privacy to the fore. In the UK, Ofcom (2009) published research showing that 54% of 11- to 16-year-olds in the UK say young people need advice about how to keep their online personal information private. A further study by Ofcom in 2015 notes that 26% of adult internet users (up from 21% in 2013) are more likely to say they don't read website terms and conditions or privacy statements, with seven in ten stating that they are happy to provide personal information online to companies as long as they get what they want (Ofcom 2015). The updates of Facebook's more than 936 million daily active users, meanwhile, could eventually provide an even richer trove of information than Twitter for the corporate giants of Google and Microsoft. Facebook users produce more than 55 million status updates each day. While most of these are private and hidden from search engines, Facebook has been campaigning to encourage users to make more of their information public, allowing access to data that can help to garner our attention for commercial gain.

As Benkler makes clear, the reversal of the economic concentrations of industrial media production is only partial; the forms of nonmarket 'sharing' Benkler celebrates, and the alternative information infrastructure they apparently enable, will, at best, exist *alongside* market-based media structures (2006: 121, 23). But that does not dim his vision of a completely new model of social storytelling; indeed he argues that 'we have an opportunity to change the way we create and exchange information, knowledge and culture' (2006: 473, cf. 162–5). But as David Harvey (2005: 3) notes, neoliberalism's endeavour to 'bring all human action into the domain of the market [requires] technologies of information creation and capacities to accumulate, store, transfer, analyse and use massive databases to guide decisions in the global marketplace – networked telecommunications and globalised neoliberalism make perfect partners'.

Thus we have to recognise that in all the radical potential of social media as social critique, as monitorial democracy and as a new way of telling, the relationship between capitalism and critique is complex. Boltanski and Chiapello (2005) suggest that critique both reinforces and transforms capitalism. Critique is always formed out of the dominant power structure and therefore always carries the socio-historic imprint of that birth. Similarly, critique must always struggle within the system that is dominant – in the cases of the UK and the US, this means neoliberalism. The internet as a technology, as a means of communication, does not transcend neoliberalism – it is part of it, although it holds the potential to expose its inadequacies. Seen in this context, it is always more likely that social media will replicate and entrench social inequalities rather than liberate them. As Marwick says:

> [a]ssuming that social networks are discretely explanatory for human behaviour, then, ignores not only the influence of systemic power relations related to gender, sexuality, race, class etc. on behaviour, but also how the subject's own ability for empirical action is influenced by the larger inter-related context in which he or she is situated. Social networking applications remove these 'webs of power' while simultaneously exposing identity self-presentation and relational ties, with the result of removing value and signification from the network.
>
> (Marwick 2005: 12)

But there is a further anxiety that rests not simply on access to resources but rather on inclusion in social networks. An article in *Wired* (June 2009) about Facebook's plans to rule the world stated:

> For the last decade or so, the Web has been defined by Google's algorithms – rigorous and efficient equations that peruse practically every byte of online activity to build a dispassionate atlas of the online world. Facebook CEO Mark Zuckerberg envisions a more personalized, humanized Web, where our network of friends, colleagues, peers, and family is our primary source of information, just as it is offline. In Zuckerberg's vision, users will query this 'social graph' to find a doctor, the best camera, or someone to hire – rather than tapping the cold mathematics of a Google search.

This is already happening in the explosion of hyper-local neighbourhood networking sites where our circle of friends, our social network facilitated through social media, becomes our primary source of information. If we accept the argument that networks online, on the whole, intensify and expand exchanges of likeminded people, this is potentially of enormous concern. Zones of exclusion established on the basis of class, race and gender sustain inequalities. Why do we think the network of networks will somehow transcend previous inequalities, when the evidence on the ground is quite the opposite? Why do we still fall into the trap of thinking about the internet as an independent factor, when, as with other earlier research on media reception, it has been shown that its use and purpose are clearly motivated by social and political background and past and present civic activities that the individual brings with them (Jennings and Zeitner 2003), although the habits of media use may have changed?

The corollary of this is the possibility that our experience of the internet itself may in some way actually hide what's going on, that it may serve to induct us into a privileged stratum of global society and blind us to the need for radical change.

This could be the outcome of self-representation through social media – the capacity to imagine ourselves only through the means of mediated self-expression and not as acting citizens (see Chapter 6). Or, when we are acting out our political citizenship online, when we sign the petitions, blog about a political issue, tweet a link to a critical website or share details of a protest on Facebook, we fall prey to the illusion that this social network, most of whom share each other's political sensibilities, can make a real difference to social and political injustices. So we end up simply preaching to the converted and ever more populating the comfort zones of our own limited echo chambers. Meanwhile the poor get poorer, the rich get richer and environmental degradation continues apace.

Conclusion

> [W]e should no longer be thinking of something called Information Society . . . but rather a Communicational Society . . . , because it is in our communication with each other that ICTs intrude most directly into the core of social existence.
>
> (Silverstone and Osimo 2005)

The communicational society that Silverstone refers to promises a new transcendental space, a cooperative society (or form of participatory democracy) that is immanent in society (as far as socio-political conditions allow) and is potentially advanced by information and information technology. But this notion of a good, equal and deliberative society isn't reached automatically through communicational means because there is an inherent antagonism between cooperation and competition in capitalism (Andrejevic 2007), and hence also in the communicational society, that threatens the potentials for participatory democracy. The means of communication produce *potentials* that *may* undermine competition but at the same time also produce new forms of domination and competition. Digital media have brought about converged platforms and converged practice – consumers are producers and can directly create meaning; meaning making is no longer the preserve of the purely interpretative but combines with the act of making/producing, but they do so in specific social, economic and political contexts. In the case of Western developed democracies, this is the context of neoliberal capitalism.

Castells (2009) may be right to stress that the internet offers *possibilities* for counter-power and the creation of autonomous spaces. But these possibilities exist within the worldwide move towards data manipulation driven by state control and surveillance and corporate interest (Lovink 2012). This does not mean that these spaces cannot exist in the future, but to understand how they might exist we have to have a critical analysis of what inhibits them.

The monitorial power that Castells (2009) sees as part of mass self-communication – the ability to monitor, reveal and hold to account – is greatly increased in a vastly expanded and speeded-up digital age. But this takes place in a context where those in power 'have made it their priority to harness the potential of mass self communication in the service of their specific interests' (2009: 414). But even as Castells acknowledges the enduring dominance of capital and state, he also sees the creativity unleashed online as having the potential to challenge corporate power and dismantle government authority (2009: 420). This is an argument that resides essentially on the basis of the politics of access to production – once you have it, then communicative freedom is yours, without due consideration of the terms on which that access is structured. Everyone can speak, anyone can blog, everyone is a producer – what wonderful plurality, what joyous freedoms. Yet the power endowed through such plurality and freedom may be hollow and fleeting. There is not a limitless stream of power that everyone can equally lay claim to. For power to be used for democratic gain, it must be wrested from those who have too much and reinvested in those who have too little. By claiming that the pluralism and freedom of an online world gives autonomy and space for resistance to breathe and grow, we put our hopes in technology – that somehow this would work despite all the evidence to the contrary.

The values of individualism and self-expression prevalent in late-modern neoliberal societies concord with a private sphere that functions as the basis for civic engagement. The mobility of this private sphere also allows everyday routines to be interwoven to render the individual permanently reachable in a manner that exerts phenomenal control over our lives (Castells et al. 2006; Ling and Donner 2009). As Jodi Dean (2009) notes, the mythic dimension of the openness of new media, which has brought about a hegemonic discourse based on the rhetoric of multiplicity and pluralism, autonomy, access and participation that apparently lead automatically to a more pluralistic society and enhanced democracy, also happens to coincide with extreme corporatisation, financialisation and privatisation across the globe.

As Norval (2007: 102) reminds us, we must avoid 'assum[ing] the existence of a framework of politics in which in principle every voice could be heard, without giving attention to the very structuring of those frameworks and the ways in which the visibility of subjects is structured'. Creative autonomy is pretty difficult to express under conditions of material poverty, exploitation and oppression. Individual particularities and political desires alone, even if they are articulated together and facilitated by new communication technologies, will not reclaim and rebuild the institutions necessary to reveal and sustain a new political order.

Genuine democratisation requires the real and material participation of the oppressed and excluded; the real and material recognition of difference, along with the space for contestation and an understanding and response to its meaning. This is not an argument simply for inclusivity, multiplicity, participation or for the creative autonomy of everyone, as these claims alone can only ever take us to first base. They may well be suggestive of possible changes in the dynamics of action. But acknowledging this should not give way to a fetishisation of technology through notions of participation, autonomy or creativity.

Networks are not inherently liberatory; network openness does not lead us directly to democracy. The practices of new media *may* be liberating for the user but not necessarily democratising for society. We would be wise to remember that the wider social contexts in which networks are formed and exist have a political architecture that predates the internet. An emphasis on creative autonomy lends itself too neatly to individualistic politics that inhibit progressive social change. While social networking forces us to recognise the destabilisation of the producer and the consumer and the blurring of the social and political public spheres, to be fully understood it must be considered contextually. In certain contexts, expansions in networked communications media reinforce the hegemony of democratic rhetoric (Dean 2009) – fetishising speech, opinion and participation. They suggest to us that the number of friends you have on Facebook or the number of followers you have on Twitter are markers of success. This networked communication may well expand the possibilities of contestation but may also increasingly embed mainstream media's priorities and interests ever more deeply into the ontology of the political. This helps to further establish the norms and values of commercial media while diverting attention from corporate and financial influence, access to structures of decision-making and the narrowing of political struggle to reality entertainment.

The key question is: do social media do no more than serve ego-centred needs and reflect practices structured around the self? The civically-motivated yet self-absorbed user of social media sees the endless possibility of online connectivity against the banality of the social order. The motivation is often fed by a desire to connect the self to society. But the above discussion shows that social media are not first and foremost about social good or political engagement; their primary function is expressive and, as such, they are best understood in terms of their potential for articulating the (often contradictory) dynamics of the political environments they are part of, rather than recasting or regenerating the structures that uphold them.

References

Agre, P. E. (2002) 'Real-time Politics: The Internet and the Political Process', *Information Society*, 18 (5): 311–331.

Althaus, S. L. and Tewksbury, D. (2000) 'Patterns of Internet and Traditional Media Use in a Networked Community', *Political Communication*, 17: 21–45.

Andrejevic, M. (2004) 'The Web Cam Subculture and the Digital Enclosure', in N. Couldry and A. McCarthy (eds) *Media Space: Place, Scale and Culture in a Media Age*, Oxon: Routledge, 193–209.

Andrejevic, M. (2007) *iSpy: Surveillance and Power in the Interactive Era*, Lawrence, KS: University of Kansas Press.

Andrejevic, M. (2008) 'Theory Review: Power, Knowledge, and Governance: Foucault's Relevance to Journalism Studies', *Journalism Studies*, 9 (4): 605–614.

Barber, B., Mattson, K. and Peterson, J. (1997) *The State of Electronically Enhanced Democracy: A Survey of the Internet*. A report for the Markle Foundation. New Brunswick, NJ: Walt Whitman Center for Culture and Politics of Democracy.

Baron, N. (2008) *Always On: Language in an Online and Mobile World*, Oxford: Oxford University Press.

Baym, N. (2015) 'Social Media and the Struggle for Society', *Social Media and Society*, 1 (1): http://m.sms.sagepub.com/content/1/1/2056305115580477.

Beckett, C. (2008) *SuperMedia: Saving Journalism So It Can Save the World*, Oxford: Wiley-Blackwell.

Bell, D. (2007) *Cyberculture Theorists: Manuel Castells and Donna Haraway*, New York: Routledge.

Benkler, Y. (2006) *The Wealth of Networks: How Social Production Transforms Markets and Freedom*, New Haven, CT: Yale University Press.

Best, S. J., Chmielewski, B. and Krueger, B. S. (2005) 'Selective Exposure to Online Foreign News During the Conflict with Iraq', *Harvard International Journal of Press/ Politics*, 10 (4): 52–70.

Bimber, B. (2000) 'The Study of Information Technology and Civic Engagement', *Political Communication*, 17 (4): 329–333.

Bimber, B. (2002) *Information and American Democracy: Technology in the Evolution of Political Power*, Cambridge: Cambridge University Press.

Bimber, B. and Davis, R. (2003) *Campaigning Online: The Internet in U.S. Elections*, New York: Oxford University Press.

Blank, G. and Groselj, D. (2014) 'Dimensions of Internet Use: Amount, Variety and Types', *Information, Communication and Society*, 17 (4): 417–435.

Boltanski, L. and Chiapello, E. (2005) *The New Spirit of Capitalism*, trans. G. Elliott, London: Verso.

Brodzinsky, S. (2008) 'Facebook Used to Target Colombia's FARC with Global Rally', Christian *Science Monitor*, 4 February. Online. Available HTTP: <http://www.csmonitor. com/2008/0204/p04s02-woam.html> (accessed 22 November 2008).

Brundidge, J. (2006) 'The Contribution of the Internet to the Heterogeneity of Political Discussion Networks: Does the Medium Matter?' Paper presented at the annual meeting of the International Communication Association, Dresden International Congress Centre, Dresden, Germany, 16 June. Online. Available HTTP: <http://www. allacademic.com/meta/p_mla_apa_research_citation/0/9/2/6/5/p92653_index.html> (accessed 1 November 2015).

Bruner, J. (2013) 'Tweets loud and quiet'. Online. Available HTTP: <http://radar.oreilly. com/2013/12/tweets-loud-and-quiet.html> (accessed 1 November 2015).

Bruns, A. (2008) *Blogs, Wikipedia, Second Life and Beyond*, New York: Peter Lang.

Calingaert, D. (2012) 'Challenges for International Policy' in L. Diamond and M. F. Plattner (eds) *Liberation Technology: Social Media and the Struggle for Democracy*, Baltimore, MD: Johns Hopkins University Press, 157–174.

Carnegie Trust UK (2010) *Enabling Dissent*, London: Carnegie Trust UK.

Castells, M. (1998) *The Information Age. Economy, Society and Culture*, Cambridge, MA: Blackwell.

Castells, M. (2009) *Communication Power*, Oxford: Oxford University Press.

Castells, M., Fernandez-Ardevol, J., Linchuan Qiu, J. and Sey, A. (2006) *Mobile Communication and Society*, Cambridge, MA: MIT Press.

Castoriadis, C. (1991) *Philosophy, Politics and Autonomy: Essay in Political Philosophy*, New York: Oxford University Press.

Cellan-Jones, R. (2009) 'Do Anarchists Tweet?', BBC News website, 2 April. Online. Available HTTP: <http://www.bbc.co.uk/blogs/technology/2009/04/do_anarchists_ tweet.html> (accessed 22 October 2011).

Coleman, S. (2005) 'The Lonely Citizen: Indirect Representation in an Age of Networks', *Political Communication*, 22 (2): 180–190.

comScore (2007) 'Social Networking Goes Global'. Online. Available HTTP: <http://www.comscore.com/press/release.asp?press=555> (accessed 7 July 2009).

Couldry, N. (2003) *Media Rituals: A Critical Approach*, London: Routledge.

Council of Foreign Relations (2008) 'FARC, ELN: Colombia's Left-Wing Guerrillas'. Online. Available HTTP: <http://www.cfr.org/publication/9272/> (accessed 23 May 2008).

Curran, J., Coen, S., Aalberg, T., Hatashi, K., Jones, P., Splendore, S., Papathanassopoulos, S., Rowe, D. and Tiffen, R. (2013) 'Internet Revolution Revisitied: A Comparative Study of Online News', *Media, Culture and Society*, 35 (7): 880–897.

Current.com (2008) 'Facebook Users Spawn Grassroots Protest of Colombia's FARC'. Online. Available HTTP: <http://current.com/items/88832752/facebook_users_spawn_grassroots_protest_of_colombia_s_farc.htm> (accessed 23 November 2008).

Dahlberg, L. and Siapera, E. (eds) (2007) *Radical Democracy and the Internet: Interrogating Theory and Practice*, London: Palgrave Macmillan.

Davis, R. (1999) *The Web of Politics: The Internet's Impact on the American Political System*, Oxford: Oxford University Press.

Dean, J. (2009) *Democracy and other Neoliberal Fantasies: Communicative Capitalism and Left Politics*, Durham, NC: Duke University Press.

Deibert, R. and Rohozinski, R. (2012) 'Liberation vs. Control: The Future of Cyberspace' in L. Diamond and M. F. Plattner (eds) *Liberation Technology: Social Media and the Struggle for Democracy*, Baltimore, MD: Johns Hopkins University Press, 18–32.

Diamond, L. (2012) 'Introduction' in L. Diamond and M. F. Plattner (eds) *Liberation Technology: Social Media and the Struggle for Democracy*, Baltimore, MD: Johns Hopkins University Press, ix–xxvii.

Donath, J. (2007) 'Signals in Social Supernets', *Journal of Computer-Mediated Communication*, 13 (1): article 12. Online. Available HTTP: <http://jcmc.indiana.edu/vol13/issue1/donath.html> (accessed 15 August 2011).

Dutton, W. (2007) *Through the Network of Networks: The Fifth Estate*, Oxford: Oxford Internet Institute.

Ellison, N., Steinfield, C. and Lampe, C. (2007) 'The Benefits of Facebook "Friends": Social Capital and College Students' Use of Online Social Network Sites', *Journal of Computer-Mediated Communication*, 12 (4): 43–68.

Facebook Group (2008) 'One Million Voices Against FARC' (English version). Online. Available HTTP: <http://www.facebook.com/group.php?gid=21343878704> (accessed 23 May 2008).

Facebook, Inc. (2008a) Create a Group. Online. Available HTTP: <http://www.facebook.com/groups/create.php> (accessed 27 April 2008).

Facebook, Inc. (2008b) Press Room. Online. Available HTTP: <http://www.facebook.com/press/info.php?statistics> (accessed 26 April 2008).

Facebook Statistics (2008) Online. Available HTTP: <http://www.facebook.com/press/info.php?statistics> (accessed 23 May 2008).

Fenton, N. (ed.) (2010) *New Media, Old News: Journalism and Democracy in the Digital Age*, London: Sage.

Ferrara, E., Varol, O., Davis, C., Menczer, F. and Flammini, A. (2015) 'The Rise of Social Bots'. Online: arXiv:1407.5225v2 [cs.SI].

Freedman, D. (2014) *The Contradictions of Media Power*, London: Bloomsbury.

Geveran, W. (2009) 'Disclosure, Endorsement, and Identity in Social Marketing', *University of Illinois Law Review*, 1105. Online. Available HTTP: <http://home.law.uiuc.edu/lrev/publications/2000s/2009/2009_4/McGeveran.pdf> (accessed 17 August 2011).

Gilbert, J. (2014) *Common Ground: Democracy and Collectivity in the Age of Individualism*, London: Pluto Press.

Gillmor, D. (2004) *We the Media: Grassroots Journalism by the People, for the People*, Sebastopol, CA: O'Reilly Media.

Golumbia, D. (2009) *The Cultural Logic of Computation*, Harvard, MA: Harvard University Press.

Gupta, A., Lamba, H. and Kumaraguru, P. (2013) '#BostonMarathon #Pray-ForBoston: Analyzing fake content on Twitter'. In *eCrime Researchers Summit (eCRS)*. IEEE, 1–12.

Habermas, J. (1996) *Between Facts and Norms: Contributions to a Discourse Theory of Law and Democracy*, Cambridge: Polity Press.

Hamelink, C. (2000) *The Ethics of Cyberspace*, London: Sage.

Hampton, K. (2002) 'Place-based and IT Mediated "Community"', *Planning Theory and Practice*, 3 (2): 228–231.

Hampton, K. and Wellman, B. (2001) 'Long Distance Community in the Network Society – Contact and Support Beyond Netville', *American Behavioral Scientist*, 45 (3): 476–495.

Hampton, K. and Wellman, B. (2003) 'Neighboring in Netville: How the Internet Supports Community and Social Capital in a Wired Suburb', *City and Community*, 2 (4): 277–311.

Harvey, D. (2005) *A Brief History of Neoliberalism*, Oxford: Oxford University Press.

Haythornthwaite, C. (2005) 'Social Networks and Internet Connectivity Effects', *Information, Communication and Society*, 8 (2): 125–147.

Heil, B. and Piskorski, M. (2009) 'New Twitter Research: Men Follow Men and Nobody Tweets'. Online. Available HTTP: <http://blogs.harvardbusiness.org/cs/2009/06/new_twitter_research_men_follo.html> (accessed 4 October 2011).

Herman, E. S. and McChesney, R. W. (1997) *The Global Media. The New Missionaries of Global Capitalism*, London: Cassell.

Hill, K. A. and Hughes, J. E. (1998) *Cyberpolitics: Citizen Activism in the Age of the Internet*, Lanham, MD: Rowman & Littlefield.

Hindman, M. (2009) *The Myth of Digital Democracy*, Princeton, NJ: Princeton University Press.

Holguín, C. (2008) 'Colombia: Networks of Dissent and Power', *OpenDemocracy. Free Thinking for the World*, 4 February. Online. Available HTTP: <http://www.opendemocracy.net/article/democracy_power/politics_protest/facebook_farc> (accessed 22 November 2008).

Holt, R. (2004) *Dialogue on the Internet: Language, Civic Identity, and Computer-mediated Communication*, Westport, CT: Praeger.

Holton, R. J. (1998) *Globalization and the Nation-state*, London: Macmillan Press.

Infographic (2010) 'Infographic: Twitter Statistics, Facts and Figures'. Online. Available HTTP: <http://www.digitalbuzzblog.com/infographic-twitter-statistics-facts-figures/> (accessed 6 May 2010).

Internet World Stats (2007) http://www.internetworldstats.com/sa/co.htm (accessed 22 May 2008).

Jennings, M. K. and Zeitner, V. (2003) 'Internet Use and Civic Engagement: A Longitudinal Analysis', *Public Opinion Quarterly*, 67: 311–334.

Kaye, B. K. (2007) 'Blog Use Motivations' in M. Tremayne (ed.) *Blogging, Citizenship and the Future of the Media*, New York: Routledge, 127–148.

Keane, J. (2009) *The Life and Death of Democracy*, London: Simon and Schuster.

Khiabany, G. (2010) 'Media Power, People Power and Politics of Media in Iran', paper presented to the IAMCR conference, Braga, Portugal.

Kohut, A. (2008, January) 'Social Networking and Online Videos Take off: Internet's Broader Role in Campaign 2008', The Pew Research Center for the People and the Press. Online. Available HTTP: <http://www.pewinternet.org/pdfs/Pew_MediaSources_jan08.pdf> (accessed 23 March 2008).

Lenhart, A. (2015) Pew Research Center, *Teens, Social Media and Technology Overview 2015*. Online. Available HTTP: <http://www.pewinternet.org/files/2015/04/PI_TeensandTech_Update2015_0409151.pdf> (accessed 3 November 2015).

Ling, R. and Donner, J. (2009) *Mobile Communication*, Cambridge: Polity.

Liu, H. (2007) 'Social Networking Profiles as Taste Performances', *Journal of Computer-Mediated Communication*, 13 (1): article 13. Online. Available HTTP: <http://jcmc/indiana.edu/vol13/issue1/liu.html> (accessed 3 October 2010).

Lovink, G. (2012) *Networks Without a Cause: A Critique of Social Media*, Cambridge: Polity Press.

McChesney, R. (1996) 'The Internet and US Communication Policy Making in Historical and Critical Perspective', *Journal of Computer-Mediated Communication*, 1 (4). Online. Available HTTP: <http://jcmc.indiana.edu/vol1/issue4/mcchesney.html> (accessed 3 October 2010).

McChesney, R (2014) *Digital Disconnect: How Capitalism is Turning the Internet Against Democracy*, New York: The New Press.

Margolis, M., Resnick, D. and Tu, C. (1997) 'Campaigning on the Internet: Parties and Candidates on the World Wide Web in the 1996 Primary Season', *Harvard International Journal of Press and Politics*, 2: 59–78.

Marwick, A. E. (2005) *Selling Your Self: Online Identity in the Age of a Commodified Internet*, Washington, D.C.: University of Washington Press.

Miller, V. (2008) 'New Media, Networking, and Phatic Culture', *Convergence*, 14 (4): 387–400.

Nielsen (2010) 'Social Networks/Blogs Accounts for One in Every Four and a Half Minutes Online'. Online. Available HTTP: <http://blog.nielsen.com/nielsenwire/online_mobile/social-media-accounts-for-22-percent-of-time-online/> (accessed 24 October 2011).

Nielsen (2012) 'State of the Media: The Social Media Report 2012'. Online. Available HTTP: <http://www.nielsen.com/us/en/insights/news/2012/social-media-report-2012-social-media-comes-of-age.html> (accessed 2 May 2015)

Norris, P. (2004) 'The Digital Divide', in F. Webster (ed.) *The Information Society Reader*, New York: Routledge, 273–286.

Norval, A. (2007) *Aversive Democracy*, Cambridge: Cambridge University Press.

Ofcom (2009) 'Children's and Young People's Access to Online Content on Mobile Devices, Games Consoles and Portable Media Players'. Online. Available HTTP: <http://www.ofcom.org.uk/advice/media_literacy/medlitpub/medlitpubrss/online_access.pdf? dm_i=4KS,1QAM,9UK2L,64F1,1> (accessed 10 January 2010).

Ofcom (2015) *Adults' Media Use and Attitudes*, London: Ofcom.

Örnebring, H. (2008) 'The Consumer as Producer of What? User-generated Tabloid Content in The Sun (UK) and Aftonbladet (Sweden)', *Journalism Studies*, 9 (5): 771–785.

Papacharissi, Z. (2002a) 'The Self Online: The Utility of Personal Home Pages', *Journal of Broadcasting and Electronic Media*, 44: 175–196.

Papacharissi, Z. (2002b) 'The Presentation of Self in Virtual Life: Characteristics of Personal Home Pages', *Journalism and Mass Communication Quarterly*, 79 (3): 643–660.

Papacharissi, Z. (2007) 'The Blogger Revolution? Audiences as Media Producers', in M. Tremayne (ed.) *Blogging, Citizenship and the Future of the Media*, New York: Routledge, 21–38.

Papacharissi, Z. (2009) 'The Virtual Geographies of Social Networks: A Comparative Analysis of Facebook, LinkedIn and ASmallWorld', *New Media and Society*, 11 (1–2): 199–220.

Papacharissi, Z. (2010a) *A Private Sphere: Democracy in a Digital Age*, Cambridge: Polity Press.

Papacharissi, Z. (2010b) *A Networked Self: Identity, Community and Culture on Social Network Sites*, New York: Routledge.

Papacharissi, Z. (2015) *Affective Publics: Sentiment, Technology and Politics*, Oxford: Oxford University Press.

Patterson, T. (2010) 'Media Abundance and Democracy', *Media, Journalismo e Democracia*, 17 (9): 13–31.

Pew Internet and American Life Project (2008) *The Internet's Role in Campaign 2008*. Online. Available HTTP: <http://www.pewinternet.org/Reports/2009/6-The-Internets-Rolein-Campaign-2008.aspx> (accessed 5 October 2011).

Porta, D. D. and Tarrow, S. (2005) 'Transnational Process and Social Activism: An Introduction', in D. D. Porta and S. Tarrow (eds) *Transnational Protest and Global Activism*, Lanham, MD: Rowman & Littlefield, 1–19.

Poster, M. (2006) *Information Please. Culture and Politics in the Age of Digital Machines*, Durham, NC: Duke University Press.

Puopolo, S. (2000) 'The Web and U.S. Senatorial Campaigns 2000', *American Behavioral Scientist*, 44: 2030–2047.

Quantcast (2008) Facebook.com. Online. Available HTTP: <http://www.quantcast. com/facebook.com> (accessed 30 June 2008).

Rainie, L. and Madden, M. (2005) 'Podcasting', Pew Internet and Life Project, Washington, D.C. Online. Available HTTP: <http://www.pewinternet.org/pdfs/PIP_podcasting2005. pdf> (accessed 3 October 2007).

Reuters Institute (2014) *Digital News Report 2014*, Oxford: Reuters Institute.

Rheingold, H. (2002) *Smart Mobs. The Next Social Revolution*, Cambridge, MA: Perseus Books Group.

Rheingold, H. (2008) 'From Facebook to the Streets of Colombia', in *SmartMobs. The Next Social Revolution. Mobile Communication, Pervasive Computing, Wireless Networks, Collective Action*. Online. Available HTTP: <http://www.smartmobs.com/2008/02/04/fromfacebookto-the-streets-of-colombia/> (accessed 22 May 2008).

Rhoads, C. and Chao, L. (2009) 'Iran's Web Spying Aided by Western Technology', *Wall Street Journal*, 22 June. Online. Available HTTP: <http://online.wsj.com/article/SB124562668777335653.html> (accessed 7 October 2009).

Sassen, S. (2007) 'Electronic Networks, Power, and Democracy', in R. Mansell, C. Avgerou, D. Quah and R. Silverstone, R. (eds) *The Oxford Handbook of New Media*, Oxford: Oxford University Press, 339–361.

Scammell, M. (2000) 'The Internet and Citizen Engagement: The Age of the Citizen Consumer', *Political Communication*, 17 (4): 351–355.

Schlozman, K., Verba, S. and Brady, H. (2010) 'Weapon of the Strong? Participatory Inequality and the Internet', *Perspectives on Politics*, 8 (2), 487–509.

Sennett, R. (1974) *The Fall of Public Man*, New York: Random House.

Shah, D. V., Kwak, N. and Holbert, R. L. (2001) 'Connecting and Disconnecting with Civic Life: Patterns of Internet Use and the Production of Social Capital', *Political Communication*, 18: 141–162.

Shirky, C. (2008) *Here Comes Everybody: The Power of Organizations without Organization*, London: Allen Lane.

Silverstone, R. and Osimo, D. (2005) 'Interview with Prof. Roger Silverstone', *Communication & Strategies*, 59: 101.

Sloam, J. (2014) '"The Outraged Young": Young Europeans, Civic Engagement and the New Media in a Time of Crisis', *Information, Communication and Society*, 17 (2): 217–231.

Smith, A. (2010) 'Who Tweets?', Pew Research Center Publications. Online. Available HTTP:<http://pewresearch.org/pubs/1821/twitter-users-profile-exclusive-examination> (accessed 25 October 2011).

Smith, A. and Raine, L. (2008) 'The Internet and the 2008 Election'. Pew Internet and Life Project. Washington, D.C. Online. Available HTTP: <http://www.pewinternet. org/pdfs/PIP_2008_election.pdf> (accessed 8 July 2008).

Smythe, D. W. (1994) 'Communications: Blindspot of Western Marxism', in T. Guback (ed.) *Counterclockwise: Perspectives on Communication*, Boulder, CO: Westview Press, 263–291.

Streck, J. M. (1998) 'Pulling the Plug on Electronic Town Meetings: Participatory Democracy and the Reality of the Usenet', in C. Toulouse and T. W. Luke (eds) *The Politics of Cyberspace: a New Political Science Reader*, New York: Routledge, 8–48.

Sunstein, C. (2007) *Republic.Com 2.0*, Princeton, NJ: Princeton University Press.

Tapscott, D. and Williams, A. (2008) *Wikinomics: How Mass Collaboration Changes Everything*, London: Atlantic Books.

Turrow, J. (2001) 'Family Boundaries, Commercialism and the Internet: a Framework for Research', *Journal of Applied Developmental Psychology*, 22 (1): 73–86.

Wardle, C., Dubberley, S. and Brown, P. (2014) Amateur Footage: A global study of user-generated content in TV and online-news output. A Tow/Knight Report. Online. Available HTTP:<http://towcenter.org/wp-content/uploads/2014/04/80458_Tow-Center-Report-WEB.pdf> (accessed 8 June 2015).

Wilhelm, A. G. (1999) 'Virtual Sounding Boards: How Deliberative Is Online Political Discussion?', in B. N. Hague and B. D. Loader (eds) *Digital Democracy*, London: Routledge, 54–78.

Williams, C. B. and Gulati, G. J. (2007) 'Social Networks in Political Campaigns: Facebook and the 2006 Midterm Elections', paper presented at the Annual Meeting of the American Political Science Association, Chicago. Online. Available HTTP: <http://www.bentley.edu/news-events/pdf/Facebook_APSA_2007_final.pdf> (accessed 27 March 2008).

Wolfe, Alexander (2008) 'Twitter in Controversial Spotlight Amid Mumbai Attacks' *Information Week*, 29 November 2008.

Xie, J. (2014) 'Influence inflation in online social networks' *Advances in Social Networks Analysis and Mining (ASONAM) conference proceedings*, pp. 435–442.

Zittrain, J. (2009) *The Future of the Internet*, London: Penguin.

Chapter 6

The internet of radical politics and social change

Natalie Fenton

Introduction: online and oppositional

The capacity of the internet to build and mobilise political networks of resistance to counter dominant power structures, both nationally and internationally, has been well documented (e.g. Downey and Fenton 2003; Hill and Hughes 1998; Keck and Sikkink 1998; Gerbaudo 2012; Roberts 2014; Castells 2015). This is a literature that goes beyond the habitual day-to-day communicative realm of the internet that focuses on the individual (albeit the individual in a connected world), and speaks to the radical collective possibilities of online political mobilisation such that the internet is claimed to have changed the nature of radical progressive politics itself (Castells 2009, 2015; Juris 2008), enabling the likes of the Arab Spring (see Chapter 2) and the Occupy Movement (see below) to materialise. Thus, the forms of mediation, the means of organising protest and demonstration, and communicating one's political passions and desires are connected to the claims of a revival of radical politics of the 21st century (e.g. Roberts 2014; Hands 2011; Alexander 2011; Juris 2008).

This chapter begins by discussing some of the key technological characteristics that have been claimed to mark out the internet as particularly suited to contemporary transnational political activism. Assessing a range of literature, the chapter organises approaches to online activism and radical politics into three dual and interconnected themes: *speed and space* – the internet is claimed to facilitate international communication among non-governmental organisations (NGOs), allowing protestors to respond rapidly on an international level to local events while requiring minimal resources and bureaucracy; *connectivity and participation* – the internet is described as a mediated activity that seeks to raise people's awareness, give a voice to those who do not have one, offer social empowerment through participation, allow disparate people and causes to organise themselves and form alliances on a transnational level, and ultimately be used as a tool for social change; and *diversity and horizontality* – where the internet is also claimed to be more than an organising tool. It is an organising model for a new form of political protest that is not only international, but is decentralised, with diverse interests but common targets, although the targets may be perpetually contested.

These three dual themes point to a heady mix of ingredients that is argued to correspond to an integral affinity between the global, interactive technology of the internet and the development of a more internationalist, decentred and participatory form of radical politics that we have seen in the likes of the Occupy Movement and is said to lead to a new *means of* and a new *meaning of* being political. Such claims go beyond a simple premise of enhanced communication aiding political mobilisation, by linking new technology to shifts in political ontology – in other words, a transformation in the very nature and practice of politics. Yet often such claims gloss over the complex social and political histories out of which these forms of resistance and political mobilisations emerge. Radical progressive politics are also connected indelibly to the political history of any one place or context. Technology is embedded in deep-rooted normative, social, political and economic forces. Thus, the chapter strives to put radical politics in a radical context by asking: what is the relationship between new media and radical politics? But also: in which circumstances are politics rendered open to contestation and revision today?

New media and transnational activism: increasing the speed and expanding the space of political activism

There seems little doubt that spaces for political engagement have expanded in a digital mediascape and that the internet is now central to an understanding of the mediation of political identities and enactments of political belief. Klein (2000, 2002) was one of the first to argue that the internet facilitates international communication among NGOs, and allows protestors to respond on an international level to local events while requiring minimal resources and bureaucracy. This occurs through the sharing of experience and tactics on a transnational basis to inform and increase the capacity of local campaigns. According to Klein, the internet ushered in an organising model for a new type of political protest – one that could cross national borders, that was leaderless, non-hierarchical and invited difference. Since Klein's description, over a decade later similar claims have been made for the Indignado movement in Spain (Castells 2015). This movement developed out of the neoliberal politics of austerity enforced in the aftermath of the financial crisis in 2008. It led to an array of protests across the country that were communicated via the internet to the rest of the world. These protests were said to have inspired the Occupy Movement that began on Wall Street in the heart of New York City's financial district to protest against social and economic inequality that then, via the internet, spread to many parts of the globe. The internet was also instilled with the revolutionary prowess that gave rise to the domino of revolts across the Arab and North African world in 2011 (Mason 2012) – all linking new media to radical political possibilities in a manner that Diamond (2012: xi–xii) has termed 'liberation technology' that can 'empower individuals, facilitate independent communication and mobilisation and strengthen an emergent civil society'.

The use of the internet for such radical oppositional purposes is described as a mediated activity that seeks to raise people's awareness, give a voice to those who do not have one, offer social empowerment, allow disparate people and causes to organise themselves and form alliances, and ultimately be used as a tool for social change. It is the ability to form networks and build alliances at the click of a mouse that is felt to be conducive to the building of oppositional political movements that can spread across national borders and merge a variety of topics under broadly common themes, though the themes may be subject to frequent change. Sometimes such radical politics takes the form of new social movements that are themselves often hybrid, contradictory and contingent and include a huge variety of voices and experiences. At other times, the oppositional politics on display is better described as an alliance of groups, organisations and individuals with a political affinity that coalesces at a particular moment in time.

The internet has another characteristic that is well suited to radical politics – it is a medium that is more readily associated with young people (e.g. Livingstone and Bovill 2002; Loader 2007); and young people, in particular, are increasingly associated with disengagement from mainstream politics (e.g. Park 2004; Wilkinson and Mulgan 1995, Sloam 2014) and engagement with the internet (Livingstone et al. 2005; Ofcom 2010). The extensive literature that discusses young people and politics falls largely into two camps: one that talks of a disaffected youth and the other of citizen displacement (Loader 2007). In the former, studies speak of the decline of young people voting in conventional national party political elections as indicative of extensive alienation of young people from society's central institutions and warn of the long-term dangers this may hold. In the latter, an engagement with traditional politics based on a sovereign nation-state is displaced:

Young people are not necessarily any less interested in politics than previous generations, but . . . traditional political activity no longer appears appropriate to address the concerns associated with contemporary youth cultures.

(Loader 2007: 1)

Rather, civil society, or certain parts of it, come to the fore as alternative arenas of public engagement (Sloam 2014). It is argued that politically motivated young people tend to look to non-mainstream political arenas often populated by NGOs and new social movements – alternative forms of political activism that work at the margins of the dominant public sphere (Roberts 2014; Sloam 2013; Kahn and Kellner 2004, 2007; Bennett 2005; Hill and Hughes 1998), now more easily discovered in an online world. As these spaces open up, they also allow for an increased diversity of views to find expression. It is further claimed that these forms of political engagement better fit the experience of social fragmentation and individualisation felt by citizens (Loader 2007) as well as being directly compatible with the structure and nature of communications via the internet – a medium that young people are commonly well acquainted with. As discussed in Chapter 5, this also relates to the internet, first and foremost, as an expressive medium that allows the felt experience of politics to be relayed without intermediaries, editing or distortion by media elites. The space given is largely (and often naively) perceived to be open and free from state or corporate control. This appeals to young people who feel excluded and misrepresented by the mainstream news but more in control of their identity and politics online (Wayne et al. 2010; Ofcom 2007).

The combined elements of the speed and space of technology, youth and counter-traditional politics – each conducive to the others – mark out the internet as particularly suited to contemporary (transnational) political activism. The expanded space and increased speed communicates protest to a far wider geographic spread of people than has ever been previously possible, opening the potential for greater national and international solidarity to form; for building alliances, organising protest and coordinating action over time and in real time. This may add to a heightened political atmosphere at key moments of protest as events unfold and new media (including digital phones) enable a broader public to bear witness to the experience through footage and reports relayed instantaneously from those actively involved in protest on the streets. In this manner, contemporary radical politics, often mediated through transnational social movements, are a combination of collective action and individual response.

To some extent this is nothing new. Radical politics has always been at the forefront of mobilising protest and demonstration. A willingness and desire to participate in such political activism is one of the defining features of 'being radical'. What is unprecedented is that this is now happening on a transnational basis and at high speed, resulting in ever more complex networks of intensely expressive and often highly personalised forms of oppositional activism (Bennett and Segerberg 2013). This is a radical politics that is fuelled and sustained through the communicative capacity of social media that generates both a public and deliberative response as well as a deeply expressive, emotional and empathetic one; it may be highly personalised (Bennett and Segerberg 2013) but it also spreads solidarity and hope (Fenton 2008).

But the speed and space of the internet is not only available to political activists to take advantage of. Those in power in political office and other elites with power through economic dominance can also capitalise on these communicative qualities, and with more resources they can do so more forcefully. Just as new media is used for liberatory ends, so it is also used to suppress dissent through state censorship, internet filtering and surveillance as noted in Chapter 5 (Calingaert 2012; Diamond 2012). Deibert and Rohozinski (2012) also reveal how both authoritarian and democratic governments engage wilfully in a range of activities that include restricting and intimidating certain forms of online content; putting pressure on internet service providers to monitor and remove certain types of content and organisations deemed troublesome; and employing 'just-in-time' blocking through distributed denial-of-service (DDoS) attacks with the purpose of freezing oppositional organisations at vital political moments as well as targeted and blanket surveillance. Social media companies are far from innocent bystanders when it comes to censoring and restricting forms of dissent (Hintz 2015) through the sharing of citizen data with state authorities and intelligence agencies. Corporate platform owners also hold the power to switch users off the networks or to switch off entire networks. This may be rare, but can be used to good effect. This is commonly understood in authoritarian regimes where the disabling of instant-messaging services during periods of unrest, and tracking, arresting and torturing protestors active online is well known (Morozov 2011; Mackinnon 2012; Deibert and Rohozinski 2012). Mackinnon (2012: 78) describes a situation akin to 'net-worked authoritarianism' in China, with its estimated 50,000 internet police, where a wide range of repressive tactics are in play: from military-grade cyberat-tacks on the Gmail accounts of human-rights activists to device and network con-trols, domain name controls, localised disconnection and restriction and engaging hundreds of thousands of people to work as pro-government online commenta-tors. But it is too easy to point the finger at China. Elmer (2015) shows how pre-dictive policing in Canada relies on social media data to plan how to limit the size, length and impact of protests. Canada is not unusual in this regard.

Communicative nirvana or political naivety?

It would be a mistake to frame the above debate as either repression or liberation. In mediated practices it is highly likely that both exist, and they do so in different contexts and emerge from varying social and political histories. Castells (2009: 300) argued that social movements that engage in oppositional politics – 'the pro-cess aiming at political change (institutional change) in discontinuity with the logic embedded in political institutions' – now have the chance to enter the public space from multiple sources and bring about change. The question then arises – precisely how will they do this? It is not enough to simply state that the *potential* of a new communicative nirvana offered by the internet *will* bring about political transformation without considering the ways in which this protest actually trans-lates into political reality, paying attention to the hindrances as well as the affor-dances. The mobilisation of protest is easy to identify, political change less so.

In Castells' argument, the multiple prospects for intervention and manipulation coming from myriad social nodes combine to create a new symbolic counter-force that can shift dominant forms of representation. The counter-political response swells to such a size online that it simply cannot be ignored offline and is, in turn, taken up by the mass media. By using both horizontal communication networks and mainstream media to convey their images and messages, they substantively increase their chances of enacting social and political change – 'even if they start from a subordinate position in institutional power, financial resources, or symbolic legitimacy' (Castells 2009: 302). Even as Castells moderates his thinking some-what to take account of 'cultural and institutional specificity' (2015: 309) as well as 'actual practices of the movement and of the political actors' to effect political change, he continues to state 'confidently . . . that significant political change will result, in due time, from the actions of networked social movements . . . Minds that are being opened up by the winds of free communication and inspire practices of empowerment enacted by fearless youth' (2015: 312).

So the argument goes: technological ease of communication leads to abundance of information that will automatically result in political gain. Such accounts put a heavy onus on the power of networked communication to meet political demand and then deliver the institutional translation of those demands into practical politics. If change is predicated on the means of communication, the danger is that we side-step a deep and broad interrogation of the conditions required for people power to overtake corporate and state power and bring about social and political transformation wherein democracy flourishes. Instead, we are left with an over-emphasis on technology as the solution to the detriment of social, political and economic context (and analysis). If the context – the conditions that both provoke a radical political response and under which a progressive politics can emerge and gain credence – dissolves into the background, then we are left with a conception of politics without base or substance. Such accounts often manage to avoid the broader framing of a dominant politics and thereby neglect the crucial issue of what is considered possible in terms of alternative social and political formations and under what circumstances.

Furthermore, whereas the economic dominance of multinational corporations is usefully discussed in depth in Castells' work, there is little critique of how such dominance may sustain the wider myths of social order, making political change more difficult. Identifying economic dominance while evading the importance of interrogating neoliberal discourse – as a powerful and largely successful attempt to reshape the ways in which the political is interpreted through the individualistic values that saturate much life and action online – leaves a theory of social change in any discussion of radical progressive politics somewhat bereft.

Constraints of a global politics subordinated to capital

Understanding radical politics in the context of the broader social order is critical. In contemporary neoliberal times, this means understanding how this social order imposes certain constraints on political change taking place. The main space for political struggles to win practical political ground remains at the national level. But currently, in many places around the world, when it comes to the economy the sovereignty of the state has been transferred from national institutions to supranational authorities such as the European Central Bank, the International Monetary Fund (IMF) and the World Trade Organization (WTO). This was made painfully clear in the aftermath of the global financial crisis in 2008 when these organisations instructed national governments on how to order their economy so that banks and financial agencies could recoup the finance they had lent to governments to resolve the problems the banks had brought about in the first place, by recklessly encouraging economic growth through individual debt (i.e. giving credit to people who could not afford to pay it back). This was made very clear in 2015 when Greece was unable to repay its loans as a result of the bailout packages it had received on the back of the financial crash, despite severe austerity policies that had seen public sector wages plummet. The Greek government, run by the populist left-wing Syriza party, was then told by the unelected and unaccountable financial creditors of the Eurozone what its next budget (and indeed, the shape of its government) should look like.[1]

Meanwhile, the likes of the WTO seek to maximise the free flow of international trade, uninhibited by 'interference' from national policies that seek to protect the public and national interest, to the advantages of mega global corporations who threaten to remove their business from national shores if individual countries do not comply with their demands. A contemporary example of this is the Transatlantic Trade and Investment Partnership (TTIP) – a comprehensive free trade and investment treaty currently being negotiated – in secret – between the European Union and the US. The main goal of the TTIP is to remove regulatory 'barriers' that restrict the potential profits to be made by transnational corporations on both sides of the Atlantic. These 'barriers' are some of our most prized social standards and environmental regulations, such as labour rights, food safety rules, regulations on the use of toxic chemicals, digital privacy laws and even new banking safeguards introduced to prevent a repeat of the 2008 financial crisis. Yet in a corporate neoliberal pact, democratic institutions become economic ones captured by the requirements of transnational traders, and at once remove any sense of politics and therefore of the public from some of the most crucial decisions that govern our lives. It is not yet clear whether the TTIP will succeed, but it threatens to further embed the structural dislocation between public power of the polity and private power of the economy.

Miller (2014) takes this a stage further, noting that elite and corporate power often occur behind our backs. His argument stresses that power is built in places we do not know about rather than where we actively or even unconsciously consent to. So theories that see publics (including protesting publics) as holding a fundamental democratic role in liberal democracies entirely miss the point that in fact our consent is now only needed in particular circumstances. More often, strong, popular, widespread and even global protest can be and frequently is entirely ignored by the powerful. He points to the global protests over the Iraq War involving millions of people worldwide to no effect. These are protests that have no political resting place or consequence or worse serve up an illusion of democracy and a fantasy of politics, a convenient distraction for those involved in where power really lies.

Supranational organisations like the IMF and the WTO offer no pretence of being democratic. Therefore, it is hardly surprising that successive and global protests against the WTO have met with a deafening silence. This political disjuncture, the way in which the global flow of capital has been severed from a politics of the state, puts acute constraints on the possibilities of being political to effect radical and progressive social change. If the ability to effect political change in systems of governance remains state-bound yet states have lost the power to do much about it because they no longer have control over their economic means, then the revolutionary potential of the internet starts to look somewhat limited.

Bauman and Bordini (2014) argue that states have been stripped of much of their power to shape the course of events. Many of our problems are globally produced, but the volume of power at the disposal of individual nation-states is simply not sufficient to cope with the extraterritorial problems they face. This divorce between power ('the ability to get things seen through and done' (2014: 11)) and politics ('the ability to decide when things ought to be done and which things are to be sorted out on the global level' (ibid)) produces a new kind of paralysis. It weakens the political agency that is needed to deal with the crisis and it depletes citizens' belief that governments can deliver on their promises. The impotence of governments goes hand in hand with the growing cynicism and distrust of citizens. States are simply not equipped with the capacities to manage the new social and economic realities of finance, investment capital, global labour markets and the circulation of commodities.

Bauman and Bordini's analysis resonates with Crouch's (2004) notion of a 'post-democracy' – whereby the representative mechanisms that underpin the state have been hollowed out as corporate power and influence have crept in. Bordini lists the chief characteristics of post-democracy (Bauman and Bordini 2014: 140) as follows:

a   Deregulation, that is the cancellation of the rules governing economic relations and the supremacy of finance and stock markets;
b   a drop in citizens' participation in political life and elections;
c   the return of economic liberalism (neoliberalism), entrusting to the private sector part of the functions of the state and management services – which before were 'public' – with the same criteria of economic performance as a private company;
d   the decline of the welfare state, reserving basic services only for the poorest, i.e. as an exceptional circumstance and not as part of a generalised right for all citizens;
e   the prevalence of lobbies that increase their power and direct policies in their desired direction;
f   the show-business of politics, in which advertising techniques are used to produce consensus; the predominance of the figure of the leader that relies on the power of the image, market research and a precise communicative project;
g   a reduction in public investments;
h   the preservation of the 'formal' aspects of democracy, which at least maintain the appearance of the guarantee of liberty.

All of these factors are interlinked, but the first sends shock waves through the rest and leaves us with greatly enfeebled nation-states that have little power to deal with the problems they face and democracies that are increasingly bereft. The state has abdicated what power it had to counterbalance insidious economic forces, and the only role left to it is to attempt to manage public opinion as best it can. Crouch's analysis takes an extreme view and tends to overlook the areas where it has been argued that the state has increased its powers largely through its disciplinary and policing roles. This analysis offers no solace – the state, having lost control over the broader economic dynamics that operate outside and above its territory, is left with attempting to sort out the problems this leaves behind. Wacquant (2009) contends that as the state has privatised its social welfare provisions, so it has also strengthened its 'penal fist' (2009: 289) as it seeks to contain those who can't work and discipline those who can, thereby weakening the capacity of subordinate groups for political action. These policies exist alongside an enormous increase in others designed to pre-empt dissent including surveillance, anti-union legislation, criminalisation of protest and incarceration.

This presents a double whammy for radical political organisations and movements – influencing those supranational financial agencies and corporations that now control our economies in ways that are often hidden from view and are fiercely undemocratic is incredibly hard. At the same time, the increasing criminalisation of dissent makes it ever more difficult to launch protests and carry out demonstrations within the law at a national level. These types of constraints illustrate the broader context in which a radical politics, albeit facilitated by global online networks of resistance, must play out. It is the sort of context that is too often forgotten, leaving our understanding of a politics of transformation in the digital age severely lacking.

Horizontality and diversity

It is hard to imagine how the sorts of constraints outlined above can be surpassed via a form of technology, even one that can mobilise large numbers of people through being inclusive and non-hierarchical. Yet the horizontality and diversity of the internet are also claimed to enhance the liberatory potential of the oppositional political movements found online. These forms of radical politics that circulate via a network of networks embrace a politics of non-representation, where no one person speaks for another and differences are openly welcomed. Such radical politics are based on more fluid and informal networks of action than the class and party politics of old. The nature of these struggles resides in the political embodiment of the diversity of social relations they embrace – an explicit contention to resist the perceived dogma of political narratives within traditional leftist politics believed by some activists to be the harbinger of outmoded understandings and values. In this vein, they often profess to be leaderless, non-hierarchical, with open protocols, open communication and self-generating information and identities. Mobilisations that are facilitated online are said to reflect this fluidity and informality: frequently they display a rainbow alliance of NGOs, new social movements, trade unions, church groups and a range of political activists from different backgrounds. The differences within and between the various approaches to the politics under contention and deciding upon a unified collective response to a particular cause or concern often raise political dilemmas for activists. They are, however, intrinsic to understanding the vibrancy of a form of politics that prefers to operate with a variety of positions and perspectives and often from a highly personalised approach, as opposed to a traditional class politics of old that may rely on established political doctrines. These networks are often staunchly anti-bureaucratic and anti-centralist, suspicious of large organised, formal and institutional politics, and want to resist repeating what they see as the mistakes of those models in the politics they practise. These acclaimed characteristics also speak to the nature of politics online, which has been associated with protest rather than a long-term fixed political project (Fenton 2008) – a bid for involvement and voice, along with a refusal to determine or even presume a singular approach or direct political outcome or end-point that may signal exclusion and/or hierarchy within any grouping or alliance. And the architecture of the internet is claimed to have enabled such diverse, leaderless and horizontal politics to emerge and thrive.

Through the work of Hardt and Negri (2004), the 'network' has been given heightened significance as an ever-open space of politics. From this perspective, the network is not simply the expression of networked individuals, but the manifestation of self-constituted, un-hierarchical and affinity-based relationships, which extend beyond state borders and have the combined notions of 'autonomy' (everyone's right to express their own political identity) and 'solidarity' (to overcome power/neoliberalism) at their core (Graeber 2002: 68). In such accounts, the internet is claimed to herald the dawn of a different type of communication, aligned with a different form of left-radical politics premised on horizontality and diversity. Here, the space of new media enables a broader range of voices and types of material to be communicated to a wider audience without the constraints of needing to comply with or follow a particular political creed or direction other than the expression of an affinity with a particular cause. It is a form of politics that cannot be identified by a party name or definitive ideology and is often liable to rapid change in form, approach and mission – it is pulsating with energy, erratic and uncontrollable by design. Many extend this argument to claim that the meta-narratives of a politics of old organised around unifying ideologies such as socialism and communism are being replaced with a type of post-foundational politics (Marchart 2007).

Perspectives that advocate contemporary radical politics as post-foundational talk not only about the materialisation of new political subjects that operate within different types of political spaces, but also claim that that the material 'stuff' of politics is changed in the process as politics morphs from formal participation in traditional representative systems to networked action as exemplified in the critical sociology of Castells (2015). These are grand arguments trying to make sense of the political zeitgeist of a particular moment in the context of rapid technological change.

Diversity or more of the same?

As enticing as horizontality and diversity may be to notions of future radical politics, we don't have to dig very deep to realise that the limitless diversity apparently on offer online is not quite so wide-ranging as many assume. Research on the digital divide notes that internet users are still younger, more highly educated and richer than non-users, more likely to be men than women and more likely to live in cities (Norris 2001; Warschauer 2003; Haight et al. 2014). These concerns not only refer to access to the internet and the huge gaps prevalent between the global North and South; they also refer to online activity within developed nations and to traditional divides between the well-educated middle class who dominate public discourse and those on the peripheries or excluded altogether (Hindman 2008). Diversity, it would seem, is strictly for the privileged.

In a survey on Digital Activism by DigiActive (2009), digital activists, particularly in developing countries, were much more likely than the population at large to pay a monthly subscription fee to have internet access at home, to be able to afford a high-speed connection and to work in a white-collar job where the internet is also available. In short, digital activists are likely to be prosperous. They also found that intensity of use, rather than simple access, is a critical determinant of digital activism. Such high use is only possible for people with the ability to pay for it or in white-collar jobs where internet access is commonplace. Similarly, respondents with more features on their mobile phone – such as internet, video and GPS – are more likely to use their phones for political activism. This is another indicator of the importance of financial resources for the politically engaged, both quantitatively in terms of greater technology access and qualitatively in terms of better (mobile) hardware. The conclusion is simple. The internet may be diverse, but more often than not differentiation is limited largely to within the global middle class. Nonetheless, the claimed diversity of communication is argued to be connected to an emergent sense of the political that resides in multiple belongings (people with overlapping memberships linked through horizontal networks) and flexible identities (characterised by inclusiveness and a positive emphasis on cross-fertilisation) (Tarrow and della Porta 2005).

Horizontality or chaos?

Claims for a radical politics that embraces multiple viewpoints and diverse identities are also subject to counter-arguments by those who interpret horizontality not as political inclusiveness but as political dissipation and fragmentation (Habermas 1998). As Diamond (2012: 14) notes, 'there are fine lines between pluralism and cacophony, between advocacy and intolerance and between the expansion of the public sphere and its hopeless fragmentation'. Those who contest the political efficacy of online oppositional politics refer to the network society as producing localised, disaggregated, fragmented, diversified and divided political identities. Problems of quantity and chaos of information challenge the way analysis and action are integrated in decision-making processes. Hence, how political change can be realised becomes difficult to imagine, let alone achieve. Writing in relation to the use of social media in the Green Revolution in Iran, Yahyanejad and Gheytanchi (2012: 151) support this view, stating that '[t]hough social media can widen the grassroots base of social movements, such media (with their open, horizontal nature) can also breed confusion when there is a need to deal with complex issues and tactics that require discipline, strategy and a degree of central leadership'.

Furthermore, in his analysis of the Purple Movement (Popolo Viola) in Italy and its extensive use of Facebook, Coretti (2014) demonstrates that while the myth of the network as open and inclusive persists, it acts as a disguise for the communication protocols of commercial social networking platforms that may well enable large-scale mobilisation but ultimately, through their very functionality, encourage organisational centralisation and fragmentation in social movements. Popolo Viola was planned and organised on Facebook in 2009 in opposition to the politics of Silvio Berlusconi's government. Along with 460,000 members on the home page, thousands of other pages and groups within Italy and beyond were established on Facebook in support of the principal aim of the resignation of Italy's then Prime Minister. Facebook both galvanised and damaged the movement. Although Facebook is a social networking platform, it is designed on the basis of individual self-promotion (see Chapter 5) and engineered to maximise consumer spend. The algorithms at work operate within a business model devised on the basis of extracting value from individuals through selling commodities and data. The inability to manage Facebook pages and groups according to commonly agreed values promoted vertical power structures within the Purple Movement that led to internal divisions and the demise of solidarity. Such fragmentation cannot solely be attributed to the technology and reflects the values and interests of the political actors themselves, but the technology did not help. Leadership and hierarchy are not dispensed with online if other controlling (structural) forces are at play. Of course, if the political organisation has a tendency towards non-dialogic politics, then it is highly unlikely that any network capability is going to change that. Politics and political organisation emerge from histories that do not evaporate in the face of technology. In fact, the technology itself is deeply steeped in a politics that operates in direct opposition to the emancipatory ideals of many social movements.

The realities of doing a politics of the multitude and effecting social and political transformation have become a central concern for many contemporary political movements. The Indignados movement in Spain was one of the first to grapple fully with the contradiction between maintaining the inclusivity and horizontality of a networked social movement with the need to claim power of the state through conventional political means to achieve lasting social and political institutional change. It is to this example that we now turn.

The case of Podemos

The financial crash in 2008 hit Spain hard. On joining the Euro in 1999, interest rates fell and credit flowed into Spanish banks, then into housing, creating a massive property boom and construction bubble financed by cheap loans to builders and homebuyers. House prices rose rapidly from 2004 to 2008, then fell when the bubble burst. The construction industry in Spain crumbled; over-indebted home-owners faced financial misery and the banks had mounting bad mortgage debts. So even though the Spanish government had relatively low debts, it had to borrow heavily to deal with the effects of the property collapse. Taxes were raised in 2011, a freeze was imposed on public sector pay and austerity measures were put in place. Unemployment soared to 25% and inequality rocketed, with Oxfam reporting that the 20 richest people in Spain had income equal to the poorest 14 million Spaniards (Oxfam 2014). Politicians were felt to be at the behest of bankers. The birth of the Indignados/15M social movement emerged from this crisis. It began with a Facebook group that brought together affinity groups such as XNet and Anonymous under the name of 'Democracia Real Ya!' (Real Democracy Now!). On 15 May 2011 they mobilised many thousands of citizens to demonstrate in the streets across Spain. On 16 May people occupied Catalunya Square in Barcelona and stayed for several months to debate issues that were being ignored in the local elections. This triggered similar occupations in over a hundred Spanish cities that then spread to over 800 cities around the world (Castells 2015). The movement became known as 15M or the Indignados – it had no formal leadership and was initially largely ignored by the mainstream media. It used the internet to spread the word and people duly came to the squares to participate. But the internet would have made no difference at all had the moment not been right, had the injustices of a failing democracy not been felt, had poverty not been visible; if unemployment had not been a common experience; had political corruption not been rife. 15M ran campaigns against cuts and spurned many protest movements (known as tides) against evictions and home repossessions, the privatisation of healthcare, cuts in education, wage cuts and attacks on working conditions, among many others.

15M laid four years of foundations for the development of Podemos, which enabled the indignation of protest to turn into explicit policies for political change (the name of their first manifesto was 'Mover ficha: convertir la indignacion en cambio politico' or 'Making a move: turning indignation into political change'). Podemos is a party against austerity measures with a commitment to a participatory popular politics. Within a year of its formation in January 2014, Podemos (which translates as 'We can') had become a populist left-wing party in Spain, with more than 200,000 members and almost 1,000 circles (horizontally organised local meetings), and frequently topped opinion polls. In May 2014, five months after it was formed, it gained five MEPs in the European elections (equivalent to 8% of the Spanish vote) with an astonishing 1.25 million votes. For a period then, Podemos posed a serious challenge to the two-party duoploy that has dominated the Spanish political scene in post-Franco years – the Spanish Socialist Workers' Party (PSOE) and the party currently (in July 2015) in office, the conservative People's Party (PP). Although these parties sound different in name, they had become increasingly similar and colluded over a change to the Spanish constitution to take away Spanish workers' rights to appease the IMF and meet the Troika's austerity measures. Podemos promised something different.

Eduardo Maura, a professor of philosophy at Complutense University of Madrid and an international representative of Podemos, notes that:

> The social movements changed perceptions, they enabled people to reconceptualise supposedly individual problems as common ones that demand collective, political responses. Podemos's ability to stand in the European elections was very much dependent on the social power accumulated by the social movements.
>
> (quoted in Dolan 2015)

In the same interview Maura talks about the need to keep the Movements separate from the Party to ensure both that the movement remains autonomous and self-regulating and that the Party is made more accountable and has a broader appeal to a wider range of people who may not identify as activists or even consider themselves to be on the left. This sense of reaching out to as wide a constituency as possible, of appealing to the unengaged and non-political, is linked to the notion of 'popular unity' (Maura quoted in Parker et al. 2014) put forward by Podemos. Popular unity refers to recognition of the need to create a new common sense to counter the dominant discourses of neoliberalism. This is an attempt at a populist left politics. To gain popularity they have discarded name tags of left and right in favour of a discourse of democracy and 'the people' that speaks to the felt experiences of austerity – disenfranchisement, resentment of the establishment and material deprivation. In doing so they have managed to gain the support of many traditionally conservative voters with about a sixth of their supporters (as of January 2015) coming from the People's Party.

Podemos took notice of the horizontality and diversity of the radical politics of 15M and the Indignados movement. They recognised that a politics of everyday life can be more fruitful than the left's traditional focus on production and labour (where production and labour are now so fragmented and insecure that they are difficult to organise around). As Harvey (in Watson 2015) notes, this is politics organised around the spaces we live in rather than the spaces we work in. Podemos focuses on people's needs and relates improved public services to enhanced democratisation in an attempt to forge a link between the particular and the universal. In this manner it has moved beyond the focus on horizontality and diversity at all costs to recognise the requirement to cohere around a common political goal that can spread solidarity while still being open to debate and difference.

As a party of the digital age, they have also adopted what they call a 'hacker logic'. To create a Podemos circle in a local area or on a particular topic requires nothing more than a Facebook account, an e-mail address and a meeting – there is no membership fee. The principle is to encourage maximum participation from members who then share in shaping the development of the party and hold it to account. They rely heavily on the internet to increase levels of participation and accountability through a Citizen's Assembly, although the principles are not so very different from the establishment of any organisation with aspirations of democratic practice. They used the social networking site Reddit for much of the process but also developed apps for voting and establishing agendas. Draft papers were submitted online relating to three areas of organisation, ethics (Podemos refuses any funding from financial institutions and representatives are subject to strict limitations on privileges and salaries) and politics; these were then debated and redrafted. There was then a period where resolutions were invited on particular topics (as distinct from strategic or manifesto concerns) that were then voted on. Drafts were then discussed at a face-to-face conference attended by 7,000 people that were voted on the following week online. The selection of party candidates to represent Podemos involved live streaming of debates and elections operating on a one-person one-vote system. This process ensured that the most committed activists, those with a vague interest, those who had precious little time to spare and those without the resources to travel could all take part.

Podemos is, however, already and inevitably facing criticism from activists that it has become a party of the elite disconnected from its roots and replicating the problems of all established parties of old. It is accused of being reformist and of the establishment; of being bourgeois and fake by entering into a state-centred political space that will ultimately reproduce the traditional politics. 15M is part of Xnet, a group of activists working for democracy and against corruption that have succeeded in taking over 100 politicians and bankers to court on corruption charges. Largely crowd-funded and aided by citizen collaboration and leaks, it has exposed fraud and financial scams. It is also critical of Podemos, seeing it as very distinct from 15M and part of a 'very old left perspective that is Gramsci centred' and still operates within a traditional political model that is closed to genuine citizen participation (interview with key activist). Their use of the attributes of the internet, they say, serves merely to conceal a centralised and egotistical politics. And it is true that those with substantial cultural capital (notably male economists and academics) have risen to senior positions within the Party. But the Party is also attempting to disrupt the dominant discourse of austerity and is trying to work out what an alternative politics might be. In doing so it has managed to create a politics that is progressively radical but side-steps the 'isms' (e.g. socialism, communism) that signify a politics felt by many to be outmoded and unsuited to contemporary times. Meanwhile, the mainstream media supported by big business paints Podemos as an economic liability and its political representatives as crazed revolutionaries. And a new law dubbed the 'gag law' has been brought in to make public protest in front of Parliament and other government buildings illegal and punishable by a fine of €30,000. People who join in spontaneous protests near utilities, transportation hubs, nuclear power plants or similar facilities would risk a jaw-dropping fine of €600,000. The 'unauthorized use' of images of law enforcement authorities or police (often taken on mobile phones by protestors as a means of protection) would also draw a €30,000 fine, making it hard to document abuses.

What this example shows is that while the internet can mobilise and involve a lot of people quickly, it does not craft a politics; it did not create Podemos. The politics of Podemos arose from a two-party system that had failed the electorate and a programme of austerity that had caused considerable hardship. Without this critical contextual anchorage a focus on horizontality and diversity runs the risk of being translated into either a liberal tolerance of difference that in fact prevents substantive questions from being asked, or an anarchic, autonomous and ultimately individualistic politics that prevents substantive change from happening.

Connectivity and participation

The dual themes of speed and space, horizontality and diversity discussed above are also intermeshed with the lauded technical capacity of connectivity afforded in a networked age. The connectivity of the internet can impact upon the internal organisation of social movements through forging alliances and coalitions, sharing best practice and the most effective campaign techniques that are said to change the way groups organise and operate.

The connective dynamics of the internet are also linked to the more directly political concept of participation. Carpentier (2011: 10) notes that the concept of participation has an 'intimate connection with the political, the ideological and the democratic . . . that is intrinsically linked to power'. Facilitation of participation by new communication technologies is seen to be a crucial factor in transnational internet activism, not least because it is largely understood as putting all internet users on an equal footing, thereby enabling a horizontal politics to be enacted and ensuring that everyone has a voice and can play a part in the movement. In these radical online settings, the capacity to maximise connectivity and interaction is seen as the political act. This reflects a further emphasis on participative decision making and the demand for concentrations of power to be broken down (Gilbert 2008). The act of participation itself, and engagement with a particular issue, is often asserted as the political purpose rather than social reform or direct policy impact.

However, connectivity and participation online have also been fiercely criticised as weakening radical politics and offering a pseudo-participation that is illusory rather than actual (Dean 2010). In other words, rather than the internet signalling a newly vital oppositional political culture, we are witnessing an era of easy-come easy-go politics where you are only ever one click away from a petition (clicktivism); a technological form that encourages issue drift whereby individuals shift focus from one issue to another or one website to another with little commitment or even thought (slacktivism); where collective political identity has a memory that is short lived and easily deleted. Collective solidarity is replaced by a politics of visibility that relies on hashtags, 'likes' and compulsive posting of updates that hinge upon self-presentation as proof of individual activism. Online campaigning organisations such as Avaaz often fall prey to such criticisms.

Avaaz describes itself as 'a global web movement to bring people-powered politics to decision making everywhere' (http://www.avaaz.org/en/about.php). Avaaz, meaning 'voice' in many European, Middle Eastern and Asian languages, was launched in 2007 and has a core team on six continents and thousands of volunteers. In August 2012 it had 15,378,229 members worldwide in

194 countries and had taken 87,772,473 actions since they began; by September 2014 this had increased to 38,778,130 members and 205,603,598 actions. They are best known for organising online petitions that can gain mass global support incredibly quickly, but their activity also extends to funding media campaigns and direct actions, e-mailing, calling and lobbying governments and organising offline protests and events, all with the intention of making the views and value of the general population matter to decision makers. They claim to be extraordinarily nimble and flexible in their campaign work, focusing on tipping-point moments of crisis and opportunity. Each year they decide which issues to focus on through all-member polls. Each week campaign ideas are polled and tested via e-mail with 10,000 member random samples. Campaigns that gain strong support in these polls are then put into action with hundreds of thousands of members often taking part within hours or days.

In January 2012 they collected over 3 million signatures for a worldwide petition opposing an Internet Censorship Bill in the US. Avaaz organised a meeting with White House officials to deliver the petition. They claim that as a result, the White House condemned the Bill and withdrew its support. In August 2012 Avaaz was working with the leadership of democracy movements in Syria, Yemen and Libya to get them high-tech phones and satellite internet modems, connecting them to the world's top media outlets and providing communications advice. They have no overriding mission or vision apart from a general and vague ideal that we are all humans and should respect each other and have a responsibility to the planet. They do not attempt to reach consensus on issues among their diverse membership, stating that this has often led to the fracturing of movements, organisations and coalitions – they simply ask members to support the campaigns they wish to.

A similar organisation, 38 Degrees in the UK, has over 3 million members (*The Guardian*, 24 September 2014, p. 42). 38 Degrees is the angle at which an avalanche happens. Their hope is that through the power of the internet, they can create an avalanche for change. Once more, they are known best for their online activism such as e-petitions and e-mailing MPs, but they too use a range of tactics from funding newspaper advertisements on their campaigns to organising meetings with MPs and hosting discussions. They use their Facebook page, Twitter, blog and website to discuss and vote for campaign ideas which are then voted on in polls of all the membership. It is important for them to take this consultation process seriously as they are funded solely by membership donations. Interestingly, one of the things the members are asking for is more offline campaigning. Their campaign against the government sell-off of Forestry Commission Estates – national state-owned forests – generated half a million strong petition, hundreds of e-mails to MPs, adverts in national newspapers and posters all over the country. After just a few weeks the government dropped their plans. 38 Degrees are keen to point out that 'there is no manifesto and no central campaign direction . . . it's a campaigning tool, not a movement' (*The Guardian*, 24 September 2014, p. 42). Again, their aims are broad:

> We provide simple and effective tools for hundreds of thousands of us to influence the decisions that affect us all. We work together to defend fairness, protect constitutional rights, promote peace, preserve the planet and deepen democracy.
>
> (http://www.38degrees.org.uk/pages/faq/)

They claim to have over a 50% success rate with 800 of the 1,500 petitions started in the UK every month, achieving their objectives. However, politicians have started to complain about the volume of traffic in their e-mail in-boxes and report a tendency to disengage with online petitions as a result (*The Guardian*, 24 September 2014, p. 42).

Other groups such as MoveOn.org and Change.org in the US and GetUp! in Australia operate on a similar basis. All focus on single-issue, easily identifiable, winnable campaigns. That means that these must be issues that can be quickly understood in a simple paragraph or two in an e-mail and have an achievable end-point. The idea of privatising woodland for the benefit of greedy land developers did not take much persuasion for clicktivists to get to work. But where does that leave campaigns on issues that are rather messier, more complicated and not so straightforwardly fixable or immediately gratifying? Campaign populism is a trap that is hard to avoid for many such organisations that are undoubtedly challenging the powerful and making public concerns heard, but nonetheless running the risk of producing a form of radical politics that favours gut reaction and quick fixes over long-term struggle. One that is all about the short, sharp referendum, a tick-box politics that prefers to avoid the complicated, drawn-out assessment of social and political systems and their consequences. One that is more likely to lead to sticky-tape solutions than genuine political alternatives. How long will politicians take notice of what can quickly be dismissed as political spam lacking in authenticity and unworthy of consideration? Do these forms of online activism add to an atmosphere of change and possibility that inspires and encourages those among us who desire a better world to continue our struggles and long-fought campaigns, or do they contribute to a politics based on consumerism and choice, that privileges the already privileged, achieving little more than self-satisfaction that one click and one's political conscience is salved?

Tufekci (2014) has argued that the lower costs associated with communication and mobilisation via digital connectivity have both empowered social movements around the world and disempowered them by pushing them into the spotlight without the requisite organisational infrastructure for being able to deal with what comes next. So it is undeniable that social media have enabled movements to spread and grow and to put into practice aspirations of a seemingly leaderless and horizontal politics, but this has also contributed to a lack of organisational depth – an oppositional politics that is speeded up but spread thin.

Connectivity may enable us to respond quickly to events and mobilise mass demonstrations with ease – functions that once required much more formal and lengthy organising – but in the race to respond, there is a danger that the movement runs roughshod over the slower process of political organisation that also builds the capacity to deliberate, build close relations and trust between participants, and consider long-term objectives, strategies and tactics: all of the things that political activism requires to work effectively. Social media works to an algorithmic design that promotes immediate, real-time and constant productivity that forces users into fast-paced iterations that are not conducive to democratic practice (Barassi 2015; Kaun 2015). Hence, Tufekci (2014) argues that movements find themselves too quickly in confrontation without prior experience of how to manage what comes next. The trade-off of speed for long-term organisational capacity building also threatens to diminish the slow-burn of skills development of activists that help push a protest politics towards being a political movement. As Tufekci (2014) notes, it is often at the end of street protests when the initial excitement and energy fades that protestors accustomed to organising horizontally and online are often unable to decide what to do next:

> Toward the end of the Gezi Park protests . . . the government requested a delegation to negotiate on behalf of the protesters. Some protesters felt that this was a disingenuous move, while others were willing to negotiate. However, the park had no formal leadership mechanism that was universally recognized by all protesters. A loose coordinating committee had taken to running many aspects of the movement, but lacking formal recognition, it also lacked formal legitimacy. There was much contestation over who should serve as delegates, and it ended up being the government that, on two occasions, invited different cohorts of delegates to represent the park. The first was composed of fairly irrelevant people within the movement and was seen as less than legitimate by movement participants. The second invitation was extended to people who appeared to have had a long record of involvement with the movement and were active in highly visible roles, which thus garnered more approval. However, this too had no formal mechanism for recognition. In the end, the second delegation was unable to negotiate or devise a strategic plan to move forward . . . In the end, no real resolution was reached because some formal institutions that had taken part in the protests decided to end them, leaving behind a symbolic tent, while many individuals and some other collectives wanted to stay. This caused even more confusion, and the government moved in shortly after with a massive police presence and disbanded the camp by force.
>
> (Tufekci 2014: 14)

The capacity of the Gezi Park movement was clearly limited beyond its impressive ability to organise a protest. Tufekci then compares this to the civil rights 'March on Washington' in 1963, which had wanted to remain leaderless and operate as a horizontal movement, but because the means of communication were simply not available to them, had they completely refused leaders or organisations the large march may never have happened because it would have been too difficult to pull off at a practical level. When it did happen it illustrated to those in power how impressive its organisational capacity was and hence the level of threat it posed. The same cannot be said of the Occupy Movement, which although it was huge in scale (taking place in over 900 cities worldwide), it was organised in a very short space of time and did not lead to any discernible policy changes – the organisational capacity it signalled based on ease of mobilisation does not pose the same danger to those in power.

Communicative means are important but of course they are not the only factor that determines the forms, intensity and longevity of political movements. A politics of protest can end up being no politics at all if the politics has not been in gestation before the protest takes place and the organisational infrastructure is absent. Protest happens first and foremost as a response to symptoms – an often visceral response to problems of the prevailing social system. As such, a protest politics rarely presents a challenge to the social order because it has no alternative proposition to make other than remedial solutions. Bookchin (2015: 180) notes that '[a] revolutionary Left that seeks to advance from protest demonstrations to revolutionary demonstrations must resolutely confront the problem of organization'. This means asking what forms of organisation are likely to be enduring and develop a programme for social change that can be translated into everyday practice. What are the conditions required (including the communicative conditions) for political organisations to endure and build capacity? Has the understandable desire for leaderless (dis)organisation fetishised horizontality and diversity to the point of political hindrance? The themes of connectivity and participation that abound in the literature on new media and political engagement also demonstrate another important lack. The connectivity and participation they refer to tends to be focused on an online setting and to avoid or ignore the social dynamics of both mediated and political practices. Understanding the social dimensions of political life – what brings people together and why they seek solidarity – is crucial to our understanding of mediated political life. This is illustrated well by the case of Syriza in Greece – the first political party in Europe to attempt to stand up to the Troika of the European Commission, the European Central Bank and the IMF.

The case of Syriza

In Athens on 6 December 2008 the police murdered the 16-year-old student Alexis Grigoropoulos. This spurred a huge uprising of students and workers who took to the streets and over the coming weeks engaged in an astonishing array of dissident activities from rallies and marches, sit-ins of police stations, occupations of a state TV studio during a news broadcast, the disruption of theatre performances to engage in discussion with audiences, to looting and rioting. Amnesty International accused the Greek police of brutality in their handling of the riots who bombarded the protestors with tear gas and flash grenades. Four days after the death of the student, the General Confederation of Greek Workers (GSEE) and the Civil Servants' Confederation (ADEY), who together represent almost half of the total Greek workforce, called a one-day general strike in protest against the government's economic policies and continued to disrupt work in solidarity with the demonstrators.

As with other uprisings and riots in the Paris banlieues in 2005 and 2007 and London in 2012, the dramatic death of an individual may have been the trigger for the demonstrations to start, but the causes were rooted in a much deeper and more difficult history. In responding to the protests in Greece, Prime Minister Kostas Karamanlis acknowledged that 'long-unresolved problems, such as the lack of meritocracy, corruption in everyday life and a sense of social injustice disappoint young people' (Kriakidou and Flynn 2008: Reuters US online). Karamanlis said income-tax cuts would go ahead. But he warned against high expectations, saying Greece would have to spend 12 billion Euros, about 5% of GDP, just to service its debt: 'Our top priority is to support those that hurt the most . . . [but] this debt is a huge burden that reduces the government's flexibility at this critical time' (ibid). The unrest was set to continue and brought about the resignation of the right-wing government and its defeat in November 2009. This gave a large majority to Papandreou's socialists, who supported the neoliberal solutions to the financial crisis that led to the onslaught of austerity measures.

These austerity measures cut deep into the social fabric of Greek society, with 26% of the population unemployed by 2015, including 50% of young people. The poverty experienced so angered a population that it enabled the collective left populism that saw the Syriza party electoral percentage increase from under 5% in 2009 to 27% in June 2012. By 2015 the Syriza party were in government in an extremely odd coalition with the populist right-wing Independent Greeks party. With 36.3% of the vote, Syriza fell two seats short of the majority required to govern alone. However, despite their ideological differences, the two parties shared a desire to end the European Commission/IMF/European Central Bank mandated cuts that were imposed as a means of 'bailing out' a debt-riddled Athens. After eventually accepting tough austerity measures insisted on by the IMF and the European Union for Greece's third international bailout, 25 MPs broke away from Syriza and formed the Popular Unity party that triggered a snap General Election in September 2015. In a low turnout, Syriza held on to office with 35.5 per cent of the vote renewing its coalition with the Independent Greeks.

Syriza is an acronym that stands for Coalition of the Radical Left. It was founded in 2004 as a federation of smaller organisations including Maoists, left social democrats, greens, feminists, gay and social rights networks and Trotskyites, but became a single party after a conference in July 2013. The largest of these groups was Synaspismos whose leader, Alexis Tsipras, went on to lead Syriza. Tsipras came from a generation whose political past developed through the anti-globalisation movement, the massive demonstration against the World Trade Organization in Genoa and the World and European Social Forums (Wainwright 2015). These experiences were formative to their politics that spurned a faithfulness to a particular ideology, preferring instead to emphasise an embrace of diversity and open and collaborative working. This was a generation who had lived through the collapse of the Berlin Wall and the fall of the Soviet Union and wanted to replace worn-out left political scripts to develop alternatives to capitalism that were deemed appropriate to the contemporary context and were as yet unknown.

The context in which Syriza was able to come to power in Greece was complex. It followed a deep social crisis and a history of elite corruption (not least among the mainstream media oligarchs) that made people angry and yearn for political change. From the first protests in 2008, Greece witnessed a growing solidarity between trade unions, left parties and social movements. As a consequence, the people involved in the rebellion were very diverse yet found a collective identity in their desire to break with the established political order. One way they have tried to do this is to set the aspirations of this newly formed coalition to be far more than a party, to have a broader political reach than just 'the left' and to build a united social front although this has been beset with difficulties. From the time it was formed, Syriza activists were not only campaigning on the streets and through neighbourhood assemblies, they were also running 'solidarity kitchens' and bazaars, working in medical social centres, protecting immigrants from attacks against the fascist group Golden Dawn[2] (who won 7% of the votes in the 2015 election), supporting actions against the cut-off of electricity supply, providing legal help in courts to cut mortgage payments and developing new relations with trade unions. They were offline and in the communities dealing with social need.

In other words, Syriza operated more as a movement than as a political party, and paradoxically this enabled their politics to be pushed to the fore. They were not concerned first and foremost with recruiting new members to their party, to push a particular line or take control, but to build a sense of shared principles with practical solutions. Syriza understood what it meant to build a movement for social change rather than simply getting a party elected to power. The movement needed to have popular backing and broad-based participation and therefore needed to present a real alternative with positive solutions. To these ends they wanted as much Greek government debt as possible, mainly held by German and French banks, to be written off. They also prioritised an end to the humanitarian crisis by measures such as reconnecting energy supplies cut-off due to non-payment of bills and subsidised food for the unemployed. To reform the country's economy, they wanted to promote workers' cooperatives and the nationalisation of banks and privatised utilities and invest in public infrastructure. And they wanted to take on Greece's political establishment by restructuring the state to squeeze out corruption, cracking down on tax avoidance, reversing the militarisation of the police and breaking up media monopolies.

This programme of work is in a document that was drawn up by Syriza members and supporters in 2012– an inclusive system that they are trying to replicate within the systems of the governance by calling general assemblies of the various civil servants in each ministry to encourage innovation and discourage hierarchies that enable corruption to thrive. This was then turned into the Thessaloniki programmme in 2014 while Syriza were still in opposition, as a national reconstruction plan for government. As a manifesto it was heavily criticised from left and right alike. They were well aware of the perils of becoming just another party that is distorted by power and disconnected from their roots, and wanted to remain open to members to bring forward new ideas and shape the direction of the party. When their economic programme was published, public assemblies were organised to discuss the party proposals. An umbrella group, Solidarity4All, was also created to link the different groups in sympathy with Syriza and facilitate the exchange of information and knowledge (Prentoulis 2015).

Regardless of the difficulties it ran in to when it found itself compromised by the new Loan Agreement as part of the third bailout package (the Economic Adjustment Programme), Syriza represented movement-inspired politics. But it is also a politics that is massively constrained by the austerity demands of the European Union, IMF and European Central Bank who wanted to claw back the money they were all too happy to lend. The powers of the Troika were not so easily brought to heel. Syriza presented a political risk that could give confidence to anti-creditor coalitions with the likes of Podemos in Spain. The European Union responded with alarm to the attempts by Syriza to renegotiate the economic terms cast by the banks. As further funds were withheld and the Greek banks faced bankruptcy, the Syriza-led government found themselves facing a possible exit from the Eurozone. The Greek Prime Minister Alexis Tsipras held a referendum and the Greek people voted overwhelmingly against austerity measures. But the democratic vote of the nation was ignored and the creditors insisted on more austerity as well as a host of national policies that would immediately bring about further privatisation and anti-trade union legislation, in the full knowledge that austerity politics does not bring economic recovery and that more debt would follow. As Koenig (2015: 1) wrote:

[T]he Greek people, the citizens of a sovereign country . . . have had the audacity to democratically elect a socialist government. Now they have to suffer. They do not conform to the self-imposed rules of the neoliberal empire of unrestricted globalized privatization of public services and public properties from which the elite is maximizing profits – for themselves, of course. It is outright theft of public property.

The vicious cycle of debt-austerity-privatisation was further endorsed by the Greek mainstream media that continued to spin a narrative that Greece was at fault: it overspent and went broke. The generous banks lent them money and the corrupt Greek government mismanaged it (Efimeros 2015). All of the mass media platforms in Greece defended the banks. Perhaps this is not surprising when it is understood that the one measure the Troika allowed to be postponed is a 20% tax on television advertising. They also overlooked the fact that television companies had not paid their taxes and had been given licenses to broadcast for free. The mainstream media wanted the Troika to win, otherwise the profits of large media corporations would lose. The story that was not told was that the banks pushed Greece into unsustainable debt while insisting that revenue-generating public assets were sold off to global corporations and oligarchs. In pedalling propaganda that supported their own interests above those of the public, Greece's mainstream media outlets contributed to public disgust of elite corruption. Greek television is watched by 95% of the public (Efimeros 2015). However, Syriza had long since nurtured a social media presence that enabled them to disseminate their message. Twitter became an important source of counter-narrative with the hashtag #ThisIsACoup being the second top trending hashtag worldwide and the top trending hashtag in Germany the Monday that the final bailout deal was struck. But the internet is used by only 60% of the population in Greece (Internet World Stats 2015). When viewers turned off their televisions, they were not all rushing to the internet; they were going to supermarkets that were short of food and many were sitting in homes with no electricity. While social networks could express solidarity and outrage, and while the counter-narratives online could offer some hope to some people, they were never going to be any kind of match for the stranglehold of the Troika.

Syriza recognised the importance of going beyond simple connectivity and participation online. Collective action requires a political solidarity that outstrips the commercialised forms of sociality on offer through social media. Mattoni and Vogiatzoglou (2014) point to how oppositional politics in Greece has shifted from a focus on actions of protest to the provision of services as well as a return to mutualism as a form of resistance to the economic crisis. In a highly marketised and globalised economy, Syriza understood social justice could only begin from below and at a local level. This was about so much more than connectivity; it was about the need to come together in a spirit of mutuality and solidarity, restoring dignity to shattered communities by dealing with the basic problems people are facing on a daily basis – housing, electricity supply, access to welfare, lack of food. In the face of ever-declining respect for politicians, the growing irrelevance of elections as parties increasingly occupy the middle ground and fail to fulfil electoral promises, and the bullying anti-democratic rulings of the Troika, they understood that a radical progressive politics needed to reconnect with the fundamental requirement of the fair(er) distribution of resources. Going into social spaces and special settings and ensuring basic social needs were met very simply put politics back in touch with the populace. Hence participating in political life stopped being about voting once every few years or signing a few online petitions; it became about doing and being at least for a while.

Conclusion

This chapter has argued that it is not enough simply to celebrate resistance through the conduit of the internet and venerate the potential of some of its technological capabilities. As new communication technologies enable disparate protest groups to forge transnational alliances and affinities, we may be faced with a new politics that is marked by the characteristics of speed and space; horizontality and diversity; connectivity and participation that demands new ways of thinking about the *means of and the meaning of being political.* The internet may well have ushered in a new form of political activism, but its consequences may not be the ones that were intended or that can necessarily deliver the democratic gains that were hoped for. Networks are not *inherently* liberatory; the internet does not contain the essence of openness that will lead us directly to democracy.

Technologies are drenched from conception to realisation to practice in the economic and political context they are part of. Technologies are never neutral. They are enmeshed with the systems of power they exist within. As Feenberg (1995, 2002) argues and as Chapters 1–4 in this book illustrate in different ways, technology and capitalism have developed together. Similarly, the practices of social media *may* be liberating for the individual user, but not necessarily democratising for society. The hyper-commercialism that configures social media platforms enhances rather than disrupts the contours of global capitalism; it encourages individual and connective responses rather than social and collective politics. In the digital age, the internet is an important component in our understanding of the contemporary representation and articulation of contestatory political identities and forms of political mobilisation. But it is only one component among many. Allowing ourselves to focus only on the technology removes our attention from where the problems really lie.

Radical politics is of course about more than communication and more than participation in communication; it is about more than protest; it is about social, political and economic transformation. The new progressive politics that are struggling to emerge in Spain and Greece are beginning to tackle how this might be possible. If we return to the question posed at the beginning of this chapter – what are the circumstances in which politics are rendered open to contestation and revision today? – we can, at the very least, reply that technology is not the best place to start looking for the answer. The example of Syriza makes this clear. When it comes to economic transformation, we need to recognise that banks, financial agencies and corporations seek increasingly to dictate the terms of our economies and the national policies that underpin them. This political disjuncture, the way in which the global flow of capital has been severed from politics, puts acute constraints on the possibilities of being political to effect progressive social change for all of us. As this removes democratic sovereignty from nation-states and they are left to deal with the fallout from a politics of austerity, so they become increasingly draconian in their response to acts of civil disobedience that fiercely, and often violently, constrain the possibilities for progressive democratic politics to take hold.

We are then left to consider what the conditions of possibility for political solutions might be. Badiou claims there will be a revolutionary revival of the raft of protests, riots and uprisings that erupted in many parts of the world in 2011 that quickly turns to radical pessimism, while he also sees the resistance shown being generated by and used by power; in the face of which the left is impotent (Badiou 2012). This dreary outlook is shared by many radical theorists initially cheered by the possibility of a resurgence of the left, only to find themselves retreating to a position of gloom and cynicism. Caygill's (2013: 208) depressing concluding sentence to his book on resistance reads:

> Resistance is engaged in defiant delegitimization of existing and potential domination but without any prospect of a final outcome in the guise of a revolutionary or reformist result or solution . . . The politics of resistance is disillusioned and without end.

This general pessimism falls back on the structuring forces of neoliberalism and the lack of any real political alternative emerging. But while subjects will always be subjected to dominant power, individual and collective identities can and do emerge from resistance over time. The emergence of subjects of resistance is usually accompanied by a huge sense of injustice, of a wrong that must be righted. It is wrong that my family should live in poverty and go hungry because of austerity measures that are nothing to do with me; it is wrong that I have no access to free healthcare; it is wrong that the state should destroy a public park; it is wrong that I am discriminated against because of my race, sexuality, gender, religion etc. This does not usually arrive with a formally worked-out plan of how justice can be claimed and applied universally, although it may result in specific claims relating to particular concerns. So it should come as no surprise that a unified left-radical front does not immediately spring forth. But it is only through particular acts of resisting particular configurations of power that the seeds of an alternative normative position can be sown, that the realisation that 'another world is possible' can come into being that then requires the engagement of a broader public.

Communicative means are part of this journey, but of course they are not the only factor that determines the forms, intensity and longevity of political movements. Organisational form shapes political action and politics just as political action and politics shape organisational form. A politics of protest can end up being no politics at all if the politics has not been in gestation before the protest takes place and the organisational infrastructure is absent. A progressive politics needs both structure and momentum. Protest happens first and foremost as a response to symptoms – an often visceral response to problems of the prevailing social system. As such, a *protest* politics rarely presents a challenge to the social order because it has no alternative proposition to make other than remedial solutions. This then means asking: what forms of organisation are likely to be enduring and develop a programme for social change that can be translated into everyday practice? What are the conditions required (including the communicative conditions) for political organisations to endure and build capacity? If we are going to begin to at least try to understand how society could be more equal, fair and democratic, how we could reclaim media, power and politics for progressive ends, then we need to insist upon an integrated, contextual analysis that places the technological alongside and in relation to its social, economic, cultural and political histories. Only then can we begin to advance an emancipatory project that aims to deepen and radicalise the democratic horizon.

In this book we have sought to situate the internet in the deceptively simple context of the societies in which we live, while also seeking to address the concerns of the specific type of communicational and technological system of the internet. We have also put forward an argument that the contemporary internet is not a democratic space per se. In the complex interrelations of the contemporary internet and society, there is potential for both democratic and anti-democratic formation. The precise manifestation of these interrelations may be suggestive of which particular strategies are appropriate for progressive political transformation in which particular context. Operationally, this creates the need to formulate mechanisms of genuine citizen participation in and control of the spaces we inhabit, with new forms of state relations that prioritise the value of the public over profit, patience over productivity and collaboration over competitiveness.

Notes

1 As part of the negotiations to remain in the Eurozone the Greek Prime Minister was told that he needed to move towards replacing the Greek government because it did not suit the views of the bankers.
2 Golden Dawn was formed in the early 1990s as a marginal semi-legal fascist organisation. Its appeal was revived in recent times by recourse to a xenophobic, anti-immigrant response to the social ills caused by austerity measures.

References

Alexander, J. C. (2011) *Performative Revolution in Egypt*, London: Bloomsbury.
Badiou, A. (2012) *The Rebirth of History: Times of Riots and Uprisings*, London: Verso.
Barassi, V. (2015) 'Social Media, Immediacy and the Time for Democracy: Critical Reflections on Social Media as 'Temporalising Practices'', in L. Dencik and O. Leistert (eds) *Critical Perspectives on Social Media Protest: Between Control and Emancipation*, London: Rowman & Littlefield.
Bauman, Z. and Bordini, C. (2014) *State of Crisis*, London: Polity Press.
Bennett, L. and Segerberg, A. (2013) *The Logic of Connective Action: Digital Media and the Personalisation of Contentious Politics*, New York: Cambridge University Press.
Bennett, W. L. (2005) 'Social Movements Beyond Borders: Understanding Two Eras of Transnational Activism', in D. della Porta and S. Tarrow (eds) *Transnational Protest and Global Activism*, Lanham, MD: Rowman & Littlefield, 203–227.
Bookchin, M. (2015) *The Next Revolution: Popular Assemblies and the Promise of Direct Democracy*, London: Verso.
Calingaert, D. (2012) 'Challenges for International Policy', in L. Diamond and M. F. Plattner (eds) *Liberation Technology: Social Media and the Struggle for Democracy*, Baltimore, MD: Johns Hopkins University Press, 157–174.
Carpentier, N. (2011) *Media and Participation: A Site of Ideological-Democratic Struggle*, London: Intellect.
Castells, M. (2009) *Communication Power*, Oxford: Oxford University Press.
Castells, M. (2015) *Networks of Outrage and Hope: Social Movements in the Internet Age. Second Edition*, London: Polity.

Caygill, H. (2013) *On Resistance: A Philosophy of Defiance*, London: Bloomsbury.

Coretti, L. (2014) *The Purple Movement: Social Media Activism in Berlusconi's Italy*, University of Westminster: PhD Thesis.

Crouch, C. (2004) *Post-Democracy*, Cambridge: Polity Press.

Dean, J. (2010). *Democracy and Other Neoliberal Fantasies: Communicative Capitalism and Left Politics*, Durham, NC: Duke University Press.

Deibert, R. and Rohozinski, R. (2012) 'Liberation vs. Control: The Future of Cyberspace', in L. Diamond and M. F. Plattner (eds) *Liberation Technology: Social Media and the Struggle for Democracy*. Baltimore, MD: Johns Hopkins University Press, 18–32.

della Porta, D. (2005) 'Multiple Belongings, Tolerant Identities and the Construction of "Another Politics": Between the European Social Forum and the Local Social Fora', in D. della Porta and S. Tarrow (eds) *Transnational Protest and Global Activism*, Lanham, MD: Rowman & Littlefield, 175–203.

Diamond, L. (2012) 'Introduction', in L. Diamond and M. F. Plattner (eds) *Liberation Technology: Social Media and the Struggle for Democracy*, Baltimore, MD: Johns Hopkins University Press, ix–xxvii.

DigiActive (2009) DigiActive.org. Online. Available HTTP: <http://www.digiactive.org> (accessed 24 April 2015).

Dolan, A. (2015) 'Podemos: Politics by the People', *Red Pepper*, February 2015. Online. Available HTTP: <http://www.redpepper.org.uk/podemos-politics-by-the-people> (accessed 23 April 2015).

Downey, J. and Fenton, N. (2003) 'Constructing a Counter-public Sphere', *New Media and Society*, 5 (2): 185–202.

Efimeros, C. (2015) 'Mainstream Media Lie in Greece', The Press Project. Online. Available HTTP: <http://www.thepressproject.gr/details_en.php?aid=79064> (accessed 5 November 2015).

Elmer, G. (2015) 'Preempting Dissent: From Participatory Policing to Collaborative Filmmaking', in L. Dencik and O. Leistert (eds) *Critical Perspectives on Social Media Protest: Between Control and Emancipation*, London: Rowman & Littlefield.

Feenberg, A. (1995) 'Subversive rationalisation: technology, power and democracy', in A. Feenberg and A. Hannay (eds) *Technology and the Politics of Knowledge*, Bloomington, IN: Bloomington Press.

Feenberg, A. (2002) *Transforming Technology*, Oxford: Oxford University Press.

Fenton, N. (2008) 'Mediating Hope: New Media, Politics and Resistance', *International Journal of Cultural Studies*, 11 (2): 230–248.

Fenton, N. and Downey, J. (2003) 'Counter Public Spheres and Global Modernity', *Javnost – The Public*, 10 (1): 15–33.

Gerbaudo, P. (2012) *Tweets and the Streets: Social Media and Contemporary Activism*, London: Pluto Press.

Gilbert, J. (2008). *Anticapitalism and Culture: Radical Theory and Popular Politics*, Oxford: Berg.

Graeber, D. (2002) 'The New Anarchists', *The New Left Review*, 13 (January/February) Online. Available HTTP: <http://www.newleftreview.org/A2368> (accessed 20 November 2010).

Habermas, J. (1998) *Inclusion of the Other: Studies in Political Theory*, Cambridge: Polity.

Haight, M., Quan-Haase, A. and Corbett, B. A. (2014) 'Revisiting the Digital Divide in Canada: The Impact of Demographic Factors on Access to the Internet, Level of Online Activity, and Social Networking Site Usage', *Information, Communication and Society*, 17 (4): 503–519.

Hands, J. (2011) @ *is for Activism: Dissent, Resistance and Rebellion in a Digital Culture*, London: Pluto Press.

Hardt, M. and Negri, A. (2004) *Multitude*, London: Hamish Hamilton.

Hill, K. and Hughes, J. (1998) *Cyberpolitics: Citizen Activism in the Age of the Internet*, Lanham, MD: Rowman & Littlefield.

Hindman, M. (2008) *The Myth of Digital Democracy*, Princeton, NJ: Princeton University Press.

Hintz, A. (2015) 'Social media censorship, privatised regulation and new restrictions to protest and dissent', in L. Dencik and O. Leistert (eds) *Critical Perspectives on Social Media Protest: Between Control and Emancipation*, London: Rowman & Littlefield.

Internet World Stats (2015) 'Internet Usage Statistics: The Internet Big Picture'. Online. Available HTTP: <http://www.internetworldstats.com/stats.htm> (accessed 26 July 2015).

Juris, J. (2008) *Networking Futures*, Durham, NC: Duke University Press.

Kahn, R. and Kellner, D. (2004) 'New Media and Internet Activism: From the "Battle of Seattle" to Blogging', *New Media & Society*, 6 (1): 87–95.

Kahn, R. and Kellner, D. (2007) 'Globalisation, Technopolitics and Radical Democracy', in L. Dahlberg and E. Siapera (eds) *Radical Democracy and the Internet: Interrogating Theory and Practice*, London: Palgrave Macmillan.

Kaun, A. (2015) '"This Space Belongs to Us!": Protest Spaces in Times of Accelerating Capitalism', in L. Dencik and O. Leistert (eds) *Critical Perspectives on Social Media Protest: Between Control and Emancipation*, London: Rowman & Littlefield.

Keck, M. E. and Sikkink, K. (1998) *Activists Beyond Borders: Advocacy Networks in International Politics*, New York: Cornell University Press.

Klein, N. (2000) *No Logo*, New York: Flamingo.

Klein, N. (2002) *Fences and Windows: Dispatches from the Front Lines of the Globalization Debate*, London: Flamingo.

Koenig, P. (2015) 'Greece – Risk of False-flagging Greece into Submission and Chaos?', Global Research. Online. Available HTTP: <http://www.globalresearch.ca/greece-risk-of-false-flagging-greece-into-submission-and-chaos/5460323> (accessed 5 November 2015).

Kriakidou, D. and Flynn, M. (2008) 'Riots Rock Greece Amid Election Calls', *Reuters UK* 9, December. Online. Available HTTP: <http://uk.reuters.com/article/2008/12/09/uk-greece-shooting-idUKTRE4B603Z20081209> (last accessed 7 April 2015).

Livingstone, S. and Bovill, M. (2002) *Young People, New Media*, Research Report. Online. Available HTTP: <http://www.lse.ac.uk/collections/media@lse/pdf/young_people_report.pdf> (accessed 28 January 2008).

Livingstone, S., Bober, M. and Helsper, E. (2005) 'Internet Literacy among Children and Young People: Findings from the UK Children Go Online Project', Ofcom/ESRC, London. Online. Available HTTP: <http://eprints.lse.ac.uk/397/> (accessed 7 October 2010).

Loader, B. (ed.) (2007) *Young Citizens in the Digital Age: Political Engagement, Young People and New Media*, London: Routledge.

Mackinnon, R. (2012) 'China's "Networked Authoritarianism"', in L. Diamond and M. F. Plattner (eds) *Liberation Technology: Social Media and the Struggle for Democracy*, Baltimore, MD: Johns Hopkins University Press, 78–94.

Marchart, O. (2007) *Post-foundational Political Thought: Political Difference in Nancy, Lefort, Badiou, and Laclau*, Edinburgh: Edinburgh University Press.

Mason, P. (2012) *Why It's Kicking Off Everywhere: The New Global Revolutions*, London: Verso.

Mattoni, A. and Vogiatzoglou, M., (2014) 'Italy and Greece, Before and After the Crisis: Between Mobilization and Resistance Against Precarity', *Quaderni*, 84. Online. Available HTTP: <https://www.academia.edu/8920266/Italy_and_Greece_before_ and_after_the_crisis._Between_mobilization_and_resistance_against_precarity> (accessed 5 November 2015).

Miller, D. (2014) 'Media Power and Class Power: Overplaying Ideology', in S. Coban (ed.) *Media and Left*, Leiden: Brill, 44–67.

Morozov, E. (2011) *The Net Delusion: How Not To Liberate The World*, London: Allen Lane.

Norris, P. (2001) *Digital Divide: Civic Engagement, Information Poverty and the Internet Worldwide*, Cambridge: Cambridge University Press.

Ofcom (2007) *New News, Future News*, London: Ofcom.

Ofcom (2010) *The Communications Market 2010*, London: Ofcom.

Oxfam (2014) *Working for the Few: Political Capture and Economic Inequality*, Madrid: Oxfam Intermon.

Park, A. (2004) *British Social Attitudes: The 21st Report*, London: Sage.

Parker, L. and Mountain, D. with Manousakis, N. (2014) 'Más allá de la izquierda y la derecha? (Beyond left and right?) An Interview with Eduardo Maura of Podemos'. *Platypus Review*, 72, December 2014–January 2015.

Prentoulis, M. (2015) 'From Protest to Power: The Transformation of Syriza', *Red Pepper*, January 2015. Online. Available HTTP: <http://www.redpepper.org.uk/by/marina-prentoulis/> (accessed 6 April 2015).

Roberts, J. M. (2014) *New Media and Public Activism: Neoliberalism, the State and Radical Protest in the Public Sphere*, Bristol: Policy Press.

Sloam, J. (2013) 'Voice and Equality: Young People's Politics in the European Union', *West European Politics*, 36 (4): 836–858.

Sloam, J. (2014) 'New Voice, Less Equal: The Civic and Political Engagement of Young People in the United States and Europe', *Comparative Political Studies*, 47 (5): 663–688.

Tarrow, S. and della Porta, D. (2005) 'Globalization, Complex Internationalism and Transnational Contention', in D. della Porta and S. Tarrow (eds) *Transnational Protest and Global Activism*, Lanham, MD: Rowman & Littlefield, 227–247.

Tufekci, Z. (2014) 'Social Movements and Governments in the Digital Age: Evaluating a Complex Landscape', *Journal of International Affairs*, 68 (1): 1–18.

Wacquant, L. (2009) *Punishing the Poor: The Neoliberal Government of Social Insecurity*, London: Duke University Press.

Wainwright, H. (2015) 'Greece: Syriza Shines a light', *Red Pepper*, January 2015. Online. Available HTTP: <http://www.redpepper.org.uk/greece-syriza-shines-a-light/> (accessed 6 April 2015).

Warschauer, M. (2003) *Technology and Social Inclusion: Rethinking the Digital Divide*, Cambridge, MA: MIT Press.

Watson, M. (2015) 'David Harvey: On Syriza and Podemos', *Verso Blog*. Online. Available HTTP: <http://www.versobooks.com/blogs/1920-david-harvey-on-syriza-and-podemos> (accessed 5 November 2015).

Wayne, M., Petley, J., Murray, C. and Henderson, L. (2010) *Television News, Politics and Young People: Generation Disconnected?*, London: Palgrave Macmillan.

Wilkinson, H. and Mulgan, G. (1995) *Freedom's Children*, London: Demos.

Yahyanejad, M. and Gheytanchi, E. (2012) 'Social Media, Dissent and Iran's Green Movement', in L. Diamond and M. F. Plattner (eds) *Liberation Technology: Social Media and the Struggle for Democracy*, Baltimore, MD: Johns Hopkins University Press, 139–156.

Chapter 7

The internet we want

James Curran, Natalie Fenton and
Des Freedman

This book has two central themes. The first is that a narrow, decontextualised focus on the technology of the internet leads to misperceiving its impact. This argument is illustrated, in the first chapter, by looking at four sets of technology-centred predictions about how the internet would change society, and then examining what actually happened. The internet did not promote global understanding in the way that had been anticipated because the internet came to reflect the inequalities, linguistic division, conflicting values and interests of the real world. The internet did not spread and rejuvenate democracy in the way that had been promised, partly because authoritarian regimes usually found ways of controlling the internet, but also because alienation from the political process limited the internet's emancipatory potential. The internet did not transform the economy, partly because the underlying dynamics of unequal competition that make for corporate concentration remained unchanged. Finally, the internet did not inaugurate a renaissance of journalism; on the contrary, it enabled leading news brands to extend their ascendancy across technologies while inducing a decline of quality not offset, so far, by new forms of journalism. All four predictions were wrong because they inferred the impact of the internet from its technology and failed to grasp that the internet's influence is filtered through the structures and processes of society. This explains, it is argued, why the influence of the internet has varied in different contexts.

The second central theme of this book is that the internet itself is not constituted solely by its technology but also by the way it is funded and organised, by the way it is designed, imagined and used, and by the way it is regulated and controlled. In the second chapter, devoted to the history of the internet, it is argued that the internet was originally shaped, after its military conception, by the values of science, counterculture and European public service. This largely pre-market formation was then overtaken by commercialisation and increasing state censorship. We are now in the midst of a battle for the 'soul' of the internet, which has a global dimension as well as a Western one.

This second theme, concerned with influences on the internet, is developed more fully in the second part of this book. Chapter 3 describes the lyrical, 'third-wave' interpretations of theorists like Chris Anderson and Jeff Jarvis who see the internet as a technology that promotes a new form of economy and a new state of being: one that abolishes scarcity in favour of abundance, replaces standardisation with diversity, and substitutes hierarchy with participation and democratisation. However, apart from a communitarian strand linked to non-commercial developments of the internet, these accounts are all based on a market model of the internet. What they overlook is the multiple distortions that a market-based internet has developed: corporate dominance, market concentration, controlling gatekeepers, employee exploitation, manipulative rights management, economic exclusion through 'tethered appliances' and encroachment upon the information commons. The internet market, on closer scrutiny, turns out to have many of the problems associated with unregulated capitalism.

Should we, then, think the unthinkable and contemplate a different way of managing the internet? This seems to disrespect the much-lauded system we have now. This system is said to be ideal because it entails soft governance rather than oppressive state control, self-regulation through experts and users rather than a regime of oppressive bureaucracy. But recent analysis has shed light on what this complacent self-presentation conceals. In fact, Western governments are not as absent as they appear to be, and retain a strategic oversight over computer networks that have increasing military and economic significance. This can take the form of arbitrary interventions, as when the US government exerted pressure on credit card companies to refuse payments to WikiLeaks in a bid to muzzle its embarrassing disclosures, or the extensive surveillance networks that were revealed by former National Security Agency operative Edward Snowden. Furthermore, control of the internet is increasingly vested in powerful internet corporations, supported by software and hardware restrictions. Self-regulation frequently means corporate regulation in a form that can threaten the freedom and public-good features of the net. So it is now legitimate to consider whether a better system of regulation – independent of government and market control – should be preferred. To this we shall return.

Chapters 5 and 6 focus on the spectacular rise of social media, which has led to speculation that they will profoundly change social relations. Technology that gives a means of communication to individuals and social networks, it is reasoned, must be collectively empowering. Positive concepts like autonomy, access, participation, multiplicity and pluralism are regularly invoked to reinforce this image of a transformative force. While it is true that social media provide a pleasurable means of self-expression and social connection, enable people to answer back to citadels of media power and in certain situations (as in Spain) may support the creation of a radical counter-public, Chapter 5 introduces a sceptical note. Social media are more often about individual than collective emancipation, about presenting self (frequently in consumerist or individualising terms) rather than changing society, about entertainment and leisure rather than political communication (still dominated by old media) and about social agendas shaped by elites and corporate power rather than a radical alternative. For example, Twitter is centred more on eavesdropping on the thoughts of celebrities than on political change. Social media, in other words, are shaped by the wider environment in which they are situated rather than functioning as an autonomous force transforming society.

What, then, is the connection between the internet and radical politics? Young people who have rejected traditional party politics, who have moved away from class-based concerns to a radical politics of identity and who express political interests and hopes that are borderless have adopted the internet as an organising and campaigning tool. There is a natural affinity between the global, interactive technology of the internet and the development of a more internationalist, decentred and participatory form of politics. But this politics is enabled by the internet rather than being the product of it. Indeed, a look at specific examples underlines the point that internet-assisted protests have underlying causes: among other things, disillusion with mainstream politics, high unemployment and continuing austerity which provide the backdrop to the rise of a highly internet-savvy party like Podemos in Spain. And while the internet has introduced a new degree of creative autonomy and effectiveness in the mobilisation of protests, with the rise of organisations like Avaaz and 38 Degrees, the radical politics with which it is associated may have limitations. Multiple voices of protest may fragment rather than build solidarity: fluid, issue-based and institution-less politics may not add up to a coordinated project for transforming society.

Of course, in acknowledging the dangers of binary traps – the internet is *or* is not transformative, that it strengthens *or* weakens existing political forces – and the importance of evaluating the internet in quite specific circumstances, we ourselves have found it difficult to contextualise everything, despite our warnings. In particular, we are aware that our chosen examples and case studies are taken from a fairly narrow range of countries and perspectives and that there may be other, countervailing arguments.

However, we stand by our approach and our conclusion: that although it was said, and continues to be said, that the internet was going to virtually single-handedly change the world, this has not been the case. Like all previous technologies, its use, control, ownership, past development and future potential are context dependent. If we are to realise the dreams of the internet pioneers, then we need to challenge that context and demand a fresh set of proposals to empower public oversight of and participation in online networks.

The internet, we have argued, is a creature of public policy, developed initially not for profit but for collaboration and communication. It has long been regulated – by governments, markets, code and communities. Subsequent developments have changed this fundamentally, so that its collaborative and communicative potential for all citizens is in danger of being enclosed and privatised. According to Tim Berners-Lee:

> the web that he helped to found is being threatened in different ways. Some of its most successful inhabitants have begun to chip away at its principles. Large social-networking sites are walling off information posted by their users from the rest of the Web. Wireless Internet providers are being tempted to slow traffic to sites with which they have not made deals. Governments – totalitarian and democratic alike – are monitoring people's online habits, endangering important human rights.

> (Berners-Lee 2010)

This, then, is a critical moment in the internet's history.

In this situation, it may be useful to draw on debates from another industry facing a similar critical juncture: banking. After the collapse of Lehman Brothers in 2008 and the financial crisis that followed, more far-sighted commentators and regulators realised that serious reforms were needed if public trust and stability were to return to the sector. One such figure was Lord Adair Turner, chairman of the Financial Services Authority that used to regulate the City of London. In a speech in 2009, he argued that the sector had to learn from its mistakes and transform the way it does business if a similar catastrophe was to be avoided in the future: 'We need radical change. Regulators must design radically changed regulations and supervisory approaches, but we also need to challenge our entire past philosophy of regulation' (Turner 2009). Two years later, frustrated by the very slow pace of reform (despite the emergence of the International Financial Stability Board and proposals for tighter control of banks themselves), he once again called for the sector to embrace 'radical policy options', including the possibility of new taxes or state intervention in the running of banks (Turner 2011).

Applied to the internet, the first objection would be that such measures would act as a brake on creativity and a distortion of market principles. Indeed, Turner acknowledges precisely these objections, noting that these proposals have been routinely rejected by critics on the basis that 'they would have a "chilling effect" on liquidity, product innovation, price discovery and market efficiency' (Turner 2011). He then dismisses these objections on the basis, somewhat surprisingly for a figure utterly embedded inside the City of London, that 'not all financial activity is socially useful' and that free and competitive financial systems 'sometimes deliver neither stability nor allocative efficiency' (Turner 2011). This is a polite way of saying that a lightly regulated banking sector has failed consumers and undermined the entire financial system.

We draw on the arguments not because the banking sector has indeed been transformed (it has not) or because, as an industry, it should somehow serve as a model for the internet (it should not), but simply to suggest that regulation of vital public resources is both possible and desirable to promote 'socially useful' outcomes and to check the power of unaccountable forces, whether they are market or government based. We are therefore calling for a particular form of intervention: of 'market-negating regulation', as the economist Costas Lapavitsas calls it (2010) in his analysis of the global financial crisis. There is no reason why principles that radical economists are proposing, not without good reason, for the banking sector – state regulation of prices, ceilings on interest rates, control of capital markets, all in the name of the public good – could not be applied to the internet. Lapavitsas argues that we have had too much of the 'wrong' sort of regulation (he calls it 'market-conforming regulation'), and this is precisely what has happened in relation to the internet as governments, supranational bodies, and large telecoms and internet companies have sought agreement on terms of trade and custom and practice that best serve them and not the public at large.

Of course this will also have to be a 'state-negating regulation' in the sense that it should not lead to the ability of governments (elected or not) to monopolise digital spaces or to use their power to direct what happens in those spaces – as evidenced by the massive surveillance programmes of PRISM and Tempora in the US and UK respectively. However, the idea that one can use the power of the state to enhance public provision, as opposed to government control, is hardly new: consider Medicare in the US, the French national health insurance system or the BBC in the UK, which, while established by the state, are certainly not the properties of any single administration. Our belief is that it is possible to establish publicly funded bodies (with membership drawn from different parts of society) and systems of oversight (which are accountable to those publics) that have an arm's-length relationship to the state.

We are aware that we cannot make any blanket recommendations, given the situated nature of the internet in specific countries. Instead, we aim to offer our own version of a manifesto for cyberspace, some 20 years after Barlow's libertarian call to arms, that seeks to resurrect public interest regulation and reverse the current relationship between markets and states that has functioned to accrue power for corporations and governments but rarely for the public whom they are supposed to serve. This approach is not counterposed to the many bills of rights already proposed by various organisations and individuals (see Internet Rights & Principles Coalition 2014; Jarvis 2011) that seek to enshrine principles of openness, collaboration and ethical behaviour. Indeed, it is an attempt to find the mechanisms by which these objectives can be protected and nurtured in an environment that increasingly rewards opacity, inequality and unethical behaviour.

We want to see *redistributional* public interventions that will foster:

- online journalism that uses the internet's ability to highlight more sources of information and better links readers and news reports, *not* the speeded-up churnalism that we have all too often seen. This could be subsidised through a tax on advertising that could generate significant amounts of money to support new journalistic ventures. Christian Fuchs, for example, estimates that a 10% tax on advertising in countries like the US, UK and Germany would yield billions of euros (Fuchs 2015) – money that could be ring-fenced solely for the production of public interest journalism;
- broadband infrastructures that are constructed as public utilities designed to serve the needs of citizens, *not* the privately constructed toll roads that governments, at a time of economic uncertainty, are keen to see built. This would involve a new Internet Works Progress Administration – on the scale of the US public works projects of the 1930s that were developed as a response to the recession of the time – dedicated to constructing a new publicly owned digital infrastructure;
- the use of 'big data' not as a commodity to be used by governments and corporations for surveillance and advertising but for the non-profit coordination of healthcare, transport and public services. This would mean, as Evgeny Morozov has argued, 'socialising' the data centres: changing the legal status of data for citizens 'to enable a more communal planning of their lives' (Morozov 2015: 65);

- the protection of privacy and the safeguarding of data. Just as there is a requirement in many cities for private developers to build affordable housing in any new development, there should be an obligation on all digital intermediaries to provide spaces that are entirely free of cookies and tracking devices that undermine people's privacy and commodify their data;
- the ability of citizens to talk within and across national boundaries through public funding of sites dealing with issues of collective concern, *not* an artificial international community of branded consumers. This could be funded by closing tax loopholes that have allowed some of the largest tech companies to pay only marginal rates of tax and the reinvestment of this additional income into funding bodies that are representative of the publics to whom they are accountable;
- the circulation of content (whether related to entertainment, news, information or education) on networks regulated in the name of the public and not controlled by major internet players like Google and Facebook with very poor systems of monitoring and accountability. This means that robust network neutrality rules must be passed that do not allow for any exceptions for 'premium' traffic to take precedence over 'ordinary' packets.

We are not calling for an international *deus ex machina* to fall from the sky to rescue the internet from today's digital robber barons. We are instead calling for constructive and achievable interventions – acts of deliberate public policy where the public will exists – to create the conditions for a more democratic internet.

This will mean arguing for redistributional policies: for taxes and levies on private communications businesses to help fund open networks and public service content; for changes to intellectual property regimes that will prevent the blockages, copyright extensions and digital rights management that disenfranchise users from networks that are best served by open access; for the creation of a set of conditions, specific to each country, that will allow the funding and regulation of the internet to benefit users, irrespective of wealth, geography, background and age. We understand that these interventions will depend on what is possible in each country at a specific moment in time *but we refuse to believe that change is not possible*. After all, we are calling for measures – for public control of a key utility – that have been applied to other key sections of the economy and society (parts of the automobile industry in the US; banks in the UK; airlines in Argentina; mortgage providers in the US).

Let us give one example of what is possible. Support is growing around the world for a tax on global financial transactions to support international development objectives – the Tobin Tax. If we are agreed that the development of an open internet environment is a policy priority for the 21st century, then why should we not press for a mechanism by which those who are benefiting from the demand for information and communication make a full contribution to building and supporting such an environment? A 1% tax on the operating profits of computer software and hardware, internet services and retailing, entertainment and telecommunications companies in the Fortune 500 list alone would raise some *$1.7 billion* annually. Let us call this a Cerf Tax in honour of Vint Cerf, the architect of the protocols that made the internet possible in the first place, but there could be many international variations. This amount of money could be distributed via participatory commissioning through non-profit agencies to support, for example, the development of non-proprietorial content, community broadband initiatives, public journalism start-ups and public access software labs.

The internet is at a turning point. This book has argued that, while many people have exaggerated and confused its real impact and significance, there is little doubt that it is a hugely important technology that has to be understood, protected and valued. The time has come to demand an internet that is run for the benefit of the public without discrimination by market or state. This means that we have to change the direction of travel and to relieve the existing institutional guardians of the internet of their responsibilities. The internet is too important to be left to the politicians, the generals or the accountants; it was born in the public sector and needs to find a home there in the future.

References

Berners-Lee, T. (2010) 'Long Live the Web: A Call for Continued Open Standards and Neutrality', *Scientific American*, 22 November. Online. Available HTTP: <http://www.scientificamerican.com/article/long-live-the-web/> (accessed 28 July 2015).

Fuchs, C. (2015) 'Left-Wing Media Politics and the Advertising Tax. Reflections on Astra Taylor's Book "The People's Platform: Taking Back Power and Culture in the Digital Age"', *tripleC*, 13 (1), 1–4.

Internet Rights and Principles Coalition (2014) *The Charter of Human Rights and Principles for the Internet*. Internet Governance Forum. Online. Available HTTP: <http://internetrightsandprinciples.org/site/charter/> (accessed 28 July 2015).

Jarvis, J. (2011) 'A Hippocratic Oath for the Internet', 23 May. Online. Available HTTP: <http://www.buzzmachine.com/2011/05/23/a-hippocratic-oath-for-the-internet/> (accessed 28 July 2015).

Lapavitsas, C. (2010) 'Regulate Financial Institutions, or Financial Institutions?', in P. Arestis, R. Sobreira and J. L. Oreiro (eds) *The Financial Crisis: Origins and Implications*, Houndsmill: Palgrave Macmillan, 137–159.

Morozov, E. (2015) 'Socialize the Data Centre', *New Left Review*, 91, Jan-Feb, 45–65.

Turner, A. (2009) 'Mansion House Speech', 22 September. Online. Available HTTP: <http://www.fsa.gov.uk/pages/Library/Communication/Speeches/2009/0922_at.shtml> (accessed 28 July 2015).

Turner, A. (2011) 'Reforming Finance: Are We Being Radical Enough?', 2011 Clare Distinguished Lecture in Economics and Public Policy, Cambridge, 18 February. Online. Available HTTP: <http://www.fsa.gov.uk/pubs/speeches/0218_at_clare_college.pdf> (accessed 28 July 2015).

Index

Aalberg, T. 10
abundance 87, 89–90, 91, 119, 153–4, 178, 204
access 8
accumulation 98, 104–7, 112, 151
acquisitions 105, 106
activism 16–21, 25, 34, 173, 196; Arab uprisings 1–2, 66–70, 86, 173, 174; authoritarian states 66; Avaaz 188–9; civil society 134; connectivity 190–1; counterculture 52, 53; digital 183; 38 Degrees 189–190; exploitation of activists 102; Greece 192–6; Internet Ungovernance Forum 135; Malaysia 31, 32; open-source movement 61; participation 188; social media 155–6; socioeconomic status of activists 14; Spain 184–188; speed and space of 174–7; women 71–2; *see also* politics
Advanced Research Projects Agency (ARPA) 50, 53
advertising 26, 56, 63, 107; commodification 101; crowdsourcing 94; Google 90, 93, 101, 111; market concentration 108; OhmyNews 29; social media 151; tax on 207
Afghanistan 8, 126
Africa 8, 49
agency 146, 147
Agre, P. 11
Ahearn, Chris 22
Airbnb 4, 92, 103, 107
Al-Saleem, Hedaya 71
Alexander, Jeffrey 70

Algeria 71
Amazon 57, 86, 91; disruptive impact of 34, 96; dominance of 6; monopoly 111; outsourcing 58; regulation 138; tax avoidance 58
America Online 139
Amsterdam 52–53, 62
Andalib-Goortani, Babak 20
Anderson, Chris 86, 91, 112, 203–204; digital logic 87; free services 90, 99–100; Google 97; 'long tail' thesis 89, 99, 109–110; market fundamentalism 95; natural path of industrialisation 139; niche economy 110, 111; open source 102–103; user-generated content 94
Andrejevic, M. 155
Ang, Peng Hwa 122, 133
anonymity 74, 128
Anonymous 185
Anwar, Ibrahim 31, 32
Apache 60
Apple 53, 57–58, 91, 105; Apple Watch 138; disruptive capitalism 96; monopoly 111; tax avoidance 58
apps 187
Arab uprisings 1–2, 66–70, 86, 173, 174
architecture 128, 129, 182
Argentina 208
ARPA 50, 53
ARPANET 50, 51, 55
Asia 49, 75, 76
Assange, Julian 62
astroturfing 149–150

AT&T 51, 60, 138
austerity 197, 198, 199n2; Greece 178, 193, 195; Spain 185, 186, 187–188
Australia 26, 126
authoritarian states 11, 12, 30, 65–6, 76, 176, 203; Middle East 68, 69–70; 'networked authoritarianism' 177; regulation 120; social media 155–156; state intimidation 10; surveillance 59
Auto Trader 93
autonomy: politics 182, 205; social media 149, 151, 152, 157, 165, 166, 204
Avaaz 188–189, 205

Bachmann, G. 74–75
Badiou, A. 197
Bahrain 67, 68, 69–70
Baidu 57, 108
Baldwin, Stanley 122
Bandcamp 93
bandwidth 89
banking 206, 208
Barlow, John Perry 117–118, 124, 129, 207
Bauer 107
Bauman, Z. 180
Baym, Nancy 152
Bebo 139
Bell, Emily 130
Benkler, Yochai 22, 95, 102, 123–124, 136–137, 162
Berlusconi, Silvio 184
Berners-Lee, Tim 54, 55, 132, 140, 205
Bezos, Jeff 96
'big data' 86, 207
BITNET 53
blablacar 92
Blair, Bill 20
Blair, Tony 88
Blank, G. 153
blogs 22, 25, 93, 99, 102, 158; Arab uprisings 69; China 75; leading bloggers 9; mass self-communication 156, 157; overhyping of 27; political activism 156; politicians 155; race hate groups 9; Reformasi 32; self-communication 148; 38 Degrees 189; women 71
Blumler, J. 35n11

Boas, T. C. 12
Boko Haram 72
Boltanski, L. 162
Bookchin, M. 192
Bordini, C. 180
bots 149
Brand, Stewart 52
bricolage 120
Brilliant, Larry 52
Brin, Sergey 96, 104–105
Brown, Derren 159
Brown, Michael 20
browsers 54–55
Bulashova, N. 6
Burma 66, 155–156
BuzzFeed 24

Cairncross, Frances 7, 88
Calingaert, D. 162
Cambodia 66
Canada 26, 126, 177
capital 5, 97–98, 139, 152, 154, 165, 197
capitalism 57, 85, 87–88, 97–99, 112; commercialisation 55; commodification 99–104; counterculture 53; critique and 162; defence of 118; discourses of 146; disruption of 95–96; hyper commercialism 151, 197; neoliberal 152, 164; net neutrality seen as threat to 131; shift to postcapitalism 86; technology and 197; unregulated 204
Carnegie Trust 154
Carpentier, N. 188
Castells, Manuel 2, 159, 182; Cisco Systems 34n6; corporations 150–151, 178; governance 121, 135; mass self-communication 23, 151, 156–157, 164–165; political change 177; regulation 125
Castoriadis, C. 152
Caygill, H. 197
CDA see Communications Decency Act
celebrities 25, 149, 157, 204
Cellan-Jones, R. 161
censorship 30, 64, 76, 118, 127; authoritarian states 10, 12, 65–66; Avaaz petition against 189; censorware filters 140; delegated 137; Egypt 70;

increase in 203; Malaysia 33; policies
  138; social media 161
Cerf, Vint 130, 209
CERN 49, 54
Change.org 190
Chao, L. 161–162
Chevrolet 107
Chiapello, E. 162
child pornography 123, 137
China: Baidu 57; censorship 12, 66;
  Chinese language 8, 35n8, 62; control of
  access 124; Foxconn factories 58, 102;
  gaming 56; individualism 75; landmine
  use 17; nationalism 10, 65; 'networked
  authoritarianism' 177; state power 127;
  Weibo 146, 149; WikiLeaks affair 125;
  women 72
Cisco Systems 34n6, 58
citizen journalism 22, 27–28, 29–30, 154
civil society 21, 25, 28, 34, 175;
  governance 122, 134, 135; Malaysia/
  Singapore comparison 31, 32
clicktivism 188, 190
Clinton, Bill 117, 124, 127
'closed code' 128, 129
co-creation 107
co-regulation 137, 138
code 128–129, 130, 134, 137
coercion 120
Cohen, Jared 86, 87, 102–103, 112, 125
Cole, G. 6
Coleman, S. 35n11
collaboration 87, 98, 112, 199, 205, 207;
  culture of sharing 92–94; Google 106;
  'New Economy' 104; open source 103
Collaborative Commons 87
Collaborative Consumption 88
collectivism 74–75
Collins, Richard 133, 136
Comcast 138
commercialisation 54–59, 64, 75–76, 125,
  139, 203
commodification 98, 99–104, 107, 112,
  150, 152
communalism 74–75, 76
communication 2, 205; communicational
  society 164; democratisation of 23;
  emancipatory potential of 121; global
  understanding 6–7; horizontal 11;

infrastructure 49; political change 178;
  social media 146, 148–152, 156–159; see
  also self-communication
Communications Decency Act
  (CDA) 117
communism 55, 132, 182, 187
Comor, E. 101–102
competition 6, 129, 131, 133–134,
  164, 203
Compuserve 139
concentration 108–111, 112, 140, 204
connectivity 173, 188–192, 196
conservatism 21
consultations 12–13
consumer power 18
consumption 55, 150
content aggregators 24, 27
copyleft 60
copyright 56–57, 60, 105, 123, 124, 130,
  137, 208
Coretti, L. 184
corporations 5–6, 21, 34, 64, 87, 204;
  Castells on 150–151; commercialisation
  56–57, 58, 59; corporate influence over
  regulation 136–137; dominance of 178;
  Greece 195; new media economy 92;
  open source 103; power of 139; social
  media 146–147, 158; TTIP 17; Twitter
  users 149
corruption 193–194, 195
cosmopolitanism 7, 11
costs 5, 85–86, 89–90, 98, 99–100, 108
'cottage industries' 55, 87, 91, 118
Couldry, N. 147
countercultural values 51–53
Coyle, D. 88
Craigslist 89, 90, 93, 96
creativity 3, 88, 112; collaborative
  approach 94; impact of regulation on
  118, 206; 'We-Think' 92
critical theory 7
Croatia 65
Crouch, C. 180–181
crowdsourcing 88, 94
Cukier, K. 86
cultural capital 9, 154, 187
cultural theory 7
Curran, James 1–47, 48–84, 157,
  203–209

cyberspace 48, 55; inequalities 11;
    regulation 117, 118, 119, 127–128, 135

Dahlgren, Peter 21
Daily Mail 159–160
data collection 58–59, 100–101; 'big data'
    86, 207; commodification 102; social
    media 146
data protection 208
Dean, Jodi 165
decentralisation 90–91, 92, 98, 130, 131,
    134, 140
Deibert, R. 162, 176
democracy 1, 11, 33, 55, 121, 198, 203;
    access to information 53; activism 21;
    Arab uprisings 68; communicational
    society 164; culture of sharing 92; failure
    to reinvigorate 12–13, 15; historical
    developments 64–66; monitorial 159,
    162; net neutrality 132; new economic 96;
    open code 129; openness 166, 196; 'post-
    democracy' 180; social media 153; South
    Korea 28; *see also* politics
DeNardis, Laura 120, 128, 137
Denmark 4
deregulation 4–5, 21, 130, 180
determinism 97, 112, 129–130, 139
Di Genarro, C. 14
Diamond, L. 174, 183
dictatorships 12, 59, 64, 77n7; *see also*
    authoritarian states
Digg 93, 99
DigiActive 183
Digital City (Amsterdam) 52–53, 62
digital divide 121, 134, 182–183
Digital Economy Act (2010) 124, 136
'digital labour' 101
digital logic 87
Digital Millennium Copyright Act (1998)
    57, 124
digitalisation 130
disempowerment 15, 21–22, 33
disintermediation 93, 111
dissent 27–28, 154, 176, 181; *see also*
    activism; resistance
diversification 87
diversity 173, 181–184, 186, 192, 193,
    196, 204
Doritos 94, 107

dotcom bubble 3, 88
'dotcommunism' 95
Downes, Larry 87, 89, 95–96, 98,
    102–103, 112, 131
Dutton, W. 8, 14, 159
Dyson, Esther 118–119

e-commerce 4, 5, 6
e-government 1, 12–13
e-mail 49, 56, 63, 156, 157
eBay 96
economic capital 154
economic policies 178–179
economic transformation 2–6, 203
economies of scale 5, 34, 90, 108, 109
economy of abundance 89–90
educational attainment 14, 153, 161, 183
Egypt 67, 68, 69, 70, 71, 156
Ehlers, Vern 6
Elberse, Anita 109–110
elites 21–22, 89, 107, 151, 154–155, 157,
    176, 179, 204
Elmer-Dewitt, Philip 22
Elmer, G. 177
emancipatory potential of the internet 2,
    104, 121, 198, 203, 204
employees 94–95, 106
empowerment 1, 11–22, 33, 134, 175,
    177; activism 16–21; collective 204;
    liberation technology 174; limits on
    12–16
English language 8, 35n8
entertainment 16, 64, 149, 153–154, 204
environmental issues 58
Ethiopia 66
Europe: countercultural values 52;
    Facebook 57; inequalities 8; net
    neutrality 131–132; *openDemocracy* 9;
    political participation 13–14, 25; privacy
    protection 59; public service 54; retailing
    4; 'right to be forgotten' 124; Television
    without Frontiers Directive 130; TTIP
    17–18, 179
European Central Bank 178, 192,
    193, 195
European Commission 57, 109, 122, 131,
    192, 193
exploitation 98, 101–102, 106–107, 112,
    165, 204

Facebook 16, 18, 61, 86, 91, 139, 163;
acquisitions 105; Arab uprisings 67, 69;
capital costs 100; commodification 101;
data collection 59, 101; democratisation
of media production 93; disruptive impact
of 96; dominance of 6; free services
89, 99; Indignados movement 185;
investigations into 57; ISIS 9; launch
of 49; 'Like' device 150; Malaysia 32;
market concentration 108; monopoly
109; network effects 98; news 157;
number of friends on 166; Podemos 186;
political activism 156; popularity of 145;
Purple Movement 184; regulation138,
208; Saudi Arabia 66; self-communication
148; social marketing 151; status
updates 162; tax avoidance 58; 38
Degrees 189; turnover and revenue 146;
word of mouth 146
Fawkes, Guido 22
Federal Communications Commission
(FCC) 127, 132
Feenberg, A. 197
feminism 68, 70, 76
Fenton, Natalie 145–172, 173–202,
203–209
FidoNet 53
15M movement 156, 185, 186, 187
financial crisis 5, 178, 179, 184–185, 206
financial deregulation 4–5, 21
Finland 23
Firefox 60
Fiske, J. 94
Flickr 61–62, 156
Foster, John 2
Foucault, Michel 128
Foxconn 58, 102
fragmentation 15, 175, 183, 184, 205
Franklin, M. I. 122, 138
Fraser, Nancy 7
free services 89–90, 99–100
Free Software Foundation 59–60
free trade 179
Freedman, Des 85–116, 117–144, 151,
203–209
Freedom Act (2015) 126
Freedom House 162
freelancers 107

Friedman, Thomas 120, 122
Friendster 153
Froomkin, A. Michael 121, 134
Fry, Stephen 25, 159
Fuchs, Christian 101, 207

G8 protests 17
G20 protests 20, 161
gaming 4, 53, 56
Garner, Eric 20
Garnham, Nicholas 98–99, 100
gatekeepers 89, 93, 111, 119, 138, 204
Gately, Stephen 159
Gates, Bill 77n6
gay men 74
Gays.com 61
GCHQ 59, 161
GDP see gross domestic product
gender 8, 70–73, 183
General Public Licence (GPL) 60
generalisation 87–88
George, Cherian 32
Germany 207
GetUp! 190
Geveran, W. 151
Gezi Park protests 191
Gharbia, Sami bin 69
Gheytanchi, E. 183–184
Gilmore, J. 118
global understanding 1, 6–11, 33, 203
globalisation 7, 88, 101, 118, 120
Globo 57
Gmail 108, 177
GNU 60
Goldsmith, J. 124–125, 129, 135, 137
Google 4, 55, 86–87, 97, 104–106, 139,
163; advertising 90, 93, 101, 111;
antitrust investigation 109; Arab uprisings
69; capital costs 100; commercialisation
56, 57; commodification 101; data
collection 59, 101; disruptive impact of
34; dominance of 6; economic recession
112; employees 94–95, 106; free services
89, 99, 100; internet logic 91, 96; market
concentration 108; monopoly 109;
network effects 98; news 24, 157; niche
markets 111; outsourcing 58; popularity
of 145; regulation 130, 138, 140, 208;

sale of data imprints 152; tax
  avoidance 58; 'tweets' 161
Gore, Al 86
GoTo 104–105
governance 118, 119, 120–122, 124;
  limitations of governance regimes
  132–135; multistakeholder 134–135; new
  forms of 136; privatisation of 137, 138;
  soft 204; technical architecture 128
governments: decline in state power
  180–181; monitoring by 205; opposition
  to state intervention 130; regulation
  by 118–119, 120, 124–127, 129, 135,
  137–138, 140, 206–207
GPL see General Public Licence
Graham, Andrew 108
Grateful Dead 52, 117
Gray, Freddie 20
Great Britain see United Kingdom
Greece 178–179, 192–196, 197, 199n1
Greengard, Samuel 85
Griffin, Nick 160
Grigoropoulos, Alexis 192
Groselj, D. 153
Groshek, J. 65
gross domestic product (GDP) 5
Gross, Larry 74
Grossman, Lawrence 11
Guardian 130, 160

'hacker logic' 186
Hahn, Harley 6–7
Haque, Umair 90–91
Hardt, M. 182
Hargreaves, Susie 123
Harvard Business School 5
Harvey, David 162, 186
Harwood, Simon 19
Henwood, Doug 103
Hesmondhalgh, D. 102
Hewlett-Packard (HP) 58
hierarchy 136, 204
Hindman, M. 25
Hintz, A. 135
historical developments 48–84, 203; Arab
  uprisings 66–70; commercialisation
  54–59, 75–76; countercultural values
  51–53; European public service 54;

individualism 73–75; march to
  democracy 64–66; military-scientific
  complex 50–51; recalcitrant users 62–64;
  resistance to commercialism 59–61;
  technical development 49–50; user-
  generated content 61–62; women 70–73
Holt, R. 153
Homejoy 107
horizontality 173, 181–184, 186, 192, 196
Howard, Philip 77n7, 86, 87
Huang, Yachien 72–73
Huffington Post 24

IANA see Internet Assigned Numbers
  Authority
IBM 60, 103, 134
ICANN see Internet Corporation for
  Assigned Names and Numbers
identity: communal 73–74, 75, 76;
  fragmented 183; political 182, 188, 205;
  young people 176; see also self
IETF see Internet Engineering Task Force
IGF see Internet Governance Forum
IMF see International Monetary Fund
income inequality 7–8
Independent Police Complaints
  Commission (IPCC) 18–19
India 72, 74
Indignados 156, 174, 184–185, 186
individualism 15, 73–75, 158, 159, 165,
  166, 178
Indonesia 65
inequalities 5, 8, 11, 203; digital divide
  121, 134, 182–183; gender 70, 72, 73;
  income 7–8; of knowledge 154; Occupy
  Movement 156; political participation 14;
  protests against 20; social
  146, 163
information 98
infrastructure 49, 207
innovation 3, 5, 85–86, 88; collective 92;
  disruptive 96; impact of regulation
  on 118, 130, 131, 206; phases of
  technological development 139
Instagram 9, 61, 91, 93, 99
intellectual property rights 56–57, 64, 76,
  104, 105, 124, 137, 208
intermediaries 111, 137

International Campaign to Ban Landmines 17
International Monetary Fund (IMF) 178, 179, 185, 192, 193, 195
Internet Assigned Numbers Authority (IANA) 134
internet-centrism 1
Internet Corporation for Assigned Names and Numbers (ICANN) 118, 121, 124, 130, 134, 135
Internet Engineering Task Force (IETF) 121, 134
Internet Explorer 60
Internet Governance Forum (IGF) 121, 133, 134–135
internet of things (IoT) 85, 86
internet protocol (IP) 49
internet service providers (ISPs) 123, 132, 137, 176, 205
Internet Society 121, 130
Internet Ungovernance Forum 135
Internet Watch Foundation (IWF) 123
interoperability 130, 134
iPad 57, 58, 128
IPCC see Independent Police Complaints Commission
iPhone 57, 138
iPod 58
Iran 65, 66, 71, 102, 161–162, 183–184
Iraq 126, 179
ISIS 9
Islam 9, 70
ISPs see internet service providers
Israel 155
Italy 184
iTunes 6, 108
IWF see Internet Watch Foundation

Japan 30, 57, 72, 74–75
Jarvis, Jeff 112, 203–204; abundance 89; commodification 101; disintermediation 93; disruptive capitalism 96; free services 90; Google 86–87, 91, 95, 97, 104, 105; niche markets 111; open source 102–103
Jiepang 61, 62
Jobs, Steve 3, 53, 57–58, 96
Johnson, D. R. 119
Jordan 67

journalism 22–28, 33, 34, 48, 56, 203; redistributional public interventions 207; social media 154, 158; South Korea 28–30; start-ups 140, 209; see also news
Juris, J. 14, 74

Kalanick, Travis 103
Kalathil, S. 12
Karamanlis, Kostas 193
Kavada, A. 73–74
Keane, J. 159
Kelly, Kevin 2, 118
Kenyon, Andrew 31
Khiabany, G. 102
Kim, Youna 72
Klein, N. 174
Koch brothers 131
Koebler, J. 131
Koenig, P. 195
Krugman, Paul 18
Kuwait 71

labour 94, 98; 'digital' 101; see also employees
landmines campaign 17
language 8, 33, 35n8
Lapavitsas, Costas 206
Leadbeater, Charles 87, 88, 91, 92, 93, 94, 95
legacy media 23–24, 27, 136
legislation see regulation
Lessig, Lawrence 128–129, 130, 134, 136–137, 139–140
Levy, D. 23
Lewis, James 126–127, 129, 135
'liberation technology' 174
libertarianism 60, 95, 117, 119, 124, 129–132
Libya 67, 68, 69, 70
licensing 76
LinkedIn 61, 100
Linux 60, 92, 99, 102, 104
Livingstone, Sonia 130
Loader, B. 175
lobbies 132, 137, 180
'long tail' thesis 89, 99, 109–110
Lott, Trent 18
Lovink, G. 152
low-income groups 13–14

Mackinnon, R. 177
Magaziner, Ira 127
Mahathir, Mohamad 31
MAI *see* Multilateral Agreement on
Investments
Malaysia 30–33, 65, 66
Mallapragada, Madhavi 74
malware 133, 162
Manning, Chelsea 62
manufacturing 6
market concentration 108–111, 112,
140, 204
market-driven approach 127, 204
market fundamentalism 95, 97
market power 57
marketing 151
markets 3, 90–91
Marwick, A. E. 150, 163
Marx, Karl 94, 97–98, 100, 102
Marxism 97–98, 131
'mashups' 91
Mason, Paul 86, 92, 95, 96
mass market 110–111
mass self-communication 23, 25, 146, 151,
156–159, 164–165
massification 87
Mattoni, A. 196
Maura, Eduardo 186
Mayer-Schonberger, V. 86
McChesney, Robert 2, 100, 108, 109, 151
McQuivey, James 96
media 23–24, 25, 26, 147, 204;
Arab uprisings 69; 'big media' 90;
democratisation of production 93–94;
Greece 195; 'new organisational
landscape' 91; WikiLeaks affair 62; *see
also* news; social media; television
Metzger, Tom 9
Mexico 4, 65
'Miami Model' of policing 20
microblogging 158; *see also* Twitter
Microsoft 57, 77n6, 105; data collection
59; Internet Explorer 60; market
concentration 108; outsourcing 58; tax
avoidance 58; 'tweets' 161
Middle East: ISIS 9; online dissidents
76; uprisings in the 1–2, 66–70; women
70–71, 73

military-scientific complex 50–51
Miller, D. 74, 179
Miller, V. 158
mobile phones 20, 49, 66, 69, 75, 183; *see
also* smartphones
mobile technology 63–64
mode of production 85, 87, 97, 104
Moir, Jan 159–160
monopoly 109, 111, 112, 151
Morocco 66, 67, 71
Morozov, Evgeny 2, 66, 77n7, 207
Morsi, Mohammed 70
Morter, Jon 18
Mosaic 62–63
Mosco, Vincent 77n7, 101
MoveOn.org 16, 190
Mozilla 60, 104
Mubarak, Hosni 67
Mueller, Milton 120, 124, 132, 134–135,
138, 140
Multilateral Agreement on Investments
(MAI) 17, 18
multiplicity 153–154, 156, 165
multistakeholder governance 134–135
Murdoch, James 130
Murdoch, Rupert 22, 100
music 6, 63, 91, 108, 110
Myanmar (Burma) 66, 155–156
MySpace 139, 151, 153

National Center for Supercomputing
Applications (NCSA) 60, 62
National Security Agency (NSA) 59, 126,
161, 204
nationalism 10, 65, 74
Naughton, John 56
NCSA *see* National Center for
Supercomputing Applications
Negri, A. 182
Negroponte, Nicholas 55, 57, 87, 91,
118, 129
Nel, F. 26
neoliberalism 126, 139, 162–163, 182,
195, 198; autonomy 152; discourses
of 146, 178, 186; hegemony of 130;
individualism 158, 159, 165; net
neutrality 131; 'post-democracy' 180;
power relations 119–120; self-regulation

122, 133–134; sharing economy 103; social media 146, 147; Spain 174; TTIP 179
Nepal 155
Nerone, John 22
net neutrality 57, 124, 131–132, 137, 140, 208
Netflix 110
Netherlands 52–53
Netscape 63
networks 86, 94, 98, 108, 158, 196; open 128; radical politics 175, 176, 181–182; social context 166; *see also* social networking sites
'New Economy' 3, 5, 34n6, 88, 91, 94, 104, 107, 112
New York Times 57, 100
New Zealand 126
Newman, N. 23
Newmark, Craig 96
news 22–28, 34, 57, 203; national focus 10; paywalls 63, 100; redistributional public interventions 207; social media 153–154, 157–158, 159–160; *see also* journalism
newsgroups 53
NGOs *see* non-governmental organisations
Nicaragua landmines campaign 17
niche economy 3, 87, 89, 92–93, 110–111
Nico Nico Dougwa (NND) 74
Nielsen, R. 25
Nigeria 72
Nike 18
NND *see* Nico Nico Dougwa
Nobody, Adam 20
Nokia 103
non-governmental organisations (NGOs) 173, 174, 175, 181
Norval, A. 165
Norway 8
NSA *see* National Security Agency

Obama, Barack 13, 126, 132, 155
Occupy Movement 14, 73–74, 156, 173, 174, 192
OD *see* openDemocracy
OECD *see* Organisation for Economic Cooperation and Development

OhmyNews (OMN) 28–30
'open code' 128–129, 134
open-source (OS) movement 60–61, 64, 76, 102–103, 128, 133
openDemocracy (OD) 9, 28
openness 90–91, 120–121, 165, 166, 196, 207; fetishisation of 112; Google 106; ICANN 121; net neutrality 131; threats to 140
Oracle 57
Organisation for Economic Cooperation and Development (OECD) 4, 6, 8, 17, 137–138
Örnebring, H. 154
OS *see* open-source movement
Oser, J. 14
Osimo, D. 164
Oxford Internet Institute 153

packet-switching 50
Page, Larry 96, 104–105
Pakistan 8, 125
Panopticon 128
Papacharissi, Z. 148
Papathanassopoulos, S. 23
'paradigm shift' 85–86
Park Geun-hye 29
participation 1, 7, 165, 199, 204; empowerment 11; entertainment-related 16; mass 93; political 13–14, 15–16, 21–22, 33, 153, 173, 180, 188–192, 196; social media 148, 204
Pasquale, F. 101
Patel, Freddy 19
patriarchy 15, 71
Patterson, T. 153–154
Pax Technica 86
PayPal 109
paywalls 63, 100, 128
peace 6, 7
PeaceNet 53
peer production 85
peer-to-peer sharing 92, 102, 128, 133
Peerby 92, 104
Perry, Katy 149
Pew Internet and American Life Project 160–161
Pew Research Center 145
phatic communications 158–159

Pickard, Victor 131
Podemos 184–188, 205
police 12, 18–20
politics 11–12, 33, 173–202, 205; blogs
    25; campaign funding 13; connectivity
    and participation 188–192; context
    178; decline in state power 180–181;
    democratisation of communication
    23; detachment from 15, 28;
    disempowerment 21; e-government 1,
    12–13; empowerment 16–21;
    horizontality and diversity 181–184;
    income related to participation 13–14;
    Malaysia/Singapore comparison 30–33;
    organisational form 198; Podemos
    184–188; 'post representative' 159;
    social and economic order 178–179;
    social media 153, 155–156, 164,
    165–166; South Korea 28–30; speed
    and space of political activism 174–177;
    Syriza 192–196; see also activism;
    democracy
polycentricity 93, 154–155, 156
Popolia Viola 184
'popular unity' 186
pornography 56, 117, 123, 137
Post, D. G. 119
'post-democracy' 180
post-foundational politics 182
post-industrialism 88
postcapitalism 86
Poster, Mark 11, 55
Postmates 107
poverty 14–15, 22, 33, 66, 165, 185, 198
power 1, 197; access to production 165;
    corporations 139, 151; economy
    of abundance 90; elites 176, 179;
    gatekeepers 119; language as medium
    of 8; Malaysia/Singapore comparison
    30–31; multistakeholder governance 135;
    participation linked to 188; polycentricity
    154–155; regulation 119–120, 137; social
    media 150, 161, 163; state 118, 119, 125,
    126–127, 180–181
PRISM 207
privacy 59, 63, 101; advertising and 108;
    loss of 139–140; protection of 208;
    regulation 126, 128, 133, 137–138; social
    media 162; TTIP 179

privatisation 136–139, 165, 195
profit 97, 98, 101, 112, 151
propaganda 66
ProPublica 27
'prosumers' 23, 94, 100–102, 107, 145
public service 54, 207
Pugsley, P. 75
Purple Movement 184

race 18, 20
race hate groups 9–10
radical politics see politics
Rage Against the Machine 18
Rainie, L. 73
Razak, Najib 32
recession 5, 112; see also financial crisis
Redden, J. 24
Reddit 93, 187
redistributional policies 207, 208
Reformasi 32
regulation 117–144, 204, 205, 208;
    banking 206; codification of 127–129;
    governmentalisation of 124–127;
    intellectual property rights 56–57, 64;
    libertarian ideas 129–132; limitations of
    governance regimes 132–135; 'market-
    negating' 206; non-governmentalisation
    of 120–124; privatisation of 136–139;
    'state-negating' 206–207; TTIP 179
remixing 93, 107
resistance 196, 197–198; see also activism;
    dissent
retailing 4, 6, 56
Reuters Institute Digital News Report
    157–158
Rhapsody 110
Rhoads, C. 161–162
Rifkin, Jeremy 85, 87
'right to be forgotten' 124
Rightmove 93
Robbins, Peter 123
Roh Moo-hyun 28, 29
Rohozinski, R. 162, 176
Romney, Mitt 13
Rose, David 85
Rosen, Jeffrey 138
Rowbottom, Jacob 136
Russia 57, 66
Rykov, Konstantin 66

Sanger, Larry 61
Sarandos, Ted 110
Saranga, David 155
Saudi Arabia 12, 66, 67
scepticism 2
Schlozman, K. 153
Schmidt, Eric 86, 105, 106, 112; digital
    logic 87; disruptive capitalism 96; open
    source 102–103; regulation 130; state
    power 125
Schneiderman, Eric 103
Schneier, B. 101, 111
Schrøder, K. 25
scientists 51, 52, 54, 55, 59–60, 61
Scott, Walter 20
search engines 55, 64, 137
self 147, 152, 158, 159, 166, 204; see also
    identity
self-communication 76, 148; autonomy 152;
    individualism 75; mass 23, 25, 146, 151,
    156–159, 164
self-regulation 122–123, 126, 128,
    132–134, 138, 204
sexuality 74
sharing 92–95, 103, 124, 162
Shirky, Clay 87, 95
Silverstone, R. 164
Sima, Y. 75
Singapore 30–31, 33, 65, 66
Skype 59
slacktivism 188
Slager, Michael 20
Slater, D. 74
smartphones 49, 57, 63–64, 73, 93, 107;
    see also mobile phones
Smith, A. 14
Smythe, Dallas 152
Snowden, Edward 59, 126, 132–133,
    161, 204
SNS see social networking sites
social capital 150, 157
social change 166, 175, 177, 178, 197, 198
social class 14, 153, 161, 183
social justice 92, 196
social marketing 151
social media 34, 85, 87, 139, 145–172,
    197, 204; Arab uprisings 67, 69;

commodification 102; communication-
    driven nature of 148–152; historical
    developments 49; horizontality and
    confusion 183–184; mobilisation of
    dissent 27–28; multiplicity 153–154; as
    new form of social telling 159–164; news
    24–25; Occupy Movement 73–74; Pax
    Technica 86; political activism 155–156,
    176, 190–191; polycentricity 154–155;
    regulation 124, 137; self-communication
    to a mass audience 156–159; sharing
    of data with state authorities 176,
    177; Syriza 195–196; user-generated
    content 107; see also Facebook; Twitter;
    YouTube
social networking sites (SNS) 146, 147,
    148, 205; Arab uprisings 69; exclusion
    150; historical developments 61–62, 64;
    news 24–25, 27; race hate groups 9; see
    also social media
socialism 182, 187, 195
solidarity 11, 176, 182, 205; Podemos
    186; Purple Movement 184; replaced by
    politics of visibility 188; Syriza 194, 196
Solt, Frederick 14
Sony 91
South Korea 23, 28–30, 72
Soviet Union 50, 55
space 173, 176, 196
Spain 156, 174, 184–188, 197, 205
spam 56, 63
Spar, Deborah 139
specialisation 87–88, 92–93
speed 173, 176, 196
Stallman, Richard 59–60, 61
Stanford University 56
start-ups 3, 5, 24, 87, 140, 209
Stephany, A. 92
Stepinska, A. 10
storage capacity 89
Stormfront 9
Stratton, Jon 7
Sun 103
Sunlight Foundation 137
Sunstein, Cass 136
surveillance 99, 164, 176, 207; advertising
    and 108; delegated 137; GCHQ 59, 161;

historical developments 58–59, 64, 65, 66, 75, 76; increase in 181; regulation 120, 124, 125; Snowden's revelations 126, 204; social media 161; state complicity with corporate interests 151
Sweden 8
Sylvain, Olivier 99, 130, 133–134
Syria 67, 68, 70
Syriza 178–179, 192–196, 197

Taiwan 65, 72–73
Tapscott, Don 91, 96, 100, 112; co-creation 107; collaboration 87, 92, 93, 106; open source 102–103; prosumption 94
TaskRabbit 107
tax: advertising 207; Cerf Tax 208–209; tax avoidance 58, 64, 208; Tobin Tax 208
Tea Party Movement 21
technology 7, 33, 34, 178; historical developments 49–50; phases of technological development 139; politics 184; radical politics 174; state surveillance 66; systems of power 196–197
Telecommunications Act (1996) 117, 136
television: EU Television without Frontiers Directive 130; Greece 195; Netflix 110; news 10, 23, 35n18
Tempora 207
terrorism 9, 59, 161
tethered devices 57, 128, 138–139, 204
Thailand 125
Thatcher, Margaret 158
Thiel, Peter 109
38 Degrees 189–190, 205
Times 100
Tobin Tax 208
Toffler, A. 94
Tomlinson, Ian 18–19
Torvalds, Linus 60
Trafigura 160
Transatlantic Trade and Investment Partnership (TTIP) 17–18, 179
'transnational ethic' 7
Trinidad 74
Tsipras, Alexis 193, 195
TTIP *see* Transatlantic Trade and Investment Partnership

Tufekci, Z. 190–191
Tunisia 66–67, 68, 69, 70, 102
Turkey 4, 102
Turkle, Sherry 2, 34n3
Turner, Adair 206
Turner, Fred 52
Twitter 18, 61, 91; active users 146, 149; Arab uprisings 1–2, 67, 69; bots 149; celebrities 25, 204; education linked to use of 160–161; G20 protests 161; ISIS 9; Malaysia 32; news 157–158, 159–160; number of followers on 166; political activism 156; politicians on 155; race hate groups 9; self-communication 148; Syriza 195–196; 38 Degrees 189; turnover and revenue 146; user-generated content 107; WikiLeaks affair 125

Uber 4, 92, 103, 107
UK Uncut 16
UN *see* United Nations
UN Working Group on Internet Governance (WGIG) 120
United Arab Emirates (UAE) 67
United Kingdom: banking 208; bloggers 9; e-government 12–13; individualism 158; inequalities 8; internet advertising 26; journalism 23–24, 26–27, 28, 48; market concentration 108; neoliberalism 162; net neutrality 131; patterns of internet use 15; political participation 13, 14, 25; privacy issues 162; regulation 123, 124, 133, 136; retailing 4; security risks 137; smartphones 63; Snowden's revelations 126; social media 145; surveillance 59, 161, 207; tax on advertising 207; 38 Degrees 189–190; WikiLeaks 62
United Nations (UN) 122
United States: automobile and mortgage industries 208; Avaaz petition against censorship 189; blogs 9, 25; conservatism 21; countercultural values 51–52; individualism 158; inequalities 8; intellectual property rights 56–57; internet advertising 26; journalism 26; landmine use 17; market concentration 108;

market-driven approach 127; military-scientific complex 50–51; neoliberalism 162; net neutrality 132; news 10, 23; patterns of internet use 15; police violence 20; political campaign funding 13; political participation 13, 14, 25; poverty 14; regulation 117, 118–119, 124, 133, 134, 135, 136; retailing 4, 6; security risks 137; smartphones 63; Snowden's revelations 126, 161; social media 145, 150; state power 127; surveillance 58–59, 207; tax on advertising 207; technical developments 49; TTIP 17–18, 179; WikiLeaks 62, 125–126, 204
UNIX 53, 60
Usenet 53
user-generated content 101, 107; democratisation of media production 93–94; historical developments 49, 61–62, 66, 76; news 154; self-commodification 152
Uzbekistan 66

Vaizey, Ed 131
values: Arab uprisings 68; commercial 166; conflicting 9, 11, 33; countercultural 51–53; embedded by code 128; individualistic 73, 178; open-source movement 61; scientific 51, 64; virtual communities 153
Verizon 138
Vice News 24
virtual communities 53, 64, 153
viruses 133
Vise, D. 106
vocabulary 3, 48
Vodafone 16
Vogiatzoglou, M. 196

W3C see World Wide Web Consortium
Wacquant, L. 181
Wales, Jimmy 61
Wardle, C. 154
Wayne, Mike 112
'We-Think' 92, 95, 103–104
Web 2.0 23, 104, 151
websites: Malaysia 32; news 23–24; race hate groups 9, 10; surveillance 58–59

Weibo 146, 149
Weiss, Meredith 31
WELL (Whole Earth 'Lectronic Link) 52, 62
Wellman, Barry 73
WGIG see Working Group on Internet Governance
WhatsApp 89, 105, 148
Wheatcroft, Patience 100
Wheeler, D. 71
White Aryan Resistance 9
WikiLeaks 62, 64, 125–126, 160, 204
Wikinomics 88, 102
Wikipedia 61, 64, 87, 91, 92, 99, 102, 104, 133
Williams, Anthony 91, 96, 100, 112; co-creation 107; collaboration 87, 92, 93, 106; open source 102–103; prosumption 94
Williams, Jody 17
Williams, Raymond 111
WIPO see World International Property Organisation
wireless networking 49, 50
Witschge, T. 24
Wolfe, Alexander 154
Wolff, Michael 111
women 8, 70–73, 76
Wong, Nicole 138
Woodward, Shaun 130
word of mouth 146
work 94–95
Working Group on Internet Governance (WGIG) 120
World Economic Forum 117–118
World International Property Organisation (WIPO) 121
World Trade Organisation (WTO) 17, 121, 178, 179, 193
world wide web 49, 54
World Wide Web Consortium (W3C) 54, 121
Wozniak, Steve 53
WSIS 134–135
WTO see World Trade Organisation
Wu, Tim 109, 124–125, 129, 135, 137

X Factor 18
XNet 185, 187

Yahoo 24, 57, 105, 108
Yahyanejad, M. 183–184
Yandex 57
Yemen 66, 67–68, 70
Yeon Ho Oh 28
young people: Arab uprisings 68;
    democratisation of media production 93;
    digital divide 183; Greece 193; hours
    spent online 1; news 35n18; politics
    175–176, 205
YouTube 11, 20, 62, 91, 105, 138;

dominance of 6; free services 99, 100;
market concentration 108; politicians on
155; popularity of 145; Reformasi 32;
self-communication 148, 156; word of
mouth 146

Zimbabwe 65
Zittrain, Jonathan 102, 123, 129, 133, 135,
    136, 138–139, 140
Zopa 92
Zuckerberg, Mark 163